RABBI
SAADIAH
GAON'S
COMMENTARY
ON THE BOOK OF
CREATION

RABBI
SAADIAH
GAON'S
COMMENTARY
ON THE BOOK OF
CREATION

MICHAEL LINETSKY

JASON ARONSON INC.
Northvale, New Jersey
Jerusalem

This book was set in 11 pt. Weiss by Alabama Book Composition of Deatsville, Alabama.

Copyright © 2002 by Michael Linetsky

10 9 8 7 6 5 4 3 2 1

Library of Congress Cataloging-in-Publication Data

Sa' adia ben Joseph, 882–942.
   [Perushe Rav Se' adyah Ga 'on li-Ve-reshit. English]
   Commentary on Genesis / [edited and translated by] M. Linetsky.
      p.   cm.
   "We present here a fully annotated translation of both the Gaon's
Arabic rendition of the Bible from the section of 'Bereshith' to
'Vayetze' and his flowing commentary thereto"—Introd.
   Includes bibliographical references.
   ISBN 0–7657–6087–8
   1. Bible. O.T. Genesis I, 1–XXVIII, 9—Commentaries—Early works
to 1800. I. Linetsky, Michael, 1973–   II. Title.
BS1235.S2913 2002
222'.11077—dc21   99–13644
                                                  CIP

Printed in the United States of America on acid-free paper. For information and catalog write to Jason Aronson Inc., 230 Livingston Street, Northvale, NJ 07647-1726, or visit our website: www.aronson.com

Contents

Introduction

Rabbi Saadiah Gaon (b. 892) was the great master of the ancient Babylonian Academy of Sura. His life story and contributions to Jewish scholarship have been the subject of a variety of works and articles. One field in which he gained especially widespread renown was that of biblical exegesis. The Gaon rendered the entire Scripture, apparently, into Arabic, the spoken language of his age. This rendition reflects remarkable scientific precision, with no word arbitrarily chosen or nuance inconsistently represented. He also supplemented this work with a profuse and lucid running commentary covering the books of Genesis (until *Vayetze*), Exodus, and Leviticus. The task of finishing off the Bible commentary was later taken on by Rabbi Samuel ben Hophni and Rabbi Aharon ibn Sarjadu.

In his commentary the Gaon lays down the rules by which the Bible must be interpreted. He shows, for the first time, the relationship between the homiletic exegesis so popular in the generations before him and the literal interpretation that can be gained from the text, and discusses the role grammar, philosophy, and rationality play in the correct interpretation of the Bible. The importance of this work is readily apparent.

The Gaon's commentary to Genesis, unlike his translation thereto, had been virtually unknown for many generations. It was only in 1984 that Moshe Zucker, after gathering manuscripts and collecting fragments from the *Genizah*, brought to light the corpus of what is known from the Gaon's commentary to this book. Zucker's *Saadya's Commentary on Genesis*, published posthumously, contains the Arabic original and an annotated Hebrew translation.

Our purpose here is to make this monumental work accessible for the first time to the English speaking audience. We present here a fully annotated translation of both the Gaon's Arabic rendition of the Bible from *Bereshith* to *Vayetze* and his flowing commentary thereto.

Unfortunately, Zucker's posthumous edition contains many errors in the original Arabic and a new edition of this text is still a desideratum. Some sections found in the translation are absent from the original and the reverse is even more often so. We have done whatever is possible at this stage to bring the entire text to the reader (see apparatus).

Various sections are fragmentary and not always comprehensible. Frequently where no sense can be made of a section we have omitted it, while in cases where some sense can be gleaned, even if dubious, we have retained it for the reader.

Rabbi Saadiah Gaon translated the Pentateuch into Arabic (at least) in two different versions. One version (henceforth: 'Translation') was an independent work consisting of nothing more than an Arabic rendition of each verse. The other version (henceforth: 'Commentary') was embedded into a lengthy commentary on the Pentateuch. Since our goal in this work is to bring the Gaon's Pentateuch commentary to light, we have based our English translation of the verses on the Arabic translation of the verses embedded in the commentary not on those found in the independent translation.

Throughout the Middle Ages many copies of the Gaon's Pentateuch commentary were made. Unfortunately, no single manuscript of the entire commentary has come to light yet. Only multiple fragments from different copies have come down to us. Fortunately, these fragments can be pieced together to reconstruct much of the Commentary. The condition of the fragments is often very poor. Some fragments are ripped in more than one place and are missing portions of text while others have segments that are unreadable due to erosion or poor penmanship. We have indicated missing or unreadable text with dotted lines.

In commenting on the verses, Rabbi Saadiah Gaon did not follow the common practice of citing verses one by one and commenting on them one by one. Instead he groups verses by context and only then begins to expound on them. Due to the lengthiness of the Gaon's works it has become customary in scholarly circles to subdivide the commentary that belongs to each of these groupings. We have used Roman numerals for this purpose. The start of each grouping is marked with the Roman Numeral I and then is subdivided until the new grouping starts, in which case the numbering starts over.

Apparatus

< > - signifies words found in the translation but absent in the original. In the Gaon's translation these symbols signify an addition to the text. In the commentary they mean that the words they encapsulate are found in the Hebrew translation but are absent in the original Arabic.

<< >> - signifies words found in the original Arabic but omitted in the Hebrew translation. (Applies only to commentary).

[ ] - signifies words added by the translator.

[[ ]] - signifies that the Gaon's Arabic rendition is supplied from Derenbourgh's edition of the *Tafsir* and is lacking in the manuscripts used for this edition.

[ ]* - signifies words supplied to fill lacuna or words that are conjecturally read.

*{ } - signifies clarifications of the editor.

* - signifies reading is uncertain.

Abbreviations

BR = Bereshith Rabba
LR = Leviticus Rabba
IPC = Introduction to the Pentateuch Commentary
IT = Introduction to the translation of the Pentateuch
BO = Book of Origination (Book of Creation)

From the Preface of the Commentary to the Pentateuch

. . . investigation because it is contingent upon it . . . despite that the quality of many of the auditory precepts is not elucidated in it,[1] He directed us to [the understanding of] command and prohibition firstly by means of what He implanted in our intellects and secondly by means of what He directs us from the Tradition. I too am of those who is obligated in this, as I am obligated not to embark on anything until I attain what is inevitable of these three notions, but I have seen [it correct] not to push off embarking on interpreting it until I exhaust every aspect of it for were I to wait for this expecting to reach perfection in these three stages, this would not be something I have seen or heard any scholar to have attained especially because I have heard what Job's friends have said "shall you find the limits of God's knowledge or reach His power's term?" (Job 11:7) according to how I rendered these verses where they are stated. Moreover, I know that only the One, the Wise may He be exalted and sanctified knows the true knowledge in its entirety, as the Prophet says as well: "but God it is who knows its way and He it is who is acquainted with its place" (ibid 28:23) whereas all the scholars have only a miniscule part of it and it is the amount endowed them according to their abilities as one of them said, exaggerating: "I have absorbed wisdom like the Nile from

---

1. See IPC.

xiii

the water of the sea." Others say "like the scent from fruit" while others "like a spark from light." The meaning is that these statements are exaggerations and extremes of subservience and devotion to Him. Each one of them has an allegorical meaning . . . as the Scripture states: "there is no wisdom or understanding or guidance with God" (Prov. 21:30). I apologize to Him because of His exaltedness and fortitude and remove responsibility from Him, that I accept upon myself these before this daring idea and I am certain of my rhetoric and my attainment of perfection and how I should suspect this perfection and how I should suspect this recognizing the incapacity in my mind and the insufficiency of my knowledge. Despite this I have heard the exalted Sages say: "he says: teach me it since I have been unknowing of men" (Prov. 30:2).

From the Introduction to Genesis

Now that I have completed what I contemplated to be a general introduction to the entire Torah, I shall embark on what shall be an introduction to [its] first part.

I say: Blessed is God, God of Israel, whose praise is above all glorification for His knowledge is above all knowledge and His exaltation is beyond any description, for no intellect can encompass Him nor can He be apprehended by any mind. As His saints exalted Him saying: "And blessed be Your glorious name which is above all blessing and praise." (Neh. 9:5) I say now that despite that fortitude and feebleness all take part in the essence and attributes of any created thing, their outset and beginning is existence, I mean [in] the existence of essence. One who is not contingent upon a creator to bring him into existence, because his essence is in existence—this being what is called "eternal essence"—no doubt is not dependent on anything [that comes about] after existence, I mean time, place, dimension that composes him, nor protection or help from what comes upon him and the like. [However] one who exists only because of a creator that brought him into existence, since his essence is dependent upon someone to give him a beginning, he likewise is dependent on someone to let him persist moment after moment, on the time in which he exists, the place that contains him, the dimension that composes him, as well as for something that will protect him from an oppressor or that will assist him in all his successful endeavors according to all the details that branch out from this principle which I have already stated.

Now all that is sensible, since the intellect determines that they are created, the mind requires them, the contingencies being what I have described, so long as the Earth stands, that they are feeble, whereas when the intellect determines that their creator may He be blessed and exalted is not created—this meaning that He is eternal having no beginning—it follows from this that His essence is not contingent upon anything for He has no need—because it is eternally existent and perpetually persistent—of a creator and sustainer for He is the creator and sustainer of all. The Scripture states of this: "You have founded the Earth before and the work of Your hand is the Heaven. They shall perish and You are the One that remains." (Ps. 102:26) Certainly there is no creator or sustainer except for Him and just as He has no need for time and dimension he abandoned this for He is the creator of place and its traversal. The Scripture says: "But will God indeed dwell on the earth? Behold the heaven and the heaven of heavens cannot contain You; how much less this that I have built?" (I Kings 8:27) Likewise, He has no need for the service of His worshippers, neither the good and the bad nor the successful and unsuccessful. Rather the success or loss return to them as the Scripture says of God being more exalted than to enter into. . . .

Introduction
to the Pentateuch Commentary

I Organization of the Pentateuch

. . . point. He will divide it into sections and after this into chapters which is for them since they are . . . like fundaments which are its mainstay so that he arranges from them sections which are like its offspring[1] and then the statement will become organized like embellished ornaments similar to what the wise one says (Prov. 25:11–12), which I have translated as "Like apples of gold inside shapes of silver is that which is said in its [proper] manner[2] and like a nose ring of gold and ornaments of fine stone is the wise man who gives direction with an agreeing ear."[3] I have a commentary in which I shall explain these two verses ad loc. In respect to the words "in their [proper] manner."[4] Now were one to ask: If

---

1. It is difficult to render this sentence accurately due to the absence of the top of the manuscript. Possibly the Gaon speaks of the way a person would organize his works.

2. In his *Beliefs* 10:14 (p. 394), the Gaon uses this verse to show the importance of obtaining "knowledge in its details."

3. Kafih (p. 202) and Derenbourgh (p. 148) read: "who gives direction to an agreeing ear."

4. The Gaon speaks there of the way letters, words, and ideas should be

this[5] is because of the importance of organizing after composing [some-thing][6] what is it with this Book, I mean the Torah, that we do not find its laws collected together or divided into chapters or sections nor arranged in any order but instead we see them dispersed and isolated [from each other]? We answer him that the One who gave the Book may He be exalted and praised, intended by this to occupy His worshippers[7] with the laborious and involved [study of] the Torah so that gradually they memorize it entirely and are versed in it, connect each statement to its kin, attribute every point to its chapter and its proper place therein so that this adds to their recompense and increases their reward.[8] God gave sound scholars the potential[9] to make these things intelligible[10] through collecting, dividing, arranging, and organizing[11] just as He gave their minds the ruse to draw water from the bowels of the Earth.[12] Indeed the Scripture associates this knowledge with {drawing water} when it says: "Man's words should be like deep waters for the fount of wisdom is like a flowing river." (Prov. 18:4) [God also] endowed [them] with the ability to pass from one side of the river to the other and [likewise] associated knowledge with this when it says: "Who is it that will pass for us to the

---

recorded. Cf. *Men.* 29b–30a. Cf. also Maimonides, *Guide to the Perplexed*, intro. (p. 11).

5. Apparently the Gaon refers to the fact that the Scripture went out of its way to emphasize the importance of organization.

6. See section V where the Gaon speaks of the virtues of organization.

7. Or perhaps "those that fear Him."

8. The Gaon follows here his recurring opinion that out of His great beneficence God creates various opportunities for His creations to merit reward.

9. I.e., wisdom. Cf. *Beliefs* 4:2 (p. 182) where he says of it: "By means of it, too, he succeeds in extracting water from the depths of the Earth to the point where it flows on its surface." Cf. Al-Qirqisani, who draws heavily from the Gaon's introduction in his *Book of Gardens* (p. 58).

10. Text: "To bring these things close to their intellects."

11. Cf. *Beliefs* 1:3 (p. 12): "It is clear, then, that the person who speculates begins with a great many things that are mixed up, through which he continually sifts . . . until all confusions and ambiguities are removed and only pure extract remains. Al-Muqameais (*Twenty Chapters*, p. 66, n. 14) also considers knowledge to be the result of a process of synthesis and discernment.

12. In his commentary ad loc. the Gaon remarks: "For that reason one should use his understanding and should sharpen it so that his words be a correct response." Apparently, he associates "sharpening," a prolonged process, with wisdom being flowing and perpetual.

other side of the sea and will take it for us and will make us hear it so that we act according to it?" (Deut. 30:13) [He also gave them the ability] to investigate geometric figures[13] in order to understand what there is of the shape and form of the celestial spheres.[14] {The Scripture} associates knowledge with this too when it says: "Who is it that will go up to the heaven and will bring it down for us and will make us hear it and we will act according to it?"[15] (Deut. 30:12). [16]Like the people of our time, feeble, lacking in many virtues and deprived of the dignity of the sciences. This is because the people of our time find the sciences and the effort in [studying] them to be difficult while boorishness and pursuit of convenience to be easy. Therefore, if the one who provides the knowledge that they seek does not provide them with it in the shortest possible manner and does not bring it to them in the easiest possible way so that it is before them like prepared food, baked bread, cooked meat, and mixed wine.[17] If only they would long for it![18] As the sage says: "Wisdom[19] has built her house and chopped seven[20] pillars for herself, made her slaughter, mixed her wine, and also set her table," (Prov. 9:1–2) as we have explained ad loc.[21]

---

13. Cf. *Beliefs* 1:5 (p. 23): "All this is demonstrable only by means of the science of geometry which shows us synthetically how one figure enters into the other. . . . This finally enables us to recognize that the figures of the heavenly bodies are spherical or circular and that some are concentric with others." See also *Beliefs* 1:1 (p. 42).

14. Cf. *Beliefs* 4:Exc. (p. 182): "By means of it [wisdom], moreover, he attains to the knowledge of the disposition of the heavenly spheres and of course of the stars and the measurement of their masses and their distances and the rest of their attributes."

15. The beginning of the pericope speaks of God's command (*miswab*) which the Gaon understands here, as in his commentary to Prov. 8:2, as "wisdom."

16. Apparently a statement to the effect that the ancient people were not in need of organization is missing here. (According to Zucker.)

17. Something to the effect that they would not even turn to it should probably be supplied.

18. Something like: "if it were provided in such a manner" must be added.

19. Manuscript mistakenly has: "Wisdom of women."

20. According to Kafih's edition; however Derenbourgh's has "many." See the Gaon's com. to Gen. 4:15 and 6:16.

21. He compares (Kafih, p. 81) those who dictate their opinions only after fully investigating and testing them to opposition to one who invites his friends to his ready house after furbishing it. The Gaon then cites this verse but only to

II Fundamental Assumptions of the Torah

After describing order and its importance, the rules that the substance of
this Book follows and the foundation upon which it stands should be
mentioned. I say: I have seen that despite the loftiness of the Torah and
its great importance, it is not God's only trustworthy source[22] nor
guidance set up for His servants in serving Him, but He has two other
sources of knowledge for us. The first precedes this Book and the other
succeeds it.[23] The one that precedes it is intuitive knowledge,[24] which is
created in one whose mind is devoid of [all] impediments and pure of
[any] defect. The one succeeding it is the knowledge transmitted by God's
messengers that His righteous prophets passed over by informing [us of]
the authentic reports. These three sources [of knowledge]—I mean
intuitive, written, and received—when they meet, give people perfection.[25]

III Necessity of Combination

[26]After [stating] God's praise and desirability, [I say]: Despite that the
intellect apprehends the simple elements of all existence and recognizes
the components of the sensibles, it does not attain this until after it

---

describe the state of an organized presentation of knowledge. Also, his discussion
(ibid.) makes mention of the Masoretes, which may suggest that he directs this
argument against some sect—not necessarily the people as a whole.

22. For preparing the people for the obedience of God (see his intro. to Ps.
[Kafih p. 14]). He elaborates on this section in his IT IV. Cf. also *Beliefs* intro.:5
(p. 19).

23. In logical precedence.

24. Literally "intellectual knowledge," which is knowledge of intuition, i.e.,
that instantly apprehended. See note. Cf. *Beliefs* 1:5 (p. 20): "By the intuition of
the intellect (lit. knowledge of the intellect [Kafih, *Emunoth*, p. 14]) we mean such
notions as they spring up solely in the mind of a human being such as
approbation of truthfulness and disapproval of . . ." This is opposed to
knowledge of necessity, which is that knowledge obtained through contempla-
tion.

25. In their worship of God.

26. See section IV where the Gaon states that the purpose of this preamble is
to show the necessity in the compositeness of speech.

separates the composite into simple components and identifies them within the composition by discerning and testing. This is [because] the primary knowledge which is knowledge through the senses,[27] i.e., {knowledge} which is associated with composite things, when it apprehends these things it passes them in front of the secondary knowledge[28] which parses and discerns them and finds that each one of them is composed of a number of components. Despite that it is possible to do without setting forth examples of what I have explained, because people can easily attest to this [themselves], I [nevertheless] shall not refrain from giving some examples. The sense of sight that comes into first contact with a book, determines at the point of contact that it is a book and directs {this notion} to the power of the intellect which discerns it. It then becomes apparent to {the intellect} that the actual writing because of which it is called a book is something accidental and that there is something which carries these characteristics called a "substance." Now, when the sight falls on a defined region and a spread-out area,[29] the intellect declares that the book has something called "quantity." Likewise, when it discerns colors and other various features, the intellect will judge that it has something called "quality." In a similar fashion it judges the rest of the categories[30] associated with matter. Now even though the senses find [all of] {the categories} to emanate from a single source,[31] [the intellect then] applies logical testing, dissects, and apprehends every component in them individually. It knows that a single subject may appear in various objects, like whiteness which appears in snow, man, stones, cotton, and the like, just as it knows that many components may meet in a single body. Now in order that the intellect have this function, [i.e.] that it discern between things that the senses gather, the Creator of all things, may He be blessed and exalted, created everything combined and composed.[32] Furthermore so that the fact that [there exist] combined and composite [things] should prove that they have a combiner and composer[33] and also so that all the components be contingent upon each

27. See note 57 and section XIV.
28. Intuitive or necessary knowledge, which involve the intellect.
29. Apparently, the contour and surface of the book.
30. Of Aristotle.
31. Text: "existence," meaning that they are part of one and the same object.
32. I.e., to enable people to be able to discern various features or facets of existence.
33. The fact that existence is composite was used by the Kalam theologians

other.[34] [Again,] with these three intentions and some beyond them declared by His wisdom,[35] God attached composition and combination to all of existence. Now despite that the mind enfolds these three reasons and the intellect embraces them, the endowed Book [nevertheless] dilates on them for it says of some of {these reasons} according to my translation [as follows:] "So that the people see this and know, demonstrate[36] and think altogether[37] that God's power made this and the Holy of Israel created it." (Is. 41:20) This is the source for [the obligation in] engaging the intellect. It also says according to my translation: "So that they know from sunrise to its setting that there is nothing other than Me; I am God and there is no other." (Is. 45:6)[38] This is the source for [the necessity in] deduction.[39] The sage also says according to my translation: "The gatherer says: I found that all things need each other so that the mind may find and apprehend it." (Ecl. 7:27)[40] This is the source for [the notion that] all [parts of] existence are contingent on each other.[41]

---

to prove the existence of a Creator. See Wolfson, *Kalam Arguments for Creation*, p. 204.

34. Apparently the Gaon means that they should prove the existence of cause and effect to show the existence of God. See his intro. to Ps. (p. 18) for proofs of the createdness of existence.

35. Cf. his *BO* 1:1 (p. 36) where the Gaon speaks of the incomprehensibility of the creation.

36. The translation ad loc. has: *yabahhathun* (investigation) as opposed to *yathbatu* (found) here. See Ratsaby, *Isaiah*, p. 89 for an alternate reading.

37. The meaning is that these scientific acts should be done together, not that the people should gather together to do them. See also *BO* 1:1 (p. 49) where the Gaon discusses this verse in greater detail.

38. However, in his *Beliefs* 2:2 (p. 98) the Gaon (as well as Al-Qirqisani, ibid.) use this verse to show God's unity. See *BO* 1:1 (p. 49) where he discusses this verse in greater detail.

39. Apparently, the Gaon takes this verse to be speaking of philosophical investigation by which God's existence may be determined from the rise and setting of the sun, i.e., observation of natural phenomena. Al-Qirqisani (ibid.) has by way of paraphrase: 'That is to infer by way of reasoning that a thing made presupposes the existence of a maker." However, he learns this lesson from the previous verse the Gaon cites.

40. Ibn Ghayyath in his commentary ad loc. (p. 250) rejects the Gaon's translation of the verse.

41. Al-Qirqisani (ibid., p. 56) has: "Proof for the existence of cause and effect through the dependence of all existing things upon the other."

IV The Compositeness of Existence and Knowledge

Since there are three principles of wisdom in things being composite, the Wise, the Great, and Exalted One, brought out everything He showed man[42] from what He created combined and composite. As far as the contingency of everything upon combination and its existence by its means is concerned, there is no difference in regards to the existence of a small particle by its contingence on a large one and the contingence of a large particle on a small one, for everything is [of] one [type of] combination. This is apparent from the animals, for their large limbs can not be upheld without the small ones.[43] This also applies to plants and likewise to the parts of the celestial spheres and the earth which exist because of each other[44] and are also a place for each other[45] as it says in God's Book that He upkeeps them together by His command as it says: "I call them and they are present together." (Is. 48:13)[46] The [application] of the principles of combination extends from the parts of the largest surrounder and its center[47] to the parts of the vessels by which service is performed[48] so that the existence of the larger vessels depends on the small ones, for otherwise the service is not valid. As the Scripture describes this type of labor: "Their makers are gathered from [among] humans." (Is. 44:11)[49]

Now that we have noted that none of the sensible [existences] is

---

42. Apparently the meaning is the world visible to man as opposed to the upper world, which is composed of pure substance. See *Beliefs* 4:2 (p. 184) and 6:3 (p. 242). See also Ibn Paqudah (*Duties*, 1:6, p. 18) for a more elaborate discussion.

43. Text has "in measurement," but since this phrase sounds superfluous in translation we have omitted it.

44. Cf. *Beliefs* 1:1 (p. 42).

45. This clause is not entirely clear.

46. See below where the Gaon uses this verse to show that the sky and the earth were created simultaneously. In his *Beliefs* 2:5 (p. 106) he again cites this verse but as a proof that each individual part of existence was created simultaneously.

47. I.e., the sky and the earth respectively.

48. In the Temple.

49. The Gaon does not refer to the dependence of the vessels on each other but speaks only of collective effort expressed by the idea in the cited verse that the men come together to work. See also ad loc. p. 98. Cf. Al-Qirqisani, *Book of Gardens*, p. 56.

without composition for if they separate they degenerate as a result and
certainly if the percepts be . . . for all knowledge is conveyed by the
senses[50] just as the only path to the second is through the first.[51] Indeed,
God may He be exalted has already made an allegory to the effect that
trustworthy proofs [are obtained] through combination [i.e.] of plants
that sprout as the result of [the following:] motion from above,[52] the
ascension of a mist from the earth, [the mist] liquefying and being
absorbed by the earth. As the result of the combination of all of these
factors the plants sprout. This is expressed in the statement: "The sky shall
drizzle from above, the constellations will overflow with righteousness
and the earth will open up because of it; help will flourish and
righteousness will grow with it. I am God. I have created this." (Is. 45:8)
"The sky shall drizzle from above" alludes to motion that comes from the
[heavenly] influence and causes mists.[53] "The constellations will overflow
with righteousness" alludes to an overflow and overabundance of what
[then] turns into water {upon descending to} the Earth.[54] "And the Earth
will open up because of it" means coming into contact with the water and
receiving it for all of {these events} are the cause of the [sprouting of]
plants[55] as it says "will grow." Since the reference with these symbols is
not to the actual rain but to the proofs and demonstration understandable
only when many things meet, it calls what overflows from the sky
allegorically as "righteousness" when it says "overflow with righteousness"
as well as what sprouts from the Earth when it says "righteousness shall
grow."[56] Now "with it" refers to everything He described together.[57] "I am

---

50. Cf. *Beliefs* 2:13 (p. 132) and Intro:1 (p. 5), where the Gaon reiterates his
view that all knowledge is through the senses.

51. Apparently this is meant in the general sense.

52. See below.

53. Cf. Ibn Ezra's com. to Gen. 2:6 (Linetsky, p. 54).

54. I.e., that it starts out as vapour and becomes water falling onto the Earth.
Al-Qirqisani (ibid.) has "Points to the precipitants upon the Earth in the shape of
rain of the part of the vapor which has been condensed into water."

55. Apparently he means that even the earth absorbing the water is a factor
for the sprouting of plants.

56. Although it is not certain precisely how the Gaon understands this
allegory, the gist seems to be to that as a result of combination righteousness shall
profess, "righteousness" apparently representing "correctness," as the Gaon says
what follows.

57. I.e., the ref. is to the entire statement not just to "help will flourish."

God. I have created this" means that [God] may He be praised set down
that proofs are clarified through combination just as He set down that the
creation exists composite and combined.[58] Now since God knew that the
allegory shows compositeness of argumentation merely by allusion, He
elucidates this without an allegory [in] that righteousness and soundness
are determined from composite things for it says (Ps. 19:10) according to
my translation: "God's judgments are just done together."[59] This "doing
together" is the combination of the five things that it mentions before
this: "Returns the soul" (Ps. 19:8) is something that the senses cannot pick
up[60] but that the soul[61] is forced to discern [things] in it.[62] "Makes fools
wise" (ibid.) is what the intellect devoid of defect attests to.[63] "Cheer the
hearts" (ibid.) are the correct assumptions and conclusions that the mind[64]
gives credence to. "Illuminates the eyes" (ibid.) is the light and radiance
[created by] speech when doubts are lifted and disappear. "Stand forever"
(Ps. 19:10) is insisting on something after challenges and invective have
been brought against it but it is [indeed] not contradicted when then the
truth manifests by combining and joining these five fundamentals as it says:
"God's judgments are just done together." Lo! how did he trod in the right
path?![65]

Indeed I have obligated myself to present the importance of combination as preamble to my interpretation of this Book before anything so that

---

58. See beginning of this section.

59. Kafih (p. 86) reads "And His judgments are all just and righteous."

60. In unadulterated form.

61. The Gaon refers to the soul's intellective faculty, but speaks of the soul
holistically because he maintains that there is just one soul with three faculties,
not a tripartite division of it. See *Beliefs* 6:3 (p. 243) and 10:2 (p. 360).

62. I.e., necessary knowledge, or that which requires deliberation. See *Beliefs*
Intro:1 (p. 16): "By knowledge derived from logical necessity, again, is meant
conclusions, which, unless they are accepted by the individual as true compel to
his denial of the validity of his rational intuition or the perception of his senses.
Since, however, he cannot negate either of the two, he must regard the said
inferences as being correct."

63. This is the definition given to immediate recognition by the Kalam
theologians.

64. Unadulterated learning ability corresponding to the definition of "knowledge" given by the Kalam theologians.

65. Text: "heart." Cf. *Beliefs* 6:1 (p. 239): "Thus wisdom is called *heart*, because
the heart is the seat of wisdom." Cf. Ibn Ezra's com. to Gen. 1:1 (Linetsky, p. 8).

one does not think that the compositeness of speech[66] is merely an embellishment and decoration;[67] it is rather as essential as creation and nature as I have previously explained[68] so that one also should not take lightly [any] minor point of a matter for without {the minor point} the entire matter will not be sustained.

V The Virtues of Organization

Now that I have revealed some of the virtues of combination, I should follow up with the virtues of organization. I say that an organized statement is much easier for the listener to comprehend than one that is in disorder.[69] This is because despite that the composer of the disordered statement has exhausted all [efforts] required for it [to be complete] and buttresses it, {the statement} will still not be fully comprehensible for most people listening to it since one will need effort and exertion to memorize it all.

VI The Types of Preparation
for the Fulfillment of the Precepts

. . . [70]command, recompense, and ethical lesson for this is because it is a book of worship and the essence of worship is the fulfillment of the precepts. We find that the most perfect [method of] preparation for people in receiving the precepts is by means of three things: Command, [telling of] recompense, and [giving] ethical lesson. [An example of] a command is: "do" or "don't do." Recompense is revealing the consequence, i.e., what doing the commanded or prohibited act will lead to. Ethical lesson is telling the events of people who observed this [command or prohibition] and prospered as well as of those that acted corruptibly and

---

66. The above section describes the process of the formation of an opinion.

67. I.e., the putting together of ideas or argumentation. This section appears to have been made as a justification for the use of reason and rationale in the interpretation of the Bible.

68. See section I, where the Gaon states that an organized statement is like an ornament.

69. This section appears to be lacking.

70. See section I, where the Gaon speaks of the importance of organization.

perished. I will give an example from the medical profession of one who has pain and whose phlegm has accumulated.[71] If the physician merely prohibits this sick person to drink milk or other cold, moist foods this would be beneficial. What would be better [however] is if he would tell him the consequence of this and would say: "If you continue drinking it, your desire will lead you to deadly disease." But [what would be] even better than these two corrective means is to tell him about someone who did so and perished and adds to these two ideas: "Just as such became ill."[72] Just as the most effective [kind of] warning is one that includes these three ideas, so the most effective [form of] urging is with three other ideas; they are that he should [then] say to him, for example: "If you eat the seeds for the stomach I hope you will be healed like such."[73] Since the Wisest One knew that when these three ideas meet we will obtain the best [form of] correction, He made them the mainstay of His Teaching. This is like when God warns against idol worship when He says: "Do not follow any worshipped objects among the worshipped objects of the nations." (Deut. 6:14–15) It tells that the consequence of this is destruction as it says: "For God your master bears the iniquitous . . . lest His wrath fasten upon you and He destroy from the face of the earth." (ibid.) It further tells of those who did not follow this and perished just as did the worshippers of Pe'or and their followers as it says: "Your eyes see everything that God did with Pe'or the idol that every man that followed him God your Master destroyed from among you." (Deut. 4:3) Just as it collected in one verse the ways of warning and said: "This is a reminder to Israel so that a foreign man who is not from the offspring of Aaron does not approach to fumigate incense in front of God and shall not be like Korah and his throng as God revealed [His opinion] regarding [Korah]," (Nu. 17:5) so also the Scripture combines the methods of urging in a single verse and says: "And God commanded us to do all these laws so that we fear God our Lord so that He endows us with long life and we live as this day." (Deut. 6:24)

---

71. The purpose of this section, which the Gaon reiterates in his IT II and *Beliefs* 3:6 (p. 155), is to show the necessity of the various nonlegal accounts in the Pentateuch, which in his opinion is essentially a book of worship (see previous note).

72. In the parallel passage in *Beliefs* 3:6 (p. 155), the Gaon uses the example of someone with a fever.

73. I.e., that he also suffered from this specific sickness.

VII The Classification of the Precepts

After this I should elaborate briefly on these three notions. I say: The primary knowledge of how God should be worshipped is divided into two parts: Commands and prohibitions.[74] The count of all of {the precepts}, combining the intellectual and auditory ones[75] is 613—248 of them positive and 365 of them negative. They also may follow a different order, by grouping together the positive commandments that are not set down for juridical matters[76] amounting to 100, negative commandments that are not punishable by death in its various forms amounting to 277, those that are punishable by death amounting to 71, and those set down for matters of accidents[77] amounting to 65.[78] . . . [79] The other prophet said: "For I too know what will be good for those who fear God, and good shall not be for the wicked." (Ecl. 8:14)[80] God set down some reward and punishment in this world[81] so that it serves as evidence and proof for us of the other reward and punishment[82] as His votary says of the delight of this world: "Make a sign for me for the good." (Ps. 86:17) God may He be exalted said of its punishment: "And they shall be for you evidence and proof." (Deut. 28:46) Reward and punishment in their essence [however]

---

74. The Gaon reiterates these levels of warning in his IT II and com. to Lev. 17:1 (see Zucker, *Genesis*, p. 172, n. 30, for an excerpt). Cf. also the Gaon's intro. to Prov. (p. 15). This division originates in the *Sifra* ad loc.

75. In his introductions to Psalms (p. 21) the Gaon expresses the opinion that these two ideas underlie all the revealed books.

76. The Gaon speaks in detail of these two categories of precepts in his *Book of the Derivation of the Precepts* (p. 18) as well as in his *Beliefs* 3:1 (p. 140). This division of the precepts derives from the Mu'tazila theologians.

77. Those related to daily living.

78. Apparently those arising between people. See IT II.

79. The Gaon reiterates this section in his *Book of Praises* (p. 156) and his *Book of the Derivation of the Precepts* (p. 190). Rabbi Samuel ben Hophni cites this passage in his *Treatise on the Commandments* (p. 222).

80. Some discussion of reward and punishment must have preceded.

81. Apparently the Gaon assumes that the lack of mention of recompense in this world indicates recompense in the world to come. See Mann, "A Karaite Tract," *Jewish Quarterly Review* 1922, p. 274 regarding a similar view expressed by Daniel al-Qumisi. (Zucker)

82. Cf. *Beliefs* 5:1 (p. 209): "It is, therefore, only a specimen and sample of these rewards and punishments that is furnished in this world, while the totality of their merits is stored for the virtuous like treasure."

are [meted out] in the other world[83] as it says: "For all the acts of God He shall bring to judgment for anything good or bad." (Ecl. 12:14) I shall discuss [this matter] elaborately when I reach the pericope of "If according to my statutes"[84] and ones similar to it, where I shall cite all the proofs found in the Scripture,[85] God willing.

Now as for the third notion, which is notion of ethics, it is not possible that I set forth the explanation of all its particulars here due to the lengthiness of the matter and because it is explained in the Scripture itself. I say only that the Scripture described the obedience of Noah, Abraham, Isaac, Moses, Aaron, Joshua, Caleb, Phineas, and the like and the rewards their acts merited them in order that we aspire to their acts and act like them as God's prophet says: "In order that you tread in the path of the good and the path of the righteous you shall watch." (Prov. 2:20) [Likewise] it describes the sin of Adam, the people of Noah, Pelegh, Lot, Pharaoh, Amalek, Meqalel, Korah, and Zimri and what each one's acts merited them so that we be careful and not act like them as God's prophet said: "In the path of evil do not go." (Prov. 4:14)[86]

VIII Types of Report and Their Purpose

Despite that these three notions are like the mainstays of the Torah they embrace another eighteen themes which, however, are entirely subsumed by the title "report" and its subdivisions. Eight of them are those that are associated with command and prohibition, which are the gist of the Torah's purpose.[87] Seven of them are of a lower level. The three remaining

---

83. I.e., in the world to come.

84. Cf. *Beliefs* 9:1 (p. 327): "All these instances indicate may God have mercy on thee, that the prophets peace be upon them, were all agreed upon this: that the reward for man's behavior is not meted out in this world but is only given in the world that comes after it." The Gaon reiterates this point in his intro. to Daniel (Ratsaby, *RSG's Interpretation of Daniel*, p. 98[2]) Cf. also *Beliefs* 5:2 (p. 210). See Zucker, "Translation," p. 173 and *Genesis*, p. 173, n. 44, for further sources and discussion.

85. See *Beliefs* 11:13 (p. 237).

86. Apparently proofs of the existence of reward and punishment in the world to come. See E. Mittwoch, "An unknown Fragment by Saadiah," p. 121 and *Beliefs* 9:1 (p. 326) for an enumeration of versus indicating this.

87. Cf. *Beliefs* 3:5 (p. 154).

ones are of the lowest level but still have use, for it is impossible that the Book embraces matters that have no use.

[88]I should enumerate the first eight themes and how they are useful. I say: The first is the report of creation in which God tells us that He created the elements, the beings, and all the kinds of sensible existences and divided them into six parts throughout six days. This has various purposes. One of them is that if we understand that He created everyone [of the bodies] we will not liken them to Him[89] nor will we worship any of them since they, I mean these individual [bodies], are created. Also in order that we believe in the signs about which God is to tell us that He made them when we say: One who had the power to create it also has the ability to create or remove accidents [from it] as well as destroy it or even revive it.

. . . . [90]God told us by means of these signs the excellence of the prophets. [91]Some of them are signs for the prophet to be certain that the words he hears are from God as God showed Moses the pillars of cloud and likewise to Aaron and Samuel so that they believe that the signs and wonders that accompany the speech are for them to be certain that the speech they heard is from God. [This is] because they are created when [the prophecy] commences and are lifted when it concludes as it says: "The God of Moses and Aaron of His priests and Samuel of those who comply with Him call God and He answers them, in a pillar of cloud He speaks to them." (Ps. 99:7)[92] Similar to this is the incident of the Bush[93]

---

88. Therefore these are the eight loftiest. In his introduction to Psalms (p. 21) the Gaon states that these two ideas underlie all the revealed books. See section VII.

89. Cf. *Beliefs* 3:6 (p. 154): "God has provided us with summary accounts of all that has happened in the past in order that we might be put into a condition for obeying Him."

90. Cf. *Beliefs* 2:9 (p. 113) where the Gaon speaks of the impossibility of God resembling anything. See section XV.

91. What preceded apparently was a discussion of the reports of the signs made by the prophets.

92. This section is elaborately reiterated in the *Beliefs* 3:5 (p. 151) and com. to Dan. (Ratasby, *RSG's Interpretation of Daniel*, p. 103[7]). Cf. also *Beliefs* Intro.:6 (p. 28). Rabbi Samuel ben Hophni in his *Treatise on the Commandments* (p. 227) adds that in lieu of a miracle the attestation of another trustworthy prophet is acceptable.

93. This verse is intended only to show that God spoke with these men in a cloud created for the purpose of verifying the divinity of speech irrespective of

and vision of the bow[94] in the incident with Ezekiel. They are also signs for the people to which God sent [the messenger] so that when they see the signs they know that it indeed[95] . . . will do it so that they be certain that He is God's messenger . . . These signs are of three kinds: For revenge, for pity, and neither for revenge nor for pity. An example of one for pity is like the manna,[96] the quail,[97] the well, and the cloud. For revenge is like the plagues that God smote Pharaoh. One that is neither for pity nor for revenge is like turning the staff into a snake and returning it to a snake[98] . . . and healthy flesh[99] and part of the water turning into blood through Moses and the like. This third part is merely for the vindication of the messenger for it causes people neither ill nor delight. The prophet predicts the creation of the signs before they come to be so that the people attribute them to him as it says: "By this peculiarity you shall know that I am God: Behold I strike the water with the staff that is in my hand, which will turn to blood." (Ex. 7:17)[100] It also says: "By this you shall know that God sent me," (Num. 17:28) and the like. The prophet [then] returns and mentions the sign to the people after it comes about and says: "Remember that you saw it with your [own] eyes,"[101] as it says: "And you should know that from today the task is not upon your children who did not know and did not see the wonders of God your

---

whether the sign and the prophecy are in confluence. Cf. *Beliefs* 3:5 (p. 156): "Yes I find that everywhere in the account given of a certain prophet in one place is not explicitly stated that God revealed Himself in a pillar of a cloud, it is made clear about him in another book of the Scripture He did thus reveal Himself to him: Thus Samuel is included with Moses and Aaron in one passage of the Scripture."

94. Ex. 3:2. This accords with the Gaon's view that even Moses did not actually see God but only His abode, despite that God spoke to him "face to face" (see intro. to Ps. p. 28). Cf. *Beliefs* 2:12 (p. 130): "As for the Creator Himself, however, there is no means whereby anybody might see Him." See also Zucker, *Genesis*, p. 175, n. 52 for further discussion.

95. Ez. 1:28.

96. Is a true prophecy.

97. Ex. 16:15.

98. Ex. 16:13 and Deut. 11:31.

99. Ex. 4:4.

100. In this lacuna the Gaon apparently speaks of Moses' hand, which turned leprous and then reverted to health. See Ex. 4:6.

101. Although Moses attributes the actual miracle to God he ascribes its activation and initiation to himself.

master and His signs and acts that He did," (Deut. 11:2–3)[102] and further "What He did to Egypt's army and its horses and chariots." (Deut. 11:4)[103]

The third is for urging. This [theme] is divided into two kinds: That which already happened before the Torah was given and that which will be after it is given. An example of this is that God told Noah that he will go through a flood which came to be, that He told Abraham that He will turn over Sodom which came to be, that He told Sarah that she will give birth and she [indeed] gave birth and that her offspring will be in a foreign land and will be enslaved and that God will judge [the nation] for their oppression which all [likewise] came to be. As for what will be after the writing of the Torah, an example of this is that Jacob told all the tribes and informed every one of them what will be their portions in the land that they will inherit as he mentioned before this: "Gather, I shall tell you what will come about you at the end of days." (Gen. 49:1) He told each one of them the place of his dwelling, dominion and conquests. Likewise what He told us of our exile and dispersion and all . . . as it says: "and it shall be when all these things shall come upon you." (Deut. 30:1)[104] Now the manner of wisdom in God telling us what will come about after the giving of the Torah is so that we endure what will come upon us in the exile and will hope for what He promised as we say: Just as the previous prophecies have come true there is no doubt that the prophecies to be will come true [as well] along the lines of what it says in a number of places: "Like everything He did in Egypt in your presence," (Deut. 1:30) that we endure patiently for the promise and not get suspicious as it says: "I am God that those who hope in Me shall not be abashed." (Is. 49:23)

The fourth type is [reports of] pity . . . that God pities His worshippers whom sorrow and straits befall when they cry out to Him and repent to Him, like He saved those that were burnt by fire as it says: "And a fire ignited in them" (Num. 11:1) [this being] because of their merit for crying out to Him as it says (Num. 11:2): "And the people cried out to Moses,"

---

102. These are the Gaon's words, not a biblical verse.

103. I.e., it is you who should know.

104. See *Beliefs* 3:4 (p. 147) and com. to Dan. 7:24 (Ratsaby, *RSG's Interpretation of Daniel*, p. 7) where the Gaon speaks of the various types of signs. See Zucker, *Genesis*, p. 176, n. 59 regarding the various requirements for the signs established by the Kalam theologians.

and like He destroyed Pharaoh when they[105] cried out to Him.[106] The
manner of wisdom in this is that they should have a proof of this[107] . . .
when . . . of one who pitied them and answered them and they repent
to Him as it says: "It is His way to save the helpless from their helplessness
and therefore does He come to them when they are pressed." (Job
36:15)[108]

The fifth type is [reports of] trials [note: cf. the Gaon's intro to Isaiah
Ratzaby, p. 248]. He told us what sorrows came upon the righteous. For
example the various kinds of trials that came upon Abraham, Isaac,
Joseph, and Moses which they endured and that . . . they endured and
directed their enemies and was kind to them to the time . . . and the
second . . .[109] its example of it in order that a person be bashful like
Adam, generous like Abraham, forgiving like Isaac, merciful like Jacob,
paying bad with good like Joseph, zealous to God like Phineas, tolerant
like Aaron, humble like Moses, quick like Joshua, and like the other
people that the Scripture recorded as having praiseworthy traits.[110] It
only records this in order to discipline the people in these traits. As
opposed to this, one should not take on the reprehensible traits that are
related of those who were condemned for having them. The prophet said
that {discipline} may be one of two kinds: True ethics in which one should
mold himself as it says: "Hear advice and accept discipline so that you be
wise at your end." (Prov. 19:20)[111] The other is discipline of speech by
name [alone] is what fools profess in as it says: "Abstain my son from
hearing discipline that will distract you from matters of knowledge."
(Prov. 19:27)[112]

The fifth kind is [reports of] prosperity in this world. The Scripture sets
forth reports in this matter because God knew that one of man's traits

---

105. Manuscript reads "He."

106. Cf. *Beliefs* 9:2 (p. 327).

107. Perhaps the reference is to Ex. 2:23.

108. In the future.

109. See *Beliefs* 5:8 (p. 23) where the Gaon uses this verse to teach a different
lesson.

110. Apparently the second reason for recording trials.

111. Cf. the Gaon's com. to Gen. 1:24.

112. The Gaon states ad loc.: "A number of principles are involved in giving
direction to the end. One is to tell the discipliner together with the disciplined
and say: 'Be patient for this [discipline] for its utility becomes apparent only at the
end."

called "laziness" detracts [from him] the zeal for work[113] and were we to take heed of what He wrote for us of the righteous engaging in work and that Jacob and Moses [for example] were shepherds we would know that this is the way of the world.[114] [This is] because the Creator fixed in the animals the desire for sustenance in order to upkeep their bodies, for the soul is like fire, and no fire can sustain itself without matter.[115] When we accustom ourselves to this we will seek the zeal in the way of the world. For that reason {the Scripture} presents the types of work at the beginning of its account of man's history. For example: "The first to live in tents and own cattle," (Gen. 4:20) "the first to grasp a tanabir and lyre," (Gen. 21) and "the first smoother of work with copper and iron." (Gen. 22). The Prophets also praised this [activity] as it says: "It shall be said to him: 'Were you to eat of the labor of your palm you are blessed and beneficence is yours.'" (Ps. 128:2)

The sixth kind is [reports of] sexual relations, I mean a man marrying a woman according to the Laws. It provides us with accounts of this subject since God knew that some of us will harbor opinions that oppose engaging in them. {The holders of this opinion} are the votaries of purity and sanctity and those who are cautious with impurity.[116] The other is the opinion that prompts us to engage in it in what ever way we like it like the view of the [. . .].[117] It obligates us to take the middle[118] of these two extremes so that we do not engage in them excessively nor should we abstain from them entirely. Instead we should engage in[119] sexual relations permitted by the normative laws.[120] The minds of some of us should not tempt us to abstain from them entirely since nature implanted

---

113. Possibly the reference is to the various extremes of ideal human conduct which leads to the distortion of knowledge. See *Beliefs* 10:14 (p. 394).

114. Cf. *Beliefs* 10:16 (p. 397) where the Gaon discusses this trait and its consequences.

115. One should be encouraged to do work. Cf. BR where working is considered a positive commandment.

116. See section XIV.

117. Here the Gaon lists ascetic groups. See Goldziher, *Introduction to Islamic Theology and Law* p. 116 regarding the various ascetic groups.

118. See Zucker, *Genesis*, p. 179, n. 71 and the Gaon's com. to Prov. 27:2 and 30:9.

119. Text reads "They should be."

120. Cf. *Beliefs* 10:15 (p. 396) and Maimonides, *Mishnah Torah, hil. De'oth* 1:7 (p. 48a). Regarding the Gaon's perception of the mean in a person's conduct, see Efros, *Studies in Medieval Philosophy*, p. 127 n. 15.

in animals the desire to sustain their kind by giving birth to another. [On the other hand] one who considers this [will realize that in this aspect he] is no better than Noah, Abraham, Isaac, Jacob, Moses, and Aaron who got married[121] and extreme desire will not bring us to sexual relations that the Laws do not look well upon. He will [then] observe the children of the nobles, I mean the Estimable Sons,[122] Shechem, Zimri, and others, how they engaged in them inappropriately and perished.[123]

The seventh is [reports of] travels. God gave them a purpose[124] when He reported them to us. For example it describes the travels of Abraham, Jacob, and Moses for various reasons, one of which is that one should not at all times attach to the land where he was born but that he may depart it because of some events that may come about. Now would God not have told us about these acts, were we to engage sound intellect it would derive {them} for us, God includes in the Scripture [anyway] in order to strengthen our deliberation and exemplification of this.[125]

Now as for the three remaining types that complete the eighteen, the first is [reports of] dates: The wise One informed us of them since He knew that the people would be happy to know them and will approach it[126] enthusiastically when they find out the [amount of] years [spanning] from the beginning of the creation of the world to their day. He also tells us their divisions and intervals, i.e., that from the generation of so-and-so there are such-and-such many years. This serves for them as an illumi-

---

121. Cf. *Beliefs* 10:7 (p. 327): "A husband should give vent to his desire for his wife in accordance with the dictates of reason and religion and to the extent required to bind them closely together, but restrain it vigorously and forcefully beyond that point."

122. Cf. *Beliefs* 10:7 (p. 371): "If sexual intercourse had been reprehensible God blessed and exalted be He would have restrained His prophets and messengers peace be upon them from it."

123. It seems according to this that the Gaon maintains that the people of Shechem were full of concupiscence.

124. See his com. to Gen. 6:4.

125. Apparently the Gaon means that because the importance of this information is peripheral in comparison to the other.

126. The Gaon discusses the uses of travels in a separate treatise dedicated specifically to this subject. See Zucker, *Genesis*, p. 431 for the remnants of this work. See also Boaz Cohen, *Quotations from Saadia's Bible Commentaries*, p. 125. Cf. See Rabbi Samuel ben Hophni in the opening of his commentary to the pericope of *wayese* where he also lists the uses of travel.

nating candle and will be [likened] in their minds to a station going from one point of time to another. This is how the people of the Torah feel!

The second is [reports of] lineage. The Torah attributes Noah to the seventy nations[127] and likewise Abraham, Ismael, Jacob, and Esau. This is because the Creator may He be blessed knew that we will feel at home knowing this lineage since our minds prompt us for us to discover them. [The result of this is] that man becomes for us like a tree that God planted in the earth and that then branched out and extended east, west, south, and north in the inhabitable part of the Earth. We will see the many as one and the one as many. [In addition to this] one will also turn his attention to the names of lands and cities.[128]

The third is [reports of] the number of people mentioned in [the Scripture] an example of which is Israel being counted in four places *where reason would find it useful to know how the nation grew after* being exiguous as it says: "As seventy people your fathers descended to Egypt." (Deut. 6:22) Also in order that we know how large the masses of the people who saw the signs of the messenger and heard God's words on the mountain were as it says: "And the entire nation contemplated the voices," (Ex. 20:18) and also so that we know how large were the masses of people whom the messenger administered with mercy, gave them a leader, and supplied them with food and sustenance as it says: "And Moses said six hundred thousand footmen of the people among which I am, and You said: 'I shall give them meat and they will eat it one month,'"[129] (Num. 11:21) and what ever fits the context. {Another} example of this is the tax of one thousand when it says: "And this is the amount that went into the tabernacle," (Ex. 38:21) and for this and the like there are reasons which I will explain in the middle of the book, God willing.[130]

IX The Necessity in the Oral Tradition

The level above the knowledge of the endowed Book completing the religion of the believers is the knowledge of what is transmitted by the

---

127. Apparently the Torah.

128. The Gaon states in his com. to Dan. 7:17 (See Zucker, *Genesis*, p. 180 n. 170 for an excerpt) that he expounded this matter in his com. to the Torah. However, this section has not surfaced yet.

129. This is something incidental.

130. Verse 24 continues to speak of the seventy men whom Moses set up for them as leaders.

messenger—i.e., preservation of the tradition.[131] I should first mention the necessity that calls for conveying and transmitting the tradition of the messenger generation after generation, before describing the transmission [itself]. I say this[132] is because the precepts[133] written in the Torah are one of two kinds, intellectual and auditory.[134] The intellectual precepts were they not mentioned in the Book, the worshipper would still come to know them and therefore if words that do not have a clear sense in the language are used in reporting them, this will not make [the report] ambiguous for us because the intellect will come to discern them and will ascertain and verify [the meaning] through judgment and correctness. As for the auditory precepts, [however,] because they were not stated in the Book we would not come to [know] them [ourselves] and therefore if words that are unclear in the language are used, this will confuse us by this since they can withstand many interpretations it would necessitate us in the words of someone who saw the messenger to unambiguate the words of the biblical[135] precept. Likewise the intellect declares that God will not give His commands ambiguously for it says: "Know that the precepts that I command you today are not concealed from you nor are they afar," (Deut. 30:11) but attests that they are lucid as it says: "They are correct for those who understand them and are like a plain for those who find knowledge." (Prov. 8:9)[136]

X What Requires One to Turn to the Tradition

By gathering we find [that there are] seven principles of the biblical[137] precepts that require us to turn to the tradition,[138] each one [of them hierarchically] above the other. The first is that the Book contains precepts whose quality was not explained, like how the fringes and

---

131. This section has not surfaced yet.
132. See introduction to translation, section II.
133. That the transmitted is above the written.
134. Al-Qirqisani, *Book of Gardens*, (p. 124) cites this section verbatim.
135. See section VII.
136. Text reads "reported."
137. Al-Qirqisani (Kitab al-Anwar) argues that these precepts were left to be determined by analogy and therefore do not require oral tradition to elucidate them.
138. Text reads "related."

tabernacle are to be made and the like.[139] The second is because it
contains commandments whose quantity was not explained. For example,
it did not reveal the quantity of the charity known as the "heave offering,"
i.e., what part of what amount[140] nor the quantity of money, wives,
horses, that the king may have. It did [however] warn him of [having an]
excess [of these things] when it says: "He just should not have too many
horses, wives, too much silver or gold," (Deut. 17:17) and the like. The
need {to know the quantity} is greater [than that of knowing quality] since
quantity is above quality in the hierarchy.[141] The third is because it contains
commandments of which it was not explained by what [means] it may be
realized what they are. For example, there is no sensible proof for which
day the day of the Sabbath[142] is nor is there one for which the new month
is. Rather he directs us for proof for {these things} to the messenger's
tradition. Were one to think that the Scripture records any [thing about]
this we will set forth the refutation of what they thought.[143]

The fourth is that it contains commandments whose very essence is not
elucidated. For example, it did not elucidate the nature of the work
prohibited on the Sabbath.[144] Indeed it merely says "any work" in
absolute form.[145] Likewise it did not explain the nature of the vessels that
may become impure for it merely says "any vessel" (Lev. 11:32) and the

---

139. Al-Qirqisani, *Book of Lights*, (p. 87) and Salmon ben Jeruhim, *Wars of the Lord*, (p. 47) dispute these principles.

140. Cf. *Esa Meshalai* (p. 46) where the Gaon reiterates this statement. Al-Qirqisani (ibid.) argues that the amount may be determined by analogy while Salmon ben Jeruhim (ibid., p. 80) claims that it indeed has no set measurement like many other commandments. The Gaon's disciple (*Schreiner, Zwei Geniza Fragmenten*, p. 91) responds to this with the claim that the Torah does not say, for example: "Make for yourself something on the corner of your garments," but uses the specific term *tzitzith* with the assumption that its specifics are known.

141. See above.

142. According to Aristotle's categories. See *Beliefs* 2:9 (p. 112).

143. Both Al-Qirqisani and Salmon ben Jeruhim (p. 81) argue that the Sabbath is known to all inhabitants of the world as a day of rest and does not require any tradition. Cf. the same claim about the seven days of the week by the Kuzari 1:57 (p. 51). See however, note 9 regarding the veracity of this view.

144. This is an allusion to the Karaites, who maintained that the establishment of the new month is according to the moon. See the Gaon's com. to Gen. 1:15.

145. Cf. *Sab.* 97b: "These thirty-four types of work were told to Moses from Sinai."

like. Now these things that the Scripture did not elucidate what they are and by what they may be recognized are above, I mean higher [in hierarchy] than what precedes.

The fifth is because the entire praying nation is [unanimously] agreed that God has [imposed] upon them commandments whose identities are not mentioned [at all], how much more so their quantity and quality. This is like prayer in regards to which we are agreed that there are three every day although [prayer] is not recorded in the Torah.[146] *[Likewise] in marriage about which we are in agreement that it can not be performed without bride price, I mean the Kethubah which is not recorded [in the Torah] and the like.*[147] This is in addition to the innumerable[148] laws that were not mentioned in the Scripture to any extent and that necessity requires to seek[149] out knowledge of them.

The sixth is the account of the [number of] years and events from the time the prophets departed from us to nowadays. This is something that cannot be obtained at all unless it is through the Tradition by which we may know how long the Second Temple stood and what events both joyful and grievous came upon us and as well as how {the Temple} was destroyed and how long has transpired from that time until now.[150]

What shows that these ideas are higher [in hierarchy] than those that precede is that since the Torah records these parts of time, those that convey it should know the amount of time that went by and he parted with it and whatever events came upon them and they were led by it.

The seventh is [reports of] what we hope God will bring about for us

---

146. Salmon states (ibid.): "But thou has erred for thou hast not considered the verse *whatever vessel it may me wherewith any work is done.* All such vessels are specified in the law if thou wouldst just turn thy heart to it." It is not certain if he thought that the Gaon should reconsider his interpretation or that he did not have this line of the Gaon's introduction.

147. In his introduction to his *Book of the Precepts* (Sklare, p. 195) and his *Book of Praises* (p. 3), however, the Gaon bases the obligation for prayer on the verse "He is your praise." (Deut. 10:21)

148. I.e., that it is of biblical origin but is not explicitly mentioned. See *Ket.* 10a and 56a–b where it is disputed if the *Kethubah* is a rabbinical institution.

149. This word is found only in one manuscript. See Zucker, *Genesis,* p. 14, n. 95.

150. Text reads *ahkam,* which are civil laws and may be attained according to judgment and analogy and not necessarily by means of tradition. (Zucker) This would then appear to be a side point, not a proof to the necessity of tradition. See Zucker, *Genesis,* n. 97.

at the end of time. I have already classified these {kinds of reports} in my explanation of some parts of the Scripture.[151] The entire nation will not apprehend all this with hope unless it is with the reliance on tradition for if they do not rely on it and apply free judgment to this, it would then be possible [to believe] that all the mentioned prophecies have already been fulfilled at the time of some king of the past like Hizkia or someone after him.[152] The same applies to the resurrection of the dead and all the promises [connected to it]. In this [case] everything they hope for would be abolished.

XI Transmission of the Oral Law

I shall [now] relate how these things were passed over from the transmission of the prophet. I say that: "The nation attested these things, i.e., quiddity, quantity, and quality from the messenger's[153] acts before the Torah was written in the fortieth year,[154,155] for God may He be magnified said to His messenger: Write from "the first [thing]" and dictated to him word by word and [Moses] would write "the first" (Gen. 1:1) until "and there you shall not pass." (Deut. 34:4)[156] God told him in

---

151. To this Salmon (p. 82) retorts: "In which sacred book is it written that it is our duty to know the reckoning of how many years shall elapse between the destruction of the temple and the Dread Gathering?"

152. See com. to Is. (Ratzaby p. 250)

153. Cf. *Beliefs* 8:7 (p. 283). Regarding its identification see Zucker, *Genesis*, p. 185, n. 101. Salmon states (p. 82) that the period of the redemption and the resurrection of the dead is well attested in the Prophets.

154. I.e., Moses. The Gaon refers to the one who brought down the Torah in the same way that the Muslims refer to Muhammad, the founder of their religion.

155. In the desert.

156. The Gaon maintains that no commandments were committed to writing before this. Yefeth states in his com. to the pericope of *Mishpatim*: "And it his deceitful claim that the commandments were transmitted from Mt. Sinai prior to the fortieth year by heart, but we find it stated 'And he took the book of the covenant,' and similarly God said to him priorly 'Write this as a memorial in a book,' and why does he claim that they were not recorded?" (cited in Zucker, *Genesis*, p. 186, n. 101). Cf. however, the Gaon's commentary to Ex. 24:4 (as cited by Rabbi Abraham Maimonides), where he states that the Book of the Covenant contained only Ex. 20:19–23:20. Cf. also the excerpt from the Gaon's commen-

brief the events of the approximately 1488 years.[157] This is the gist of what we believe regarding the writing of the Torah—that its reader should be able to find out to his satisfaction all the reports and commands that he wishes. From the first year[158] the messenger taught the nation all the commandments and laws that he was commanded. By setting up for them officers of one thousand, officers of one hundred, etc. so that they adjudicate what he taught them.[159] It is impossible that he should command them to eat matzah without explaining to them which grain it is [to be made from] or to abstain from impurities without having explained how much is [required to be considered] a zav,[160] and the like. As long as the children of Jacob (!) were agreed on it in the chosen land the king and the priest would preserve and guard the transmission and particularly during the presence of the prophets. However, when we were first exiled and prophecy had been lifted the Sages feared that the oral law[161] would be forgotten so they turned their attention to it and committed it to writing, calling it the Mishnah. They left off the branches with the hope that they will be preserved after this with this commitment in writing of the gist and this was so: The remaining branches were preserved until we were exiled a second time when we were dispersed even more than the first. The students then feared that what these predecessors did not commit to writing would be forgotten so they committed it to writing and called it the Talmud.[162]

Were one to ask how do they, I mean the Mishnah and the Talmud, contain statements attributed to individuals?[163] We say because they were

---

tary to this section as preserved by Rabbi Mubashshir Gaon, Criticisms, p. 108.

157. The Gaon follows the opinion that Joshua finished off the narratives of the Torah that follow Moses' death. See Sifri 487 and Baba Bathra 15a.

158. Since the creation of the world.

159. From the giving of the Torah.

160. See Deut. 1:15.

161. Text reads "how much a zav and zava is."

162. Text reads "instructional knowledge."

163. The Gaon expands on this section in his com. to the pericope Mishpatim (see Zucker, Genesis, p. 187, n. 103 for an excerpt of Yefeth's verbatim citation of this section) where he states: "That these laws and teaching remained with our people from the time that employed them and ruled with them were not fixed nor recorded but they were preserved in the minds of the entire nation, but when they were exiled the first time the Sages feared lest it be forgotten and dressed them in words and committed them to writing and called it the Mishnah.

the ones who reminded the people of them,[164] not that they invented
them. This is like the Torah attributes the pericope of "Anything that is
able to go into fire" (Num. 31:21–23) to Eliezer because he mentioned,
it not because he composed it.[165]

Were one to ask how did disputes between the transmitters come about
in them, I mean the Mishnah and the Talmud? We say they are not true
disputes, but [only] what appear to be disputes when they first reach the
listeners. However, in truth they are one of three kinds: The first is that
one of the sages pretends to dispute and twit him so the he may know the
gist of his view.[166] This is like Moses peace be upon him pretended to be
upset with Aaron and his children for burning the Goat of Expiation[167] so
that they reveal to him what is in their mind since he did not believe that
they would burn it unknowingly. The second is that what they heard from
the prophet may have two aspects, one permissible and one prohibited.
One of the sages came forward and related the permitted aspect and the
later related the prohibited one. [But in truth] they are both correct in
their statements for it is permissible in one way but prohibited in the
other.[168] This is like it says in the Torah: "You shall not destroy its trees,"
(Deut. 20:19) but then: "Only trees that you know are for food shall you
destroy." (Deut. 20:20)[169] [The same applies to] the statement: "And if a
daughter of a priest is to marry a strange man," (Lev. 22:12) and then "she
shall not eat," when it then says: "A daughter of a priest if she becomes a

---

Whoever first gave direction in any of them, they fixed it in their name in order
to encourage the students to preserve it." He implies that the Mishnah was
written after the Babylonian exile. See note above for a citation. Cf. Rabbi Sherira
Gaon in his *Epistle* (p. 14). An anonymous Karaite (see the Gaon's *Exiled Book*,
p. 153), however, cites the Gaon as of the opinion that the Mishnah had begun
to be recorded already in the days of Simon the Just.

164. If it is a true tradition, not the invention of individuals.

165. Al-Qirqisani, *Book of Lights* (p. 132) says: "His statement concerning this
implies that these statements that are attributed to those people—the entire
community forgot them—while all of them remembered some of it . . . we do
not believe that all of them should forget [every]thing."

166. Cf. *Ber.* 33:2: "To sharpen he wishes."

167. Lev. 16:16.

168. See Zucker, "On the problem of the disputes in the traditions," p. 64.

169. The first is a general statement, while the second specifies which trees in
particular.

widow,"[170] and then "from the bread of her father she shall not eat." There is no difference if what balances {two similar verses} is close to them or is far and [that only] then [is the idea] explained.[171] The third is that a scholar may have heard a partial statement and thought it to be a complete one while the rest heard it in its entirety[172] and when that scholar mentions how he understood it they claim against him that they heard the entire statement in which what you heard and thought to be a generalization concretizes.[173] An example is like one who reads in the third book of the Pentateuch of the Torah: "And clothes of different types clanged together,"[174] (Lev. 19:9) and thought it to be a general statement, but when he would come across someone who read the entire Torah he would inform him that it concretizes {this statement} in the fifth part and makes it specific when it says: "You shall not wear clothes blended from wool and linen," (Deut. 22:11) and whatever else is along these lines.

XIII Deniers of the Oral Law

You should know, God make you prosper, that those that deny this notion[175] when they are compelled to [admit] that there are some auditory precepts whose quiddity, quantity, and quality are not written [in the Scripture], they say that the Wise One left them since He directed us to them by analogies. I have already composed a book that rejects what

---

170. The Gaon's student (Schreiner, Zwei Fragmenten, p. 49) cites this verse in the Gaon's name in response to Salmon ben Jeruhim.

171. The concretization of a law may even come in a later pericope. This is opposed to the view of the Anan that the generalization must be juxtaposed with the concretization. The Gaon disputes this view in greater length in his com. to Lev. 18:17. See Zucker, "The dispute between the Karaites and the Rabbinates regarding the rule of 'a positive commandment displaces a negative commandment,'" Dine Israel VI, p. 181.

172. Rabbi Sherira Gaon (Epistle, p. 6) states that because of the disturbances and upheavals students did not spend enough time with their masters and this led to an increase in argument.

173. See Zucker, ibid., for a possible Islamic source for this argument.

174. This is the Gaon's rendition of sha'atnez.

175. I.e., the third notion, which is tradition, the reference being to the Karaites.

they say.[176] It is inevitable that I mention major sections of it when I reach the middle of [my] interpretation of this book.[177] I shall make it known that the categories of analogy are four: The analogy of the logician, which takes its force from the four causes—substance, form, action, and aim.[178] I shall explain that the auditory precepts are not sustainable by any of these. The analogy of the polemicist, which is applying a law [that is contingent upon a particular] cause to anything that has this cause. I shall explain that this too has no relevance to our precepts. The analogy of the jurists,[179] which is that a new precept is connected with one that has the most similar features to it. I shall reveal that this cannot apply to our precepts, apart from the inherent lacking {of this type of analogy} [alone] for there is no set limit for how big or how small a similarity may be. The analogy of the dissenters, which judges the individual of each kind like that which applies to something else of this kind and applies to all categories the law that is found in one of its kind by whatever kind and type is similar to it and applies to all.[180] This however has no place in any case for it requires that each person be a scribe and analogizer just because we find individuals with these traits. Furthermore, this would necessarily [create] contradiction since we [certainly] find [some] individuals who do not have {these traits}. I shall also reveal that since we see that our precepts discern between the laws of things that belong to one category and [yet] compare them to things that belong to two categories the Scripture rejects what they adhere to. This is like it distinguishes between an ox and sheep that are stolen and sold even though they are [both] animals while it compares [the law of] the ox and a garment that are

---

176. The reference is to *The Book of the Derivation of the Precepts*, mentioned above. See note 81. Rabbi Samuel ben Hophni in his *Treatise on the Commandments* (pp. 218–19; see ibid. 143), however, admits anological derivation if it is guided by tradition.

177. Likewise in his *Book of Guidance* (pp. 130–31) Rabbi Samuel ben Hophni states that the Gaon spoke of the invalidity of analogical derivation in his com. to Lev. This section, however, has not surfaced yet.

178. As expounded by Aristotle.

179. I.e., that of the Arab jurisprudence.

180. These types of analogies were performed by the Karaite Anan. See his *Book of Precepts*, p. 4: "It said 'ox' which is a pure animal and said 'donkey' which is an impure animal. It wrote [them] together (Deut. 22:10) which means an ox and all its kinds—an impure animal—and a donkey and its like which is an impure animal." See also ibid., p. 6.

disclaimed[181] even though one of them is an animal and the other [is of] a growth [from the ground].[182] When I explain this and an observer with a sound mind understands what I have presented previously, all that they claim will be rejected and they will necessarily seek refuge by the necessity to return to the tradition.

Now some of them also used the denial of part of the nation [of the tradition] as a claim against it.[183] But were this as they argue, then the denial by part {of the people} of the oral law should also be an argument against it [as well]. Others use the failure of some of our people[184] to preserve it as an argument against it. But were this as they argue, the fact that some failed to preserve the written law should be an argument against it. Indeed I have only spoken of minor points of what they adhere to and rely on the understanding of one who analyses this book.[185]

This has been an elaboration of the three notions that make the observance of the believers complete and these again are the intuitive, written, and transmitted [knowledge].

XIV How the Bible is to Be Interpreted

Now that I have finished explaining these three notions that are inevitable for anyone interpreting the Torah to consider, I shall begin in preamble with the way in which the Torah as well as the other books of the prophets should be interpreted. I say: Since those three notions that I have previously mentioned[186] are the mainstay [of the Torah] and since any word may either be clear or obscure,[187] for every language is built

---

181. See Ex. 22:8.

182. Cf. Book on the Derivation of the Precepts p. 398 for a parallel statement.

183. This constitutes the first of fifteen arguments advanced by the Karaites against the oral law which the Gaon lists in the above work. The response to this is found in the Gaon's com. to Est. (see Zucker, p. 190, n. 128) where he claims that the minority may indeed obligate the majority.

184. See Zucker, Genesis, p. 190, n. 128 where he determines that the reading should be "some of the people (i.e., nations)."

185. I.e., the Scripture, not his commentary.

186. See section II.

187. More specifically, tolerating only one meaning (clear) or tolerating various meanings (obscure). See Gatje, The Quran and Its Exegetes, p. 56 for a citation from Zamakhshari, and Zucker, Genesis, intro. p. 38.

according to this structure and the same applies to the Torah since it is written in one of the languages, anyone who [comes to] explain the Torah should render it according to the notions that precede[188] it and the tradition that succeeds it as clear, and should render whatever disputes one of {these notions} as obscure. Discussing this matter further I say:[189] One who has a sound mind should take the Book of the Torah at all times to be [understood] in the manner apparent from its words, I mean one that is known and frequently used among the people of its language, for every book is composed so that its ideas reach the mind of the listener entirely unless [1] knowledge of the senses, or [2] of the intellect opposes the popular explanation of the statement, or [3] that this popular explanation would contradict another verse [whose meaning is] clear, or [4] one of the traditions. If he sees that were he to leave this statement according to the literal meaning of its words that this would lead him to believe one of the four things that I have expounded,[190] then he should know that this statement is not to be [understood] according to its popular meaning but that it has a word or words that are metaphorical[191] and that he should deliberate which type of metaphor it is until he brings it to its definite meaning. This verse will [then] return to agreement with the senses, the intellect, the other verse, and with tradition.[192]

Along the lines of this subject I shall give examples of these four things: What relates to the first kind is that the Torah says: "And Adam named his wife Eve because she was the mother of all living." (Gen. 3:20) Were we to leave this [the statement] in its sense that is known to the masses, we deny the senses for this would require that the lion, the ox, the donkey, and the rest of the animals be Eve's children and since there is no trickery that agrees with the senses,[193] we believe that this verse contains an

---

188. I.e., the intellect. See section II.

189. Text reads "Were I to discuss this further I would say . . ."

190. I.e., something contradicting one of these four principles.

191. See Mordechai Z. Cohen, "The Best of Poetry," *Torah U-mada Journal* VI, 1995–1996, p. 27, notes 59 and 60.

192. Rabbi Samuel ben Hophni Gaon echoes these principles in his introduction to the pericope of *WayeSe*. He adds that the necessity to interpret all verse literally is based on the rabbinic dictum "A verse does not depart from its literal meaning." (*Shab.* 63a) See Zucker, *Genesis*, p. 455 for the text.

193. The Gaon here draws on his belief in the utter reliability of the senses. Cf. *Beliefs* Intro.:5 (p. 19): "We say then as for knowledge [derived] from sensation is concerned, whatever is correctly perceived with our senses by virtue of the

elliptic word by [the addition of] which it will agree with that which is visible [in reality] as I shall explain. To the second category belongs the Scripture's statement: "For the Lord your God is a consuming fire." (Deut. 4:24) Were we to believe that this is according to what appears from the words, the intellect rejects and annuls it for the intellect declares that every fire is created for it is feeble and contingent[194] and prone to change.[195] After this it determines that it is not possible for the Creator to have any of [these traits] whereas were we to believe that the statement contains something metaphorical,[196] the intellect would adjust {this statement} to what is written. The third kind is like what it says: "You should not try the Lord your God." (Deut. 6:17)—an unambiguous statement, but since it says later "Take out your tithe and give charity from your money,"[197] we know that these are ambiguous words that have a meaning that is not popular by which the words will be in agreement with the unambiguous statement in the Torah, as we shall explain its place.[198]

What belongs to the fourth kind is God's statement where He warns: "Do not cook a kid in its mother's milk." (Ex. 23:19) Whereas, the Tradition prohibited eating any [kind of] meat with any [kind of] milk.[199] However, those that conveyed the Tradition did so according to what they experienced and saw it we should seek an explanation the nation accepts which accords the tradition of the prophets as I shall explain in the middle of the book.[200]

I have set forth words for every type [of ambiguity] to serve as a model and example. If the interpreter is to use these assumptions in the way I

---

connection existing between us and the object in question must be acknowledged by us to be in truth as it is perceived by us without [the admission of] a doubt." See Efros, *Studies in Medieval Philosophy*, p. 9.

194. Cf. *Beliefs* 5:4 (p. 247): "Fire can make an appearance only by being attached to something else."

195. Beliefs (ibid.) the Gaon has "subject to extinction."

196. Accordingly he translates it as: "For God's punishment is a consuming fire." Cf. *Beliefs* 2:7 (p. 144), 7:2 (p. 266), and "Appendix" 7:2 (p. 415).

197. This is a paraphrase of Mal. 3:10, which continues: "and test me by this."

198. Cf. *Beliefs* 7:1 (p. 135): "I will state moreover, that He is not subject to allusion or change, as Scripture says: 'For I the Lord change not.' (Mal. 3:6) Cf. *Ta'anith* 9a, where this case is considered an exception to the prohibition against testing God.

199. In his translation the Gaon removes "its mother's" to make it include *any* milk.

200. This section has not surfaced yet.

described them, his explanation will not flourish with errors of malice and [those of] hurling into a matter without looking. However, errors resulting from not being certain will not come upon him only if he is among those whom God knows will not err and chooses to be messengers because He knows that they will not fail in this.[201] Should the verse or pericope demand transference of a statement from a popular explanation that is much used to one that is metaphorical and little used, one should not apprehend a letter or a word to be different than its literal meaning unless [he,] the one who changes and transfers it is proficient in the methods of metaphor [i.e.,] by which the statement becomes unclear and by explaining it, it becomes clear. I will also mention that . . .[202] as it says: "And the king Ahasaurus said, and he said to Esther the queen," (Est. 7:5) and as it says: "I, my brothers, my lads, and the people of the watch are after me—we do not remove our clothes." (Neh. 4:7) The smallest [distance] that may exist between such repetitions is two words dividing between two statements, one of which is repeated. The fourth kind is the word that fills two places.[203] This being common [found] with the word "no,"[204] as it says: "Giving in concealment reduces anger and a bribe in the sleeve great anger," (Prov. 21:14) which means "reduces great anger."[205] The first represents the second as it says: "For there our revilers asked words of praise and our executioners rejoicing," (Ps. 137:3) which means "and our executioners asked for rejoicing." The first "asked" takes the place of the second and the like.

The fifth is the omitted letters, some of which are servile like "which" in the statement: "The One who gives a soul to the nation upon it" (Is. 42:5) [which] means "to the nation which is upon it," [and] "For all that comes your [mightiness]," (Ps. 51:5) [which] means "[that] all which will come."[206] The same applies to "from it": "To the rock you have been hewn and the spade of the boron you have been poked out of," (Is. 51:1)[207] which means "the rock from which you have been hewn and the spade of

---

201. Cf. Rabbi Samuel ben Hophni's parallel statement in his intro. to Deut. (appendix to com. on Gen., p. 462.)

202. This section deals with the repetition of words.

203. Cf. his com. to Gen. 2:19. See also Zucker, *Translation*, pp. 276–268.

204. This clause seems to be parenthetical unless the examples are lacking.

205. The Gaon, however, ad loc. translates it as "eases great anger."

206. He translates the verse as follows: "For all the generations that are to come and your glory . . ." connecting this verse to the next.

207. Cf. Ibn Janah, *Riqmah*, p. 287.

the boron you have been poked from." There are also independent words as it says: "And David finished (techal)," (2 Sam. 13:39) which means that David's soul[208] finished,[209] and likewise "from it" is omitted as it says: "I shall go from tent to tent and from tabernacle," (I Chron. 17:5) which means "from tabernacle to tabernacle," and as it says "from which man fears" (I Sam. 17:7) *you should hint until you reach the fear of God and the like.*

The fourth way of explaining what is unclear is conjoining. The most common [in this category] is apprehending [the words] according to how they are conjoined.[210] This means that every word that is conjoined in reading should yield one [unit] of meaning without dividing between them when rendered. Likewise one should not connect in the rendition words that are separate as I shall explain of *seraphim om'edhim mima'al lo* (Is. 6:2) where there is a considerable difference between if you connect two words together or a number of them.[211] However if the need to separate what is connected or to connect what is separated in reading should arise in order to preserve the meaning this is possible just as the statement: "Then God said: Lo man has become one who of himself knows the good and bad (Gen. 3:22) is separated and connected [as needed] so that the meaning be in its place.[212] The same applies to connecting: *uvammenorah arba'ah gevi'im meshuqqadim kaftoreha ufraheha* (Ex. 25:34); *meshshuqadhim* modifies *the first [clause] not the second,*[213] *and the like. The . . . part . . .*[214]

---

208. This addition is needed because *techal* is feminine while David is masculine.

209. So already Jonathan ben Uziel. Rabbi Samuel ibn Nagdila (*Epistles of the Friends*, p. LXI) and Ibn Janah (*Riqmah*, p. 265) follow this view. Ibn Ezra vacillates in this matter; in his *Moznayim* p. 5a he recognizes this ellipsis, but in his LR to Gen. 2:2 and com. to Deut. 28:32 he opposes it.

210. By the Mesoretic cantillations.

211. Cf. his com. to Prov. 25:11 (p. 199): "If he connects three words together and separates the fourth, the assertion would be that God has angels in the heavens but if he connects each two words and reads the first *seraphiim 'omedhim* and then *mi'ma'al lo* this would lead to heresy," because the verse would mean that God has angels above Him.

212. The word *mimmenu* (of himself) is accentuated with a *zaqeph* which separates it from the following word. Ibn Ezra ad loc. (Linetsky, p. 91), however, argues that this separation against the cantillations is not permissible.

213. I.e., *gevi'im,* not *kaftoreha u-feraheha.*

214. The following section is highly grammatical and hardly sensible in English translation and has therefore been omitted.

XV The Uses of Wisdom

. . . . The primary use of wisdom is enjoying it as it says:
"When wisdom shall come to your heart and knowledge shall be pleasant
for your soul," (Prov. 2:10)[215] and further the understanding [attained] by
it in serving and obeying God as it describes . . . also the reward for it,
for there is reward for any effort as it says: "So you should know wisdom
for it is for your soul if you find it you found its end."[216] (Prov. 24:14)
Likewise, some people are more estimable than others in this world as well
as in the one to come[217] as it says: "Who is wise and will understand this,
has understanding and will know them." (Hos. 14:10) It says further:
"Wise people inherit nobility and fools increase contemptibility." (Prov.
3:35). *When discussion of this comes to an end it will need explanation* . . .
wisdom will avail them . . . the book . . . the book . . . quality . . .
in the . . . clearly . . . by declaration . . . It began with it that . . .
in his thought . . . in his thought . . . that which is desired but it was
given in the language that the messenger will inform his people so that
the yoke of learning a[nother] language be lightened for them so that
only the meaning remains for them to study.[218] As for the querist who
claims regarding lifting doubt[219] He only places these [metaphorical]
expressions in the Book, because He directs us to the explanation of the
messenger from which we hear a generally accepted meaning [of the
expression] and see what he does clearly without any doubt or uncer-
tainty.[220] Since His intention was to direct us to the tradition of the
messenger to decide in anything undecided it does not matter if . . .

---

215. See *Beliefs* 10:14 (p. 393): "Among the scholars there are some who
maintain that there exists nothing with which an individual ought to occupy
himself in this world except the quest for scientific knowledge." They go on to
cite this verse as proof. See ibid. for the Gaon's rejection of this view.

216. I.e., even wisdom.

217. Cf. Ibn Gabirol (*Improvement of the Moral Virtues*, p. 30) for a similar
statement.

218. The matter here is a little garbled. This is a response to why the Scripture
uses ambiguous language. Cf. Rabbi Samuel ben Hophni's intro. to Deut.
(appendix to com. on Gen., p. 494) where he says that the purpose was to
conceal matters from those who do not have the capacity to apprehend it.

219. Apparently the reference is to one who claims that ambiguous language
should not be used.

220. In juridical matters.

some of them are in the book entirely to the tradition . . . it is permissible for him to judge and will not be in the statement . . . will say . . . this . . . decides between the dubious words in the book . . . some and what he will inform him. . . . His question would have no place for he had indeed asked of the creator not the created despite *that he would believe in regards to this that if he would follow this opinion that the essence is merely in approximation of the statement*.[221] Our response would also be by means of approximation and the summary not by analogy to the created beings. We said that He is something without beginning and end, wise, able, creates everything He wishes in justice, nothing is comparable to Him according to the conditions that we have previously mentioned so that the querist will not probe these words of ours. Our statement that God is a thing is to ascertain that He is an existence and to negate the statement of the one who denies this. The Scripture calls what exists *yesh*.[222] We say that He has no beginning to negate that He has a "before" or "after," as we have explained.[223] We say "wise" to attribute wisdom to Him and to negate any unknowingness [from God] as it says: "For He is sage in understanding, mighty in power." (Job. 9:4)[224] We say: "able" to attribute full strength to Him and to negate any weakness in Him as it says: "In your hand is all strength and glory." (I Chron. 29:11) Now neither the eternity, the wisdom, nor the power is something other than Him for the reason that we have already explained.[225] [This is] like the Scripture says: "There is no other except Him." (Deut. 4:35). We said that He creates what He wishes [the meaning is] ex nihilo as we have

---

221. See Efros, *Studies in Medieval Philosophy*, p. 51.

222. There was some dispute between the Kalam theologians if God is to be termed a "thing" or not. In his *Book of Discernment* the Gaon says: "The polemicists were taken by dispute if an absence is a thing or not but concluded that it is a thing. However, it is not possible that something should be found and absent simultaneously, rather they speak of this by means of exaggeration and hyperbole and say 'an absent thing.'" See Zucker, *Genesis*, p. 196, n. 182 for the citation and further discussion. See *Beliefs* 2:9 (p. 112) for a discussion of God's substantiality. Cf. also Ibn Ezra to Ecl. 4:3.

223. This section has not surfaced yet.

224. In his commentary (p. 221) the Gaon states: "I rendered 'wise of heart' as '(sage in) understanding' because it is the manner of the Hebrews to call 'understanding' 'heart' since understanding develops in the heart."

225. This section has not surfaced; however, in his BO (1:1, p. 37) the Gaon has some discussion on this matter. See Efros, *Medieval Jewish Philosophy*, p. 54.

explained previously[226] and as the Scripture says: "All that He wishes He does." (Ps. 115:3) We said nothing resembles Him as we have proven[227] and as the Scripture rejects that He resembles even the greatest things and how much more so things below Him, which are [of] four [kinds]. The greatest of the speaking [existence] are the angels[228] of which it says: "For they will say who among the hosts will match God or will compare to Him among the able." (Ps. 89:7) The most estimable [part] of the [heavenly] spheres is the luminaries of which it says: "To whom shall you compare and shall be similar the Holy One shall say; lift your eyes to the sky and see who created these." (Is. 40:25–26) The most estimable of the growths is the cedar. It says: "And to whom are the able comparable and by what likeness will they describe Him. Does the idol which the carpenter chooses . . ." (Is. 40:18–19) The most estimable of the inanimate is silver and gold of which it says: "To whom shall you liken Me, equate Me, or compare Me and I shall resemble him like those who pull gold from their pockets." (Is. 46:5–6)[229] When we say "just" we mean that He will not place upon His worshippers what they are unable to bear as it says: "My nation what have I done to you? What have I forced?" (Mic. 6:3) and does not force them to do anything for which they will be punished as he relinquished [His responsibility] for their iniquities and said: *"Lo rebellious sons God says since they give council, but not from me,"* (Is. 30:1)[230] and attributed [the sin] to them when it says: "From you this was." (Mal. 1:9)[231]

---

226. This section has not surfaced yet, but see *Beliefs* 1:1 (p. 40) and BO, p. 18. See also Wolfson, *Kalam Arguments for Creation*, p. 196.

227. See *Beliefs* 2:9 (p. 113).

228. The Gaon likewise asserts that the angels are the most estimable creations in his responsa to Hiwya al-Balkhi. On the other hand, in his *Beliefs* 4:1 (p. 180) he states that man is the most estimable creation because he is found in the center of the universe. Likewise in his commentary to Ex. 23:1 he asserts that angels were created for guarding man. Rabbi Mubashshir Gaon (*Criticisms*, p. 123) and Ibn Ezra (short com. to ex. 25:4) point to this contradiction. The latter states that the Gaon did not impart his opinion on this matter in its entirety. See Ibn Ezra's com. to Gen. 1:2 (Linetsky, p. 9); Zucker, *Genesis*, p. 197, n. 191; and Efros, ibid., p. 67 for further discussion.

229. Cf. *Beliefs* 2:9 (p. 113).

230. I.e., God calls them rebellious not because they violate His laws?

231. Cf. *Beliefs* 4:4 (p. 189).

. . . It is not possible that He resemble[232] them and since His essence creates and innovates it is impossible that His [supposed] created essence [also] be so. This is because we have seen only something created but not a creator. Therefore [the possibility] that they resemble Him is eliminated. [Now] the Scripture warns us of these two things as it says of God: "To whom shall you liken Me, equate Me, and compare Me so that I be likened?" (Is. 46:5) and "To whom shall you compare Me and I shall be similar the Holy One shall say?" (Is. 40:25) [?] with these two immediate statements I shall annul these two false notions as I have interpreted them in their place.[233]

The believers should know regarding this matter that after we establish His existence to be eternal unlike the sensible existence, then anything— i.e., one of the three exalted attributes: "able," "living," and "knowing"— that we may attribute to Him beyond this is like [that which is] in the essence of existing things. The necessity to attribute to Him that He is able is that we have not seen one perform an act unless he is able, and likewise "living" we have not seen anyone perform an act unless he is living. The same applies to "knowing" since He knows that the things . . . and commands . . . and His Book has already made us aware of all this for it says of living: "And I have said I am living forever." (Deut. 32:40) Of being able it says: "I know that You have power over all." (Job 42:2)[234] Of "knowing" it says: "There is no limit to His knowledge." (Is. 40:28) These three attributes do not imply variation in Him[235] despite that each one of them imparts to the listener something the other does not. This is because of the language, i.e., because of the weakness of language in its inability to combine three words into one expression and how much more so because it is the inability of the language to have one word that will combine these [three words] [coupled with the fact that] the intellect apprehends it at once.[236] This is because by the [very] same way that one

---

232. See Efros, ibid., p. 50.

233. This entire section is reiterated in *Beliefs* 2:9 (p. 113).

234. Rabbi Samuel ben Hophni Gaon (*Treatise on the Commandments*, p. 225) cites the same verse for the first case but Deut. 32:41 for this case and Deut. 6:16 for the last case.

235. See Wolfson, *Saadiah on the Trinity and Incarnation*, p. 552[6]. Al-Muqameais (Twenty Chapters, p. 200) already states along these lines: "God has neither diversity nor variety. His attributes vary and differ in the linguistic expression, but not in meaning."

236. See Efros, *Studies in Medieval Judaism*, p. 52.

ascertains that God created, one can ascertain that He is "able," "living,"
and "knowing." The Scripture supports [this] for it says many times in
mentioning Him: "There is no other than He," [i.e.] It is not possible that
we should think that the quality of His wisdom is different than that of
the created beings.[237] The same applies to Him being "able" and "living."
For were we to think this we would admit that something in concealment
is other than that which is in sight[238] and it will be easy to the heretics
to claim against us[239] with [the] doubts [they express] that [attempt to]
destroy our truth. Rather we should believe that the type of wisdom is one
and the same. I say the same regarding "able" and "living."[240] Were one to
set forth the claim against us that [now] "He knows," "is able," and "lives"
is in accordance to what exists,[241] we explain that this does not
incriminate us [to agree] for not by virtue of [the fact] that the created
beings are living have I declared upon God that He is alive, nor by virtue
of [the fact that] the created beings are knowing have we declared upon
Him that He is knowing, nor by virtue [of the fact that] the created beings
are "able" have we required that He be "able," but because we see that at
times {a person} is alive while at others dead we know that there is a
reason because of which he is alive. Likewise when we see {a person} at
times knowing and at other unknowing it becomes clear that there is a
cause because of which he is knowing and when it is removed he no
longer knows. Likewise because we discern that at times one is able and
at others one is feeble, it becomes clear for us that the cause that made
him able has departed from Him and for that reason he is feeble.
However, since none of these things applies to the Creator of all, He is
knowing, able, and living because of His essence[242] not because of

237. Apparently, the Gaon means that were we to consider the quality of
God's wisdom, etc., to be different than ours, our entire theological system would
collapse. (Zucker)

238. Now that he has established that the quality of God's wisdom, etc., does
not differ from that of the existing beings.

239. I.e., that something is different just because it concealed.

240. Cf. Maimonides, *Guide* 1:35 (p. 80).

241. I.e., among humans. The question is: How can we say that the quality of
the Supreme is the same as that of flesh and blood? Al-Muqameais (*Twenty
Chapters*, pp. 200–202) refutes this criticism, which he attributes to the Dualists,
in a similar fashion.

242. Cf. Rabbi Samuel ben Hophni Gaon, *Treatise on the Commandments*, p. 225.

something other than Him[243] for these [attributes] as metaphorical of approximate [meaning]. He has already mentioned this to us [i.e.] in His Books that this strength, knowledge, and vitality do not change and become other than Him for they have no bounds as it says: "Our master is great and has much power and there is no amount to His knowledge," (Ps. 147:5) and "You are the one who has no years to come to end." (Ps. 102:2) It will be upon one who seeks the truth to consider these four notions and to immerse in investigation until it is revealed to him that the intellect proves that it is impossible that this Creator be more than one. This will be clarified for him from the impossibility that He should be[244] . . .

XVI God's Grace in Creating the World

[245] . . . a means of preferment for He created us at first in a world of riches and gave us of it amenity without making us work for anything. The other is by giving reward for He created us first in a world of labor obligating us [to do] what is within our ability and transfers us from it to the world of recompense where He rewards us with the fruit of our labor. Since the most fortunate between the potential of what the deserving that did not do work receives and the one that comes from his master for doing what he was commanded to do is the one who receives benefit for what he did,[246] God predilected us with the most abundant kinds and

---

243. Meaning that He acquired it from something else. Al-Muqameais (*Twenty Chapters*, p. 192) similarly already makes this point. He directs his argument, as does the Gaon in his *Beliefs* 2:5 (p. 104), against the Christians. Here, however, the Gaon uses this line of reasoning against the Dualists.

244. See *Beliefs* 2:1 (p. 96).

245. See the Gaon's intro. to Job (p. 127) where he speaks of God's grace in creating the world.

246. Cf. *Beliefs* 3:1 (p. 138): "God's making His creatures' diligent compliance with His commandments the means of attaining permanent bliss is the better course. For according to the judgment of reason the person who achieved some good by means of the effort he has expended for its attainment obtains double the advantage gained by him who has achieves this good without any effort but merely the result of the kindness shown him by God." On the other hand in 4:5 (p. 192) the Gaon states: "I have further encountered men who asked in this connection: 'What reason could have prompted [divine] wisdom to issue

created us in a world of labor to recompense us for it in the world of recompense. The prophet elucidates this to us: "I said in my heart the righteous and wicked, God shall judge for there is time for everything and for all acts a name." (Ecl. 3:17) He does not command anything that we do not have the ability to fulfill.[247] The proof for this is that each one of us knows in his soul that he is able to move and rest, act and abstain from what we usually do or abstain from respectively. Our acts are arranged in three levels. The first level is the things that are pleasant for us so our intellect demands doing them, like righteousness and fairness. The second level consists of things that are unpleasant for us and we find that our intellect negates and warns against them, like deceit and extortion. The third level is those things that are optional that the intellect neither prompts to do . . . nor does it preclude them, rather it is something possible like standing, sitting, combining, and separating.[248] There is no doubt for anyone of us who is sound of mind that the Creator implanted in our intellects righteousness and justice as being truth for He commanded us in them, and deceit and iniquity as bad, for God has already prohibited us from them as for composition . . . where it is optional it is possible that He will command us in some of them and will prohibit us in others . . . reward. His Book elicits this as it says: "God wishes that He be made righteous." (Is. 42:21)[249] Were someone to think that his

---

commandments and prohibition to the virtues of whom God knew that they would not turn aside from serving Him . . . to pay his full reward, for, if he were to serve God without having been commanded to do so he would not receive any reward for it." Apparently, the Gaon speaks of the satisfaction obtained from the reward (see Kafih, Emunoth, p. 229, n. 174)—a view sanctioned by Rabbi Nissim Gaon (Book of Savior, p. 345) but apparently rejected by Rabbi Samuel ben Hophni Gaon (Treatise on the Commandments, p. 220. See ad loc. 118, who maintains that one who performs a commandment because of rational obligation, not in service to God, still merits rewards. These differences in opinion give rise to various interpretations of the talmudic axiom: "Greater is the one who is commanded and performs than the one who is not commanded." (Kid. 31a) See Book of Precepts (Bennet p. 473).

247. See IT II for a parallel statement.

248. See section I for a similar assertion.

249. I.e., that God wishes the best for His creations (see his Book on the Obligation of Prayer, p. 33). Cf. Beliefs 3:1 (p. 140): ". . . consists of things neither the approval of which nor the disapproval of which is decreed by reason, on account of their own character, but in regard to which our Lord has imposed

intellect deems iniquity to be good and justice to be bad because it gives delight to the one who does it, He is deviant and pompous[250] and exceeds in self-aggrandizement.[251] Now the strongest and most compelling proof that reveals his deviance and manifests his pompousness is that he declares that the intellect finds cheating good because it delights the deviator—despite that to the same degree it grieves the cheated. However, according to this claim cheating should be both good and bad at the same time[252] for he both grieves and delights. The same applies to justice and righteousness.[253] The Scripture says of these: "And those who rejoice in doing evil and they will rejoice when they dispose of it." (Prov. 2:14)[254] But to the community of believers, the indignity of deceit and the pleasantness of truth are for us like pillars upon which we base every necessary conclusion and obtain a desirable opinion. As the pious one says: "Therefore in all your commands I stood just and all false ways I despise." (Ps 119:128) As another pious man says: "Hate bad and love good." (Am. 5:15) Another continues to denigrate those who love bad and hate good.

XVII The Tradition

Now the faith of the believers will not be perfected until he believes that in this world there are trustworthy traditions. [This is] because being that the precepts commanded upon the worshippers are of the third kind, which are optional, [i.e.] there is no way to know them unless it is through the messenger who provides them for {the people} and lets {the people}

---

upon us a profusion of commandments and prohibitions in order to thereby increase our reward and happiness." See IT II and section above.

250. The argument is against the hedonists who maintained that one who takes delight is fortunate while one who grieves is unfortunate. The Gaon reiterates this argument in *Beliefs* 3:2 (p. 142).

251. The text is difficult and this translation merely reflects the gist.

252. The argument is based on the Aristotelian principle that opposites cannot act on the same subject simultaneously. Cf., however, David Raw, *Monatschrift*, 1912, p. 23, and Altman, *RSG's Divison of the Precepts*, p. 634.

253. *Beliefs* 1:2 (p. 40).

254. The Gaon apparently directs this verse at the beholders of the foregoing opinion.

understand them.[255] Since they are only obligated to receive from the messenger if there is a verification by which it is certain for them that God endowed him with it and thus he does something that the other creations cannot do like them He required that there be trustworthy traditions in order that the person that was with the messenger, when he tells one who was not present with him which of his acts he saw and which commands he heard, it is upon the one to whom it is transmitted to accept his statement of the knowledge and fulfilling it just as the one who was present and saw {it}.[256] The Scripture already describes this for it says: "Which we heard and knew it of what our fathers related us." (Ps. 88:3)

XVII Reports and How to Ascertain Them

When the one who seeks the truth wishes to find what the path to recognize the trustworthy reports is he finds at the outset that the path to this is first to recognize the deceitful reports, which may be one of two kinds. They are: that the one who is reporting either [1] intends to lie or [2] [just] conjectured something but it did not turn out as he thought. For example one who came into somebody's house and tells {the people} [in the house] that there is a solar eclipse. As a result of the two reasons that I have mentioned, they are not obligated to believe this [report] even though he is the only one reporting [it] and even though this is on a day that there may be an eclipse. The first is for the reason that he may have intended to lie and the other is that he may have seen a cloud forming[257] under the sun and thought it to be an eclipse. But if those who spread the rumor are many it is not possible that they should [all] commit the same error nor would they make {the error} intentionally for it would manifest if they invented the report[258] . . . my heart . . . since he himself saw . . . in the Torah: "His heart softened and cried like . . ."[259] when he heard the reproach of God to him like Yoshiahu praised when he says: "Because your heart was tender and you humbled yourself in front of me,"

---

255. See Rabbi Samuel ben Hophni, *Treatise on the Commandments*, p. 221, who states similarly that the auditory precepts are attainable only through revelation.

256. I.e., the minority obligates the majority.

257. Text reads "creating a shield."

258. Cf. the words of the *Kuzari* 1:48 (p. 49).

259. The Gaon cites this verse in Arabic translation.

(II King. 22:19) and also: "You have rent your clothes and wept before me," (II Chron. 34:27) for God scrutinizes everything he does as the verse ends and says: "I have heard, God spoke."[260] (I Kings 22:19)[261]

XVIII Closing Remarks

One should not neglect the precepts of the Torah when he sees direction for paupers, like a man selling his daughter to maid servitude and giving half a shekel every year for [it is with] sound wisdom that the precepts be essentially easy and then to add whatever is possible . . . and richness[262] nor when he sees many of the enemies of the prophets and righteous men and sorrow and straits befall them,[263] like Abraham, Isaac, Joseph, and Moses, peace be upon them for this is for their glory and esteem for they aspire for the world to come not for this one,[264] nor when they see this nation lowly and humiliated in this generation despite that it is loyal to its faith for in this state reproach is stronger and clearer.[265] Nor when one sees in the Torah statements that have no [apparent] meaning like the passages about the Awites[266] and Siddonites[267] for all of them have import as I shall explain in what is to come.[268] Nor when one sees us say in some cases: "It is probable," "may be," and "possibly" for I say this only in reverence to God's words and only in places [requiring] intellectual proof or transmitted statements do I declare and speak affirmingly of {the interpretation}. The listener should study all these things and convey them according to the exalted rules that I have set forth

---

260. Our translation of *ne'um yyy'* follows the Gaon's usual rendition of the phrase in other places.

261. Possibly the Gaon accounts for the abundance of the curses found in the Torah. Cf. *Mishna Baba Bathra* 8:2, Lev. *Rabba* 35:1. Cf., Rabbi Bahya ibn Halawa.

262. See Zucker, *Translation*, pp. 122 and 129.

263. Apparently because of the seeming injustice of this.

264. See *Responsa to Hiwya*, p. 28.

265. Cf. *Beliefs* 3:10 (p. 179): "Our answer hereunto is that the adherents of the Law had been granted perpetual sovereignty; the non-believers might have said about them that the only reason they served their Lord was in order to preserve their favorable situation."

266. Deut. 2:23.

267. Deut. 3:9.

268. See the Gaon's *Exiled Book*, p. 176 and Zucker, *Translation*, p. 18, n. 45.

at the beginning of the book and {these rules} shall push aside all doubts
and remove any false thoughts. Since completion for the believer will
come to be when he preserves the truth and clarifies and verifies [it with]
intuitive knowledge, believes in the endowed Book and has belief
undenying belief in the transmitters and pays attention to His worship.
The Wise One says of these five themes: "[1] Turn your ear and hear
words of sages—and return your mind to My knowledge [2] for it is
pleasant that you preserve it in your mind[269] and it stays together in your
lips [3] and in God shall be your trust. Informed you today—you
too—[4] have I not written for your kings in council and [5] knowledge
so that you know matter of truth and verity," (Prov. 22:17–21) as I have
explained these verse in their places.[270]

---

269. Text reads "stomach," which the Gaon renders as "breast." The reference
apparently is to the heart, which is seated in the chest. Cf. Job 15:2 (p. 263),
15:35 (p. 266), and 32:18 (p. 349), where the Gaon renders "chest" as "heart."

270. In his com. ad loc. the Gaon explains the sections of these verses as
follows: (1) tradition; (2) what is absorbed by the senses; (3) discernment,
foremost of which is knowledge of God, which cannot be sensed; (4) knowledge
of the Scripture; and (5) analysis and investigation of the previous sources of
knowledge. Cf. his com. to Ex. 25:39 ("Some interpretations of Rabbi Saadiah
Gaon to the Book of Exodus," Ratzaby, p. 12), where the Gaon lists seven general
stages of wisdom.

Introduction to the Translation on the Pentateuch

In the name of the Lord we shall do and succeed.

The Interpretation of the Torah by the Head of the
Academy Rabbi Saadiah in Blessed Memory.

Which is the translation of the rendition of the holiest book of prophecy
called the Torah from the *ancient[1] language into the language that is
dominant among *the *people of the time of the translator and his
birthplace.

[The author] said: Since praise to the Lord may He be exalted and
gratitude to Him for all his beneficence is limitless, for the strength for
which He is praised and the acts for which He is thanked is endless, the
greatest [form of] praise is exaltation and the loftiest [form of] gratifica-
tion is elevation. Praise to the Lord and blessed is the One Whose
existence is eternal, the true One Who has absolute wisdom, Whose
ability is complete, Who is totally beneficent, and Who is exalted above
all praise and glorification.

---

1. Words added or changed based on alternative manuscripts provided in
"some new sources" are marked with asterisks.

I Purpose of the Torah

[2]Now after [this we say]: When the Wise One wished with this Book to teach the people[3] and to lead them to obey him and since teaching is of three types, some more important than others. The first, which is the worst of them, is that it be said to the one who is intended to be taught: Do this! but do not do that! without revealing to him the consequence for [following] what he commanded or [ignoring] what he warned against, for the person knows that with this act he will bring the other to do what he commanded and will distance him from what he warned against. The second is to reveal to the one who is commanded and warned together with the commandment and warning the result of the act that he chooses, i.e., he would say to him: Do this and you will have complete recompense and do not do this for you shall be punished in such and such a way. This way is better than the first for {the person} will imagine to himself by means of this what good or bad will come upon him as a result of the action he chooses. The third is that together with informing the one who is commanded or warned of the good recompense for obedience, he tells him incidents of people who have obeyed this command and that [as a consequence] he improved their lot and they prospered.[4] [Likewise], together with informing him of the most stringent of punishments for his wickedness he tells of the incidents of people that were negligent with that sin and were punished and made wretched. Now this type is better than the first two types since test and trial impress the mind of the one who hears this and is for him in place of sight. For this reason God thought to give this Book, which is intended for preparing humanity,[5] including [in it] these three types in order that {the Book} be most accurate and orderly. In it He commanded humanity to do righteousness and warned them against wickedness. [He] also promised them what they will bring upon themselves for the good that they will do and intimidated them from unfavorable actions as well as informed them of people that came before them that did good in the land and prospered and [likewise of] people that corrupted their path in {the land} and were destroyed. This is in order that there be no element of teaching that His Book not

---

2. See IPC VI.

3. Text reads *ibadah*. Ginsburg translates all the like as "servants."

4. Cf. *Exiled Book*, p. 174.

5. For worshipping God. See IPC VI.

encompass. An example of these three types in the Torah is the statement of the Exalted may He be elevated, to Aaron: "And do not go during many of the times to the Holy." (Lev. 16:2)[6] He then reveals to him the consequence for this and says: "You shall not die," (ibid.) and mentions to him what happened to his sons when they did this when it says: "After the death of the two sons of Aaron." (Lev. 16:1) Similar to this is also what Solomon said when he warns about laziness in matters of belief and the world as he says: "Do not like sleep." (Prov. 20:13) He then explains that the consequence of this is the severance of good[7] as it says: "The desire of the lazy is liable to kill him." (Prov. 21:25) This is the instance of one who is lazy from overseeing his field until thorns grow in it to the point that its fence collapses. This is [what is meant when] it says: "When I passed over the field of a lazy man . . . and it has grown thistles." (Prov. 24:30–31) Now the most correct and proper order and arrangement would be for the command to precede, followed by the consequence and then the recollection.[8] However, since the giving of the Torah was not at the beginning of time, for His Wisdom declared that its giving be at the time that the population reach a constant number at which they will stay,[9] God the Lofty be blessed and exalted was required to inform them of the substance of the events that preceded them so that they follow the [acts] that God praised that their predecessors did and distance themselves from the actions of the predecessors that He condemned and [that] He order and arrange this from the beginning when all things were created to the time of the giving [of the Torah]. Afterwards He commands, prohibits, warns, and promises relying that He speaks to people of pure and sound understanding.

II Prerequisites for the Understanding of the Torah

You the reader of this Book should know that despite its great value and exalted level that the rest of the books of prophecy cannot compare to it and despite that from the literal meaning of the text one can explain what is obscure and obstruse, it is not permissible for people to believe that

---

6. The Gaon cites this verse in Arabic translation.
7. The verse continues: "lest you be bereaved."
8. I.e., that the Torah should contain only these three elements.
9. See his intro. to Ps. (p. 24) where he expands on this subject.

God may He be elevated and exalted has no other demands,[10] but it is upon them to know that He has two other demands for them. The first is prior to Torah and is intellectual proof by which they should know that [1] visible substances and other sensibles are created ex-nihilo,[11] [2] that their Creator is eternal having no beginning nor end, [3] that He is One and that He is not comparable to [any of] them, [4] that [none of] them is comparable to Him, [5] that He is Wise and knows what will be before it occurs, [6] that He is the Creator who created what He wishes without any material, [7][12] that He is righteous and does not impose on his servants what they cannot bear and likewise the rest of the fundaments of belief derived from intellectuals proofs like the intellected precepts such as righteousness and uprightness. I will restrain from citing the proofs for anything from this [subject] in this book for I did not write it for this purpose. The second demand, which comes after the Torah and is knowledge of the tradition handed over by the prophets—how they would rule in every new case that would occur between men and how they would fulfill the auditory precepts that the intellect neither prompts to reject or require them. However, although their imposition on man is optional,[13] when the prophet taught them they became obligatory. Nevertheless the quantity and quality are not recorded in the Book like the amount of prayers and the measurement of righteousness and the kind of work on the Sabbath and whatever else known by Tradition that is commanded. I also will restrain from explaining any of this in this book of mine for I did not write it for this purpose and also because I have already explained elaborately in the large book of the interpretation of the Torah these two notions, I mean *what *is *by *proof and what came down by tradition.

III The Reason for Composing the Translation

Indeed, I only wrote this book because a student asked me to write a separate book containing the interpretation of the Torah that does not

---

10. Other than studying the Torah.

11. See IPC XV.

12. Ibid.

13. Apparently he means that the auditory precepts, because they are ambivalent to the intellect, would have been left for the individual to decide whether to follow or not.

weave into it anything relating to the usage of the language, [i.e.] absolutes, substitutions, transformations, and metaphors.[14] It will not contain any questions of the heretics *nor *the *dissenters[15] or criticisms of them nor the branches of the intellectual precepts or how to perform them. I shall only translate the meaning of the text of the Torah. Now I saw that what he asked of me was useful for the listeners [to be able] to understand the meaning of the Torah, the stories, commandments, and recompense in an orderly, arranged, and brief fashion. And [further that] the effort [expended] by one who seeks [to know] a certain idea not be increased because of the proofs mingled in this so that it not be a burden on him. And if after this he wishes to understand the legislation of the intellectual precepts and how they are to be performed and by which means criticisms of the Scripture may be rejected, he may seek this from the other book since this short one will make him aware of this and will lead him to his goal. When I saw this I wrote this book—an interpretation of just the plain meaning of the Torah delimited by the notions of the intellect and tradition. When it is possible for me to add some word or letter by which the meaning and intent would be revealed for those for whom a hint instead of elaboration is sufficient, I did so. In God I shall find aid which I seek for all good concerning this world and the next.

14. See IPC note XIV for examples.
15. I.e., the Karaites.

Chapter I

[[1) The first thing¹ God created was the Heavens and the Earth.]]

I

[I rendered *bereshith* as "the first thing" for]* were I to render *bereshith* as "in the beginning" this would imply that there was something before the creation of the Heavens and Earth. But this is impossible.[2,3]

II

The heretics asked in regard to the creation of the world: Why did God not create the world prior to the time that it was created? For they

---

1. Ibn Janah (*Kitab al-Usul*, p. 659) gives this translation of the verse verbatim, which may indicate the grammatical explanations of the Hebrew texts that he sets forth are also drawn from the Gaon. He maintains that the *beth* is additional (*Riqmah*, p. 66, n. 3) and that either the particle *asher* (which) is implied as if it stated *Reshith asher bara* or that the word *bara* is to be taken as an infinitive, i.e., *Reshith bero*.

2. Maimonides (*Guide* 2:30, p. 349) also rejects this interpretation, claiming that it implies the pre-existence of time although he does not explain how this is so. See also *Beliefs* 1:4 (p. 86).

3. This section was preserved by Yefeth ben 'Ali in his commentary ad loc. (Ben-Shammai, *Doctrines*, p. 65).

thought this question to have place and began analyzing it and said: Was it because of some delay or because of something that had held Him back?[4] But they do not know that the question is essentially unfeasible for if we say that He created a time that includes every "before" and "after" and they suggest to us that this be before that time, they then suggest one of two things: either that time is non-time or that non-time is time.[5] . . . Now if we would wish to think that all things created themselves we cannot escape the fact that their creation of themselves would be either prior to or after them existing. Now were we to think that they created themselves prior to being created then something that is absent cannot create anything, and were we to think that they created themselves after them existing then what reason is there for them to create themselves for their former existence would already suffice?[6,7] We therefore would know necessarily that something else created them. . . .

III

[8]He indicates with the definity of the *hes* in *ha-Shamayim* (the Heavens) and *ha-Ares* (the Earth) that they are created according to God's plan and wisdom.[9] Since it states here "the Heavens and the Earth" and elsewhere "I call them they are ready together," (Is. 48:13)[10] it teaches us that they were created simultaneously in the minutest possible time.[11] Therefore, the possibility that one may think that the creator of the Heavens did not

---

4. I.e., was it something on God's own part or something exterior to Him?

5. This section was preserved by Rabbi Mubashshir Gaon in his *Criticisms*, p. 18.

6. This is preserved in ibid. p. 19.

7. This section is reiterated in *Beliefs* 1:2 (p. 46) in a slightly expanded form.

8. The problem treated here is that "the Sky" and "the Earth" are definite, as if they are specifically mentioned before or are somehow previously known.

9. This homiletic explanation originates in *BR* 1:3 (p. 12): "He built the Heaven, i.e., the Heaven that He originally contemplated and the Earth that He originally contemplated," i.e., each creation was premeditated, none created without a purpose. See his com. to Prov. 16:4 and *BO* 1:1 (p. 37).

10. In *BO* (p. 32) the Gaon attributes this view to the Sages (in *Hag.* 12a) and refers to his commentary here. See however Ibn Ezra (Linetsky, p. 18), who rejects this interpretation of the verse as unilateral.

11. In *Beliefs* 2:5 (p. 106) the Gaon explains that God's speech (in this case

create the Earth is eliminated.[12] It is not unlikely that the circumference and the center should come about simultaneously,[13] for we see [that] all bodies come about in this manner.[14] As for plants, their skin does not precede their meat nor their seed nor stem and likewise in embryos the bones do not precede the flesh nor the limbs, but everything starts at the same time and ends at the same time.[15]

IV

Now these Heavens that God created at the first instance of time[16] were the celestial spheres without any stars in them.[17] He created them to be a place for the stars just as He created the Earth without any growths on it as space for growths like plants and animals.

V

Now, as for the statement that God created the Earth (Eres), He did not name it Eres at the moment He created it, but it was named so on the third day when the water was removed from it as it says: "And God called the dry land[18] Eres.[19] (Gen. 1:10) The meaning is rather that He created the place that He shall name Eres. There are many examples of this in the

---

"calling") in the context of creation merely indicates creation "with one blow not within a certain interval of time or piecemeal."

12. Because it states: They are ready together.

13. The comparison is to the Heavens and the Earth respectively as the Gaon explicitly states in his com. to Ps. 19:2 (p. 83).

14. Some text appears to be missing here.

15. I.e., even the rest of the elements were created simultaneously with the Sky and the Earth as the Gaon affirms in the BC (p. 32). There may be a lacuna here, as in BC (ibid.) he states that he mentioned here the example of fire whose properties come about simultaneously.

16. There was no time prior to this since time comes about by means of the motion of the spheres. See Beliefs 1:4 (p. 85) and BC (p. 21).

17. They were inserted on the fourth day when they were created.

18. I.e., the Earth that was revealed.

19. Ibn Ezra, however, objects as follows: If the "heavens" mentioned in the first verse and in the fourth are not time same ones, then the earth mentioned

Scripture, for Moses states: "Across from the Gilgal," (Deut. 11:30) but it was only called so afterwards.[20] The meaning is: "The place that shall be called Gilgal."[21] In my explanation of the section of "and these are the names,"[22] I shall have a lengthy discourse on this subject concerning the pericope of the Mountain of God (Ex. 3:1)

2)[[And the Earth was inundating (*tohu*) and engulfed by water (*bohu*) and darkness on the face of <the> [23] inundation (*tehom*) and God's wind blowing on the face of the water.]]

I

[24]Since the Earth and the Sky were . . . His goal at the beginning of creation[25] was to mention them, why does He mention the Earth in the second verse and says: "And the Earth was inundating and engulfed by water?" [We answer:] His intention in this second verse was to let us know us that the water and the air were created and therefore He mentions them explicitly and associates them with the Earth.[26] Now before the explicit mention of the creation of the water and the air, we would undoubtedly have known [anyway] that they were created from the verse of "The first thing," etc. alone, for from reason we would not doubt such an obvious notion. That is, had it stated only "The first thing" and restrained from saying "And the Earth was inundating and engulfed by water," since we would know that the two borders[27] are created, it would

---

here and in the latter verse should not be the same either. However, it is not possible to assume the existence of two earths.

20. Josh. 5:15.

21. See also his com. to 2:13 where he elucidates this subject.

22. This section remains unpublished in a Jewish Theological Seminary manuscript.

23. The Gaon adds the definite article as though the reference is to the inundation already mentioned, since he derives *tehom* from *tohu*. See section III.

24. The question here appears to be: Why repeat "Earth" in our verse?

25. Apparently the meaning is: in the first verse.

26. See *BO* 2:1 (p. 77) where the Gaon mentions this section.

27. The Sky and the Earth.

follow that everything in between them be created [as well]; for water and
air are things that can only exist by means of something created[28] and the
Heavens and the Earth are created![29] However, God did not suffice with
this since He wrote the verse of "And the Earth," etc., by which He refers
to the Earth whose creation had just preceded, as if to say: "That the Earth
that preceded, I created it, I do not mean just the ground, but the ground,
the water, the air, the wind[30,31] and everything in between the celestial
spheres and the Earth as well."[32]

III

Tohu refers to the Earth and it is the ground that covers the Earth from all
its sides. What indicates to us that *tohu* refers to the circumference[33] is
that it says of the land of Edom: "And He stretched around it a *qaw* of *tohu*
and stones of *bohu*." (Is. 34:11)[34] Now *qaw* is a band that the builder
stretches and by which he records area and measurements[35] as it says:
"And yet the measuring line shall yet go out straight forward." (Jer. 31:39)
However, the ground was covered with water and I have translated *tohu*
accordingly.[36]

---

28. Apparently because they need to be contained. See also *Beliefs* 1:1 (p. 43)
and *BO* Intr:1 (p. 26). See also note 80.

29. As is indicated by the first verse; furthermore the belief in a created world,
according to the Gaon, is a pillar of Judaism. See *Beliefs* 1, EXCORDIUM (p. 40).

30. See com. below regarding the creation of the element fire.

31. This is in accordance with *Hag.* 12a: "*Tohu, bohu,* darkness, wind, and water
were all created on the first day."

32. In his *Beliefs* (ibid.) the Gaon states further that this verse indicates that all
things were created ex nihilo. His statement here, and much more so in his *Beliefs,*
implies that this verse speaks of the creation of the entire world. It does not seem
to fit his translation of the verse according to which the "it" speaks of the creation
of the Heavens alone. On the other hand in his com. to Gen. 2:1 and in his intro.
to Ps. (p. 19) the Gaon does interpret this verse so.

33. I.e., the exterior surface.

34. The Gaon translates the verse periphrastically as follows: "Its circumference, which is stretched like a band of desolate Earth and desolate stone."

35. In his commentary to verse 7 the Gaon defines it as a "rule."

36. I.e., as "inundating."

IV

Bohu refers to the center, i.e., the center of the Earth, in the middle point of its inside[37] and it is the hard stone on which all sides of the Earth are founded. Another proof that the word has this meaning is that it says "And the stones of *bohu*." (Is. 34:11)[38] However, it was engulfed by water like anything that is so, i.e., that it is at the bottom of the water.[39,40] Now *tohu* and *bohu* make up the diameters of the Earth and its boundaries[41] and the water surrounds them.

V

What is meant by "darkness" is the air[42] for darkness is not a substance as the deceitful Dualists think.[43] [44]For when light hits the air it turns bright and if there is no light it darkens. Now what proves the correctness of our statement is that the dark air receives light which is a substance, which removes the darkness. However, since darkness is not a substance, the illuminated air does not receive it and the light [in the air] is not removed

---

37. I.e., the center of the sphere of the Earth, not the middle of its surface.

38. The definition of *tohu* and *bohu* that the Gaon sets forth here is based on the following statement in the *BC* (p. 123): "*Tohu* is a green line that surrounds the Earth and *bohu* is the immersed stones that are inside the Earth from which water comes out and the proof for this is that it says regarding the land of Edom, etc." (The rendition of the original text is according to the Gaon's translation of it.)

39. From each side respectively. See *Hag.* 12a and *BO* p. 85.

40. This section is difficult to make sense of. It appears that the Gaon maintains that both *tohu* and *bohu* means "desolation" but that *tohu* generally refers to the circumference and *bohu* to the center. Accordingly, he translates the first as "inundating" (i.e., on the surface, around the Earth) and the second as "engulfed" (i.e., in the center). It is not certain in which case these terms refer specifically to the corresponding parts of the Earth.

41. Apparently he means: respectively—i.e., that it makes a solid sphere.

42. There may be Pythagorean influence in the association between darkness and air.

43. The reference is to the Manicheans, who believed in the existence of two deities: one of evil and one of good. See Wolfson, *Repercussions of the Kalam*, p. 137. However, many Karaites also followed this view: So Yeshuah ben Yehudah (ad loc.), Ali ben Sulaiman (Skoss, p. 46), and possibly the Gaon's Karaite rival Benjamin al-Nahavendi. See Mann, *Early Karaite Commentaries*, p. 455.

44. Cf. Aristotle, "On the Soul," vii (p. 105).

by it, but the air reverts to darkness when the light is dimmed. This[45] also becomes evident if we look at light: The closer the carrier of the light approaches the more the light intensifies and penetrates the air, while the more it distances itself the more the light weakens. However, we do not see darkness act on any body! In truth darkness is merely an absence of light just as the absence of voice and wind is not a thing but rather air vacant of them.[46] Again the meaning of "darkness" here is the air and this is the third element.[47]

VI

For what reason does it state "on the face of the Earth" and not "on the Earth" or "on the[48] inundation" or "on the entire inundation"? We say that it does not say "on the Earth" because nothing was visible of the actual Earth since the water covered it and for this reason it says "inundation" [altogether]. This statement supports the fact that we derived *tohu* from *tehom*.[49] It did not say "on the entire inundation" either since the light was created simultaneously with the Sky and the Earth[50] at the first instance of time[51] as I shall explain afterwards[52]—but at the same time was concealed from the face of the Earth as I shall explain in what is to come.[53] It must then be that the face of the Earth, which is the inundation, was dark at the beginning of its creation until this light endured the period of a watch of night[54] and appeared on the face of the

---

45. That darkness is not a substance.

46. See also *Beliefs* 1:3, p. 65 where he reiterates this entire section.

47. In his *Kitab al-A'tabar* the Gaon refers to this section. See *Criticisms*, p. 130.

48. We insert the definite article according to the Gaon's translation of the verse.

49. Which he translates as "inundating." This derivation was accepted by Rabbi Abraham bar Hiyya (*Meditations of the Soul*, p. 42) but rejected by nearly all commentators following him. Cf. Ibn Ezra and Yefeth as cited by Skoss in *Ali ben Sulaiman's Commentary to Genesis*, p. 43.

50. Light emanates from fire. See note 70.

51. See note 10.

52. This section is lacking.

53. This section has not yet come to light.

54. See below (Zucker, p. 372) where the Gaon discusses the watches and their measurements.

Earth at the first instance of day as I shall likewise explain.[55] Now since darkness[56] did not encompass the entire Earth but only the face of the Earth for the light was on the opposite side, it says: "And darkness on the face of the inundation," and not just "inundation."[57]

I say further that if the entire Earth is spherical[58] and is round,[59] where is the face and where is the back? I say that its face is the side on which God declared with His wisdom that man be created. This is the inhabitable quarter of the land, I mean the quarter between the equator and the North. It is a quadrant[60] and this is what is called the face of the Earth. Also the revolution[61] of the celestial spheres during the six days of creation began from it. Now when the light appeared upon the Earth[62] it would be called "morning" and when it was concealed from the Earth this period of time would be called "evening," as the night and the day were measured according to what would be after the creation of man.[63]

VII

Wind which is blowing wind[64] is of the third element but was singled out from it for two reasons. The first: because of its movement and powerful action. The second because it brings the ground water.[65] Furthermore[66] it

---

55. This section is lacking.

56. I.e., the dark air.

57. The Gaon apparently wishes to explain why evening precedes morning in the verse.

58. This was the accepted view since Aristotle.

59. Perhaps he wishes to emphasize that it has no flat surfaces.

60. I.e., a 90-degree surface.

61. He probably means the starting point of the measurement of its movement.

62. The Gaon appears to maintain that originally the light emanated from the spheres and was distributed on the fourth day when the stars were created.

63. Even though in the future the light will be distributed among the stars. See note 7 above.

64. Not a spiritual wind.

65. Cf. *Beliefs* 2:8 (p. 111): "Again the wind although finer than the water is nevertheless more powerful than the earth because it moves it and even causes it to rise."

66. The Gaon indulges in giving reasons and specifying differences and often gives more that he states.

aligns the ground in the center and for that reason[67] God attributed it to
Himself and said "the wind of God" for unlike the wind none of these four
elements fix and align the Earth and furthermore God's power appears
more by its intermediacy than by anything else. God attributed it to
Himself just as He attributed the mountain of Sinai to Himself as "the
Mountain of God," (Ex. 3:1, etc.) the Holy Temple as "the House of God,"
(Gen. 28:17, etc.) and the messenger of God as "the Man of God." (e.g.,
Deut. 33:1) Similarly, the wind that guards the elements in their center it
calls "the wind of God."[68] Now even though our statement that the wind
oversees the water so it does not run off the Earth is evident, the Scripture
says regarding it: "So I broke upon My constraints as though I set bolts
and doors upon it," (Job 38:10) i.e., that God made the wind bind the
water to the face of the Earth. It also says along these lines: "Who scribes
a veil on the face of the waters." (Job 26:10) Again, this wind sustains the
Earth itself as we have explained. I shall bring this out in further detail!
The wind moves together with the celestial sphere[69] and since it
surrounds the Earth from all its sides equadistantly, it effects that the Earth
be in the center.[70] [This is because] were we to take a round jar and put
a small round stone inside of it and turn it on a potter's wheel it will stay
in the middle of the jar and will not touch any part of it and will keep
equidistant from all sides as long as the motion of the jar persists. The
Wise One said of the movement of the celestial spheres and the Earth
being in the middle [of them]: "It revolves and revolves; the wind goes on
its revolutions the wind returns." (Ecl. 1:9)

---

67. The Gaon shows influence of the Stoics, who maintain that air keeps the
Earth immobile in the center. See Freudenthal, *Stoic Physics in the Writings of Rabbi
Saadiah Gaon*, Arab Sciences and Philosophy, vol. 6 (1996) p. 129.

68. The Gaon explains this in greater detail in his commentary to Gen. 1:26.
In his *Beliefs* 2:8 (p. 111) the Gaon speaks of 'fire' instead of 'celestial spheres'
because he maintains that the celestial world is composed of fire.

69. I.e., the movement of the largest sphere is the cause of wind. See his com.
to Gen. 18:1 sec. II and BO (intro) p. 27.

70. Cf. Freudenthal, ibid., pp. 128–129, n. 54. See also Zucker, p. 370, where
the Gaon attributes another function to the wind.

VIII

Were one to ask: For what reason does it not mention the creation of the fire?[71] We answer him as follows: If he asks about the celestial fire, the Scripture already mentioned it in the creation of the celestial spheres[72] and if the reference is to the fire that is concealed in the parts of the Earth,[73] i.e., water,[74] stone,[75] dust,[76] trees,[77] and the like, for, because the Scripture mentioned the creation of the carrier[78] to us it suffices without mentioning the creation of the fire itself. The case is similar regarding the water. Would the Scripture not have mentioned the creation of the water we would have sufficed with just the mentioning of the creation of the carrier[79] alone, for water itself is a feeble body that cannot persist independently.[80]

IX

Now as for the people who think that the darkness,[81] the water, and the wind are eternal because the verse states: "And the Earth was,"[82] it is this verse itself that lets us know that they are created, for it associates these

---

71. The Gaon reiterates this entire section in BC (p. 29), where he adds that those who advance this question maintain that the fire is eternal and is the material from which all of existence was created.

72. In his Beliefs 1:3 (p. 70), the Gaon rejects Aristotle's view that the celestial region is made of the quintessence in favor of Plato's belief that it is made of fire. The Gaon's refutation is cited by e.g. Rabbi Bahya ibn Paqudah (Duties of the Heart).

73. This distinction between celestial and terrestrial fire also appears to be Stoic in origin. See Freudenthal, ibid., p. 129.

74. When it is warm.

75. Apparently he speaks of volcanic rock.

76. Apparently ashes that are still aflame.

77. When set afire?

78. The sky.

79. The Earth.

80. Because it needs at all times to be contained. See note 28 above.

81. However, in the parallel passage in Beliefs 1:3 (p. 68) and intro. to BO (p. 27) the Gaon does not mention darkness as that thought to be eternal.

82. I.e., that this verse describes what existed before the Earth was created. Possibly the reference is to the Jewish Heretic Hiwya al-Kalbi. See Zucker, Genesis, p. 212, n. 213.

things with the Earth whose creation is mentioned prior to this and did not associate them[83] in such a way as being prior to the Earth.[84] Despite this the Scripture does not restrain elsewhere from stating explicitly that these things in this verse are created. Of darkness it says: "I create light and darkness," (Is. 45:7)[85] the wind: "For behold He creates mountains and wind,"[86] (Amos 4:13) and regarding the upper waters: "And the water which is above the firmament for He commanded and created them," (148:4–5) and the lower waters: "To Whom the the sea is and He made it." (Ps. 85:5) This is the explication of the creation of the four elements. I say further if each one of these four elements is an independent existence what wisdom is there in associating them with the Earth and saying: "And the Earth," etc?[87] We respond: This is because it would be impossible to associate the water with the celestial spheres.[88]

X

[89] . . . The living creatures cannot exist without them.[90] The Earth is the place where they dwell and live. The celestial spheres—since by their means the Earth stays fixed at the center.[91] The air because anything that breaths lives through it. The water—because the air adjacent to the Earth

---

83. I.e., with the Earth.

84. In his *Beliefs* (ibid.) the Gaon reiterates this sentence in a slightly different form.

85. The Gaon maintains that this verse refers specifically to that darkness (i.e., the air) spoken of in our verse, not to darkness in general which is a mere absence of light. See ibid. (p. 66) where the Gaon states that the purpose of this verse is to offset the view of the Dualists.

86. Our translation of this verse imitates the method of the Gaon in the previous one.

87. I.e., that just as Earth they are elements all in their own right.

88. Apparently what the Gaon means is that in order to indicate the createdness of the elements (see note 25) it would not have been possible to associate them with the celestial spheres since they have nothing in common with water and therefore the Earth was the only possible alternative.

89. The question appears to be: Why were these specific things singled out?

90. Apparently, the elements.

91. Since they move the wind. See note 67.

is moistened, balanced, and adjusted to the air of the soul[92] by means of the water. The proof for this is that the air is destroyed when the water above the Earth is destroyed and in deserts, which are far from water, living animals cannot sustain themselves. Since these four elements are essential for the existence of living creatures at every . . . the Creator mentioned them first and indeed they are the most worthy for God to have called them "very good."

[[3) and God wished that there be light and there was light]]

[93]I translated "and God said" as "[and God] wanted,"[94] for "speech" has a number of meanings, one of which is "wanting" as is the case here and similarly in: "What your soul shall say I shall do." (I Sam. 20:4)[95]

[[4) and when God knew that the light was good God divided between the light and between the darkness.]]

Hiwya al-Balkhi said that "and God saw the light that it was good" indicates that God had never seen light prior to this. But this is due to his boorishness in the language of the Hebrews for they refer to "knowledge" as "vision" as it says: "And Jacob saw that there was a hunger in Egypt." (Gen. 42:1)[96,97]

---

92. See *Beliefs* 7:7 (p. 279), 1:3 (p. 66) and 6:1 (p. 238): ". . . the purpose of this respiration is to temper the natural heat of the heart wherein the soul has its heat." Cf. Ibn Ezra to *Gen.* 2:7 (Linetsky, p. 56, n. 36).

93. This excerpt is preserved by Rabbi Yahya Dahari in *Seda la-Derekh*. (Kafih, Perush, appendix)

94. Such is the Gaon's translation of "And God said" in the entire story of creation with the exception of the creation of man in verse 26. In his *Beliefs* 2:5 (p. 106) the Gaon explains that when the Scripture states that something was created by God's word the meaning is simply that it was done according to His wish, not by necessity. His rendition of our verse, however, was criticized by many scholars after him. Ibn Gikatila, followed by Ibn Ezra (Linetsky, p. 23), claimed that this is an over-allegorization since "And God wanted 'let there be light!'" is senseless. Al-Qirqisani, however, uses a different line of reasoning.

95. The soul obviously does not speak, but desires.

96. The meaning is obviously that he knew that there was a hunger since he could not possibly see Egypt from his location.

97. This section is preserved by Rabbi Mubashshir Gaon in *Criticisms*, p. 21.

5) [[and God named the times[98] of light "day" and the times of darkness He named "night"[99] and there[100] had passed of night and day[101] one [complete] day.[102] 6) And God wanted that there be a firmament[103] in the middle of the water and that it be a divider between the two waters.[104] 7) And God made the firmament and divided between the water that is under it and the water that is above it and it was so 8) and God named the firmament Heavens and the second day [consisting] of day and night had passed.]]

I

. . . [105]This is apart from the other necessary uses they have. These celestial spheres [for] by means of their power and solidity, screen the

---

98. The Gaon adds this word for the sake of clarification.

99. The distinguishing and naming according to the Gaon may possibly be two separate actions Cf. Ibn Ezra, (Linetsky, p. 25, n. 136). See Rivlin, *Perush Rav Saadiah Gaon la-Torah mi-Toch Targumo*, p. 134.

100. The translation of verses 5–8 as indicated by the brackets has been supplied according Derenbourgh's edition. However, in verses 13 and 19 there is some discrepancy between the two editions. Whereas our version reads: "And there had passed . . . and God wanted," Derenbourgh's edition has "And when there had passed . . . God wanted," merging the two verses together. We have, in consideration of this, altered the reading supplied from Derenbourgh's edition, although by conjecture, to conform to the parallel cases.

101. The Gaon changes "evening" to "night" and "morning" to "day" in order to create a parallelism with the first part of the verse.

102. Text reads *Yawm*, which means "day" in the sense of a 24-hour period. This rendition is rabbinic in origin. See *Pesiqta Rabbath* #17, but also Ibn Ezra's objection! (Linetsky, p. 26, n. 142).

103. Text reads *Jald*, a congealment or the like. Ibn Ezra states disapprovingly in his long recension to Gen. that he maintained that it is like the water under an eggshell. Apparently, the Gaon took it to be some solid substance, a view found already among the early Rabbis. See *BR* ch. 4 and Tal. *Jer. Ber.* 1:2.

104. The Gaon reformulates the original "between water and water" as if to indicate that it is the upper and the lower waters, spoken of respectively. Apparently he speaks of the utility of the things mentioned in the opening verses, perhaps as a justification of their mention.

105. This section has been placed here by mere conjecture.

heat of the Sun and the stars from the Earth.[106] Regarding this the Scripture states: "For the Sun He placed a tent in it." (Ps. 19:5) These are the three spheres below {the Sun} and the . . . as it says: "He stretches the sky like a tent." (Is. 40:22)[107] It is also serves to delight the people's eyes with the color of sky blue, the color in which the *Mishkan* was made like . . . We shall explain in the making of the *Mishkan*[108] . . . The Earth for the plants, plowing, and building and whatever else relates to this. The water is for drinking, watering, and for carrying loads in it and whatever is similar to this. The wind to improve seeds, to disperse chaff, and to set boats into motion and the like. Now regarding this it says: "When it was good." By informing us . . .

II

We say now that all of existence, despite that its multitude cannnot be counted, consists of two kinds—simple elements and composed [things].[109] As for the elements there are four and they are fire, air, water, and earth. All things are composed of them.[110] They persist and do not desist until the time that God's wisdom declares it[111] as it says regarding the time of their desistance: "For the Sky like a smoke shall be evaporated." (Is. 51:6) However, the decomposition of the simple and composed elements into parts that we see in our times[112] is nothing more than the breaking down of the pieces and their . . . elements reverting one to the other.[113] This accords the statement regarding the righteous whose soul is elevated until it reaches below the Throne of Glory in the loftiest place for ever . . . in the most exalted of luminaries and will

---

106. Following Aristotle.

107. The Gaon apparently understands the *raqi'a* here to be the celestial sphere or spheres.

108. See Ratsaby.

109. See also IT.

110. I.e., at least one of them.

111. The Gaon maintains that the world will desist in messianic times. See *Beliefs* 7:7 (p. 281).

112. As opposed to messianic times.

113. See *Beliefs* 7:5, treatise on resurrection 1:1 (p. 413) and *BO* intro (6th opinion).

dwell in the most exalted of places.[114] Now when we see something like fire that consumes wood, it is nothing more than the the parts decomposing and each of the elements reverting to its corresponding element.[115] Whichever of them is moist, I mean the air which is moist and hot[116] and the water which is moist and cold, ascends in its entirety [in a vapor] and mixes together with the air. An example is air that is hot and moist in nature [which] reverts to its elements and water that was subjected to the accident of heat which softened it to the point that it turns into the nature of air and ascends as vapor. But if the accident, I mean heat, departs, it cools down and reverts to the nature of water directs itself to the Earth immerses in it, mixes with its element and reverts to water. Likewise the earthy element remains in wood and turns to ash and all that fire does is divides into parts and brings every part to its element.

III

[117] . . . one of them is that we should consider that "It was good" was not written regarding the division between the two waters so that we do not separate in the camps and have disputes between ourselves, [2] because the death of the Messenger[118] about which it is said "that he was good" (Ex. 2:2) came about because of water, I mean the Water of Dispute, (Num. 20:13)[119] and further [3] because fire[120] with which wicked people are punished was created as it says: "The plan ready from the night before." (Is. 30:33) When it says "from yesterday" it refers to a day before, I mean *temol* and not *shilshom*.[121] And [4] further because the created [beings] do not know any command derived from anything created on

---

114. Cf. *Beliefs* 6:3 (p. 242).

115. Cf. *Beliefs* 7:7 (p. 278) and app. 7:1 (p. 412). This is in accordance with the view of the Rabbis in BR 4:7 (p. 32).

116. I.e., when it is vapor.

117. In this section the Gaon speaks of the reason why "it was good" was not mentioned in verse 8. The opinions that he cites are midrashic in nature but it is not certain where they originate.

118. I.e., Moses. See IPC section XI.

119. Following the Rabbis.

120. Fire is the element of which the celestial existence is composed.

121. See Pes 54a and *BR* (ibid).

this day.[122] However, the most probable explanation is what I shall relate,[123] that the Scripture's manner is not to state "that it was good" in connection to essential [things] since the creation cannot exist without them. Now since God made the firmament an essential as it says: "And He called the firmament *Shamayim.*" He did not state {"that it was good"} of {the firmament} but entered it in the general [flow] as He did with the elements in the general.[124]

IV

The implication of it first stating "And He said"[125] but then "And God made the firmament," and likewise "And God said: Let the waters swarm and God created the Sea Monsters" (Gen. 1:20–21) and so also "And God said let the Earth bring forth" and then "And God made," (Gen. 1:24–25) is that all this indicates . . . its words to inform us that the meaning of "and He said," "and He called," "and He made," and "and He created" is one and the same, i.e., "wish" as it says: "What He wishes He does," (Ps. 115:3) and "desire" as it says: "What His soul desires He does." (Job 23:43)[126]

V

The meaning of "and it was so"[127] is that it remains so forever, similar to the statement "and he was there to this day." (II Chron. 5:9)

VI

It is now necessary that we explain when the angels were created. We say that most probably they were created on the second day together with

---

122. It does not teach any lesson or law.

123. This section has not surfaced yet.

124. Since it only says that it was good regarding the creation of light.

125. Before stating that He did the act.

126. See com. to verse 3. Cf. also Al-Muqameais (*Twenty Chapters*, p. 272) who states that command and wish are one and the same thing.

127. See also Rabbi Abraham bar Hiyya (*Scroll of the Revealer*, p. 48).

the Heavens.[128] This is because after stating: "He stretches the sky like a bow," etc. (Ps. 104:2) David says: "He makes His angels winds and servants blazing fire." Furthermore, the entire second psalm of *Bless my soul* (Ps. 104) refers to the act of creation each day according to its sequence[129] and this is one of the things that is attached[130] . . . and further observing the parts of angels . . . [131]to the extent that they become the color of addax as it says regarding some of them: "And the essence of its body is like pearls," (Dan. 10:6)[132] and furthermore since some of them appear to the prophets carrying the firmament its shape being like that of awesome ice as it says: "And a likeness on the heads of the animal a firmament like the awesome ice." (Ezek. 1:22) Despite that their names change and we certainly know that the forms of *Seraphim*, *Hayyoth*, *Ophanim*, and *Malakhim* differ from each other as I shall explain in various places,[133] the rendition of everyone [in Arabic] is *Mala'ikah* since in the language of the Arabs there is no equivalent to the word. Similarly, the color of fire that Daniel[134] saw was in a simple body. We shall expound on this in its place so that our discussion here not be too lengthy.[135] However, what is most surprising is that "wind" is mentioned of the angels for it says: "He makes His angels wind," and it also says: "For the wind of the beast is in the wheels." (Ezek. 1:20)[136]

VII

Now in mentioning that God created the firmament that He made the cause of rain[137] there are four purposes as is customary for me to mention.

---

128. See his com. to verse 27.

129. Cf. Ibn Ezra to Gen. 1:2 (Linetsky, p. 28).

130. Apparently to the first day, the reference being to the angels.

131. In this section the Gaon appears to speak of the various realizations of the angels arguing against the view that they are of various kinds.

132. See his com. ad loc.

133. See his com. to Dan. 10:6.

134. Manuscript mistakenly has "Ezekiel."

135. Apparently he means that it was a corporeal fire, not a divine one. Cf. his com. to Ex. 19:18 (Ratsaby, p. 5).

136. The Gaon maintains that the angels are made of fire. Cf. Ibn Ezra ad loc. (Linetsky, p. 11) who claims that the regular elements are spoken of. See his com. to Gen. 3:8, where he explains the wind to mean "motion" in that text.

137. The latter point is not stated in this section.

The first is that we should worship Him since He created these things as He says contendingly: "Have you at some time reached the storehouses of the snow or seen the magazines of hail strife and battle . . ." (Job. 38:22, 26)

The second is that we do not serve the Heavens which is the largest body since we know that it is created as the early ones said: "Are there among nations those who . . ." (Jer. 12:22)

The third is that we believe in the signs that He did with the rain which He shall describe to us and we should say: He who created the cause of rain is able to do these wonders by their means. An example of this is [1] the waters of the flood as it says: "And the rain lasted forty days and forty nights on the Earth," (Gen. 7:21) [2] God's raining on Sodom and Gamorrah sulphur and fire as it says: "And God rained sulphur and fire on Sodom," (Gen. 19:25) [3] that He made the rain come out of its time because of Samuel's prayer as it says: "Is it not wheat-harvest today? I shall call unto the Lord," (I Sam. 12:17) [4] and that He held back three years of rain because of Elisha's and Elijah's prayer as it says: "And Elijah the Tishbite said there shall be this year no dew and rain," (I Kings 17:1) and it says: "And God's word was to Elijah on the third year saying: Go show yourself to Ahab and I will send rain upon the Earth." (I Kings 18:1)

The fourth is that we observe that which God commanded us regarding the water; meaning that [1] at the time when rain comes down we should praise Him [as follows]: "Blessed is the Good and the Doer of good."[138] [2] If lightening and thunder and lightening bolts accompany it we bless: "Blessed is He Who made the Genesis and Blessed is He Whose strength fills the world,"[139] as we have explained in the *Book of Praises*.[140] [3] If the rains cease twenty-four days before their time we pray over it."[141,142] [4] If God holds the rains back longer we gather together and fast seven days three after three, thirty days in sum, and during these days we add six chapters to the eighteen chapters amounting to twenty-four chapters. The names of the additional chapters are: "The one who answers in a time of distress," "Hearer of joyful shouting," "Hearer of cries," "Remembers the

---

138. *Ber.* 9:2.
139. *Ber.* 59a.
140. See *Book of Pearls*, p. 90.
141. I.e., from the 7th of Heshwan until the beginning of Kislew.
142. Cf. *Ta'anith*, 10a.

forgotten," "Hearer of prayer,"[143] and "One who pities the Earth." This is in public prayer but in private {the prayer} should only include "In the time of distress."

9) And God wished that the water gather from under the firmament to one place and [that] the land should appear and it was so. 10) And God named the dry land "earth" and the gathering of water "seas" for God knew that it is good.

I

I have translated *yiqqawu* as "gather" since these two letters[144] combine to have four meanings. [1] "Gathering," e.g., "And the rest of their gatherings of water." (Ex. 7:19) This is one of the things that indicates that it does not call the water *miqwe* but rather that which is above the ground.[145] [2] "Hope," [e.g.] "The hope (*miqwe*) of Israel," (Jer. 31:39) which is derived from: "All the time I have hoped (*qawe qawethi*) for God," (Ps. 40:2) and the like. [3] *Qaw*, which is a builiding rule and measurement[146] as in: "And the measuring line (*qaw*) shall yet go out opposite him." (Jer. 31:39) [4] *Qaw* [as in] *qaw umvuse* (Is. 18:2), [which means] a trampled and meted-out nation—the first word is in the absolute.[147]

II

The first thing we shall investigate {in this matter} is that—being that the water covered the Earth—if some of {the water} was above the firmament, would not the rest of it fill up {the space} between the Earth and the firmament so that [when] God would have wished to reveal it was the firmament (*raqi'a*) lowered or the Earth raised? We answer [by asking] how

---

143. Cf. Mishnah *Ta'anith*, ch. 2, where the order differs.
144. I.e., *qof* and *waw*.
145. The containment itself.
146. See com. to verse 2 sec. III.
147. I.e., *qaw*. Apparently the Gaon's reading the first was vocalized with a *qames*.

can the firmament be raised? For the celestial spheres surround it from all sides; and likewise [how can] the Earth be lowered when it, I mean the firmament, is surrounded by them from all sides? Rather the most probable [answer] to this [is] that when the water was first created . . . it was finer than it is now. It reached the firmament and when God wanted that {the water} gather it gathered and thickened, nested, and obtained the form it [has now].*

III

<Now there are four types of use in mentioning the creation of the water. The first is that we should worship the One Who Created this large body [I mean] the sea and prevented it from flooding the world as it had[148] as it says: "Just as I gave it the clouds for clothing and the mists for swaddling bands," (Job 38:9) [and] "so the depths You have covered." The second is that we should not worship the water since we know that it is created and has a ruler that moves it[149] as it says: "That I have placed the sand to be a border to the sea." (Jer. 5:20)>[150] The third is that we should believe in the signs that God made with water about which He will tell us and that we say that He Who is able to create them ex-nihilo is able to create these things. [An example] of this is the splitting of the Red Sea as shall be explained [in its place]*[151] . . . holding back the water of the sea for Elisha and Elijah as we shall explain[152] . . . one and taking the water out of the rock as He did in Rephidim and Kadesh[153] and the like.

The fourth is that we should accept what God commanded us concerning the water [i.e.] what regards impurity and purity according to its many aspects as we shall explain in our commentary to Leviticus[154] that water may be of a number of kinds.[155] [The first is] drawn [water] which in many cases is the cause of impurity. The second is non-drawn

---

148. Apparently in the Flood.

149. Apparently, the Gaon refers to Aristotle's universal principle of motion, the idea being that God controls the water.

150. The section up to here is drawn from *Seda la-Derekh*.

151. This section has not surfaced yet.

152. This section has not surfaced yet.

153. See Ex. 17:6 and Num. 27:14, respectively.

154. This section has not surfaced yet.

155. See *Miqwaoth* 4:1.

which is either from a non-constant or constant source; slow-moving water which is pool water, spring water, sea water, and fast-moving water. I have [just] introduced them here in short.

11) **and God wished that the Earth produce herbage and offspring with seed, and trees and fruits producing fruit according to its kinds and [according] to the seed that it is from on the Earth and it was so; 12) and the Earth produced herbage and offspring with seed according to its kinds and a tree producing fruit according to the seed that it is from 13) when God knew that it was good and there had passed of the night and the day a third day.**

I

I translated *mazri'a zera'* as "with seed"[156] exactly and added *waws* in *'Oseh Peri* and *asher zar'o bo* in order that the latter be connected to the former.[157] The meaning is that what was God's desire [is what] shall be in reality.[158]

II

[159] . . . in order to inform us that they are divided according to individual and kind so God wanted that they be divided[160] and despite that there are many, there are four {fundamental} kinds of herbage (*deshe*). The first is offspring, which has no seed in them but grow directly from the ground like herbage as it says: "And brings forth the sprouting grass." (Job 38:27) The second is *'esev mazri'a zera'*, which is that which has seed and grows from it like vegetable. The third is "tree producing fruit," which is a tree that in itself is a fruit of the Earth and does not carry anything. The fourth is "producing fruit," which is that which brings forth fruit from time

---

156. I.e., not "producing seed."

157. So that *asher zar'o bo* modifies "fruits," not kind, i.e., as opposed to fruit tree producing fruit.

158. For in verse 12 these two clauses are independent modifiers.

159. The aim here appears to be to account for the items singled out in the text.

160. "According to its kinds" modifies "herbage" as well.

to time. But we do not have the need to present their number and description.

III

It adds "according to its kinds" in order [to indicate] that the tree should not bring forth at times a pomegranate, another an apple, a fig, and yet another an olive.[161]

IV

It adds "whose seed is in it" [to indicate] that the seed of the tree should sprout into a tree of the tree [it sprouted from]. An example [of this is] a fruit tree. Among these are those whose seeds do not sprout but a branch is cut from {the tree} and [then] is planted, e.g., a pomegranate.[162] Some say that a cabbage is a kind of herb whose leaves grow.

V

And the Earth brought forth not because of its own power but because of God's command[163] as it says: "And the Earth opened," (Num. 17:32) [which opened] not of its own power but by God's command.

VI

The Scripture states "to its kind" regarding the plants but not when telling [God's] wish [that it be so] not because the things turned out different in reality than that which was wished but rather [the Scripture] was brief and elucidated [this] at the end.

---

161. I.e., an instruction that it should consistently produce one kind.

162. "Whose seed is in it," not "according to its kind" as would be expected, indicates the command to produce its own kind.

163. So also Yefeth, however, Al-Qirqisani (Doctrines, p.), Rabbi Abraham bar Hiyya (Med. p. 49), and Ibn Ezra (Linetsky, p. 32) maintain that the power was already given to the ground but the Scripture omits this.

VII

We shall explain after this that these plants number many rather . . .
[164][I shall not elucidate]* any of the types that heal man as I have in the
incident of "Every tree of the field" (Gen. 2:5) . . . first the one who
impressed this [made it] that the tree and its nourishment . . . and the
hardstone so that the sower can not sow it and the plower can not plow
it nor can the planter plant it . . . rather the Creator created it ex-nihilo
and as God wanted the plants to be, so they were, [i.e.,] differing in form,
length, width, and circumference and different in their time of [growth
and ripening]* from twenty-two days from the sycamore tree to herbage
differing in color and taste . . . differing in their time of growth and
sprouting by twenty-two days like[165] . . . after being planted as long as
seventy years like the carob.[166] All this at the beginning of time . . . in
its full.[167]

VIII

"Since it was good" [said] of the plants [means that it was] for the good
and benefit of mankind.[168] The ones that are nourishing like the seeds of
wheat and barley. They sustain bodies[169] and give their souls binding
material as it says: "Brings forth herbage for the animals and grasses for the
service of man and brings bread out of the Earth." (Ps. 104:14) "Brings
forth herbage for the animals" refers to animal fodder and grasses. "For the
service of man"[170] refers to flax as . . . dry herbage and the like. For that
reason it says: "for the service of man" as it says there: "The makers of flax
will be disappointed" (Is. 19:9) and [also] "the house of the makers of

---

164. The bracketed words are added conjecturally.

165. The missing growth may be restored according to *Bech.* 17:32 to be the
almond that ripens after twenty-two years.

166. According to *Bech.* 8:1.

167. Apparently he wishes to say that all the plants were created full-grown.
See section X.

168. See also Ibn Ezra.

169. Of animals.

170. The translation of this verse follows the Gaon's immediate interpretation
of it. His translation ad loc., however, has "for the beholders of man's service"
where he adds "beholders."

linen," (I Chron. 4:21)[171] i.e., so that they spin it to weave [it] and [then] wear it. "And brings bread out of the Earth" refers to actual bread. The statement afterwards, "and wine gladdens man's heart," (1s. 19:9) refers to beverages and afterwards "and oil which brightens the face of man" refers to oils. "The trees of the Lord shall be satisfied" (v. 15) refers to the fruits collectively, meaning that they shall be satisfied by the trees of the Lord,[172] and "the cedars of Lebanon that He planted (ibid.) refers to the teak . . . and the pine from which people chop pillars and shade their dwellings. He also did a great good for the animals as it says: "in which many birds that are there shall make nests." (Ps. 19:17)[173] Were one to think that God created something harmful for people like opium, euphorbia,[174] Colocynth,[175] and [][176]. We say that everything He created is beneficial, either for sustenance or building [materials] as we have explained. The medicinal ones He created to clean out all pieces of food in people's bodies [as well] all moldy mixtures like myrobalan,[177] scammonium,[178] hellebore, ribes siculum, and the like do if a person combines them correctly, as the Scripture describes that Solomon the prophet[179] spoke of their benefits from big to small as it says: "And he spoke of the trees and the stones from the cedar which is Lebanon to the hyssop which sprouts on the wall." (I Kings 5:13)[180] However, they cause sickness and pain [1] if not used wisely, [2] if one ruins their properties, [3] adds to or detracts from their [correct] amount, [4] consumes them at the inappropriate time, [5] with the incorrect medical powder, [6] in the inappropriate time of the year, [7] in a land that is not fit for them or in

---

171. The point of these verses is that flax and linen is produced by man, i.e., for his own use.

172. Here the Gaon adds a *mem* in order to change the subject to "man." Ad loc., however, he renders it literally.

173. This is a question posed by the heretics, as Al-Qirqisani (see Zucker, *Genesis*, p. 225, n. 84 for an excerpt) attests in his commentary ad loc.

174. "Designates the sponges with resin and other plants that grow at the southern border of Mount Atlas in Morocco." (*Medical Works*, p. 21).

175. See Lane, p. 657.

176. The Gaon cites other growths which are not readily identifiable.

177. A laxative mixture (*Medical Works*, p. 87).

178. See also BO 2:5 where the Gaon discusses scammonium.

179. The Gaon considers Solomon to be a prophet. Cf. However, Maimonides Guide 2:45.

180. The Gaon takes it that he spoke of their uses.

any way that is against their nature. Also placing them in the [incorrect] place.[181] Even grain, wine, and oil, if a person takes {a greater amount} of them than necessary, may even kill him as it says: "Just as when you find honey you should only eat enough for you so that you do not have too much of it and vomit it out." (Prov. 25:17)

IX

Now God informed us that He created the plants for four reasons, as I describe, in the entire act of creation. The first is that we should serve Him since He is the Creator of the plants as it says: "Which brings forth herbage in the mountains," (Ps. 147:8) and obligates prior to this [as follows]: "Answer to God with thanks." (Ps. 147:7). The second is so that we do not worship any of the plants according to what it says: "Do not plant any evergreen tree,"[182] (Deut. 17:21) and condemns "those who prepare and adorn themselves [to go] in to the gardens." (Is. 66:17)[183] The third is that we trust in what He shall tell us of the wonders that He shall do with the plants. An example of this is that a barren tree grew fruits, branches, and leaves overnight as its says of Moses and Aaron: "It brought forth leaves and blossomed flowers and formed almonds." (Lev. 17:23)[184] Similarly, Jonah's 'kikayon' which God made sprout and [so] removed overnight.[185] He also brought together fire and the thorn bush[186] and turned Moses's staff into a serpent.[187] [Therefore,] we should say that He Who is able to create {a plant} to start with is able to create with it what He decribed. The fourth is that we should accept the commandments that God commanded us regarding the plants since He is their Creator. An example of such [commandments] is [as follows:] [1] That the first three years after planting trees {their fruits} should not be eaten. [2] That we do not sow in the year of Shemittah[188] and the

---

181. In the body.
182. This is how the Gaon renders *ashera*. See "perushe" Kafih, p. 143, n. 11.
183. To worship.
184. Cf. Maimonides' com. to *Sheb.* 7:5 and *Kil.* 6:9
185. See Jonah 4:7.
186. Ex. 3:2.
187. Ex. 4:3.
188. Ex. 23:11.

Jubilee.[189] [3] That we should not attach an ox with a donkey in our field work.[190] [4] That we should not sow two composed species as it says: "Do not plant your vines from two kinds so that the first juice of the seeds that you shall sow with the produce of the vines not be prohibited to you." (Deut. 22:9) [5] That we should leave for the pauper what is forgotten, gleanings, and that corner of the field.[191] [6] That we should not muzzle an animal that is threshing.[192] And [7] we should take out heave and tithe every <<year as I shall explain these precepts lavishly in their place>>; [8] hallah, [9] <<two blessings on food [one] before [eating] it and after as it says [of the blessing] that precedes [eating]: "Because he blesses the sacrifice and afterwards they eat the bidden." (I Sam. 9:13) It says of [the blessing] following [eating]: "And if you eat and are satisfied and you shall bless the Lord your God." (Deut. 8:10)>> We say that it is appropriate that we obey the Creator of all these plants because of all of this. . . .[193] <<"Plant your vines from two kinds so that the first juice of the seeds that you shall sow with the produce of the vines not be prohibited to you," (Deut. 22:9) and that we take heave from seeds as well as tithe and hallah together with what He adds for us that when we obey Him the Exalted, He gives blessing to our seed>> as it says: "Bring all the tithes into the storehouse . . . and I shall pour you out a blessing." (Mal. 3:10)

And as we see the blessing that God endowed our father Isaac's produce as its says: "Then Isaac sowed in that land and found on that year one hundred times the measure that he sowed." (Gen. 26:12)[194] The verse contains three things which need to be uncovered. The first is that it says "in that land" when it could have done without mentioning this. The second is [that it says] "on that year" when it could also have done without mentioning this but just: "and Isaac sowed one hundred measures [more]." The third is: What is the Scripture's intention when it says "one hundred measures?" We say that the intention of "and Isaac sowed in that land" is

189. Lev. 25:11.

190. Deut. 22:10. In his translation of this verse he renders lo teberash as "You shall not connect" in general, to include hybrid mixtures in accordance with the Sifri. See Zucker, Translation, p. 434.

191. Lev. 19:8.

192. Deut. 25:4, as opposed to Anan who interpreted it as "before it threshes." See Ibn Ezra to Gen. 2:2 (Linetsky, p. 50) and Sifri ad loc.

193. The following paragraph appears to be a part of a different version of the preceding one.

194. See Derenbourgh ad loc.

to give notice to the fact that the ground of that land was desolate, that he obtained no benefit from its seed and that it did not even bring forth what was planted in it. Do you not see that as soon as Isaac went out and settled in that land Abimelech expelled him as it says: "And you hated me and sent me away from with you." (Gen. 26:27) Were it not an affluent land why would it not have been permissible for him to live there? Now although there were fields and villages, nevertheless there were no wells because it was barren land and for that reason it says "in that land."[195] The meaning of "in that year" is that that year had little rains. Do you not see how Jacob's servants dug a well for water and

X

. . . how God brought them[196] out from absence into existence in the six days of Genesis and that He may He be blessed brought them out holistically, I mean in a manner of completeness and simultaneity, not one thing growing after the other. He brought about the trees [together] with their offshoots, branches, leaves, and fruits in them.[197] As the Sages said: "All of the creations of Genesis were made in their full grown stature with their consent and their pleasure."[198] "According to their consent and their pleasure" means in the most complete form that God wished everything sowed and planted from tree to branch, leaf, and fruit to be at the end. The same applies to the plant with its seed whose coming to be was simultaneous.[199] The Scripture explains this since it says: "And God wished that the Earth shall bring forth offspring with seed and fruit producing fruit according to its kind," (Gen. 1:12) and as wisdom decreed [it] God brought [it] about in its fullest. Likewise, what it declared to have fruit God brought out with its fruits in the fullest size that it can attain. Also what wisdom declared to create for a specific purpose He created [it] to its fullest utility and what He created to be sustenance for the creation

---

195. Apparently the fact that the Scripture goes out of its way to emphasize what land he sowed indicates that there was something about the land such that it would be unexpected that one would plant there.

196. Apparently the reference is to the trees and the plants as the Gaon states in the immediate.

197. See com. to verse 1.

198. Cf. *Rosh. Hash.* 11a and *Hul.* 60a.

199. Following *BR* 5.

He made it sustenance for them[200] and what He created for a purpose He made it useful for them and taught them their specifics and their utilization. He revealed this to His prophets as it says of Solomon: "And he spoke of the trees from the cedar of the Lebanon the herbage which sprouted on the wall." (I Kings 5:13) As for the second start in time to come,[201] God made plants so that they grow by birth from a seed or branch like the pomegranate or palm tree or from a grain by plowing the ground like wheat and barley or legumes as it says: "Does the tiller have the entire day to sow?" (Is. 23:10) and "Six days you shall sow." (Lev. 28:3)[202]

14) And God wished that there be luminaries in the firmament of the Heavens that will divide the day and the night and the two of them shall be signs and times (re-othoth ul-mo'adhim) and days and years; 15) And there shall be luminaries in the firmament of the sky to shine on the Earth and it was so; 16) and God made the two large luminaries, the large luminary to illuminate in the day and the small luminary in the night and the stars; 17) and God made them in the firmament of the sky to shine on the Earth 18) to illuminate in the day and the night and they divided between the light and the darkness since God knew that this is good; 19) and there passed of night and day a fourth day.

I

Now in this matter our dissenters from the followers of Anan and others erred for they thought that [the lamedhs in] le-othoth ul-mo'adhim are indicators. They say this statement refers to the luminaries [i.e.] that God made them indicators for the holidays.[203] However, they were unaware that it is entirely impossible for {the statement} to refer to the luminaries. This is because it should refer to something that itself is able to be signs, times, days, and years but it is impossible that the luminaries themselves

---

200. There is some difficulty in the reading of the preceding passage.

201. I.e., the next generation.

202. The purpose of these verses is to show the existence of sowing, not to distinguish between the two kinds of plants.

203. See Al-Qirqisani (*Book of Lights*, p. 631). The Karaites maintained that the new month is sanctified according to the sight of the moon. Accordingly they interpret the verse to mean "And the stars shall indicate signs and holidays, etc."

become signs, times, days, and years.[204] Were one to think that [the stars] are indicators of the mo'adhim [we say] that there is no such thing in the language, rather any body connected to a body with a *lamedh* is either possessive or is itself. Were there in the Scripture for example one thousand *lamedhs*, 999 of them having the sense of indication and one having another sense, their claim[205] would [still] not [necessarily] be valid for it is something requiring proof and his dissenters may dispute him on his claim by the *lamedh* that remains.[206] How much more so if there is not even one that is as he thought.[207] Rather what *we-hayu le-othoth ul-yamim we-shanim* refers in truth to is the night and the day, which are both mentioned before it for it says: "To divide between the day and the night." The Scripture says regarding the day and the night together: "And they shall be signs," for they themselves are indicators and become times.[208] However, were we to say [that mo'adhim] means "holidays"[209] we would not object.

II

I rendered *le-othoth ul-mo'adhim* as *ayatan wa-awqatan* (signs and times) not as *li-ayat wa-l-awqat*, according to the norms of the [Hebrew] language. [This is] not a conjecture but a certainty! This is because when its people wish to say that wool became a garment they say: *haya ha-bbaghedh li-Semer*, and if they wish to say that the seed became food they say: *haya ha-zzera' li-lehem*, always adding a *lamedh* to the second [unit]. They do not mean by this that the first should be an indicator of the second;[210] rather they

---

204. The argument here appears to be that according to the literal meaning, were we to accept for a moment that the *lamedhs* are indicators, the verse would read: "The luminaries will be for signs etc." in the possessive. This reading would only be possible if the luminaries themselves were able to serve as units of signs, days, etc.

205. That it has the sense of indication.

206. I.e., by the claim that it has another sense.

207. I.e., in the sense of indication.

208. Al-Qirqisani (*Book of Lights*, p. 793) argues against the Gaon's interpretation that it would imply that the day shall be days. Cf. also Ali ben Sulaiman (Genesis, p. 115), but see next note!

209. Not times.

210. I.e., that one is for the other.

mean that this becomes that. An example of this from the Scripture is the statement: *wayehi ha-adam le-nefesh Haya* (Gen. 2:17), and likewise regarding the stick: *wayehi le-thanin* (Ex. 2:6), and the dust: *wayehi le-khinnam* (Ex. 8:12),[211] and the like—they all mean that the first thing as it is the one that became the second not that {the first} is an indicator of {the second}. Now a stronger [example] than these—and I shall explain what it means—is what God says: *wayehi lachem le-lodhim* (Lev. 26:12), which is God Himself not an indicator of someone else. [Likewise]: *we-attem tihyu li le-'am* (ibid.), i.e., you yourself: [this is] not an indicator of someone other than you. Whenever words are formulated [like this] they may be either with or without a *lamedh* as it says: *wayyasimennu le-av le-far'oh ul-adhon le-khol betho u-moshel be-khol ereS MiSrayim* (Gen. 45:8) and so here: *le-othoth ul-mo'adhim ul-yamim we-shanim.*

III

"And they shall be days"—each two of them constitutes a compete day.[212]

IV

"And they shall be years"—according to the definition of year. Were "luminaries" closer to "And they shall be signs" and "the day and night" were farther from, this would require us to connect this statement to the farthest one because of the impossibility of it being connected to the closest. How much more so if "the day and the night" is closer and "luminaries" is farther. Apart from this they also decided that *mo'adhim* are holidays. This word appears in the Scripture in seven senses as we shall explain in the pericope of "this month." [Indeed] among these is "times": "Until the time of their times," (Dan. 12:7) and "Even the stork knows her times," (Jer. 8:7) and the like.

---

211. Our texts, however, have *wehaya.*
212. So also in his *Book of Discernment,* p. 437.

V

The first thing we should speak about in this connection is: What is the manner of wisdom in the stars not being created at first together with the sky? We say: So that we not think them to be eternal. The point of observation despite that the change and coming-to-be is visible in the four elements, people have thought them to be eternal, misinterpreting "and the Earth was,"[213] how much more so the stars which are balanced not expanding or reducing as if of the quintessence.[214] If He would have created them first they would have thought them to be eternal.[215] Furthermore, why did God create them multifarious? We say in order to prevent [us from] serving them when we see that one covers the other and one holds back the act of the other. Do you not see that the moon according to its measurement is parallel to the Sun and goes under it and its light is concealed? If the worshippers see it as such they will not believe that one of them has dominion over the other. Further from what did God create them? We say, as we have already mentioned He created them from the first great light.[216] I have compared [this] to a bar of gold that the goldsmith casts and of which he makes various kinds of jewelry, or diamond or corrundium from which he makes various kinds of crystals and this creation was similar to it. . . . .

VI

I mean the sphere of the fixed stars to exclude these seven mobile stars. *He placed one of them in parallel in the sphere that is under it.* One should not err because of the [Scripture's] statement "in the firmament of the Heavens" to think that they are all in the firmament, I mean the surrounder[217] which was created on the second day, for it says this because their light reaches us, meaning that God made their light penetrate the firmament just as it penetrates the spheres and as [the light] of the large luminary will reach

---

213. See above, verse 2.

214. Ibid.

215. Cf. *Ber.* ch. 6.

216. This view is expressed by the Rabbis in *Hag.* 11:1: "These are the luminaries that were created on the first day but were not put up until the fourth day."

217. See note 108, regarding *raqi'a*.

the Earth on the second and third day for the Scripture often describes [things] according to what the eye sees as it says regarding the birds: "And a bird shall fly against the face of the firmament of the sky." (Gen. 1:20)[218]

VI

"To divide beween the day and the night" refers to the Sun alone for the day is distinguished from the night by means of {the Sun}[219] according to what man is accustomed to[220] and the Scripture described [it] so as well. Now this statement[221] is said of places that are populated,[222] i.e., between the equator and the northern side which is divided in the manner that I have [described]*.[223] Despite that night and day may be longer or shorter [in the various] {climates} even if {the day or the night} are at their greatest length or shortness [respectively] it is not possible that the celestial spheres turn one revolution during twenty-four hours without light and dark falling in {the climate} if the duration of the day and night increases or decreases it does not reach more than *a third of the the day or two-thirds* for trial shows clearly that the median of the first climate is thirteen hours and the middle of the second is 13.5 and the median of the third is 14 and the median of the fourth is 14.5. The median of the fifth is 15.5 and of the seventh[224] is 16. The reason for this is that the Sun moves in the celestial sphere specific to it for would it reach the maximal distance from the upper horizon to the southern side the day reaches its shortest length. <When it reaches this distance from the north, the day is at its longest.> But when it is in the middle and its sphere and the sphere of the constellation intersects at two parallel points and day and

---

218. I.e., they are not literally against the firmament in outer space.

219. Apparently the Gaon wishes to exclude the stars from this function. He maintains that "the stars" is the object of "and God made" independently of the interceding clause. Cf. Ibn Ezra ad loc. (Linetsky, p. 37) for an opposing view.

220. As opposed to the stars and the moon.

221. I.e., that the Sun distinguishes between day and night.

222. The populated area is used as the reference point for the periods of day and night.

223. This section has not surfaced yet. Apparently he speaks of Ptolemy's seven climates.

224. Zucker's arabic original here (p. 38) reads "four" but this appears to be an error.

night become equal. However, in places that are uninhabited, the day reaches its greatest length of up to twenty hours and likewise the night down to four hours. What indicates this is that from the ascent of the northern star and further it ascends to the point until there becomes one day of summer that is entirely day and in the winter that is all night. It can also go up two or three days until a month of the summer is all day and likewise a month in the winter that is all night. It may also go up until six months become all day and all six months all night since they are together.[225]

VIII

. . . When the axis is on the place which is on the head. The rotation of the sphere of the fixed stars in these places [that are uninhabited] inverts and is made like the rotation of a grinding mill, i.e., from the south to the north from the rotation that is in the inhabited places <inverting the rotation that is in the inhabitable area which is from east to west. Regarding those same risings and settings that are in the climates of inhabitable and unihabitable areas God challenges His creations saying: "Or in what way the light is cleft or its rising rays spread out upon the earth." (Job 38:24)—this is in inhabitable areas in which there is sunrise and sunset every day. He says further: "And have you comprehended the expanses of the Earth. Then tell of it, if you know aught," (Job 38:18) meaning a place where there is always light and no darkness mixed into it as well as a place of constant darkness. This is for six months and six months like half the revolution of the sphere. This is the measurement by which it has become clear that the two axes, which are the [extreme] points, one of which does not move in the direction of the southern horizon and the second is opposite conceals under the Earth.

"And they shall be for signs"—"for indicators," for any indication is a sign. Both of them, I mean the day and the night, are divided into hours and seconds, according to the Pentateuchal calculation each hour having 1080 seconds and according to the astronomical calculation each hour has sixty seconds. According to these parts [of time], more or less people measure their travels and any act or craft that they do and all their turning. Likewise they have marks in hours in steps and ascensions and with beams

---

225. Cf. *BO* p. 62 and com. to Job 39:19.

of wood they are measured and the like. Just as the the kings of Israel had markings* for hours of which it says: (Is. 38:8). . . . It exists now according to the various agreements between people or according to what he commanded. As for determining what is agreed there are those people who determined every month to be thirty days and ignore the five days remaining at the end of the year. Others determine every month to be thirty-one days and four [months] having thirty [days each] and one twenty-eight days—this excludes those who agreed [determining the months] according to the Moon.

"And for days" [means] that each day and night are a complete day. According to the division of day and days that I have described.

"And years" [refers] to the number of days called a "year." This means the return of the Sun to the place where it was and the beginning of the cycle of the year. Its recognition in the Heavens is by the course [of the Sun] and its reflection on the Earth [i.e.] in openings and windows, and all days . . . because the two of them. . . . >

Then it says "the large luminary" despite that both of {the luminaries} are large. [This is] because the light of the moon is from the Sun for the moon is a dim planet like a mirror which receives the light of the Sun and directs it to us in the corresponding place similar to the pupil of the eye which reflects the shape of man from inside the entire eye.[226] Since it is illuminated by the light of the Sun it follows that only half of its body, which is the half opposite the Sun, is always illuminated and the other half is always dark. At the time of intersection since it is under the Sun equally its light hits the upper half of its body and none of its light is visible since we see the lower half of its body. However, when {the Moon} separates from it, the revolving half deviates from the top part and turns a little in our direction and we see from this this measurement . . . after the place that the light hits is directed more at us . . . and the Moon with our sight until it reaches in its path half the sphere and is parallel to the Sun its light hits half the body which is all from our side and we see it all illuminated unless it happens that the Earth intersects between it and the Sun, then its light is concentrated from all its body or just some of it and there is an eclipse of all of it or part of it [respectively]. However, this will be only on the night of a full moon because when it is positioned opposite the Sun then the light begins to reduce from our [view] . . . all that it

---

226. Theory of vision.

began . . . light in inclination . . . shall become . . . only in its essence {?} and shall become. . . .

VIII

"To illuminate in the day and in the night" means by their light and nothing else[227] . . . side . . . with the enlargement and reduction of the moon . . . so that the night becomes extended . . . and those who travel visiting and reveals to us the essence of the stars and the wonder of their nature when it reduces.[228] By it the seas are expanded[229] and the bodies of animals are changed by it in the *blood and marrow*. By it trees are saturated and moistened or dried like the effect of the Sun during the spring, summer, fall, and winter. The Torah already attributes the ripening of the plants to the power of the Moon just as it attributes it to the Sun as it says: "And from the delight of the produce of the Sun and from the delight of the grains of the Moon." (Deut. 33:14) Furthermore, the Moon is God's indicator that everything has a beginning as well as an end,[230] a contraction and expansion,[231] and likewise the Scripture says of the one who takes away . . . as it says: "And you, were you to conceal your pity from them, they shall be frightened and if you take their wind they die and return to dust and when You send Your wind in them they gather and collect and You shall make anew the face of the Earth with population and building." (Ps. 104:29–30) . . . as it says: "For the sky like smoke shall evaporate," (Is. 51:16) and then it says . . . "For like the heavens and the new Earth that I have created stay before Me God said so shall your offspring and your name stay." (Is. 66:22)

IX

<"And He placed them in the firmament of the Heavens" . . . the stars. We say that the Sun is the last star of the constellations that remains

---

227. Not astrological influence. The original reads "for ruling of the day. . . ."
228. In visibility.
229. Tides?
230. See *BR* 15:26 Torah *Shelema* to Ex. 12 item 41 (Zucker).
231. Apparently the Gaon wishes to compare the phenomenon of the moon which becomes new, grows, and then diminishes to existence which came to be anew, generates, and then corrupts.

[visible in the sky] until three hours of light of the fourth day . . . the beginning of the fourth hour to the beginning of Libra while the Moon is at the end of the < . . . . . . > revolves entirely above the Earth . . . goes the Sages said that the reason for mentioning *kesil* before *kima*[232] and in another place it says: "Because He makes *Kima* and *Kesil*," (Amos 5:8) because . . . cold to cold. Now Kesil is the star called Canopus[233] to the . . . one of these air to the Earth and balances them. The same applies to all of . . . But God made these exemplary for everything.

X

One of the dissenters clung to [the statement] "to shine during the day" and fancied to invent that [God] the Exalted wished that we determine the months according to the Moon for the Sun alone determines the day and the stars alone at night and the Moon has no use. However, since it is impossible that it be created futilely[234] it must be that it should indicate the months. This, however, opposes God's division[235] since He made the Sun for the day alone and then firstly the Moon and then the stars with it for the nights as it says: "And the small one to shine in the night and the stars."[236] It also says: "The laws of the one Who separated the Moon and the stars from the light of the night," (Jer. 31:35) and "The Moon and stars to illuminate in the night," (Ps. 136:9) then the division of the One Who divided as we have said is nullified.

XI

The statement "To divide between the light and the darkness" requires that any light that appears before sunrise is at the time of darkness and its domain until the Sun itself appears. Someone thought that there may be morning at two times before sunrise. The first is within the darkness that

---

232. Job 9:9.
233. See *Ber.* 58b.
234. See com. to verse 2.
235. Of time alloted to the celestial bodies.
236. I.e., together with the stars.

is near [this time of] the morning star. He[237] adduces support for himself from what is said in the pericope of Boaz: "And she lay under his feet until morning and got up before one could recognize his friend." (Ruth 3:14) However, this is not definite for it is possible that there is a contraction here [i.e.] that the meaning is before she [could] sleep the entire night until the morning she arose in the the night.[238] The other is at the time of the morning star. He adduces support for himself from the statement "The morning illuminated." (Gen. 44:7) However, the deficiency in this is that this light is the light of the Sun as it says: "So said God One Who gives the Sun as light for their day." (Jer. 31:34)[239]

XII

"For it was good" means good and beneficial for mankind.[240] Firstly, {the luminaries} shine to the benefit of {mankind} day and night, {people} calculate according to their motion, [i.e.] according to the times [measure from it], [the cycle of] their sustenance and produce as well as the length and periods of their lives, dates, loans, and the rest of their dealings as He commanded: "From the number of years after the year of release you shall be from your friend," (Lev. 25:15) and also: "And its buyer shall count how much of the year has passed." (Lev. 25:50). Also {the luminaries serve to} ripen their fruits and their seed. Some {of the luminaries} act upon them by means of their moisture as it says: "Do you bind the sweet influences of the Pleiadas," (Job 38:31) and others pull, ripen, and warm them as its says: "Or loose the drawstrings of Canopus." (ibid.)[241] Also {people} sail in the sea with their guidance and they balance their bodies and their fruits and founts when they rise and fall and the like.

---

237. See Anan's *Book of Precepts*, p. 175 for citations from Benjamin al-Nahavendi, who maintains that morning may be at two or three times.

238. Cf. Ibn Ezra's *SR* to Ex. 14:24, where he opposes the Gaon's claim that morning in all cases is at sunrise and cites this verse (in Ruth) against his view.

239. I.e., not the morning star.

240. See also Ibn Ezra LR to Gen. 1:4.

241. Cf. Maimonides, *Guide*, 2:10.

XIII

The purpose in letting us know that God is the Creator of the stars is of the types common in the account of Genesis. The first is that we worship God because He is the Creator as it says: "Lift your eyes to the sky and see Who created these stars." (Is. 40:26) It refers with this to the fixed stars whose motion is uniform. It says eleswhere: "One who takes out their armies in a number and calls all of them by name," (Ps. 147:4) which refers to the mobile stars each one of which has a specific motion or motions.[242] The second is so we do not serve any of them since it is clear to us that they are created, equalized [by] and submissive [to God] as it says: "Lest you lift your eyes to the sky and see the Moon . . . and shall bow to them," (Deut. 4:19) as I shall explain in my interpretation of "Which the Lord your God divided" (ibid.) in seven ways. The third is that we trust in the signs that God made with them which He will describe to us which He did with them from the breaking of the two luminaries for Joshua as it says: "And the Sun stilled and the Moon stood." (Josh. 10:13). This was [done] by stopping the eastern motion of the spheres[243] as it says: "And He said in the sight of Israel, Sun, stand you still upon the Gibeon and you the Moon in the valley of Ajalon," (12) for only eastern motion is visible to the eye of man because of its rapidness while all of the other motions are reduced when compared with it. Another [example is] the return of [the Sun] ten levels for Ezekiah says: "Behold I return the shade of the levels," (Is. 38:8) and that He raised {the} heat {of the stars} upon the enemy army as it says: "The stars in their courses fought against Sisera." (Jud. 5:20)[244] We should say there is no doubt in that He Who is capable of creating them is able to do with them these acts and even more. The fourth is that we accept the ordinances and commandments that God commanded us with them. An example of this is that there should be prayers twice daily after sunrise and before its setting as we have explained[245] and as the early ones have transmitted: "Its performance

---

242. The Gaon referes to Ptolemy's epicycle, trajectory within trajectory. See IPC section I.

243. So Ibn Bal'am in his com. ad loc. (Perez, p. 103). However, he cites his rival Ibn Gikatilla as of the opinion that they did not actually still, but that God shaded the Sun's light. See *Beliefs* 7:1 (p. 411).

244. See Midrash *Tehilim* 11:5 and R. David Qimhi to Josh. ad loc.

245. See *Book of Praises*, pp. 12–13.

is with sunset."[246] That we bless the Sun in the day that it is the fullest on the day of the cycle of Tammuz:[247] "Blessed is the Maker of Genesis,"[248] and that we bless the Moon once whatever time during these eleven days that we see it, I mean [that] from the fourth to the fourteenth we bless: "Which by His word created stars," according to what is in [my] *Book of Praises*[249] and that the new years be close to [that of] the solar year and that we do not calculate the year of the Sun according to [the Sun] itself as we all agree that some years are twelve months [long] while others are thirteen. When we calculate the beginning of our month it should be according to that of the lunar month, not by the sight of the actual Moon as our Ancients have transmitted that of the twelve months, ten are fixed at thirty or twenty-nine days except for Marheshwan and Kislew, which alternate. God has indicators telling us every month what [length] He wishes us to make these two months as I shall explain in [my] interpretation of the pericope of: "This month is for you the head of years." (Ex. 12:2)

XIV

Our dissenters divide into nine groups which branch into ten views. Some of them say that the duration of the month should be calculated as twenty-nine days, twelve hours, 963 minutes and when the day that they have calculated is reached, it is ordained as the head of the month even if only a minute remains of it. He adduces proofs to this[250] from [the fact] that [for the *Niddah*] part of the day is counted as a [full] day.[251] The response to him is that the *Niddah* does not impurify everything that she touches on the same day before the flow of the blood.[252] How [then] can it be considered holy from the beginning of that day? The second group says the same regarding the calculation [of the month] as the first ones but maintain that if [only] one hour and one minute remain of the day we establish {the new month} on that day otherwise we establish it on the

---

246. *Tosefta Ber.* 1:4.
247. I.e., the summer solstice.
248. *Ber.* 59:2.
249. See Book of Praises p. 90.
250. I.e., that even a fragment of a day is considered a day.
251. See *Niddah* 33a.
252. See Zucker, *Translation*, p. 222 n. 859.

next day. The first are the Tiflisites and his students and the others are the Samaritans who claim that they received this [as a tradition] from the Israelites. However, there is nothing of the like in reality among the Israelites. The third group follows the solar months and does not heed the Moon at all. They adduce proof from the story of Noah and the Ark and the 150 days. I shall refute them there after I state their argument and these are the Sedducees.[253] The fourth are the Boethisians who say that it is according to the Moon alone and if it is not visible they count thirty days. I shall refute them and whoever else relies on the Moon whether they add or remove from their condition. The fifth are the Badarites who are the ones who < maintain that the new month is [on] the night that the Moon is at its fullest and avoid [the problem of the Moon] being concealed but I shall prove to them> in what is to come <that> the most perfect [part] of anything is its middle not its beginning. The sixth is Anan's statement regarding the Moon and when it is concealed he counts thirty days and if it is visible in Nissan or Tishri at the night of the Sabbath the eleventh day will be made the twelfth. Although I have written a separate work on this [subject][254] it is inevitable that I mention in this book many of the arguments against him after delivering his opinion. The seventh is Benjamin and his colleagues who say that the months are always [determined] according to an order, i.e., twenty-nine, thirty except for Nissan and Tishri [which are determined] according to the sight of the Moon and if it is not visible during {these months} they are also [determined] according to the aforementoned order. According to his opinion at times when the Moon is concealed they determine the month to be twenty-nine [days]. This is [also] when Tishri is visible on the twenty-ninth so then the second Adar is established as thirty. The refutation of him is similar to that of the Boethisists and Anan adjusting to what they differ in. The eighth are the people of Sivan. They maintain similar to Benjamin that [the length of] the month is [determined] according to the order of thirty and twenty-nine and the test is the month of Sivan which balances the year. They turn to {Sivan} because the air, according to them, during it is pure and there are no clouds. However, they are not certain that what they believe in is as they thought. The ninth group is the people of the calendar. Since they knew of the

---

253. Cf. Al-Qirqisani, *Book of Lights*, p. 796.

254. See Zucker, *Genesis*, p. 436 for an excerpt from the *Book of Discernment*, where this subject is covered in great length.

completion . . . the Moon in the lands and they necessitated with this that since thet when it is . . . in a climate they make if the new month . . . also since the Moon will not appear at the time between sunset and darkness but after this . . . themselves . . . the work according to the chart and they make . . . requiring it . . . since it is said to them they are . . . the new month . . . how was the intention of these people known . . . and it is always full in the sky. I mean that half of the [Moon]* will be illuminated . . . the tenth path is the path of . . . and the truth that I have already mentioned is if Israel will have a year close, but not exactly like the the solar one and likewise have months close to, but not exactly like lunar ones. Just as the years have conditions to let us know if we should make the solar year earlier or later so the Moon has conditions educating and desired . . . the Moon or if we belate it. This part of the precepts regarding the luminaries. One of them is accepting the year, I mean the periods, and it has part in the knowledge of the . . . the great and this is in the matters of the luminaries and because He knew that He will command us with His precepts and laws regarding the luminaries. He informed us that He created them in order that we obey Him through them . . . on the fourth day He created the Sun the Moon and the stars . . . we knew that . . . the luminaries were created before it necessitated . . . a few things result from this that the Sun was created . . . in this . . . the west and when it was first created it set . . . and the entire night passed then it set in the west at the first . . . the first light.

20) God wished that the waters swarm creatures with living souls and a bird flying on the Earth opposite the firmament of the Heavens. 21) And God created the great monsters and the rest (kol) of the crawling creatures which the waters swarmed according to its kind and every winged bird to its kind and God knew that this was good; 22) and God blessed them and said to them by decree: "Be fruitful and multiply and populate the water in the sea" and the bird shall multiply on the Earth 23) and there had passed of the day and the night a fifth day.

I

"That the waters swarm" does not mean that the water itself should move [around] but that the creatures born in it should swarm and move [around] on the Earth as it says: "And the frogs swarmed from the Nile," (Ex. 7:28) and also: "And God made their land swarm [with] frogs." (Ps. 105:30)[255]

II

I have interpreted kol as "the rest" and not as "all" since the monsters are also living souls. This is because the word kol may have [one of] six meanings: [1] "All" as it says: "I am God maker of all (kol)." (Is. 44:24) [2] "Thing" as it says: "Your family does not have anything (kol)." (I Kings 4:2) [3] "Much" as it says: "And much (kol) of Egypt's cattle died." (Ex. 9:6) And [4] "the rest." It is [used] when some of the whole has previously been mentioned as it says: "And God spoke to Moses saying: Speak to Aaron and to his children and to the rest (kol) of the children of Israel." (Lev. 17:1) [5] "So long as" or "every time" as it says: "For so long (kol) as my soul is in me." (Job. 27:3) [6] "Opposed to" in short as it says: "Kol kovel" (Dan. 2:12, etc.) which is the Aramaic translation of neghedh as it says: "As opposed to what they have replaced Me for a nation which shall not did they." (Is. 30:5)

III

Now since it did not say "living soul" of the plants but of the fish and the birds it says: "Wished that the waters swarm creatures with living souls," (Gen. 1:20) and of the animals: "God wished that the Earth produce living souls," and of man: "And man became a thinking soul," (Gen. 2:3) we know that the plants do not contain a soul but that all animals do. This eliminates two erroneous opinions. The first is of the one who maintains that the plants [do] have a soul in them and the second is of the one who maintains that the animals breathe without a soul. Both of {the beholders of these opinions} support themselves on the common characteristics between plants and animals, i.e., growths. The former maintain that just as the animals grow without a soul so do the plants. <The latter maintain that just as the plants grow without a soul so do the animals.> According to the latter {the soul} has a force {in both} except that in animals its activity is more visibly apparent. The former maintain the opposite of

---

255. The Gaon renders wesharas in a causitive sense. Cf. Ibn Ezra ad loc.

this, that the soul is a spirit which both have but that in plants it is less visible. However, were a watchful person to observe, he would find that the difference between the plants and the animals is that animals have sensation and movement but the plants have neither of these.[256] This concept gained through observation we correctly attribute to the soul (*Ru'ah*) to the spirit (*Ru'ah*). The definition of sensation is the recognition of one body of a[nother] when it clashes with it. The definition of movement is: {something} transfering from place to place, filling the first and vacating the second. Now this *Nefesh Hayyah* (Gen. 2:17) mentioned of man means "a cognizant soul" and this distinction is what [having] intellect distinguishes man from the rest of the animals in existence as I shall explain in [the pericope of] "and God said Let us make man."

IV

The fact that it says "And He said" and then "And He created" informs [us] that speech is creation and nothing else as I have previously explained that "And He said" and "And He made" mean the same.[257]

V

Now even though in the first verse it mentions "crawlers" and "a bird flying" and does not [mention] "sea-monsters" nor "a winged bird" as it does in the second verse, since these verses are identical, we should put them together collectively, yielding: "Let the waters produce creatures, living soul, large monsters, crawling creatures, and winged birds flying on the Earth." We should also apply this to [the verse] "eighteen cubits is the height of one pillar and a strap of twelve cubits surrounds the second pillar." (I Kings 7:15)[258] This is called: "The subject has two objects and the object two subjects."[259] Would it have [just] said: "Let the waters

---

256. Cf. Aristotle, "On the Soul," I (p. 19): "There are two qualities in which that which has a soul seems to differ radically from that which has not: these are movement and sensation."

257. See com. to verse 6.

258. The first pillar is also surrounded by the strap.

259. See Zucker, *Translation*, p. 256.

swarm" and silenced it would mean that the water itself moved. For that reason it added "swarming creatures," [i.e.] to indicate that there is some other body in the water that alone moves in it. Would {the Scripture} have limited itself to this [statement] it would be possible for {"swarming creatures"} to be an inanimate one and for that reason it added "living soul" making it two kinds: fish and birds.[260] He made the fish of two kinds: large and small, [i.e.] large monsters and "living souls" [respectively]. The birds are also of two kinds: "of Kanaf"—winged, which is "winged birds," and wingless which are trampling birds. [Again], there is no other way than to bring all these verses together . . . . . . We say that just as at the beginning of creation it begins with the largest body which is the surrounder [the Heavens] and says: "the Heavens and the Earth," so in the creation of the luminaries it begins with the largest of them which are the two luminaries, so it begins with the largest fish which is the sea monster. It did not include it with the rest of the fish because it is an extremely large being. Indeed, God exalted mentions it when He says to Job that He made a large creature in the sea just as He made a large creature in the desert. This is what it says: "Behold, one of the beasts that I created along with thee eats grass like cattle," (Job 40:15) and "he is the first of the beasts that God created." (Job 40:19) Likewise, it explains regarding the creation of the sea that the {sea monster} is the first fish that He created as it says: "And He created the large sea monsters." Its greatness is expressed in the verse: "He looks upon all the lofty, and he is like a king over all the wild kind," (Job 41:26) meaning when it raises its head it sees all the high places like the mountains, etc. This can only be described by the height of one one hundred persangs. The Scripture describes its teeth as hard as a shield and when they cover each other air cannot pass between them as it says: "They have a strength like the hardness of a shield, and lock tightly as a seal. When they meet one another, air passes not between them." (Ibid. 7–8) Flames of fire issue from its breath as it says: "Out of his mouth sparks seem to come," (11) as well as from its organs as it says: "His nose seems to flash forth light," (10) "Out of his mouth sparks seems to come," (11) and "Smoke seems to issue from his nostrils." (Job 12) No sword, bow, or weapon can injure its skin as it says: "What sword could reach him would not quell him, nor the battle ax, lance, or mace. He deems iron as straw and brass as rotten wood." (Job 18–19). As a result of its motion the sea roars and on its

---

260. Making it two kinds seems to be a side point.

banks it erupts and storms like turmoil as it says: "He causes the deep to boil." (23) It plays in the sea in its depths and widths as it says: "And the Leviathan which You have created to play in it." (Ps. 104:26) The reference is to the sea.[261] It is possible that He created [many] monsters in the sea, but it is necessary that one of them is the largest one in all of the water as it says: "He is like a king over all the wild kind." (Job 41:26)

It is possible that it writes *taninim* [without a *yodh*] in the sense of "their sea monster" that it is one from among all of them the head and the largest of them. Despite its largeness its size in the eyes of the Creator is like a small fish whose flesh we can pierce with a hook as it says: "Or pierce his cheek with a thorn." (Job 40:26)

<Now after this large creature it mentions the rest of the fish and says: "All the crawling creatures which the waters swarmed," [which] are of various kinds as it says: "according to its kinds." Some have scales and always live in the uppermost and purest part of the water while others do not have [any] scales on them and always live in the lowest and most shallow parts of the water. Some, like the alligator, the snake,[262] and the swordfish, are predators. Alligators are distinguishable in many ways. {The alligator} lives off of air for it leaves the Nile and sleeps on its coast and often runs on its shore [the distance of] many cubits, and [likewise] locates its mate in the wilderness. Another is that it lays eggs on the shore near the Nile and when the time for the egg to hatch has come, those that enter the water become alligators and those that go out into the wilderness become crocodiles.

VII

Now what the heretics claimed regarding the creation of the fish is: What is the manner of wisdom in God creating large monsters that overtake the other harmless creatures and scorch them? But indeed how great is the manner of wisdom in this and in all [kinds of] destructive [creatures] that God shows and endows us with! For He intimidates us of the severe punishment in the world to come. [This is because] were we never to see any retribution and suffering, this would not be impressed in our minds. However, when we see these venomous and deadly [creatures] as well as

---

261. Cf. *Avod. Zara* 3:1.
262. Aristotle, "History of Animals," II, p. 123.

the harsh suffering [that they cause] in this world, they set for us [an example] of {the suffering}[263] and [this] is impressed [in our intellects]*[264] as something we already know and whose bitterness we have already tasted as it says: "Like the vehemence of the sea monsters is their wine." (Deut. 32:33) If we fear this we will obtain good.

They also asked: What is the manner of wisdom in that God made some [creatures] strong and others weak, some large and others small, and did not require that [all] creatures be of equal size, strength, and other characteristics? However, this [demand] is contrary to wisdom, for were things equal so that they are all the same the intellect would not be able embrace or discern them and we would think that God made them according to their nature[265] like fire which burns according to its nature and does not cool and [like] snow which cools by nature and does not burn. Therefore, in order that we know that He makes a thing and its opposite, God made them distinct as we have previously explained at the beginning of the book.[266] Another difference is that some of them are small while some are large and some are strong while others are weak.

Were one to ask: Why do some animals eat others? We state the full implications of the statement: Since it is necessary that some be strong while others weak, the strong eats the weak. Were they to ask: Why did God place this in their nature? We respond to them that this is to our benefit for the large [animals] like the lion and the sea monster [serve] to intimidate us so that we be filled with the fear of the punishment of our Master when we see them. The smaller of them, like the birds as well as the edible animals living in our domain [were created] for us to hunt them. Were they not to eat meat we would not be able make any prey.

VIII

We now speak about birds and their definition and that . . . "according to its kind" and . . . fundament? "All winged birds" . . . its definition is "wing." This is the wondrous nature they have . . . God made the wings [capable of] staying in the air without resting. Were one to say that [this

---

263. In the world to come?
264. Supplied according to Al-Qirqisani.
265. Not His wish.
266. See IPC, but this section has not surfaced entirely.

is] because of their light feathers scattered over them. We say that God placed the feathers themselves [on them] in order that one wonder how this became so.[267] As God says to Job: "Or do you know how the wings of little songsters bear them aloft or the feathers of of the kite or falcon?" (Job 39:13) It calls the birds [chirping] *ra'ananim* since they bewonder us by their chirping like the turtle pigeon, the paks, and the rest of the chirping birds, which are all called *himam*—"Doves." Now from the statement "There is a bird that abandons its eggs on the ground and warms them on the dust foolishly," (Job 39:14) we learn that there is a bird that lays eggs on the ground and sits warming the ground instead of its eggs ignorant of this. Even though the philosophers [of nature] do not know about it, the Creator of all knows what He created. The calling bird whose practice is to steal another's egg and warm it and when the chick hatches and comes out it resembles a calling bird*. They[268] knew about this: "Like this calling bird that embraces that which it has not given birth to." (Jer. 7:11) The same applies to the one who makes riches not in its normal way, meaning that just as the calling bird will not obtain anything from this except for the effort so no despoliation remains for the despoiler except for the sin [accruing from it]. From the statement "She acts callously toward her children as they are not hers," (Job 39:17) we know that there is a bird that is tyrannous with its children as if they are not its. This is the bearded vulture. If it gives birth to two[269] its practice is to kill one but to sustain the other. As for the eagle, that does not kill its offspring, but abandons them when it sees that they are still white and flies away hovering over them. [Then] when they endure a little and grow feathers that turn black it returns to them, but until the time it returns to them God provides them with their sustenance as it says: "Who provides for the eagle's sustenance." (Job 38:41) From the statement "And at the time that it ascends to the height," (Job 39:18) we know that there is a bird that ascends into the air and lands only on hard large objects.[270] This is called a phoenix. There are also birds that migrate from land to land in

---

267. Apparently because they are extra weight.

268. The philosophers?

269. Aristotle, ibid. (p. 247), says this of the eagle: "The mother ejects one of the two chicks from the nest as they get bigger because she finds them too much trouble."

270. This does not seem to be indicated by the verse but is a characteristic of the bird that has the former traits.

the winter as it says: "And the pigeon, the crane, and the swallow watch the time that they come." (Jer. 8:7) Now from the statement "Is it from your understanding that a hawk shall grow a pinion or shall spread its wings to the south," (Job 39:26) we know that the hawk and other predatory birds are propelled in flight by the northern wind for it says: "Or spreads its wings for the south or at your command that the eagle takes the high or raised his nest on the high," (Job 39:27) indicates that the eagle carries its chicks on its back unlike the practice of the rest of the birds which carry their chicks between their legs for it does not fear any birds above it since there is none greater than it. For that reason it states in the Torah: "On his nest he shall hover." (Deut. 32:11)

IX

[271][It says: "And God blessed them," [which means] that He blessed them by them being fruitful and multiplying. [This] is by decree not through speech, meaning that He planted this in their nature. This is the meaning of every blessing] of God in regards to the plants and animals as it says of Sarah: "And I shall bless her and I shall provide for you from her a son." (Gen. 17:16) Likewise, regarding the plants it says: "And I shall command by blessing to you." (Lev. 25:21) God placed in the midst of all the animals the desire for nourishment in order to sustain the first form[272] and to perpetuate it. He [also] planted in them the desire for copulation to provide a substitute for themselves after they become feeble and deteriorate. For that reason the Tradition has conveyed that in wedlock we bless: "And he fixed for him from it a building[273] forever in humanity."[274]

X

The meaning of "be fruitful" is that they should produce in their like and the meaning of "multiply" is that one [of them] should bring forth ten,

---

271. This section is supplied according to Al-Qirqisani.
272. The form from which all subsequent ones stem.
273. The Gaon apparently understands "building" to refer to procreation.
274. See *Keth.* 8a.

twenty, or more. This is because we all agree that the first humans were two in number, Adam and Eve. However, as for the first individuals of the rest of the animals—the Scripture does not record the quantity of the individuals of each kind. It is possible that God created two individuals of each kind, male and female, or possibly more. Were one to say that God created seven pairs of all clean animals and two pairs of all impure animals by analogy with the amount that remained with Noah in the ark, this would not be obligatory since God left eight[275] people but only two people were created at first. The analogy [therefore] is abolished. Rather because we cannot know the number of the individuals our fathers have [indeed] transmitted the number of species from the prophets and said that the number of clean fish was seven hundred species, crickets were eight hundred and the impure birds twenty-four species, but for the impure fish, impure crickets, and [of] the clean birds they did not hear anything from the prophets for they said: "Seven hundred kinds of fish, eight hundred kinds of crickets but for the clean birds there is no number."[276,277]

XI

I rendered "and fill" as "populate" since this word may have [one of] five meanings. [1] "Fill" as it says: "And he filled his palm." (Lev. 9:17) [2] "Granting" [as it says]: "And he granted them" (Ex. 28:41)[278] the ram of completion (Ex. 29:22). [3] "Arrangement" "And you should arrange it an arrangement of stone," (Ex. 28:17): and "And the stone of arrangement." (Ex. 25:7) [4] "Courageousness and daringness" [as it says]: "Which he dared," (Est. 7:5) and the opposite—"How frightful is your heart." (Ez. 16:30) [5] "Covering" [as it says]: "And the house was covered by a cloud." (Ez. 10:4) Now even though we shall render it[279] as "full" it means "cover" for the cloud did not cover the house entirely.

---

275. After the flood.
276. Not that they were innumerable.
277. *Hul* 63:2.
278. In the translation he adds "perfected."
279. I.e., in com. his translation of this verse—which has not surfaced yet.

XII

It says "And the birds shall multiply on the Earth" for despite that at times the birds dwell in the water they multiply and give birth on the ground.

XIII

It tells us that God is the Creator of the birds and the fish first in order that we worship Him for it has become certain to us that He is the Creator of these awesome monsters and the land eagles and [also] that we contemplate and say: If these creations are so big, how [big] must the Creator be as it says: "And if no hunter can flush him." (Job. 41:2)[280] God says of the sea monsters "if a hunting dog is unable to kill it, how much more so Me, who shall stand before me?" (ibid.) [meaning]: "Who will opppose me?" The second is that we should not serve any of the created creatures since they are created ex nihilo and even something that is in their image as it says: "So that you do not corrupt and make for yourself an idol in the image of any [human] male or female or in the image of any animal on the Earth or [in] the image of winged birds that fly in the sky or [in] the image of anything that crawls on the earth or [in] the image of fish that is in the water under the ground." (Deut. 4:16)

The third is that we believe in the wonders that He shall tell us about that He did with them and we should say: Indeed the One Who created them is able to do with them what He described. An example of what He did with the fish is [that] He confined Jonah three nights and three days in [a fish's] stomach and he did not die as it says: "And Jonah was in the fish's stomach." (Jon. 2:1) Also what did with the birds is that seven pairs of each kind was gathered for Noah, [i.e.] by God's command, without [any] effort on Noah['s part] as it says: "From the birds of the sky too." (Gen. 7:1)[281] The fourth is that we accept the commandments that God commanded upon us concerning {the fish and the birds}. As for the fish He prohibited any fish that has no fins or scales on it as it says in the Book of Leviticus (11:9): "And this is what you may eat anything that has fins and scales in the water, etc., but anything that does not, etc., is disgraceful for you." As for the birds . . . it prohibits twenty-four kinds, twenty by

---

280. See Goodman, Job p. 409, n. 1.
281. See com. ad loc.

name and four additional because it says: "according to his kinds" and "according to her kinds."[282] He permitted the rest as I shall likewise explain in the Book of Leviticus except for slaughter and decapitation applying to birds[283] and whatever else He commanded us of them.

XIX

It says [here] as usual: "And there had passed of the night and the day a fifth day" and informs us by this that all the species of the fish and birds were created in the minutest [fragment of] time according to their varieties and characteristics before the fifth night and the day connected to it were completed and returned without any of them passing at all.[284]

24) And God wished that the Earth produce living souls according to their kinds, beasts and crawlers and Earth dwellers according to their kinds and it was so; 25) and God made the rest of the Earth crawlers according to their kinds when God knew that it was good.

I

"That the Earth produce" indicates that at that time God created non-speaking beasts from {the Earth} and explained that they are born from it.[285]

II

"And it produced" does not [mean that it did so] by its own [innate] power but that God created it and brought it out from it. As we have said of "that the earth produce herbage," (Gen. 1:11) despite that at times the Earth produces herbage with the power that God implanted in it, it never produces trees [by itself].

---

282. See *Hul.* 63a.
283. See *Criticism* of Rabbi Mubashshir, p. 87.
284. The implication is that this passage of time occurred after their creation.
285. In the future.

III

Our explanation of "living souls" here is similar to that of "that the waters produce living souls," (Gen. 1:20) that they are mobile and move their antennas feeling other things.

IV

"According to its kinds" means that each kind should not produce anything other than its [own] kind. Similar to "according to its kinds" that is [said] of the plants. {The Scripture} divides the non-cognizant animals that walk on the Earth into three categories [as follows]: [1] animals, [2]crawlers, [3] and beasts of the field. This is after excluding the fish and the birds.

V

It adds a *waw* to *haytho* for glorification for it is the practice of the Hebrews to aggrandize nouns and verbs in this manner. An example of the aggrandizement of nouns is *beno be'or* (Deut. 24:28) and *beno Sippor* (Deut. 23:18) where [*beno*] means *ben*. [Likewise] *le-ma'yno mayyim* (Ps. 114:8) means *le-ma'yan mayyim*. An example of the glorification of verbs is the statement *wayyako ha-ehadh et ha-ehadh*, [which] means *wayyakh ha-ehad eth ha-ehadh* (II Sam. 14:6) and also *wayshanno eth ta'amo* (I Sam. 21:14) which is like *wayshanneh eth ta'amo*. Likewise [here] *haytho areS* means *hayyath AreS*.[286]

VI

Behema is whatever eats herbage like the ox, sheep, donkey, and horse, and also the deer and the gazelle despite that they are steppe animals for the

---

286. These types of *waws*, as in the former examples, following the Gaon, were generally accepted as additional. Cf. Ibn Janah, *Riqmah*, p. 69 and Ibn Ezra ad loc. (Linetsky, p. 40) although in cases where the actual number of the verb is affected, the Gaon's suggestion did not gain much acceptance.

gist is that they are not carnivorous. For that reason it says: "These are the animals that you may eat," (Deut. 14:4) . . . and combines some of the steppe animals with the domestic ones because they are not carnivorous.[287]

VII

Remes are small crawlers also called *ShereS* and may be [one] of three kinds: [1] ones that crawl on their arms like the mouse; [2] ones that crawl on their belly like the snake as it says: "And anything that walks on its belly" (Lev. 11:42); or [3] ones that have four legs or more although their legs do not resemble those of animals. An example is the scorpion and the millipede which is called "many legged" as it says: "And anything that walks on all fours to anything that has many legs." (ibid.)

VIII

Haya are animals that rip and eat meat, from the lion and the like to the eagle and the rat and the like. All these are termed here by the name *hayya* and it says "according to its kinds" of all of them.

IX

The animals are divided into four types: The first are those that have split hooves and chew their cud. These are the ten pure animals permissible [for consumption] that are written in the pericope of: "And these are which of the animals you may eat." (Deut. 14:4) The second are those that do not have split hooves but do chew their cud and are three: [1] the camel, [2] the rabbit, and [3] the hedgehog. This is despite that some say

---

287. As opposed to *Sifri re'eh* 100 and *Hulin* 71a, which maintain that *haya* is included in *behema*. See also Rabbi Abraham Maimonides, who disputes the Gaon's view. In his commentary to Lev. 11:39 (Saadiah Manchester studies, Jacob Levine, p. 87) however, the Gaon interprets *behema* as clean birds in accordance to the rabbinic view. Cf. Ibn Janah in *Riqmah* p. 416 and *Roots BHM*, which apparently also follows this interpretation. (Zucker)

that the hedgehog is [a hybrid] of two species and is not an original creation and is among the predatory animals like the place of the mule among the animals.[288] The third are those that do have split hooves but do not chew their cud, which is the swine alone. The fourth are those that neither chew their cud nor have split hooves like the horse, the donkey, the lion, etc.

X

Now despite that it does not mention in the Torah that the first animal that God created was a large, awesome one that is high in the mountains as it does specify that the first fish that God created was the sea monsters as it says: "And God created the monster," God did already say to Job in contest with him that the first animal that He created was the large behemoth as it says: "He is first of the beasts that God created." (Job 40:19) This is after it mentions it and says: "Here is one of the animals that I have created with you," (ibid.) and described [it] as needing many trees to shade it as it says: "The shady foliage shades him," (Job 40:22) many mountains to produce sustenance for it when it says: "And the willow of the river bed surround him," (ibid.) as well as many rivers to water it and it drinks it entirely when it says: "He oppresses the river without grief trusting when the Jordan reaches up to his mouth." (Job 40:23) And even though it describes it as one whose bones are like bronze and whose tail is like the cedar its sustenance is only herbage as it says: "Herbage like cattle he shall eat." (Job 40:15) Now the special characteristics that God gave it are the ones that add [greatness] to it and for this reason God distinguished it from all the beasts and said: "For all the beasts of the wilderness as well as the behemoth in many mountains." (Ps. 50:10)

Below this behemoth [in stature] is the wild ox, which is a large creature of such length and such width that an elephant compared to it would be dwarfed. It has horns that are so long [that] God compares His defense of Israel to the defense of the wild ox's horn as it says: "God that took you out of Egypt with horns of a wild ox He waged wars for you." (Num. 23:22) It also says of it: "Does the wild ox long to serve you or lodge upon your manger." (Job 39:9)

Below it [in stature] is the elephant. One of its wondrous natures is its

---

288. See *Hulin* 79a and *Pes.* 54a.

long trunk through which it obtains food and water. One of its special characteristics is that it never crouches to sleep [but] only [does so] while leaning. Now if the female wants to give birth it enters the water to its stomach so that the child falls into the water not onto the ground for because of {the elephant's} great height {the child} will die.[289] Because of its wondrous nature it was brought to Solomon as it says: "Bringing gold and silver, ivory, apes, and peacocks." (I Kings 10:22)

After this is the buffalo, which is a genus of the bovine. It was sacrificed as it says: "And he sacrificed oxen and fatlings." (II Sam. 6:13) This is for a sacrifice. It says in another place: "And he had slain oxen and fat cattle." (I Kings 1:19 and 25) Its fat is prohibited.[290]

The ram has the special characteristic that it eats vipers without their heads . . . and because of the strength of their poison it heats up and thirst takes him and burns him and it calls for help in search of water. For that reason the Scripture uses this as a comparison and says: "Like a ram that calls for help to the springs of water so my soul calls to you for help." (Ps. 42:2)

Now the special characteristics of the mountain goat and some rams is that when they give birth they fear that their children will abandon them and flee, they dislocate enough of their bones to prevent them from walking so that they remain with them and grow up as God says to the entire creation: "Do you know when the wild goats of the rocks give birth or mark the calving of deer? Do you know the months they must complete that you know the time they will deliver?" (Job 39:1–2) Now when this child matures and grows up and is no [longer] in need of its mother, God heals it of this ailment so that it awakens and gets up by itself as it says: "Which recuperates in the field." (Job 39:4) The word *yaHlemu* means "to recuperate." It is derived from the word *watahlimini* stated in Ezekiah's words: *wala* (Is. 38:17). And when it walks it does not return to its mother [anymore] as it says: "And when it goes forth it does not return." (Job 39:4)

The unicorn is a small riding animal that has only one long horn. The

---

289. Cf. *History of Animals*, VI, p. 333.

290. This opinion is cited in the name of the Gaon by Ibn Bal'am and Rabbi Isaac ben Samuel (Zucker, *Genesis*, p. 249, n. 233) in opposition to Rabbi Hai Gaon who maintained that its fat is permitted. Cf., however, Ibn Ezra to Amos 5:22 where these opinions are swapped. There is some possible corruption. Cf. his com. to Is. 1:81.

Firsts said of it: "A unicorn even though it has only one horn its fat is permissible."[291] The lion, and even larger animals than it, fear and tremble because of its greatness as God compared it and said: "A lion roars who shall not fear." (Am. 3:8)

The horse does not fear war and the flash of the sword nor the sound of thunder and clamor as it describes in the pericope of "And do you give the horse his strength or clothe his neck with terror?" (Job 39:19) "He laughes at menace and crumbles? Not before the sword he turns not his back," (Job 39:22) "but saying at the bugle 'Ha' and from afar he scents battle," even though this is clear from the verse.

Now each animal has something wonderous and this is [that] the domestic ones [i.e.] living with man in his dwellings do not resemble each other like the horse, the donkey, cattle which bears features by which Reuben's animal is distinguished from Simon's while wild animals are mostly similar to each other for they are ownerless[292] and if they do have an owner this is only occasionally as it says: "Who but I send the wild ass free or loosen the oneger's bonds just as I make them desert his home and his dwelling place the salt flats." (Job 39:5–6) . . . Are those that grow without any copulation[293] . . . among them are those that are part flesh and bones and sinews and whatever other similar limbs and its other part is in the form of limbs not of flesh and it nevertheless moves about. Regarding it the Rabbis said: "A mouse half of which is flesh and the other is earth, one who touches the flesh is impure and one who touches the earth is pure."[294] Among them is the salamander. It is an animal that grows in volcanous mountains and enjoys fire and can exist in it for an extended period of time without getting burned by it. It is called in Hebrew *Salamandria*.[295] In the commandment of the eight crawlers I shall elucidate as much [of this matter] as is appropriate. Among them is the hedgehog, which according to its special characteristics lives in a hole having two openings. One of which opens if a northern wind blows and the other if the southern blows . . . the swift camels in order to go faster for they go [the distance of] forty Parsangs per day. Dogs for hunting and guarding.

---

291. *Hul.* 59b.

292. See *Hul.* 59b.

293. Spontaneous reproduction. In the Middle Ages it was believed that some creatures reproduce without copulation.

294. *Hul.* 9:4. See Lieberman, *Hellenism in Jewish Palestine*, p. 183.

295. See *Hag.* 27:1.

Now the benefit of all these, I mean animal, crawler, and beast, in medicine is immeasurable [as] for example the benefit of their fats, biles, and bones. From their skin, carpets, sandals, shoes, and the like can be made. From their wool, fur, and hair—something to cover oneself with for protection from chill for these [materials] return to the body mists coming up from its pores. From the elephant teeth, bones, ivory [may be made] as is described of Solomon: "And Solomon made a large chair of ivory." (II Chron. 9:17) And even the lowliest of things like the beetle may be used to fumigate congealed blood until one puts a spider web or *shiqna'm* on wounds and fats of vipers and snakes as an antidote to absorb whatever poison one's body may have. There are much more [uses] that I shall not mention here. However, above this in importance of the characteristics found in animals that a person should adopt for himself is in the service of God as our Ancients have taught us: "Be strong like a tiger, swift like an eagle, run like a deer and mighty like a lion to do the will of your Father in the Heavens." (*Ethics of the Fathers* 5:20) The meaning of their words is: Use the might of a tiger and the swiftness of an eagle and the quickness of a deer and the bravery of the lion in doing the will of the Master of the universe. The prophets spoke of all these traits. Of mightiness in the service of God it says: "Therefore I have placed my face like a stone." (Is. 50:7) Of lightness it says: "I have hurried and have not delayed and have preserved Your precepts." (Ps. 119:60) Of quickness in work it says: "To the path of your commandment I shall run in them." (Ps. 119:32) Of power it says: "I have filled with power from the spirit of God justice and might." (Mic. 3:8) Likewises the intelligent will use the rest of the praiseworthy qualities of the animals in the positive manner as the animals use it by the nature implanted in them without [intellectual] distinction.

XI

The Scripture informs us that God created the animals walking on all fours and the crawlers for the four [types of] reasons found recurring in the entire account of Genesis: The first is that we should serve God because He is the Creator of all these bodies as it says: "I made the Earth, man, and the animals, etc." (Jer. 27:5) The second is that we should not worship anyone of them since they are created and brought about from nil as it says: "So that you do not become corrupt and make for yourselves . . . the shape of any animals on the Earth," (Deut. 16:47) and then says: "The shape of any crawler on the Earth." (Deut. 16:48) The third is that we should believe what He is destined to tell about the signs that He did with these animals, i.e., the accidents He created or removed. An example of this is the speech that He created in the ass which Balaam heard [as if it] pass[ed] through {the ass's} tongue as its says: "And God opened the ass's mouth." (Num. 22:28)[296] And that He made [to serve] as a screen between the lion and Daniel so that they do not harm him and the like as it says: "My master sent His angel and closed the mouth of the lion." (Dan. 6:23) The fourth is that we fulfill what God commanded us of the consumption of animals and beasts and that we pass them through five tests. [1] [To distinguish between] the species in general, I mean the entire species and they are the ten pure animals mentioned [in the Torah].[297] [2] To check them when slaughtering them and whichever does not fit the process of slaughtering we set it aside.[298] [3] To put them to the third test which is to check if the animal is well or ill and whichever we find to be ill in any way that there is no living one like it we should not eat it. The healthy [animals] we set aside to put through a fourth test, i.e., we extract from it the prohibited fats, the veins, and the sinews that carry blood or covering fat . . . and whatever is left of [we put through] the fifth test which is that we salt it.

26) And God said: We shall make man in Our form as Our likeness in dominion they shall rule over the fish of the sea, the birds of the sky, the animals, and the entire Earth and the rest of the crawlers that crawl on it; 27) and God created man in His form, in an estimable form to rule He created him, male and female He created them; 28) and God blessed them and said to them: Be fruitful and multiply and populate the Earth and reign over it and rule over the fish of the sea and the birds of the sky and the rest of the animals that crawl on the Earth.

I

[It says "We shall make man" in plural for this is for aggrandizement and honor as is the practice of the language of the Arabs that the king and the

---

296. See Rabbi Mubashshir's criticisms of the Gaon (*Criticisms*, p. 38). However, Ibn Bal'am (*Kitab al-Tarjih*, p. 85) and Ibn Ezra in Gen. 3:1 (Linetsky, p. 76) cite the Gaon as of the opinion that an angel spoke instead of the ass.

297. I.e., Deut.

298. I.e., that it is prohibited to eat.

official and the distinguished person say: "We commanded," "We said," and "We did," and so Laban says: "And We shall give this one to you also," (Gen. 29:27) and Amazia said: "Did we place you as an advisor." (II Chron. 25:17)[299] Afterwards it says: *be-Salmenu ki-dhemuthenu*. This too is plural in the fashion that we have previously translated as "in our form as our likeness."

II

The Christians cite a proof from this verse in support of their view of the trinity[300] [and claim] that were God one without hypostases it would say: "in My form, as My likeness." It should be said to them: Do you maintain that this pericope has allegorical words or is every word in it literal? If they say that they are literal they would be forced to say that man is indeed in the form of God. [Thus] according to them God would be of flesh, blood, bones, etc. But this is something none of them maintain. Likewise they would be forced to say that God is male and female like man for it says: "in the form of God He created him," . . . and "male and female He created them." They would also be forced to say that all the hypostases created man for it says regarding this: "We shall make," and that only one of them created Eve for it says: "I shall make him a helper opposite him." (Gen. 2:18) But these are all [things] from which they turn aside and reject. It is then inevitable to admit the necessity that this sequel contains allegorical words and that we do not have here a true form nor a true likeness but only a form and likeness of action.[301] This being so this should oblige them to admit the same regarding the trinity, i.e., "We shall make in Our image as Our likeness," and that this is allegorical as we have previously stated. Like one who says: "We worked" and "We did" even though he alone did it. But no matter how they should attempt to revert the singular to the plural, we have greater [grounds] to turn {the plural} into the singular.

The second is one who [indeed] did not maintain that in the essence of

---

299. See *Beliefs* 2:6 (p. 107) where the Gaon cites other verses to this effect. Cf. Ibn Ezra ad loc. (Linetsky, p. 42) who rejects this view as well as the Gaon's interpretation of the verses he cites.

300. Cf. *Beliefs* (ibid).

301. I.e., emulation.

God there are separate units for {the beholder of this opinion} is of our people but attributed this section to an angel[302] <and he is Benjamin of Nahavend.>[303] This is because he was confounded by the two expressions [found] in this pericope.[304] It is inconceivable according to him for them to refer to God and therefore he refered them to the angels. He said that the meaning of God's statement: "We shall make man" is: "And the angel said: 'let us create man,'" and for that reason it states: "in our form, as our likeness,"[305] for man is similar to angel as it says: "And He reduced him a little from angels." (Ps. 8:5) But this interpretation did not suit him [completely] so he said that [Elodhim in] "And Elodhim created man in his form" is the angel who created him. He saw that since he made the creator of man an angel, this interpretation would not suit him unless he would say that the creator of the beasts and the carnivorous animals too is an angel and that it is the one that said "Let the Earth produce," (Gen. 1:11) and "Let the waters produce." (Gen. 1:20) This would unfold until: "Bereshith bara elodhim," for these are those things that are interconnected. So the fool believed that the creator of the Heavens and the Earth and what is between them[306] was an angel. He mustered the strength to say something to justify this view; this is that God almighty and lofty gave this angel the power to create with it so that he created at God's command. He thought that he will be rescued by this. [However,] this opinion is totally erroneous from [the aspect] of the intellect, what is written [in the Scripture and in] the Tradition.[307] From the intellect, were it possible for something created ex-nihilo to come from something brought out ex nihilo, I mean created,[308] then it would be possible for God to give man the power to create and create ex nihilo as well as in regards to them being brought out ex-nihilo and created, there is no difference between man and angel.[309] Furthermore, this would also be possible with any other animal that has the ability to function [and] even

---

302. I.e., the creation of man. Cf. *Beliefs* 5:8 (p. 232).

303. Al-Qirqisani (*Book of Lights*, p. 55) also attributes this view to him.

304. "Let us make man" and "our form and likeness."

305. It is uncertain how he interpreted the Hebrew words and therefore we follow the Gaon's translation.

306. The elements.

307. See IPC section II.

308. See IPC section III.

309. Here the Gaon implies that the angels are incapable of creating. See, however, note 319.

the animate objects.[310] Moreover, if the argument from creation and composition would be an argument for the angel that God created, the arguments for [the existence] of God may He be exalted are invalid.[311] This matter is too meager that we should depart in contradicting it. [The arguments against it] in what is written in [the Scripture] are that God said that He is the Creator of all for it says: "The portion of Jacob is not like them for He is the Creator of all," (Jer. 10:17) and also: "So said the Lord Creator of the Heavens which is God Creator of the Heavens and its Maker," (Is. 45:18) and also: "Creator of light and darkness I am God Maker of all these," (Is. 45:7) and also "For behold He is the Creator of the mountains," (Amos 4:13) and [verses] similar to this that it would be too lengthy to specify. From tradition our Ancients said: "All admit that on the first day nothing[312] was created so that you do not say Michael stretched the south of the firmament and Gabriel its north and God measures in the middle, rather 'I am God maker of all,' (Is. 44:24) I stretch the sky Myself and spread the Earth. 'I am God maker of all.'"(Bereshit Rabba ch. 3) It is written *mi-itti* meaning: "who was a partner with Me in the creation of the world."[313] Observe may God guide you in the right path, how strong roots are attached with such easy error may God preserve us from evil and arbitrariness of the heart.

The third is one who refers this statement to the Master of the universe, as we do, but does not understand "the form" to be corporeal and also does not give "We shall make" a plural [meaning] but nevertheless misleads the translation and meaning. These are the people who interpreted this matter, I mean the form and likeness, in three ways. [1] Those that said that it means with this "the form and the likeness God made" and when he says to them "This is the form of God" he means that God formed it, or that "This is God's likeness" he means "that God likened or created" it like when Reuben draws the shape of a lion or tree on the wall this shape it is said [that it is]: "Reuben's form." The action is his, not that this is the shape of his body. The meaning is that the shape is his from the aspect of

---

310. I.e., they too would be able to create because they are created ex nihilo.

311. See *Beliefs* 2:1 (p. 96).

312. I.e., nothing angelic.

313. Text: *m'ty* which is the *qere* meaning "of myself" whereas the *kethiv* is *my 'ti*—"who is with Me." The Gaon renders this word as *mn'ndy*, which could be rendered either way. Here the Gaon follows the kefib to show that God had not partner in creation. In this *BO* intro (p. 22) and *Beliefs* 1:1 (p. 40) where he cites this verse to teach that God created everything ex nihilo he follows the qeri.

[his] acting [with it]. This explanation which is more plausible than the other three would be sustainable if not for God making the reason for killing anyone who killed a man "for in the form of God He made man," (Gen. 9:6) for would the explanation be so an animal would also be in the image of God in the manner that God formed it from dust.[314] [This would also] obligate death to one who kills an animal. Furthermore, a tree too is in the form of God from the aspect that God formed it and one who uproots the tree for this reason would be liable death. A mountain too is in the form of God from the aspect that God formed it and for this reason one who would remove a stone from it would be liable death. But all this is absurd!

[2] There are also those that say that the meaning of "in Our form as our likeness" is [in] "the form that God brought out from Himself for the first time there being nothing the like [of it] at all." They say that the purpose of this [statement] is that at the time that the Torah was written people saw only the people who came before them. Therefore it informs us that God created the first man in the form created for the first [time] for him and did not bring it out from something that preceded it. Nor did He make his form in imitation of the form that preceded it. But even this opinion, despite that it is more probable and does not undermine the roots of belief, does undermine the Law like the first one, for this cause is found also in substances, trees, and stones that God created from Himself as well in an original form, neither did it resemble what preceded it nor did God bring it out or extract it from [some]thing [else]. [Therefore] death should be upon one who destroys them for they [too] are in God's form according the view [that] binds {the beholders}.

[3] There is also one who maintains that "in Our form as Our likeness" refers to the form of angels for he found that the angel is called *elodhim*. When he would be asked about "in Our form as Our likeness" and that he has established that "and *elodhim* said we shall make man" is the Master of the worlds—he would say that the meaning of "in Our form" is "in our forms," meaning the forms of the animals that God formed, and the meaning of "as Our likeness" is "as the likeness of the one who was created before us," i.e., the angels that preceded man. This opinion would have had place were it not for it being improbable and distorted. Do you not see that he is lost and confounded. When they say that *be-Salmenu* is "in Our image in Our form" they mean by this that it should be the archetype

---

314. Ibn Ezra repeats this argument in his com. to verse 26.

of all forms and apply it to all forms and [when] they say *ki-dhmuthenu* they attach to it words that are "one who was created before us" and so what remains of this verse for them? I would not have mentioned them did they not reject the Scripture and uphold that which is not [attested] in it.

Now as for the one who says that "in Our form" means "for its utility" and and derived it as meaning "forced labor" from "But in the darkness (*BeSelem*) a man walks," (Ps. 39:7) or one who says that {"as Our likeness"} means resembling [what was revealed] to the prophets similar to what is written: "and on the likeness of the Throne," (Ezek. 1:7) or one who says that ["as Our likeness"] means "as a wise form."[315] These are things that are not worth and do not require a response to them.

Now, the explanations that appear correct to me are two: The first is that "in Our form as Our likeness" as well as "in the form of Elodhim" are said as a form of singling out and raising to distinction, i.e., just as God created all parts of the Earth and raised one land to distinction saying of it: "This is My land," as it says: "And I shall bring you to My land," (Ezek. 38:17) and also: "And they shall not dwell in God's land." (Hos. 9:3) So, He created all the mountains and made one mountain special [and said]: "This is My mountain," when it says: "I shall say that this is God's mountain," (Ps. 68:16) and "We shall say I formed all the mountains on the ways." (Is. 49:11) God [also] created all houses and raised one house to distinction and said: "This is My house," [as it says]: "For My house shall be called for all the nation a house of prayer," (Is. 56:7) and also: "That God's house shall be ready on the top of the mountains." (Is. 2:2) So also [He created] all the forms and singled out one of the forms [and] said: "This is My form." This is [what is meant] when it says: "We shall make man in Our form, as Our likeness," as it likewise says: "And He created man in His form." . . . The second [explanation] is that which the Torah sanctions . . . that man is in the form and likeness of God in the sense of dominion and rulership, not [in the sense of] the mold or the likeness of the face. This is like one who says: "Today such is in the form of a teacher" and "such is in the form of a heretic," refering not to the form of the body but to [his] status and position. From among all other beings God made man in the position of a master over everything just as He [Himself] be exalted and aggrandized is a ruler over everything. What supports this is that it says: "And they shall reign over the fish of the sea," where it informs us that {man} resembles God in the aspect of "and they

---

315. I.e., that man is intellectually above the rest of the animals.

shall reign" over others. Therefore, David says: "You have made him a ruler over [some] of your creation," (Ps. 8:7) and before that: "To the extent that You have reduced him a little from the level of angels." (Ps. 8:6) [This means] that God deprives him of [the ability] to create, bringing out anew, and the like.[316]

III

<"And populate the Earth" refers to the inhabited part of the Earth.>[317]

IV

"Ruling" includes the [use of] equipment by which man may gain dominion over the animals. Over some of them [he has dominion] with mines and hobbles and over others with cords and reins and yet others with pits and collar, hunting equipment and *adbaan*. Others are with cages and towers and the like until God teaches {man} everything [about this].

V

[Ruling over] "Fish" includes [the use of] tactics in hunting fish from the bowels of the sea and rivers, preparing those permissible [for eating] with cooking utensils so that {one} can eat it, taking pearls from the shell, benefitting from the parts of the skin and bones that one prepares, and whatever applies to this.

VI

It adds "the sea" in order to include man's dominion over the water in this so that he can take it out from the bowels of the Earth and raise it out until

---

316. Implying that angels do have the ability to create. This appears to be in direct contradiction to his criticism of Benjamin, who maintains that an angel created the world. See above.

317. Not the entire earth. In the Middle Ages it was maintained that half the earth was sea.

it is visible[318] with buckets or basins or pressing or pushing machines. Likewise he dams in rivers in order to transfer from one side to the other and uses it for turning grindstones and mills. As when it says elsewhere: "And many of those who pass on his ways." (Ps. 8:9) It alludes to making boats and ships to pass in them from side to side. He too makes large *Daramin* which hold thousands of men to cross the widths of the sea and in a place where there are stones they make vehicles of papyrus in which to travel so that they do not break. Like Isaiah explained: "And in vessels of papyrus." (Is. 18:2)

VII

"[Ruling over] the birds" accords the [various] tactics to hunt birds that fly in the air and to make them work for us until they [actually are used to] hunt each other. The benefit from them is [also] to prepare food for {man's} sustenance and herbs for his medicines and the like.

VIII

It adds "the sky" to include in this {man's} ability to know the celestial spheres, their structure and composition.[319] Also to forge copper in a shape, to construct the astrolabe for [investigating] the descent and the ascent [of the stars] and to make the various equipment so that one be able to calculate hours and their parts.

IX

<By [ruling over] "animals" God gave {man} the power of leading, the power to make use of every one of them, to eat their meat that is fit[320] for eating by means of various preparations and the kinds of various foods, to be healed by whatever healing potential it has, to ride on those fit for this like mules, and to know all their sustenance and how they sustain?>

---

318. Cf. IPC section I.

319. See IPC section I. The Gaon speaks here of the celestial spheres in detail; however, because the medieval terminology which he uses is senseless to the reader, we have omitted it.

320. Apparently by Jewish law.

X

"And in the entire Earth" alludes to God's giving him the wisdom [to know] how to build houses, fortresses, and castles and to plow the Earth with various seeds and plants. Also how to extract gold and so with silver and bronze and copper from mines; how to make vessels and ornaments in crafts, and also how to make equipment for farm work like ropes and the plow and making carpentry equipment like saws and axes; [making] equipment for sowing clothes like pants, like the weaver's beam, and [making] writing utensils like pens and inks and the like as it says of Bezalel: "And I completed in him the knowledge from God with wisdom and understanding and with knowledge of all the crafts and the carving stone to arrange," (Ex. 31:3–4) and "In the heart of the rest of the wise men I have placed wisdom." (Ex. 31:6) I have been brief and have not cited proofs from the verses for each one of these.

XI

In the statement "and all the crawlers" it refers to giving the understanding to man [of how] to capture bees in their hives so that they make honey for him and surround it some . . . .

XII

<Now the reason that it mentions here "the fish of the sea" before "the birds of the sky" and "the birds of the sky" before "animals" is that it follows the order of creation. However, the reason David peace be upon him mentioned animals before the birds and the birds before the fish of the sea in his statement "And you shall have made him ruler over part of the creation . . . the birds of the heavens and the fish of the sea," (Ps. 8:7–10) is that he looked at what was near and [then] far from him.>

29) And God said: Behold I have made for you herbage and seed that is on the face of the Earth and all trees that have fruit with seed in it [it] shall be for you as food; 30) and for the rest of the beasts of the Earth and the birds of the sky and the rest of what walks on the Earth that has a living soul green vegetables shall be for food and it was so 31) when God knew that all that He created was very good and the sixth day and night passed.

I

Here too I have said . . . would they use wisdom. "Behold I have given you" indicates that God implanted in the intellect of man the knowledge of all plants that are for sustenance whether grains, trees, or vegetables. Likewise the knowledge of those [plants] by which he may be healed. He did not make man rely for this on trial and test for he would perish if he would hasten to eat something that would kill him or would die of hunger if he would delay until he checks everything. Likewise the statement "and for all the beasts of the field" tells that God told {man} of the fodder of every kind [of animal] for the preceding reason. One of the wonders of wisdom is that the animals that lack speech and understanding, God placed in their nature the knowledge of what is beneficial and nurishing for it . . . sustenance and fortifies the body [is] from . . . and it changes in the third level [of digestion] I mean in the [intestines]* until its hard part disintegrates to bones and fortifies them and the intermediate is for meat and fortifies it. The smallest is for fat and fortifies and the remaining water is directed to the organs of excrement until it comes out of the body. Now, all the nourishing [materials] are of two types: that which is vital like grains and the like, or [what is just] a need like wine and oil as it says: "And wine gladdens the heart of man." (Ps. 104:15)

II

Herbage [indicates the knowledge] that God informed him of the types of plants and trees that are medicial, gave direction in [determining] their [proper] weight and the components of their mxture as well as their preparation. Necessity prompted for composing medicines since there is no healing drug or medicines that are uncombined. God placed in man's wisdom [the ability] to compose them until the desired effect is reached.

III

With the word "seeds" it alludes to [the fact] that God placed [in man] the wisdom [to understand] how to sow with every kind, at what time to sow anything composable until he attains the desired effect and how to press out from it whatever is possible like wine and oil and to preserve them.

IV

"That are on the face of the Earth" is God's telling [man] which ground is fit for wheat and which of it for vineyards and which for cucumbers as well as which lands will bring forth. . . .

V

It did not say "Be fruitful and multiply" nor "And He blessed them" of the plants because it connected them to man like it did with the animals.[321]

VI

There are two [questions] that people ask and both of them have the same answer. The first concerns the statement to man: "Behold I have given you all the plants." They say that this implies that He did not permit them to eat meat. The second is [concerning the statement] "for all the beasts of the Earth." They say how [can] this [be] do we not see that lions, hawks, and the like do eat flesh [and] not plants. For these two questions there are two answers. The first is that {the Scripture} speaks only of the majority and abandons the minority as we have already explained in the introduction to this commentary.[322] Being that the majority of man's food is plants for they are something that he needs by necessity and eats meat less frequently for {people} have no necessity in it. Most animals too eat plants and only the minority of them eats meat. {The Scripture} speaks of what is most commonly found and abandons the minority.[323] What buttresses this is [the fact] that some of the predators and fish eat dust[324] but {the Scripture} does not mention this for it alludes only to the majority. The second answer [is] that [it is possible that] God prevented man from eating the meat of the animals and prevented animals from eating each other only at this beginning stage because there were only a

---

321. See verse 22.
322. This section has not surfaced yet.
323. See Zucker, *Translation*, p. 444.
324. E.g., the serpent (see Gen. 3:14).

few individuals of each kind [in existence] and would He permit this they would all perish. For this reason God pushed off [giving] permission [for eating meat] until they multiplied and [only] then did He permit [it to them].[325]

---

325. According to *Sanhed.* See also Ibn Ezra ad loc. (Linetsky, p. 47).

Chapter II

1) The Heavens and the Earth were complete. 2) And God completed on the seventh day His creation that He made and 3) He restrained on it from creating anything of the kind of His creation that He made. 4) This is <a detailing of> the products of the Heavens and the Earth when they were both created at the time that God made the Sky and the Earth 5) and when all the trees of the wilderness before they were on the Earth and all its herbage before it sprouted since God did not rain on it nor was there man to work it 6) nor would a mist ascend from it to water the entire face of the Earth.

I

. . . He intended with this if he did not use this allegorically.[1] Likewise, I say that the completion of creation indeed took place on the seventh day. This is because since God determined the order of {the days} to be seven, the sixth is incomplete and would be completed only on the seventh.[2] Now with what was {the creation} complete? [We say:] With

---

1. Apparently the Gaon speaks of some verse whose meaning he was not sure was allegorical or literal and gives both possibilities.

2. Apparently this is an answer to the question: Did God indeed complete His work on the seventh?

the blessing of the seventh holy day. This is because "and He blessed" and "and He sanctified" said during creation are similar to "and He said" and "and He made" mentioned in the six days for all [these expressions] mean "desire" [and] nothing else.[3, 4] Now this seventh day in truth is separated from the eighth and ninth as well as from the rest of the parts of time and is attached to the six [days] preceding it by means of blessing and sanctification which separate it from {the days} following it and attach it to {the days} preceding it.[5]

II

Now I should explain the four expressions "and He completed," "and He rested," "and He blessed," and "and He sanctified." I say: [1] "And He completed" refers to the completion of the substances and accidents of which there exists none other than [those that] His wisdom planned as I have explained.[6] [2] "And He rested" means abandonment of creation of things the like of which had never been in existence [before]. We say that "He did not create anything" in a metaphorical sense while in truth [it means the same] as "nothing more remained to be created."[7] Now shevithah encompasses [one of] eight meanings: [1] The first one is "abandoning creation," as investigation indicates, as well as [2] destroying and removing as it says: "And I shall destroy her mirth," (Hos. 2:13) and "And I shall remove from the cities of Judah." (Jer. 7:34) [3] "Abolishing all work"—this is on the Day of Atonement: "And you shall abstain from work," (Lev. 23:32) and particularly it being a fast-day. [4] "Abolition of most kinds of work" as on the Sabbath as it says: "It is an abandonment of work sanctified for God tomorrow." (Ex. 16:23) [5] "Abolition of work done for the sake of profit," which is on the holidays [as it says]: "And on the fourth day is abstinence from work." (Lev. 23:39) [6] "Abolition of one

---

3. I.e., that God wished that it be sanctified and blessed, not that He pronounced any word. See the Gaon's com. to Gen. 1:3.

4. Apparently the Gaon maintains that the creation was completed by the seventh day, which closes the cycle of days that precede. CF BR 10:2.

5. The question is why the seventh is attached to the day preceding it and not the one succeeding it.

6. See his com. to Gen. 1:1.

7. Beliefs 2:12 (p. 128). See also Responsa to Hiwya (p. 48). Cf. also Guide 1:61, where Maimonides cites this opinion.

[kind of] work," like working the ground on the seventh day [as it says]: "And on the seventh year is abstinence from work for the Lord." (Lev. 25:4) [7] "From a condition even if it is [just] speech" [as it says]: "And the three persons ceased to answer Job. (Job 32:1) And [8] "abolishing greatness and honor": "And laughed at her loss of esteem." (Lam. 1:7) I shall expound these matters in the middle of [my] commentary in the pericope of "On the morrow of the Sabbath" (Lev. 23:11) because of a need to show that the Shabbath is not the word for the day of the Sabbath specifically but a term for any day on which abandonment of work has been commanded . . . three times "seventh" only and after resting has been commanded on it in connection to the time of the manna it is called "Sabbath."[8] Being that the abandonment of work is the reason for it being called Sabbath, if the effect is found its cause is found too [i.e.] that every day that has resting is called Sabbath. [3] Now as for "And He blessed," it means glorification of the day itself [i.e.] that it is distinguished from the days after it by means of blessing since it is not separated from them by means of work.[9] [4] As for "And He sanctified," it means that He designated it to command upon it the estimable nation so that we do not think God commands them of the seventh day arbitrarily, rather it is in the seventh day itself.[10] Those who believe in the antiquity of the auditory precepts maintain that since the Torah gives the creation of the Heavens and the Earth as the cause of the Sabbath as its says: "For God created in six days the Heavens and the Earth and gave them rest on the seventh day, for that reason God blessed the seventh day and sanctified it," (Ex. 1:2) it follows that God commanded it to His servants from that time. [However,] investigation shows that it gives the creation of the Heavens and the Earth as a reason for the Sabbath [only] for the exaltation of the day itself as it says: "And for that reason God blessed the seventh day and sanctified it," (Ex. 20:11) whereas the commandment of resting on it is the result of the Exodus from Egypt as it says: "And remember that you were slaves in the land of Egypt but God your Lord took you out." (Deut 5:15) Then came the Tradition and combined these two reasons in the Kiddush of the Sabbath as it says: "A memorandum for the act of Genesis and a memorandum for the Exodus from Egypt."

---

8. Perhaps the Gaon cites here some proof to the effect that "Sabbath" is a general term.

9. This differs from how Ibn Ezra (Linetsky, p. 52) cites the Gaon. Cf. BR ch. 11.

10. See Mekh. to Ex. 16:1.

III

We should know the manner of wisdom in that the one who has the ability to create at the blink of an eye created it only in the duration of the [six] days. We give various reasons [for this] despite that God's wisdom is beyond them. The first is that God wanted that the things be arranged in front of us one to one since it is not within our ability to apprehend them simultaneously.[11] The second is that God wished to teach us how to classify the sciences and to arrange them into categories so that every idea should be connected to its kin [and placed] in its proper context. [Accordingly,] in order to give us the key to know how the sciences are to be classified, God arranged His teaching into parts.[12] I shall expound on this at length in my explanation of "apples of gold in ornaments of silver." (Prov.)[13] He also intended to prepare our hearts to correct our acts because of our desire for[14] . . .

IV

. . . [15]And that it is the one also called in it not the second . . . it continues after the same name [with] which He created it and increased the distress of trial. Now one of them has confused the matter because of the variety of words [used] [to denote] "creation" He said, since it says: "For behold the Creator of mountains and Creator of winds," using *yeSirah* in regards to the mountains while *beriah* to the wind, instead of grouping them with one word, and likewise it says: "creator of darkness and creator

---

11. The Rabbis, however, maintained that the world was created simultaneously. See Optowizer, HUCA, VI, pp. 205–206. See the Gaon's com. to Gen. 1:1 (III) where he himself seems to imply that the world was created simultaneously.

12. See *Git.* 60a and *Sifra* ch. 1.

13. See IPC section I.

14. Possibly the Gaon wishes to say that God created the world in an extended period of time in order to give the world importance and that man should await perfection in the world. Cf. *Fathers*, ch. 5 and *BR*, ch. 10. (Zucker)

15. This appears to belong to the verse "for on the day." The question may possibly be supplied from Al-Qirqisani as follows: Were various names mentioned in the previous chapter it would be possible to think that various things were created by different gods. Cf. Ibn Ezra to verse 15 (Linetsky, p. 63).

of light." [This means] that the one who created one did not create the
other. It should be said to them: So as for his claim, would you not say
that "The one who implants the ear" is not "The one who creates the eye,"
since it singles out one with "implanting" and the {the other} with *yeSirah*.
Were you to think so you would be forced to say if one should wish to
destroy the limb that is his and the other should wish to sustain the limb
that is his then the ear would be destroyed and the eye would remain
intact.[16] How [much more so] if the variation would be in many names
would the matter be greater and more profound. However, because of this
it mentions only one name during the entire act of Genesis without
variegating it and when the creation ends it begins with another name to
teach us that God has many names and that they all have the same
meaning. <We also have not seen> that it mention the second name . . .
and will also believe that the statement . . . and said: "It is upon you to
know that God is the Lord no other except Him," (Deut. 4:35) and this
is the path we must tread on in regards to all of God's names and would
it also have said: "The first thing God created was the Heavens and the
Earth," (Gen. 1:1) and "And God wished that there be light," (Gen.1:3) it
would not occur to us, the monotheists and people of analytical thought,
that one is not the other, for it would be recognized with the aid of the
intellect that "The Lord" is [identical to] "God" as they do not think . . .
it says already: "And Jacob arose from the well of seven and the Children
of Israel carried," (Gen. 46:5) because it is clear [to us] that these are the
names of one and the same man. Similarly, we do not believe that Jerubaal
is not Gideon despite that it says: "And Jerubaal the son of Joash
went . . . and Gideon had three score and ten sons." (Jud. 8:29–30) It
places the second name . . . before it mentions . . . and calls anyone
names so. This is not a homily that gives names for God rather God
informed him . . . and therefore whenever He creates something important it is called by the Estimable Name as we shall explain in the
pericope of "The primordial that has no end." (Ex. 3:14)[17] Now in every
language the names set for God Exalted are like the names that He is
called [in Hebrew], in respect to oath, desecration, and blasphemy. For
this reason Daniel praises his Master with the term "Heaven" as it says:
"You O the king, you are the king of kings, since the Master of the

---

16. See *Beliefs*, ch. 2 and *Guide* 1:72.

17. See *Beliefs* 2:3 (p. 99) and *BO* 1:1 (p. 43) where the Gaon speaks of this
subject again. See also *SR*, ch. 3 and *BR*, ch. 33.

Heavens has endowed you," (Dan. 2:7) according to the agreement between the people of that language.

V

It mentions here the Earth before the Sky after it mentions the Sky before the Earth in "the first thing" (Gen. 1:1) for various reasons. The first is that it is possible that it mentions the Sky before the Earth in [the account] of creation because the account of the creation comes from God[18] Who is loftier than any of His things and for that reason it started with that which is lofty because it comes from it, whereas it mentions the Earth before the Sky after the [actual] creation because the [view of the] observer falls on the Earth first and then on the Sky. This is the manner of all speakers. The second . . . therefore it mentions it after the Sky. It is also possible that it mentioned the Earth first because it comes to specify first the things about which . . . about the speech . . . in the history of the Sky it writes (*Toledhoth*) in full . . . and "the history (*Toledhoth*) of Perez," (Ruth 4:18) it writes *Toledhoth* in full [because fullness] returns during the return of the seed of Perez to its initial condition.[19] Every other *Toledhoth* is written in three ways: lacking both *waws* or lacking just one of them at the end or the beginning of the word or both of them together.

VI

. . . [20]the balance and addition of every, and its detraction is . . . and its lacking [results] in foolishness and an addition is [boldness]* . . . and a detraction is laziness.[21] All the forces of the soul serve the five known

---

18. I.e., from this perspective.

19. This fragmentary section is based on *BR* 12:6 (pp. 91–92): "All Toledhoth found in the Scripture are defective except two . . . Rabbi Berekiah said in the name of Rabbi Samuel ben Nahman: Though these things were created in their fullness, yet when Adam sinned they were spoiled and they will not again return to their perfection until the son of Perez comes."

20. This section probably belongs to "and man became a cognizant being."

21. This sentence is particularly difficult to render because of the lacuna. Zucker has: "and balance, and addition in each one, in man any addition in

senses which are: hearing, vision, smell, taste, and touch. The sense of vision directs the brain in which imagination, thought, and memory are formed. The sense of hearing directs the heart in which knowledge is born. The sense of simple smell is breathing and the composite is. The sense of taste reaches the digestive organs. The sense of the soul for the entire body. Speech comes about from feelings and belief which is in the heart except for natural utterances which result from the activity of the windpipe which is like of any limb. {The characteristics} by which man is singled out is not my intention to specify here. I offer here just some of them in order to tell of their importance and estimability, for God did not [compare]* any rough body to this fine one which can not tolerate the severity of attack that other [animals] can . . . it enters it until it becomes capable to . . . in it because of its delicateness and fineness.[22] This is because there are many questions here that [people] have raised regarding the nature of man and he is not . . . the first . . . the parts and we say that the soul receives . . . how . . . we say they are because of its fineness he mentions it and the establishment from what because . . . is not . . . the clothing of man . . . innumerable types. Likewise weapons like horn or claws and likewise he lacks [the ability to] trample like horses and the like. Likewise also that man is damaged when he eats raw meat or unbaked grains . . . that both of them are . . . the soul and the resting place of the . . . and that both of them not be low and disgusting thing like dirt and filth. So also regarding man's weakness that he is unable to stand on his feet when he is first born as opposed to the other animals. This too is because of his fine temperament and structure. So also regarding his degree of timidity and [that he] is fast to bend over or crouch because of fear. This [too] is because of his sensitivity and awareness so also regarding his upward stance and his dull vision. These [characteristics] are also due to the his fine structure. The same applies to man being stricken with diseases that do not effect other [animals]. Praise be to the Lord the One who collected these innumerable qualities and benefits that are in a single minuscule body.

---

thought is an evil thought . . . and an addition is boldness . . . and detraction is laziness." Cf. *Beliefs* 10:16 (p. 399).

    22. Cf. *Beliefs* 4:2 (p. 184) and *BO* (p. 106).

VII

You should also know, may God guide you on the right path, that the Sages called man a microcosm for everything is in him.[23] He bears similarity to the large [scale] features of the world. You should also know that this special nation, I mean the children of Israel, resembles all of humanity in the sense that I have described here. I am brief and do not contrast every characteristic of theirs to humanity as a whole. For that reason the Scripture singles them out from all people and says: "When the eyes of man as of all the Tribes of Israel shall be toward the Lord," (Zack. 9:1) and: "And you My flock, the flock of My pasture I am your God says the Lord God." (Ex. 35:34)[24]

Afterwards it speaks of the history of man and says:

7) and that God created man dust from the earth and blew into his nostrils the soul of life and man became a thinking soul. 8) And God planted a garden beyond the east to place there man that He created. 9) And God made sprout from the earth trees of good appearance and good for food. The healing tree [was] in the middle of the Garden and the Tree of Knowledge of good and bad.

I

I rendered *mi-qqedhem* correctly as "in the east" for the false interpretation that it is [derived from] *qedhem* in the sense of "priorness"[25] for if the reference with it is to before [the creation of] all the plants then it is not before.[26] If the intention is before the elucidation of the history of Adam and Eve then the same applies [as well].[27]

II

I translated *ES Hayyim* as "the healing tree" because healing from a sickness is called so as it says: "If I shall live from the sickness," (II Kings 1:2) and

---

23. See Ibn Ezra to 1:26 (Linetsky, p. 45, n. 238).
24. See *Mekh.* Jethro, ch. 4.
25. So Onqelos.
26. *Pes.* 54a.
27. *BR* 15:2.

it says regarding the ulcer: "And they shall stroke the boil and it will heal," (Is. 38:21) and says. . . .[28]

III

. . . And we should know that there was [indeed] wisdom in making all the trees sprout in the Garden before God set man down in it. [This is] in order that man come to the Garden when it is blossoming, full and pleasant. However, being that "And He made sprout" happened before "And he placed," *wayyasem* should be interpreted as "in order to put there." [This is] similar to what it says of Jacob: "And he went to Haran," (Gen. 28:10) which means "to go to Haran," of Shim'i: "And he went to Gath to Achish,"[29] (I Kings 2:10) and of Reuben: "And he saved them from their hand," (Gen. 37:21) which means: "in order to save him from their hand to return him to his father."[30] Likewise *wayyasem* means "to place man there."[31]

IV

Now what manner of wisdom is there in that God created {man} at first in this inhabitable area and [only] afterwards transferred him to this Garden? We say to make him aware of the kindness [that] He [did] for him. This is because would He not have created him at first dwelling in this garden[32] {living in the Garden} would not be [on] so high of a level and so great a delight for him because he [already] lives in it. However, when he was created in a place of lower [status] and then God transferred him to a more estimable place, he recognized [God's] kindness and found himself obliged to thank the One Who endowed him with this and to accept [His] commandments.[33] So also regarding Abraham: For what

---

28. See ch. III, sec. II, where the Gaon speaks of this word again.

29. I.e., to go to Gath.

30. Ad loc. he translates: "and sought to save him."

31. Apparently, the Gaon maintains that the planting of the Garden in Eden ocurred on the same day that the plants were created.

32. And therefore accustomed him to something other than it.

33. It appears that the Gaon maintains that man, and possibly also Eve, was created outside of the Garden and after a time was transferred to the Garden.

reason was he deprived of his father's goodness? In order that God do kindness for him so that he be endowed and recognize in truth the One Who endows him. The same applies to the nation of Israel: For what reason were they first enslaved and then redeemed? In order that they be obliged to thank [God] and to accept [His] commandments for He multiplied them after being exiguous as it says: "Your fathers went down to Egypt as seventy souls," (Deut. 10:22) and gave them greatness after they were lowly as it says: "And God had chosen and took you out from the likeness of the furnace of iron from Egypt." (Deut. 4:20)

V

Now in which horizon of the Earth was man created or from which dust was he taken? There is no decisive proof for this. Some say that he was created in a place of holiness and goodness, I mean in the Temple, and was placed in the Holy Land, i.e., the Land of Israel.[34] There is no claim against this opinion.[35]

VI

The Scripture expands here [and says]: "Trees of good appearance and good for food," as a preamble to what it will tell us afterwards [i.e.] that the tree of which the man was warned: "For the tree was good for food and desire for the eye." [This is] so that it does not come to our minds to justify man and think that he was turned to its goodness because he could not find a tree as good in taste as it. For that reason it mentions first: "Trees of good appearance and good for food," [i.e.] to tell us that God created for him good and pleasant trees that will relinquish his need in that [tree's] pleasantness and goodness. So the measure of justice is that one does not prohibit one from anything that one is in need of until one gives him its equivalent. So although God made us in need of sustenance and perseverance of form, He did not prohibit this in all aspects but

---

This is in opposition to the view of the Rabbis that he entered the Garden on the same day he was created. See *Sanhed.* 38b for example.

34. See T.J. *Nazir* 7:2, BR 14:8.

35. See however, Ibn Ezra ad loc. (Linetsky, p. 64) who does in face object to this view.

prohibited some and permitted the other. [Likewise,] although He made us in need of copulation to sustain the seed, He did not prohibit this in all aspects but permitted it in one fashion but prohibited it in another. According to this principle we say that when a man finds himself in need of some act it should be clear to him that the One Who made him in need of this permitted it to him except for what is elucidated to him that God prohibited it to him. Then all things we need are permitted for us except for what the prophet conveys to us is prohibited. This means that it is not upon one who says that this thing is permitted to cite a Scriptural proof, it is only upon one who says "This is prohibited." This is a matter in which the [Rabbinate] congregations and its opponents [are divided]. The [Rabbinate] congregation says everything is permissible except for what was prohibited [explicitly] while {the others} say everything is prohibited unless it is permitted [explicitly]. But I say to them: Find me the permission in the Scripture to wear linen and the like but they will not [even] find its mention in the Scripture at all. Another person would say to them: Where have you found [in the Scripture] explicit permission to eat truffles and the like?

Now in the history of creation it also says:

10) And a river came out of Eden to water the Garden and from there it separates and becomes four heads. 11) The name of the first is the Nile which is the one that surrounds the entire land of Zawila where there is gold. 12) And the gold of that land is good and there are pearls and there are stones of onyx, 13) and the name of the second is Jihan which the one that surrounds the entire land of Ethiopia, 14) and the name of the third is the Tigris which is the one that goes through the west of Jeriah, and the name of the fourth is the Euphrates.

I

It first says: "To water the Garden" and afterwards: "And from there it separates" to tell of the largeness of this Garden. This is because what we are used to seeing is geysers which water the ground reaching [in size] one sixtieth [of the land] and if there were four large rivers watering that Garden it would have sixty times more of them.[36] Were one to say: We

36. See Tal. Pal. Ber. 1:5 says 1/60.

see the origins of these [rivers] but where is their origin? We say since we do not see where the springs flow from . . . for that reason the Torah recorded for us their origin of flow where it is from when we do not see . . . and in this . . . the rivers to no numbers as it says: "The one who sends springs in the rivers," (Ps. 104:10) but none of them except these four come out of the Garden. Were one to ask: Where does this water flow to? The decisive and known answer of people to this question is: To the place it flows from, especially because the Scripture states: "All the rivers go to the sea," (Ecl. 1:7) but we shall explain and elucidate this: We say: God created the water so that by its nature it should be in the bowels of the earth for cold things staying for a while become liquid if they collect [in the bowels of the Earth] and the bowels of the Earth are not able to contain them, then overflows . . . and gushes out until it . . . and afterwards . . . every liquid collects and attaches there. This is the reason that God contested with Job and all the people when it says: "Have you at some time come to the wellsprings of the sea." (Job 38:17) Likewise all drawn water spilled on the face of the Earth, the {earth} absorbs it and it reaches its bowels. If there is a chilly place in the vicinity {of the water} it seeps inside of it and if there is no standing water it collects [it] and turns to mists and then rain or until it explodes in a geyser. Of this the Scripture says: "To the place that the rivers go they go to return." (Ecl. 1:7) This [fact] appears to us clearly when we look at the rain . . . whatever water and whatever [water] collects in what flows out of it.

II

Many interpreters understand Pishon as [the river] Beloch because the Scripture mentions of it a cluster of gold and stones of onyx. However, it is not in the vicinity of Hawilah. This is because there are two Hawilahs. One is the son of Cush[37] and the other the son of Yaqtan[38] and neither of them is in its vicinity.[39] Likewise, there are two Arams; one is the son of Cush and the other is the son of Nahor. Two Dedans; one is the son

---

37. Gen. 10:7.

38. Gen. 10:29.

39. I.e., the territory occupied. The latter Hawilah is between Mecca and Medina. See the Gaon's trans. of Gen. 10:30.

of Re'ema[40] and the other is the son of Yaqtan.[41] And so three Shebas, the son of Tema,[42] Yeqtan,[43] and Yaqshan,[44] and also three Us's: the son Aram the son of Sem,[45] the son of Dishan the son of Se'ir,[46] and Nahor.[47] However, the Nile is in the vicinity of the places called Hawilah, I mean Habasha and Yemen and in its vicinity is a large cluster of gold. It is [also] possible that in its upper part there are onyx and pearls while in the lower part there are none.

III

Now just as there is in the land clusters of gold it has clusters of silver. Some say that clusters of gold surface once in five hundred years while silver once in fifty and for that reason gold is usually many times more precious than silver, I mean ten [times]. The meaning of surfacing is that some dust turns to a mass during the duration particular to it and according to the conditions created for it by nature and it turns to gold or silver. In this period . . . fire they say that their practice is to collect stones and dust and to mold them in the particular way in the duration they have determined and at times too gold and silver as nature penetrates the bowels of the Earth. This [however] is far improbable and doubtful for would it be possible to create a mesh from inanimate objects by some unusual manner it would then be possible to create animals from a mesh in manners we are unaccustomed to.

Now, just as there is in the depths {of the Earth} springs of cold water so there are springs of hot water which we shall mention in the section of the Flood, and just as it has in its depths springs of fire whose openings appears in one of three places. The first is the land of Siqliah which is [in] the mountain where the salamander that I have already described appears. The second is in Naples which is the passage to France. The third is in the

---

40. Gen. 25:3.
41. Gen. 25:3.
42. Gen. 6:7.
43. Gen. 6:28.
44. Gen. 25:3.
45. Gen. 10:23.
46. Gen. 36:28.
47. Gen. 22:21.

wilderness for which I do not know a name. So also the Earth has springs
of wind growing like water does. And when they erupt from one side
there is an earthquake and when from both sides then there is a mountain
slope like of *miq'alu*[48] and the like when only the winds are blowing the
Earth opens up because of this heat and trembles but nothing is covered
up. Apart from what is in its depths like tar and chromium there are similar
things which are not found in every land but I shall not go to length to
describe [it], because they go beyond the initial subject.

IV

Were people to ask: How does it say Cush (Ethiopia) and Ashur for were
these two men not in existence yet? They assume that this text was
written at the time of creation of the world. We mention to them that it
was written only at the fortieth year.[49] God told His messenger what
occurred from the beginning of [the creation] of the world until his
days.[50] This is our response [also] in regards to their question regarding
"All of the field of the Amalekite," (Gen. 14:7) for Amalek was not yet in
existence in their opinion and likewise regarding "And he pursued them
until Banias,"[51] (Gen. 14:14) and the like.

V

The {Scripture} mentions the Nile before {the other rivers} for various
reasons. The first is because it is the largest of them. This is because its
extent in Egypt is four hundred parsangs and we do not know what is
above this. It is divided into two bridges in its width with an island in
between them and every bridge has sixty boats. It is different than the
other rivers [1] because the three flow from north to south while it flows
from south to north. [2] Also its waters swell from Asereth to Sukkoth

---

48. The reading is not certain.
49. After the Exodus from Egypt. Al-Qirqisani (Hirschfeld, *Qirqisani Studies*, p.
51) actually formulates this as one of his exegetical principles.
50. See BR 17:11 and 14 as well as *Keth.* 10b. See also IPC section XI.
51. A river in Syria. See Kafih, *Perushe*, p. 26.

while their water reduces and it reduces from Sukkoth to Asereth at the time that theirs swells; [3] it is not dependent on rain while the others are. [4] This is the river that the nation for which the prophet recorded this statement knew about [i.e.] because they were in Egypt.

VI

Now the Gihon (Jihan) which Ezekiah plugged[52] is not the same Gihon mentioned in this section but is the Gihon known in the vicinity of Ethiopia.[53]

VII

It says of Perath: "And the fourth river is Perath," something that it does not say of the other rivers is because it is at the border of the Estimable Land, I mean the Land of Israel. For that reason it is called "the large river," [i.e.] because there is no river in the vicinity of the Land of Israel larger than it[54] similar to what Daniel calls the Tigris "large" in his statement: "I stood on the shore of the large river which is the Tigris," (10:4) because in Iraq there is none larger than it.[55]

Afterwards it tells us of the auditory precepts and says:

15) **Then God took the man and placed him in the Garden of Eden[56] to serve and preserve it 16) and God commanded him saying: From all the trees of the Garden you are permitted to eat 17) but from the tree of the knowledge of the good and the bad you shall not eat for on the day you eat from it you shall be deserving of death.**

---

52. II Chron. 32:30.

53. See however Ibn Ezra ad loc. (Linetsky, p. 60) who argues that they are one and the same.

54. See BR 41:7. CF Nahmanides ad loc.

55. Cf. his com. ad loc. (Zucker, Genesis, p. 272, n. 354).

56. The pre-Saadianic translation renders Eden as a noun meaning "enjoyment."

I

The statement "And God took" does not imply coercion for [God] Exalted takes no direct effect on the actions of people[57] rather {the placing} is [merely] an instruction. The most probable [explanation] is that God sent an angel and commanded it to transfer [him] into the Garden.[58] And so: "to work it" is the command to service this Garden with the task of cleaning, for example, as well as sweeping the hyssop. Also collecting fruits from the trees whereas collecting and dispersing what is needed for it in actual agricultural work and labor there was no need because of the arrangement of the Garden.[59] And so: "to watch it" is His command not to depart from it as long as {man} is by himself but when Eve was created with him the Garden should not have been left without one of them, he or she, remaining for watching the Garden was unnecessary[60] . . .

II

The statement "From all the trees of the Garden you are permitted to eat" comes not because he needed the tree to be permitted for him and that otherwise it would be prohibited. Rather this statement comes because of what is [mentioned] afterwards[61] as it says: "Six days you shall work," (Ex. 20:9) because of "And the seventh day is a Sabbath," (Ex. 20:10)[62] and: "Six years you shall sow" (Lev. 25:3) because of "and on the seventh year you shall abstain from work.[63] Likewise it says here "from any tree of the Garden" because of "and of the Tree of the Knowledge." Also to mention to him I did not prohibit you anything until I gave you its replacement and also that that which I permitted you is more abundant that what I prohibited you.

---

57. Here the Gaon follows the Mu'tazila notion that no coercion on the part of God may be executed even if it is not in a matter of good and bad. (Zucker)

58. The connection appears to be that in both instances a command was issued.

59. Apparently because it was naturally watered by the rivers.

60. See *Sifri Eqeb* ch. 41. Apparently the Gaon maintains that animals could not enter the Garden.

61. "And from the Tree of the Knowledge of Good and Bad you shall not eat."

62. As opposed to *Mek.* ch. 292 and the *Fathers* of Rabbi Nathan (ch. 11), where there is an actual commandment to work during the week.

63. See Zucker, *Translation*, p. 334, *Kid.* 20a and *Mek.* to Ex. 21:3.

III

You should know that <the matter of the tree is literal> and those who understand this tree allegorically interpret "good" and "bad" to mean that he knew by [means of] it what is good and bad for man, i.e., his reward and punishment for would he abstain from {the tree} he would be rewarded and when he would eat from it he was punished.[64] But this is not possible, for we see that when he eats from it his mind indeed broadens and his understanding improves as it says: "And the eyes of both of them opened."

IV

I say [now] if this tree indeed could sharpen the mind and add to the intellect what is the manner of wisdom that God restrained him from it? For it would be more correct, in our opinion, that He should not only permit him to eat from it but should command him to do so in order that his intellect is broadened and specifically because the aim of {man's} creation is for knowledge. I shall give two responses to this question, but I shall make a preface to them first. I say: Adam and Eve were not lacking in the knowledge of all good and bad before they ate from the tree, for they were commanded and warned and only one who has intellect can be commanded and warned. And how could it be that they were blind as appears to the masses because it says: "And their eyes opened," for God brought in front of man all the animals and he gave them names and he saw and even named Eve.[65] Moreover, it was inevitable that he should see the tree itself before he was warned of it. Rather he [indeed] had most knowledge of good and bad but a few things remained that would come to him either by means of instruction from God or with the understanding that this tree sharpened.

Now we give the first answer and say: Despite that this tree developed man's intellect it caused him other damage in the manner that its use came

---

64. This interpretation is cited in the name of Rabbi Phineas ben Yair in Midrash *Tadshe*, p. 150.

65. Ibn Ezra ad loc., however, uses this argument to prove that Adam had intellect.

to his loss and God restrained him from it in order to protect him from
the bad that it has. Indeed He has the ability to endow {man} with the
good of its like as it says: "For God is the giver of wisdom and from His
utterances is knowledge and understanding." (Prov. 2:6) The second
answer I say: For was the tree only constructive and not destructive it
would be be better and easier for man to abstain from [eating of] its fruits
for God Augmented and Exalted was destined to teach whatever sciences
were allotted him as it says: "The One Who teaches men knowledge." (Ps.
94:10) From this he would have derived a dual benefit. The first is that
God would be his teacher not his [own] mind and the second is that his
attempt in learning would be greater so the reward for this effort would
be grander. [For that reason] God restrained him from obtaining this
remaining knowledge by means of nature for he would relinquish the two
goods together. [1] He would not be the student of his Master and [2]
would lose the greatness of his recompense. [The fact] that [God]
restrained him from any tree is with various facets of wisdom [i.e.] were
it not [even] called the Tree of the Knowledge of good and bad; [1] in
order to merit him reward for distancing himself from it; [2] that when
man goes around the tree from all its sides he should remember the
mastership of his Master and His commandments and warnings; [3] he
should also warn the others of {the tree} and should merit a second
reward.

V

It repeats "from it" after it says "And from the Tree of the Knowledge of
the good and the bad you shall not eat," for this is one of the ways of the
usage of the language—that it starts with a word and when the statement
until the end of the subject becomes lengthy it repeats {the first word} as
it says: *eth yyy Seba'oth otho taqdishu* (Is. 8:13) [and] (Lev. 25:46), where it
repeats the *beth*. Likewise here it repeats "with him."

VI

God's statement to {the man}: "For on the day you eat of it you shall be
deserving of death"—informs him of his punishment. Now this is the

most perfect form of correction that one who warns tell the warned: Do not do such so that such does not come upon you.[66]

VII

Now some have also been confounded by the interpretation of "You shall surely die," for they saw that the man ate [of the fruit] and did not die on the day he ate. Some say it means "You shall surely be iniquitous,"[67] while others say [that it means]: "You shall surely be punished."[68] However, these depart from the literal meaning. Some say that he indeed died but this was on a day the measurement of which is one thousand years and for that reason the man did not live a complete one thousand [years] but lacked seventy.[69] These two are also close to the first for [they deny that]* the statement "on the day you eat" {means} a known day.

There are those that say that it indeed is a known day but when it states "for on the day you eat of it" it makes a condition: If you do so and so with the intention of angering Me—you shall die—but he did not do this with the intention of opposing his Master but only because of his evil and his desire. The contradiction to this opinion is evident in that [according to this] anyone who does an iniquitous act without the intention of angering his Master but only because of his desire and evil, the punishment due him is not generally given to him. But I say that "on the day you eat" is literal, but that the meaning of the statement "You shall surely die" is: "You shall be deserving of death,"[70] as I have noted in [my translation] of the verse. Being that "You shall surely die" is [nothing more than] informing him what he deserves, God may pay him immediately or delay it or may [altogether] forgive him if he repents for this is not a definitive decree from God that it is inevitable for it to occur and this is similar to what is said to us of one who eats on the Day of Atonement: "Any person who reaches thirteen years and does not fast on this day he shall be cut off from his people," (Lev. 23:29) and of one who does work on {this day}: "And any person who does work on this day I shall destroy this person

---

66. Cf. IPC section VI for a parallel idea.
67. This rendition is found in the anonymous translation (Tobi, p. 117 [31]).
68. See Ibn Ezra to 3:8 (Linetsky, p. 83) who cites this opinion as well.
69. See BR 19:8 and *Jubilees* 4:36. See also Ibn Ezra (ibid.).
70. Ibn Ezra (ibid.) cites this opinion anonymously.

from among his people." (Lev. 23:30) These two statements are not something that should inevitably occur because of a sin but only informing him
of what he deserves. It is possible that God will quicken or delay {the
punishment} as we see[71] from these two as well as from the rest of the
Kerithoth that some of them come immediately while others occur in a
time. However, that if he would not have eaten of the tree he would not
have died in a natural manner is something no one who practices
investigation at all would say.

Now let us investigate the use in man being commanded[72] of the Tree
of the Knowledge while he was still alone before Eve was created with
him[73] for at first glance it would seem correct to us that they should both
be commanded. We find various arguments in this. The first is that his
intimidation would be upon her when her Master's command reaches her
and her fear of him shall grow and so through Him the man should have
additional reward for conveying His teaching to her while she loses
nothing by this. [3] To emphasize the wisdom of man by him making a
fence for her and prohibiting something permissible as a guard from the
fundamental prohibition as I shall explain in [connection with] "You shall
not touch it." [4] And that this should be a sign and example for all
auditory precepts that the men should hear them and bring them to their
wives, children, and all those accompanying them as it says in some
places, i.e., "and your household," (Gen. 45:12) and "you and your friend,"
(Zech. 3:8) and the like.

The Scripture tells us of the beginning of the history of acts and names
and says:

18) **It is not good for man to remain by himself I shall make an assistant
opposite him 19) and when God created from the earth all the beasts of
the earth and the birds of the sky He brought them to man to show him
what he should name them and whatever living soul man names so this
would be its name until now. 20) And when Adam gave names to all the**

---

71. See *Mak. 13b.*

72. I.e., warned. The Gaon apparently maintains that "commandment" and
"warning" fall within one and the same category. See Maimonides, intro. to the
Book of Precepts, principle #8 (p. 30).

73. The Rabbis, however, maintained that Eve is included with Adam. Cf.
Sanhed. 38b for example.

animals and the birds of the steppe[74] he did not find <for himself[75]> a helper opposite him.

I

Before I explain the meaning of these three verses, I shall preface: What is the reason for introducing [the giving of] the names between the history of the Heavens and the Earth with which {the Scripture} began. I say that the intention of {the two things} is one. This is because this history comes to inform us how their beginning was because we only see plants from plants, God [therefore] told us that they were originally created out of nothing and [because] we only see animals from animals it tells us how their beginning was and [since] we only see people, male and female,[76] only by the coupling of a male and female it tells us that the first male was created from the dust of the Earth and the first female from his rib.[77] Likewise, since we only see speech as something passed from one who preceded us and for that reason it told us at the outset that the first language was created as I shall explain.[78]

II

It introduces into the flow of the story of the creation of Eve and says at its outset: "It is not good for man to be by himself." The meaning of this is not that there is no good at all for man to be alone for God created him at first by himself and the intellect would reject [the thought] that [God] would create something that is not good. The text also [rejects this] because it says of every creation: "When God saw that it was good." Him being alone at first was for his good in a number of aspects which I

---

74. This rendition of the usual "field" is already found in the anonymous translation (Toby, p. 117).

75. Devenbourg's edition as the anonymous translation (ibid.) has "for Adam" as an addition.

76. See com. to 1:26.

77. As opposed to the Rabbinic view that he was a hermaphrodite.

78. This section has not surfaced yet. See the Gaon's "Book of the Hebrew Language," Vol. I, p. 96 for further discussion about his view about the development of language.

mention: [1] So that when he shall see Eve created after him and especially from his rib as I shall explain[79] he should have no doubts that he is created like her since [they] are of one kind. [2] So that he should precede her in ruling over all things when she comes afterwards and finds him ruling over everything she will see herself as secondary to him and will attach to and obey him. [3] So that he will feel loneliness from the solitude and will ask for her in his heart. [Then] when his request is filled he will be grateful and will not complain when temptation comes.[80] [Nevertheless] continuing in solitude was not good for various reasons because of the benefits obtained from a partner and furthermore it would not be beneficial because of the cutting off of offspring.

III

I say: [it says] "I shall make a helper opposite him" and did not make each one of them helpers for the other. It follows that man should do the start of things and the woman should be the one who supports them. He makes the roots of the work and she the branches. The explanation of these two things is lengthy and known.

IV

It says "opposite him" for there are things in which she is equal to him, the children are from both of them equally as well as the lineage and total trustworthiness is upon both of them alike.

V

The [mention of the] word "to him" indicates that she should be subservient to him and that he not be so to her and also that he should supercede her in thirty kinds of precepts as I shall explain in the pericope of "the heads of the tribes" (Num. 30:2) God willing.[81]

---

79. This section has not surfaced yet.
80. Cf. *Sifri Deut.* 1 and *Ab. Zar.* 5b.
81. See *Responsa*, p. 120.

VI

"And God created from the Earth" is not a second creation but a repetition of what it said, [i.e.] that after God created the animals on the days of completion[82] and the birds created on the fifth He brought them to Adam.

VII

It intends with "To see what he will call them" that man himself should commit their names to memory.[83] The meaning is: "for man to see[84] what he will call it," and will be diligent over them so that today he will not call a load carrier a horse and tomorrow an ox and that today he should not call a pomegranate a pomegranate and tomorrow a fig.

VIII

Now despite that the first verse only mentions beasts and birds and the second adds animals, we should know that he named all the animals. The proof for this is that we see that they have names [today] and the proof for this is that we have names for them. The same applies to all the plants for all plants and inanimates for we find many of them having names. Likewise for all [types of] labor and the equipment with which work is done and so all the stars that have names and likewise the specialized terms that are used in the art of logic and all the names given to determine the level of things whose meaning is clarified by the philosophers, all of them the man gave names that they have until this day so that there is nothing that has a name that {Adam} did not name[85] as it says: "And

---

82. I.e., the sixth.
83. I.e., not that God should see what he shall call them. Cf. BR 17:4 (p. 135) and CRE, ch. 13 (p. 91), which interpret this passage literally—that Adam gave his own names to the animals.
84. The Gaon takes lir'oth in the causative sense of "to show."
85. See Kuzari 2:68 (p. 125).

whatever living soul man would name so this would be its name until today."[86]

IX

Now in which language did he name them? [We say] in the Holy Tongue for it is the desired and preferable language as I shall explain in the pericope after this.

X

It repeats "And the man called names" for it means that at the time that he named them he deliberated them and saw that none of them would befit him and for this reason he mentioned of all the things named only the animals for they are closer to man whereas plants and inanimates are between them and men in many levels.

It then tells us how [God] created the woman from a rib and says:

21) and God placed a sleep on the man and he fell asleep and He took one of his ribs and filled in its place with flesh. 22) And He built from it a woman which He brought to him. 23) And Adam said: This time <I have seen> a limb from my limbs and flesh from my flesh and this should be called "woman" for she was taken from man. 24) For this reason a man should leave his father and mother and will attach to his wife and they shall be like a single body.

I

When some of our people read first: "Male and female He created them," and then here a second creation when they read: "This time," they came to believe that two wives were created. <One of dust like him and the second from his rib.> When they read "This time" they say [that] this refers to another wife before her.[87] I have already mentioned what I have

---

86. This applies only to forms.
87. Cf. *Alpha Beta of Ben Sira* and BR 22:8. See Ibn Ezra ad loc. (Linetsky, p. 71).

argued against this deceitful opinion at the beginning of God's statement "These are the offspring," [that it] teaches us that all of this section is an explanation and detailing of what was said before in general form and just as the repetition of the creation of man here does not indicate the existence of a second man but is merely a detailing of his existence for not and . . . said only "Male and female He created them."

II

[88]<The meaning of "This time" is not that he had a second wife but that this was a second sight after he saw all of the mute animals and did not find among them even one similar to him as it says: "And he did not find a helper opposite him," he saw that Eve was similar to him and said: "This time.">

III

Now as for the manner of wisdom in God placing a sleep upon him We say that this was by necessity for when God's power reached him [it had enough] to detach a thing from his structure so He placed a tiredness upon him similar to death and it was also by way of providence in order not to put pain on any of his limbs.[89] One of the heretics claimed that this, I mean: "And He took one of his ribs," is theft. But the fool did not know that one who takes a little but returns much is not a thief.[90] We say further that the ribs were not lacking when this rib was taken away from him for God created {man} with an extra rib designated for this purpose[91] and when it was taken from him he was made complete without [any] detraction or addition. The same applies to the circumcision of which the heretics claimed saying: How is it possible that when something is cut off someone's body he be complete? The response is: The foreskin is an addition that God created in the body to be trimmed off and as long as it exists in the body the body is incomplete but when it is trimmed {man's body} becomes complete because he has no additions or detractions.

---

88. This section seems to repeat the previous one.
89. Cf. his trans.
90. See *Sanhed.* 3a and BR 17:7.
91. Cf. Ibn Ezra to 2:23 (Linetsky, p. 71).

IV

Now the manner of wisdom in God creating her from the rib is in order that [1] he should watch it like one of his own limbs, [2] she should watch him as the foundation of her body, [3] he should be her preserver because she comes from his body, and [4] she should follow him like a limb does the entire body.

V

He says "a limb of my limbs" knowing that she comes from his limbs for he knew that he had an additional rib and when {the rib} awoke him and he felt its absence and saw the woman in front of him he deduced that the rib that [God] removed is the woman that he found.

VI

He says "flesh from my flesh" because of the flesh God returned to him for it says: "And He closed the flesh under it."

VII

"For that reason she shall be called 'woman'"—he derived for her a name from the name of the man and we have already said that there is a proof in this that the Hebrew language is the ancient one.[92]

VIII

"For that reason a man shall leave his"—two interpretations of this have been said. One is that these are the words of Adam and are a continuation of his statement: "This time." Other people thought that these are the

---

92. See BR 18:4. See above section II. This was the accepted view in the Middle Ages. Cf. Al-Qirqisani (*Book of Gardens*, p. 62), Ibn Ezra to Gen. 11:1, Rashi ad loc., and *Kuzari* 2:68 (p. 124).

words of the teller of the Torah, I mean Moses[93] in blessed memory for the Creator Exalted and Magnificent that because of the story of Eve and that she was created from the rib of something foreign a man must marry a woman that is not his relative like his father and mother and the like, i.e., daughters and sisters and brothers and sisters-in-law[94]

IX

"And shall attach to his wife" implies faithfulness of the couple to each other similar to what it says: "As his soul has attached to Your obedience." (Ps. 63:9)

X

It says "his wife" to separate, [i.e.] to exclude him from [copulating with] his friend's wife.

XI

"And they should be one flesh"—prohibits copulation with a male or an animal or copulating with a woman where there can be no offspring for there is no place for something to be destroyed because of this.[95]

25) And they were both naked together, Adam and his wife, and were not abashed <of this>.

I

It says in the beginning that both of them were naked because it wished and mentioned afterwards that "They were naked" after eating of the fruits. {The Scripture} tells that they were not aware and did not know

---

93. See IPC section IV.
94. See *San.* 58a.
95. Following *BR* 18:5.

that it was disgusting until their understanding was broadened by eating of this fruit. Similar to this is found that a person should do something that is disgusting in the eyes of the Sages and not to know that it is disgusting and after he obtains education and his knowledge broadens the disgustingness of his act becomes clear to him and he restrains himself from [doing] it [again].

Chapter III

[[1)And the snake became wiser than all the beasts of the steppe that God created and said to the woman: Had indeed God said you may not eat of all the trees of the Garden. 2) The woman said to the snake: Of all the fruits of the trees of the Garden we may eat, 3) but of the fruits of the tree that is in the middle of it God said: You may not eat of it or touch it so that you do not die 4) and he said: You shall not die 5) for God knows that you, on the day you eat of it your eyes shall open and you shall be like angels knowing the good and the bad.]]

I

[1]On it . . . in it[2] that equating animals with angels under the title of *Seraphim* does not necessitate that their names be identical [as well] but rather would this be [so] it would be possible for snakes to be called

---

1. This section apparently is the rejection of the view that since both snakes and angels are called *Saraph*, then the snake was a satanic being, not an actual creature. (Zucker) The identification of the snake with the Satan or at least involving the Satan is found in various sources. Cf. *Book of Adam and Eve* 16:7–17, Chapters of Rabbi Eliezer #13, and *Book of Enoch* 2:11. See Rabbi Hai Gaon, *Responsa*, p. 214 and Ibn Ezra ad loc. (Linetsky, p. 75) for examples of others who oppose this view.

2. The translation of these words is doubtful. From the context it appears that

147

angels this being one of the most probable possibilities. Rather what concerns any things called by the same name it is possible that the [individual] should be called by another name as we say[3] . . . a tall house and a tall man and as we say a true *dirham* and a true loaf of bread, a complete statement and a complete day, etc. This is something the intellect rejects. However, if we say a holy and pure Nazarite and a Holy Priest it is possible that they be compared.[4] The same is true regarding God the Mighty and Awesome and the like of these names except if this were to require to attribute envy to angels as well as emotions of anger and desire and [to believe that] the angels may chose to mislead the messengership to the prophets as I shall explain in the matter of the Satan in [the Book of] Job and [in my] argument against the one who thought that it is an angel <not a man>.[5] Apart from this they would be forced to consider the punishment of the Snake to be an allegory and accordingly the punishment of Adam and Eve would also be allegories. According to this also the Garden and the tree would [also] be [just] allegories and so the possibility would be endless for them to the point that they will be forced to take the entire account of creation out of its literal meaning and to say that it is an allegory as are forced those that say that the Tree of the Knowledge is some prohibited substance not an [actual] tree.

II

You, may God make you prosper, should know that what lead both of these [camps] to divide in these views is their disbelief that the known snake should speak and how much more so that it should be rewarded and punished. This is because {reward and punishment} accords only one who is commanded and warned.[6] If so, it follows that the animals [too] are commanded and warned and rewarded [and] punished for according to investigation there is no difference between snake, camel, and the frog in

---

this read something like: "There are various points in this section that need to be discussed."

3. There appears to be an omission of text by the copyist.

4. Apparently he means that in the former instances the adjectives, although identical, do not have the same implications as opposed to the latter instances, where they are similar.

5. See Job 1:6 (Goodman, p. 154 n. 30).

6. Rabbi Hai Gaon (ibid.) reiterated this idea.

this aspect and it will not matter then that they have commandments and warnings, reward and punishment; but whether they have intellect or not! <If they do not have intellect it is possible for them to have command and warning> and if they do have intelligence man has no advantage over them. This distinction brought them to such a disposition in these matters. This is what they distinguished . . . regarding this I say that it is impossible that this known snake should be commanded [or] warned from the aspect of the intellect nor from anything else according to what I explained, according to what the intellect necessitates, and according to what the Scripture states, [i.e.] that the commandments and prohibitions are all for people. These are as [follows]: "To inform people of His valor," (Ps. 145:12)[7] "Then He said to the offspring of Adam: 'Fear of God that too is wisdom and to shun evil too is understanding'" (Job 28:28)[8] "And I shall bring distress upon men, that they shall walk like blind men because they have sinned against the Lord," (Zeph. 1:17)[9] "How estimable and honorable is Your Excellence and people that are under the shade of Your wings shall take shelter," (Ps. 36:8)[10]—it singles them out with "knowledge," "commands," "reward," and "punishment." However, I shall say regarding [this] something with which I shall free myself from all of what they claimed: The first is that God Exalted and Magnified created many snakes just as He did the other animals and when He wanted [to put] man [through] a test, He fixed one of the snakes and covered him with the form of a man so as to place upon him commandments, warnings, and recompense. He recognized its punishment and warned it that if it defies Him He will revert it to its original state[11] similar to what it says: "For you are dust and to dust you shall return." (Gen. 3:19) For that reason I have rendered *haya arum* in my translation as "became wise." Indeed, he turned wise for man's test! For us the word *heyoth* [indicates] a necessary

---

7. Cf. *Bel.* 1:4 (p. 86) where the Gaon cites this verse in an attempt to show that such an elaborate world was created in order to manifest God's wisdom. It is possible that the Gaon wishes to say that command and prohibition can only be given to someone with an intellect.

8. Cf. *Beliefs* 4:2 (p. 183) where the Gaon cites this verse and says: "Nor did the All-wise endow man with superiority in these respects for any other reason than that He had made him the bearer of His commandments and prohibitions as the Scripture states."

9. Cf. *Beliefs* 9:3 (p. 332).

10. Cf. *Beliefs* 9:8 (p. 347).

11. Rabbi Hai Gaon, *Responsa*, p. 15, maintains a similar opinion.

sense as it says: "Your Holy Cities have become (*hayu*) desert and Zion too like a desert," (Is. 64:119) "And I will be when you shall become (*wehyoth*) a curse." (Zech. 8:13) Likewise, for us the word *heyoth* may mean "persistence" as it says: "And it was there until this day" (Josh. 4:9) of the stones and: "There shall not be a bereaving [woman] nor a barren one," (Ex. 23:26) and as we have said already regarding: "It is not good for man to remain by himself." (Gen. 2:17)

The word *arum* which I have rendered as "wise" is commonly found particularly in the Book of Proverbs. It says: "The wisdom of the alert will understand," (Prov. 14:8) "Any alert person will make his decisions with knowledge," (Prov. 13:17) "You shall see the alert if he sees evil he conceals from it." (Prov. 27:12)

Now this [has been] the response to the first question.

The second [question] is: How did {the snake} change? The response is: In the manner that the Creator at times changes accidents in bodies when He shall bring about wonders with them so that His creatures believe in Him. This is like God took water and turned it into blood. Now some analysts say [that] He destroyed the water and created blood and then destroyed the blood and created water anew. But were it as they thought it would not say: "And all the water in the Nile turned to blood." (Ex. 7:20) Rather, we say that He lifted all the characteristics of water from the water, [i.e.] its white color, its pleasant smell, and its sweet taste and left [only] its liquidity intact and [then] created the accidents of blood in it: its red color, its stenchy smell, its bad taste to the point of total transformation. This is the correct opinion as we shall contradict their view too regarding the staff of Aaron. They say that God removed the tree and created a living being [instead of it]. He then removed the animal and created the tree. However, the statement: "And the staff turned into a snake" indicates that this opinion is annulled because it annuls the transformation.[12] But we say that God lifted all the accidents of the tree and left the substance intact and put in its place the characteristics of an animal and by this the transformation took place. According to this we say here regarding the snake that the Creator lifted from it the accidents of a snake and put in place of it the accidents of bodies that carry humans for that reason it says here: "became wise" just as it says there: "and it turned to blood" and "and it became a snake." Were one to ask: how [is it that] {the Scripture} calls it a "Snake" after God transformed it? We say

---

12. The Gaon keeps to the literal sense of the words.

that it called it by {the} first name [it had] just as it said at the time that Moses' *tanin* swallowed the staves of the magicians:[13] "And Aaron's staff swallowed their staves," (Ex. 7:12) which was a Sea Monsters[14] because it calls it by the first name [it had].

The third question is: Why did God transform it? As we have already said, this was to test man by it.

Were one to say: Indeed transforming it was wise would man have passed its trial, but since God knew that {man} would not pass [it] but would be tempted so that he and his inciter be punished, what wisdom [then] is there in this? We respond saying: The same wisdom that there is in God creating heretics and giving them the ability for heresy, for had He not have given him the ability for this he would not deny Him. The answers that we all the monotheists respond here regarding the matter is: It is upon a wise person to act [only] according to what his wisdom dictates. [I.e.] that it should direct us to the greatest good if we be tested so that if we pass [the test] we are rewarded. [Therefore] our choice of heresy does not necessitate the ruin of God's wisdom. This is what I respond regarding the incident with Adam. One who thinks himself to be an analyst proffered that God gave the ability of speech [to the snake] so that it arouses [man's] attention to the Healing Tree so that they[15] eat of it for they were not warned of it. Therefore the snake began saying: "Had indeed God said: 'You shall not eat.'" However, this abandons the text. Apart from this we shall not escape from what has been claimed against us[16] which is that [God] gave the snake the ability to tempt Eve?[17]

The fourth question is: Where did the snake come into contact with Eve? For did it, together with the rest of the animals, not enter the Garden?[18] The response to this is according to what I have laid down that Adam and Eve were not obligated to remain in the Garden forever but God permitted them [to be] in it for [their] esteem and He instructed them with the statement "to watch it," i.e., that they should not leave it together but that at all times one of them, either Adam or Eve, should be

---

13. This appears to be a question posed by Hiwya al-Balkhi (Shirman).

14. "Sea Monsters" in plural.

15. Adam and Eve.

16. Apparently the beholder of this opinion, a predecessor of the Gaon, already responded to this question.

17. I.e., how could God do so?

18. The Rabbinic sources, however, maintain that the snake did indeed enter the Garden. See BR 19:3. Cf. Ibn Ezra ad loc. who thought this question invalid.

in it. According to this it is possible that at the time when Eve went out of it and left Adam the snake met her and spoke to her according to what was described.

The fifth question is: On what grounds did Eve say that God said: "You shall not eat from it and you shall not touch it," for God did not say: "And you shall not touch it" to Adam? The response to this is: since God restrained Adam from eating of this tree the man made a guard for what was commanded him by holding himself back even from touching it so that if a stumbling block should come about him it should occur [only] to this addition not to the prohibited essence itself. Like the expert physician when he wants to distance the sick person from meat he warns him of bird meat so that if a stumbling block perchance him it will occur to the bird meat not to the [actual] meat. On the basis of this our Ancients have taught us: "Make a fence for the Torah." (*Fathers* 1:1)[19] As an example of this I say that pure water that was poured into a vessel defiles food that fell on top of it [but does not defile] people. However, we make a guard by saying that it defiles people so that [people] do not purify the food that fell on it. Likewise we do not permit one to sell something that is worth a *sela* for something worth less than the [normal] price so that this does not lead to the cheating of *ribbith*.[20] We rely regarding this and the like on what the Torah prohibited for watching and guarding as it says: "He shall not have too many wives," (Deut. 17:17) and the like.

The sixth is: From where did the snake know that this Tree expands the mind and adds knowledge to say "for God knows." The response to this we say since God said to Adam: "And from the Tree of the Knowledge of Good and Bad you shall not eat of it," it is possible that he explained to Eve that {the tree} adds knowledge and so the rumor left from between the two of them and the snake heard it.[21] Were one to say: Do we not see that {the Scripture} says: "And the woman saw," and that she did not know this [before]? We say [that] this is like a person knowing theft and prostitution but does not pursue them until someone incites him.

The seventh is: What is the meaning of: "And their eyes were opened," and what is stated afterwards: "and the eyes of both of them also?" Were Adam and Eve blind? We say how could Adam be blind when the

---

19. In *San.* and *BR* 19:3 this addition is taken negatively.

20. *Bab. Mez.* 60b.

21. The assumption appears to be that God's communication to Adam was prophetic, not verbal.

Scripture attests that he gave all the living creatures their name and memorized them[22] if it is not possible that he should distinguish between their names he could not distinguish between their bodies? Furthermore, when she was brought to him he saw her and said: "this time" and further God should have shown him the actual tree when He warned him of it. All the conclusions that follow from this regarding man follow regarding Eve as well. Rather we say that this opening of the eyes is a term for a person realizing what he did not before this time. Indeed our language calls this idea *piqebuth*. And there is nothing in this that takes the verse out of its literal sense nor do we enter the opinion which we alienate. For we find this usage in the stories of the Scripture [in] words that are clear where there is no place for allegory[23] like that which it says of Hagar: "And God uncovered her eyes and she saw a well of water," (Gen. 21:19) but she was not blind! And of the disciple of Elisha it says: "And God uncovered the eyes of the blind lad," (II Kings 6:17) and: "For bribery blinds eyes of the wise from the truth." (Ex. 23:8) The meaning is that bribery dims their vision because they do not give heed to the point of proof and there are many [examples] of this. There is [also] opening that comes after dazzling preceding it like that which is said of the army of the king of Aram: "For bribery blinds the vision of the acute,"[24] (Deut. 16:19) and: "And God open their eyes and they saw," (II Kings 6:20) according to what we have mentioned of Adam and Eve realizing after they ate the fruit what they did not realize [before this] and [this] again is called *piqebuth*.

The eighth is: Did Adam and Eve not know good and evil for God says to them: "And you shall be like angels knowing good and bad," (Gen. 3:5) and if this was [indeed] so this matter contains claims [against it] which I shall describe, i.e., what the heretics defiled in length and said: How is it possible that God should hold back the knowledge of good and evil from the servant, and further said: It is the snake that vindicated and did good for them for he taught them something from which they obtained use? They further say: Punishing someone who seeks to flee straight to profit and from darkness to light is something repulsive and strange. They further say that punishing someone who shows someone something useful is even stranger. [Indeed] because of all this they are God's foes. They are

---

22. See ad loc.
23. See IPC section XIV.
24. Some manuscripts have "the wise of the truth." Derenbourgh p. 114, n. 5.

incriminators and are biased.[25] But I am the first to explain and reveal this [matter]. I say: [The knowledge] of good and evil that God described Adam as not knowing is not the knowledge of all good and bad but of some of it. For I find [in] the language of the people of Israel that they use "good and bad" regarding an act. An example of this is Moses' statement to Israel about their sons that had not reached twenty years: "And your children that today do not know good and bad." (Deut. 1:39) It is known that every nineteen-year-old knows all good and evil that a [grown] person knows lacking only [knowledge in] warfare because they do not go out . . . to it under twenty.[26] It follows that tactics of war are called "good" and "evil." And so Barzilai's statement to David: "I am eighty years old today, do I know the difference between good and bad?" (II Sam. 19:36) He knows all good and evil that [grown] people know except that he lacked some pleasures like sexual copulation or the like because of [his] feebleness. Also Laban and Bethuel's statement to Abraham's servant: "We cannot tell you of it neither good nor bad" (Gen. 24:50) is not one that includes all good and evil but is a specific statement regarding whether Rebecca will journey with him or not. Likewise [in] the statement of God may He be Exalted to Laban: "Guard yourself from speaking with Jacob from good to bad," (Gen. 31:24) ["good" and "bad"] is not general but only specific in that kidnapping his child or his wealth and acting righteously with him. Likewise, the wise woman's statement to David: "Like the angel of God so is my master to hear good and bad." (II Sam. 14:17) However, she only meant good and bad that is in the claims of plaintiffs. There are [also] many other kinds of good that do not relate to this discussion but to the interpretation [of the verse] "This travail God has given to the son of man to be exercised thereforth" in the book of Ecclesiastes (1:13). The partial goods and evils like those[27] were lacking in Adam and Eve, one of which was ashamedness of nakedness as it says: "And the eyes of the two of them opened," not emptiness of good and bad.

The ninth [question] is: Would they not have eaten of the fruit would their Creator have informed them of whatever else they lacked [in the knowledge] of good and bad? The response is: It would be inevitable that

---

25. This appears to be a question of Hiwya al-Balkhi (see Shirman, p. 35) originating in the Gnostic idea that God sought to take away knowledge of good and bad because of jealousy.

26. See Num. 1:3.

27. Cf. Ibn Ezra's intro. to Ecl.

He would teach them this so that their knowledge should be complete especially being that man is called "full of wisdom and a vessel of beauty." (Ex. 28:12) They would have had fortune would they have remained in that state for [then] they would be students of their master. When one says to a wise man: You shall be the disciple of a prophet if you refrain from such, he is obligated to refrain from it and how much more so [to be] a disciple of God and not to stumble from errors and be burdened by doubts and not to suffer from forgetfulness . . . as it reached us regarding how He taught Moses His messenger <since he learned directly from God>[28] When he refused to wait for this and was hasty with haughtiness in relation to his Master to obtain what remained for him by means of nature and deprived himself of his reward because of the lack of the engagement[29] in learning, it is [then] just and appropriate that his Master should punish him and his inciter. Were a king to say to [his] officer: Do not eat today until you eat food with me at my table similar to what David says to Mefibosheth.[30] [Then] some people that knew about the king's commandment came and incited the commanded officer to eat before the time the kings eats and he eats and no [longer] has need of the king's food, [then] the intellect necessitates [that he] punish <both him>, and the official cannot save himself by [claiming] any of the things that aroused his desire for food that the inciter told him and mentioned him of its goodness and good taste and usefulness for the king promised him something better, more important, and estimable [in return] than it. However, these boorish heretics attach to the first impressions and do not investigate the matter to the end.

Afterwards it says:

6) And when the woman saw that the tree was good for food and desirable to sight and endowment for the intellect she took of its fruit and ate and gave some of it to her husband also and he ate with her[31] 7) and their eyes opened and they knew that they were naked and he sewed from leaves from which he made for them belts 8) and when they heard the voice of God gently moving from side to side in the Garden

---

28. Cf. *Tem.* 15b and *Zeb.* 101b and 66b.

29. This appears to be in response to Hiwya al-Balkhi (p. 38).

30. See II Sam. 9:10.

31. The Gaon moves the "with her" to the end of the passage, as did Ibn Ezra after him.

like the motion of the day and Adam and his wife hid from in front of God in some of the trees of the Garden <out of embarrassment>³² 9) and God called man and said to him <reproachingly>: "Where are you?" 10) and he said: "I heard Your voice in the Garden and I hid for I was naked"; 11) He said: "Who told you that you are naked, have you eaten of the tree that I have commanded you not to eat from it?" 12) Man said: "The woman that you have made with me, she gave me of it so that I eat it"; 13) and God said to the woman: "What is this that you have done?" She said: "The snake enticed me so I ate it."

I

I translated *leru'ah bayyom* as "[like] the motion [of the day]" because this noun may have [one of] nine [other] meanings in our language: [1] "wind" as it says: "And God's wind hovering" (Gen. 1:2); [2] "side" as it says: "From the side of the east" (Ezek. 42:17); [3] "measuring rule" as it says: "The measure of the west he measured" (Ezek. 42:18); [4] "man's spirit" as it says: "In whose hand is the soul of every living thing and the spirit of the body of every human being" (Job 12:10); [5] "description and structure" as it says: "And the pattern of all that was in the plan with him" (I Chron. 28:12); [6] "council" as it says: "And council dressed Amishai" (I Chron. 12:18); [7] "air" as it says: "And air passes not between them" (Job 41:8); [8] "wrath" as it says: "For you return to the Almighty your anger," (Job 15:13) and "Where shall I go from your wrath?" (Ps. 139:7); [9] "lie" as it says: "Does a man put forth intelligence that is empty" (Job 15:2); [10] "motion" as it says: "For the motion of the beast is in the wheels." (Ezek. 1:20)³³

II

{The Scripture} elaborates how Eve was glorified by the pleasant taste of the tree, its beautiful color, its benefit, and attaining its good . . . it

---

32. As opposed to out of fear. This addition is found in the anonymous translation.

33. See, however, com. to Gen. 1:5. See also *BO* 2:1 (p. 71) where the Gaon speaks of this verse.

wished by this to make it clear to us by which of these things <was she incited> . . . this is because inciting her is prevented for the five senses and the strongest <of the five senses are vision and taste> . . . <and now> . . .

III

In regards to this matter there are three questions. The first is: We know that Adam and Eve knew that they are the first people created, that on Earth there are no intelligent beings other than them. When Eve saw the snake in the form of a man how is it that she did not find this strange, was not uneasy with his words by which he incited [her] to eat [as to] withdraw the question of who and from where he was? The response is: The story implies that man did not see the snake for it says: "That she gave some of it to her husband and he ate," and his, I mean the man's statement: "The woman that you have given with me," makes no mention of the snake. For what reason was the snake not strange in the woman's eyes so that she did not ask about his nature? There is no doubt that she did [just] that but the Scripture did not mention this nor what went on between them in regards to conversations, [i.e.] questions and answers from [contained in] it.

It then elaborates on this and says: "Even if God said." It is not possible that "Even" be the opening of a conversation for this is not the manner of the usage of the language. Rather this word comes as a continuation of something. What is possible is that the {snake} spoke to her of himself as the messenger of the Master of the World or an angel or prophet and for that reason she was turned to him and received his words. He turned to her without Adam [being present] because of the weakness of the woman's nature and because they are quicker to accept to be enticed by empty and misleading things and [also] because women tend to mislead men[34] like with Solomon and Ahab.[35]

The second question is: How was the woman certain that the fruit of this tree is good when she had not [yet] tasted it nor had the snake told her that it was good? And from where did she recognize that it is beneficial that she should believe [the snake's words]? The response is that

---

34. Cf. Maimonides, Yad Hil. Talmudh Torah.
35. I Kings 11:4 and 21:8 respectively.

despite that the Scripture [did not mention]* that the snake said to her that the fruit is good, it is possible that it did so when it described it. Since his intention was that the woman and her husband should eat of it, the first thing that he should have done is to describe [it] as having good taste. It is [also] possible that it cited a proof to this, i.e., how nice its appearance is to which the statement "For it is desirable to sight" alludes [meaning that] it is desirable in appearance. Indeed the desire of Adam and Eve to eat of it preceded this for two reasons: Because of the pleasant appearance and good smell and also because it is man's tendency to desire what is prohibited.[36] Therefore, she judged that it is good for food. But how did she know and determine that it was beneficial for the intellect when she said: "And endowment for the intellect?" This she realized from the name of the tree itself—that it is the Tree of the Knowledge.

The third question is: [How did the woman believe what the snake told her: "You shall not die," after God said: "For on the day you eat of it you shall be deserving death." The response to this is: We have already said in the response to the first question that the snake told the woman what he said only after he announced that he is an angel or a prophet, and God's words to the man: "You shall be deserving of death" were [in fact] by means of an angel and the snake's words: "You shall not die" were said for certain in one of two ways: Either that he wished to say that these words: "You shall surely be deserving of death" were [only] for a particular time and that that time had already transpired or it is possible that he intended to say that this angel added to what [God] said and what proves his claim is: "For God knows." This means that since God knows that this tree shall add to the intellect it is impossible that He should hold it back [from you] and that this angel that said this to you jealously had incited him to do this so that you do not reach a status of importance. His practice was like that of the elderly man that misled God's prophet because he said to him: "I too am a prophet like you," (I Kings 13:18) and the rest of the incident. Now when she heard this, the desire to eat in her brought her to eating and feeding her husband [as well].

IV

"And He said to him: Where are you?" This is not a question, for nothing escapes God Exalted and Magnified as it says: "Shall anything escape Me."

---

36. Cf. "Stolen water, how sweet it is?" (Prov. 9:17)

(Jer. 32:27) It is rather an opportunity for his servant so that his confession be an opening for his repentance when he informs Him that he lacks an answer.[37] There are many similar cases in the Scripture like this. For example: "Where is Abel your brother?" (Gen. 4:9) and many others.[38]

V

<<Now why did God have to ask Adam for him to tell Him about Eve and Eve about the snake? [We say:] So this should be a lesson for us so that we know that God does not the enticed just as he does not do so with the one who entices him. Their punishment was the same along the lines of what it says: "And they shall bear their iniquity, the iniquity of the prophet shall be like of him that seeks." (Ezek. 14.10) Were one to say. If the snake transformed for man's trial then this is a courtesy and no denigration or punishment should come upon him! We say: It was not the intention that {man} should be tested and {the snake} should add and lie, but he lied in his statement: "You shall not die." Furthermore, he is deviant to God in that he sought to annul His statement. For that reason he was obligated in denigration and punishment.>>

[14) **God said to the snake: Since you did this <knowingly> you are cursed from all the animals and all the beasts of the steppe and on your chest you shall crawl and dust you shall eat as long as you live; 15) and hatred I shall make between the woman and your offspring and between her offspring and he will smash you on the head and you shall bite him on the heal; 16) He said to the woman: I shall increase your hardship, with hardship you shall give birth to children and to your husband shall be your obedience[39] and he is the one who has dominion over you as he wishes; 17) and He said to man: Since you hearkened to the voice of your wife and ate of the tree [of] which I have commanded saying: "You shall not eat of it," cursed is the Earth because of you, with toil you shall eat of it as long as you live; 18) and thorns and elm shall sprout for you**

---

37. See the Gaon's trans. and com. to Job 1:6.

38. A question of Hiwya al-Balkhi. See Ibn Ezra ad loc. (Linetsky, p. 84, n. 58).

39. The same rendition is found in the anonymous translation. See Nahmanides ad loc.

and you shall eat the plants of the steppe; 19) with the perspiration of your face you shall eat the food until you return to the ground from which you were taken for you are dust and to dust you shall return.]

I

. . . God made the lioness' pregnancy 350 days, which is seven times greater that that of a cat, which is a kind of [snake]*. God made the snake's pregnancy period seven times more than that of a lioness, reaching seven years.[40] This is not something that came anew [with the snake], rather this was its nature [from the beginning and God returned it to its nature.[41]

II

In this section there are nine questions: The first is: How did God make the snake's crawling on its belly a punishment for it for do not many [other] animals crawl on their bellies and [if] this is a punishment for them too what [then] caused {the punishment} [and if this is not a punishment] then this is not a punishment [for the snake] either? The response to this: We say that this is not a punishment for anyone whose nature is such and was not accustomed once to any other nature [at all]. However, for the snake this was a punishment since it was accustomed not to crawl and then was made a crawler which was then a punishment for him.

The second is: How is it possible that God should make its food dust but do we not see that it eats all that it finds? The response to this is that it eats all that it finds according to its nature but He added to it eating dust[42] in order to lower him by this and to set an example for any inciter and subverter like it as it says: "They have sharpened their tongues like the snake," (Ps. 140:4) and "A snake shall bite without enchantment and a babbler is no better." (Ecl. 10:11)

The third is: How did God make the [snake's] hatred of man a

---

40. See *Bech.* 8a.

41. See *Sanhed.* 29a.

42. So also in a responsum to Hiwya al-Balkhi (p. 37). Cf. *Yoma* 75a which maintains that everything it eats has the taste of dust.

punishment for we see that many are his enemy like wild animals and scorpions? Either these too are a punishment or that [for the snake] this is not a punishment. We say regarding this the same as [we said in] the first response: [Because] for all the animals that are enemies of man by nature this is not a punishment but [because] the snake which [at first] was not man's enemy but was made an enemy for it,[43] this becomes for him a punishment [for him] and were . . . man we would consider this a tragedy.

The fourth is: How did it mention the snake's fighting with man as a punishment; does it not fight with all the other animals? Either [all] the animals are punished like man or that man is punished like them. We say that the snake attacks all animals because of its nature but man he feared and *coped with but* when his fear and dread of him was lifted he began stinging him like he stings the rest of the animals and the punishment is [in this].

The fifth is: How is Eve's pain in pregnancy and birth a punishment for do we not see the females of all the animals suffering this pain? Either all of them are punished or all of them are not? We say to them according to this response that [for] all the females from Eve [and on] <the pain was natural> while Eve was designated to be pregnant and give birth easily but when she sinned [and] was made like all the other animals this was her punishment. I shall give a parable for all these five: Natural impairments are not a punishment, but only ones that come about beyond nature. Moreover, they do not involve any pain at all. Accordingly, one is not called blind if he does not see with the back of his neck nor mute one who does not speak with his ear nor is one who does not hear with his hand deaf for the nature of these limbs is not to see or speak or to hear [respectively]. However, this is said of organs that were created with this function and if something unusual happens to them then this is called a defect. Similarly, [as for] one whose nature is to crawl or give birth in pain this is only a punishment for one whose nature was not so [before] and was made his nature. Further, I speak of a rulership, a king who was angry at his vizier and made him a servant [at first] for this is a punishment for him because he was not a servant [to start with] and became one. But it is not a punishment for one for whom this is customary. These parables suffice for each of the five questions.

The sixth is: Why did the punishment fall upon all the offspring for it

---

43. This appears to be a question of Hiwya al-Balkhi (ibid.).

says: "with the sweat of your face." [We say that for his offspring this was not a punishment]* *for* "with the sweat of your face" *is like* "with pain you shall eat" because he was alone in all labors as I have explained.[44]

The seventh is: How is it that man sins and the earth is cursed for it says: "Cursed is the Earth because of you"? Now boors said that it is crooked that Reuben should sin and Simon should be punished[45] but they do not remember that the Earth is not a body capable of recognition for the curse to give it sorrow nor does it have senses for the plague to make it suffer. The curse applying to the ground is just dryness and drought just as the blessing applying to the ground is abundance and satisfaction for it says: "And He blessed His land of the delight of the Heavens," (Deut. 33:13) and the opposite of this: "Like the scent of a meadow that God blessed," (Gen. 27:27) "When their party was blamed in the land," (Job 24:18) and the like. Just as the blessing of the ground is for the specific benefit of man for it {means} abundance so the cursing of the ground is for the loss specifically for man. According to this explanation it is man who is punished by this statement not the ground.[46]

The eighth is: That He said: "With the sweat of your face you shall eat food," but we see that some or [even] much of {Adam's} offspring eat their food at leisure. The response to this has already preceded and we have already said this [i.e.] that the toil of Adam and the sweat of his face is different than that of his offspring since he had no assistance yet.[47] But we shall expand and say if this would encompass his offspring too then there are two possibilities. The first is that it alludes to the actual sustenance created only by man toiling in it whether the individual worker is the one who eats or someone else — This was not decreed on every individual but on the species.[48] The other is if we were to assume the decree to be on [each] individual the man cannot escape from toil which is his sustenance each person according to his status and even a king as it says: "The profit of the Earth is for all, the king himself is served by the field." (Ecl. 5:9)

The ninth is: Why is it that it does not mention the return I mean the resurrection of the dead? We mention that we have said previously that [this was said] specifically of Adam [and] he was the first to hear that {his} body will turn to dust after death and this was something to give him sorrow and worry him, but the rest of his offspring already encountered

---

44. See *Tosefta Ber.* 7:5 and *Bab.* 58a.
45. This is a question of Hiwya al-Balkhi.
46. This is apparently a question of Hiwya al-Balkhi (p. 36).
47. For him it was toil.
48. I.e., mankind.

this in their maturity and already came to grips with it as it says: "And the dust shall return to the Earth as it was." (Ecl. 12:7) This is not an evil rumor that originated with them.[49] If we consider this to be a general statement referring to all of man's offspring inclusively it would only refer to the span of his life in this world in which he does not cease to ask for life until he dies. When it comes to the statement of "And to dust you shall return," it is not possible that it should mention the life of the other [world] for then it would come to mind that toil and worry exist in the next world as well, but this is not so. On the contrary it is a world of pleasure as it says: "He shall greet them with peace and they shall be settled in their couches," (Is. 57:2) and "And you shall find rest for your soul." (Jer. 6:16)

III

<<"And between your seed and his." We say that the punishment mentioned in this first pericope is: "You shall be deserving of death." The second is: "On your belly you shall crawl." The third is: "And dust you shall eat." The fourth is: "And hate I shall place." The fifth is: "With hardship you shall give birth." The sixth is: "And to your husband is your obedience." The seventh is: "And he shall have dominion over you," and the eighth . . .

. . . As for "You shall surely die," [it means] you shall be deserving destruction before the deadline as we have explained that he should be punished and it is clear.

As for "On your belly you shall crawl" and "And dust you shall eat" and "And hatred I shall place," I have already explained that this statement is not in regards to all the snakes rather that specific one alone for God transformed him to this condition and would return him to his natural [state].

It then says:

20) And he named his wife Eve for she was the mother of all living <[and] speaking>; 21) and God created for the man and his wife body garments and dressed them; 22) then God said: Behold man has become as one from whom [there is] knowledge of good and bad. Now so that

49. The offspring.

he does not extend his hand and take of the Healing Tree, eat and live for eternity; 23) God expelled him from the Garden of Eden to work the ground from which he was taken; 24) and when He expelled the man He set in the East of the Garden angels and flashes of an inverting sword to guard the path of the Healing Tree.

I

I have added "and speaking" in the translation of "the mother of all living" in order that this statement not include in this expression the rest of the animals like the horse and the donkey and the like, something that the senses deny.[50]

II

I translated *eS Hayyim*—as "Healing Tree" for the word *Hayyim* in our language can mean [one of] eight things: [1] "life in this world" as Rebecca says: "Why do I need life," (Gen. 27:46); [2] "living people" as it says: "And living they shall go down to the ground" (Num. 16:30); [3] "rich people" as it says: "What it is for a poor man who knows how to go against rich [ones]" (Ecl. 6:8); [4] "healing" as it says: 'The healing heart is the life of the body" (Prov. 14:30); [5] "reward in the world to come" [as it says]: "See [that] I have placed in front of you today life and the good and death and the bad" (Deut. 30:15); [6] "knowledge" as it says: "Words of the wise is the fount of knowledge" (Prov. 10:11); [7] "return of immediate desire" [as it says]: "And the tree of life is immediate desire" (Prov. 13:12); [8] <<"blessings" as it says>>:[51] "For God commanded there blessing and life

---

50. See IPC section XIV.

51. The Gaon details these definitions in his com. to Lev. 13:10 (Ratsaby, "New Chapters from the commentaries of Rabbi Saadiah Gaon," p. 16) in a slightly different form. A parallel fragment completing this chapter is found in an Antonin manuscript of the St. Petersburg library. See also ch. 2 section III where the Gaon already defined this word.

for eternity." (Ps. 133:3)[52] Likewise, I added "healthy" in my translation of "And he shall live for eternity."[53]

III

I shall [now] return to these verses to explain: "And God made for Adam and his wife." [I Say that it] is not the creation of a garment from nothing[54] for them but that He caused them to know how to make something by which they may cover for themselves the shame of the organs of nudity as well as from the heat and the cold. God showed him linen and wool as two [representative] growths and created [in him] the thought that it is possible to warm himself with them and [the man] tried it and found it to be so. He then thought about wool, camel, and goat's hair and found them [fit for] this [too]. God brought a silkworm to him and the man saw how silk comes out of its mouth and accustomed it for himself. The same applies to clothes and plants, anything from which clothes are made. [By this] He absolved him of the need to cover himself with tree leaves since they are impermanent. Indeed the [Hebrew] language terms "causing" as "doing" as it says: "And I shall make it that you shall go according to my laws," (Ez. 36:27) which is nothing more than causing.

IV

It says "garments of skin" not "garments for the flesh" because the reference is to the upper layer of the body which comes into contact with clothes and this is the skin.[55] Likewise: "The clothes of his body (oro)," (Ex. 22:26) and so: "skin for skin" (Job 2:4) which means "limb for limb."

---

52. Here the Gaon apparently interprets "life" as "blessing." This may reflect a different rendition than ad loc.

53. However, this addition is not found in the translation.

54. As opposed to the Rabbinical view. See *Sifri ShnH* and *Sota* 14a.

55. Ibn Ezra cites this opinion anonymously.

V

It says "skin"[56, 57] [which is] what the senses feel. And so when a person presses his hands against his face the initial pain falls onto the skin and when he scratches there usually is no wound. [Along these lines it says]: "He shall eat the shoots of his skin,"[58] (Job 18:13) [which means] shoots of his body, which are his children,[59] and did not say "the shoots of his flesh" because it is the skin that senses and is the cause of creating seed. Likewise "our skin like a furnace was scorched" (Lam. 5:10) refers to the entire body.

VI

Its addition "And He dressed them" is for various reasons: One is that He turned their attention to sewing shirts,[60] pants, hats, and all other dress as well as to sewing threadless clothes according to their kinds like belts and headdresses and the like. He also told them how to undress at one time and to dress in another so that they do not change. It also includes the knowledge of [how] to cover [with them] in the winter, in the summer, and in the intervening [seasons].

VII

The statement of God may He be blessed: "Behold man has become like one of who of himself [has] knowledge of good and bad" reveals to us the reason for man's expulsion which is: "That he already has become a teacher of himself and does not need [any] more of My teaching." For that reason [God] was forced to expel him. The true meaning of *ke-eHadb mi-mmennu la-da'ath tov wa-ra* is like one who by himself knows the good

---

56. Not "flesh."

57. "Man and does not say" may be a dittography.

58. The Gaon renders "skin" as "flesh."

59. See Job, p. 285, n. 12.

60. I.e., they dressed themselves. Cf. *Sota* 14a, which states that the garments were created.

and the bad.[61] This is something with reason for a wise man would say to his disciple: This amount that you still need to learn, do not learn it from such until I myself teach you it, but he does not comply and goes and learns it from such, he deserves to be punished and expelled. According to reason there is no difference between such and the tree in this aspect. We do not see any of the snake's words to have come true except for the first statement which he did not invent, which is: "And your eyes shall open," for God usurped him in [telling] man [of this] when He said: "But of the Tree of the Knowledge of the Good and the Bad you shall not eat," as I have explained, but the other two ideas that the snake invented, the first being: "You shall not surely be deserving of death," and the other: "And you shall be like angels," the opposite of them happened to the man, [i.e.] he deserved to die and was restrained from the Healing Tree. Moreover, it is not enough that he did not ascend to a [lofty] status but was lowered to the level of animals as the Scripture states about a person who was deprived of honor: "And man with his honor shall not slumber and is compared and likened to the animals," (Ps. 49:13) and when he was deprived of simple medicine God implanted in his intellect [the ability] to compose herbs whose healing [power] is similar to that of that herb. The manner of his punishment in this matter is that if he is unable to obtain ingredients or measure their measurement how much is appropriate or that he will not figure out how to make the medicine properly or that the remnant that is necessary for preparing the medicine a second time he will not be able to do so or that if he will prepare less of the herbs than the necessary quantity or more of them he will perish. When all the conditions are fulfilled there is medicine close to the specific uncomposed medicine [in the Tree of the Knowledge] will be procured and we humans that have never seen that medicine at all, that he lacks is not a punishment for it is like the parable I gave of the council of the king and the servant.

VIII

Were one to ask: If Adam's punishment were he to sin, is to be restrained from the Healing Tree which gives him blessing were he to eat of it—and

---

61. The Gaon follows Onqelos as well as *Mekhilta, Beshalah*, and *BR* 21:5 in this rendition. See Ibn Ezra (Linetsky, p. 91) who opposes this view on the grounds of the division of the cantillations. See IPC section XIV.

it was prohibited to him before the sin as its says "of all the trees" to exclude the Tree of the Knowledge—we see that were he first to have eaten of the Healing Tree and then the Tree of the Knowledge that he would have removed this punishment as God said to him: "Of all the trees of the Garden you are permitted to Eat"? We respond to him that the Scripture did not explain that the Healing Tree has the ability to protect man from God's power and it is impossible to say so [at all] for the function of the Healing Tree was to strengthen his nature against things that could harm him but when {man} rebels against God, He has the ability to take away that power that he obtained from the Healing Tree and {this power} would not be more powerful than the bodies and the essences that annul it.

IX

"And God sent him" is by command just as his entrance into the Garden was by command whether He commanded man Himself or an angel to take them out.[62] The man was closer to the place where he was found.

X

It adds "which he was taken from" to allude that man already worked that ground and toiled in it for some time and tasted toil and rest and afterwards he was returned to his state of [toil] just as the snake reverted to its original state.

XI

There is here yet another question that is one of the thirty questions asked about the pericope of Adam, Eve, and the snake: What is the manner of wisdom in God appointing guards for the Garden so that man does not enter [it]. Why did He not [just] destroy the Garden or make man forget the way to it or divided between them with a river or mountain or the

---

62. Cf. Rabbi Abraham bar Hiyya (*Scroll*, p. 12) who says that man and his wife were accompanied. Cf. also Ibn Ezra ad loc. who opposes this view.

like.[63] The answer is would God stop the man from entering [the Garden] by one of these ways man would reconcile with the situation and would be consoled since there would be no turning against it but when he leaves the Garden in its original state he longs [to return] to it. He gets up and does not stop going until he reaches its entrance and [there] he finds angels that have a sword or burning swords in their hands <<to prevent him>> [from entering], he then returns full of sorrow, lowly and [feeling] expelled. This would have a greater effect on him and he would pay more attention to everything that happened to him <<so he remembers what was commanded upon him>> and will not return to rebel against his Master. Along these lines the Scripture expresses "placing guardians" with the expression "and He set" to add to man's distress when he sees others inhabit his estimable place where he was but has been expelled[64] and is [thereby] prepared for obedience.

XII

How much time did he reside in the Garden? This was not established in the Scripture nor in Tradition[65] and needless to say that it is not possible to reach it by intellect. We do know that he was there many days and serviced and guarded the Garden for some time until the snake became jealous of them and sensed [Eve's] separation from Adam and whatever [else] that falls in this section. Something like this occurs to every person. God brings him into something of a Garden for his goodness and kindness and gives him commands and warning. There are those that mislead him and he sins and is taken out of it.[66] This is similar to what God condemns the king of Tyre and says: "You have been in Eden the garden of God, precious stone was your covering . . . you are the anointed cherub." (Ezek. 28:13–14). The meaning is: You are an anointed person, i.e., honored, to defend your people. It then describes his sin: "By the multitude of your merchandise they have filled your midst with violence; and you have sinned . . . your heart was lifted up because of your

---

63. A question of Hiwya al-Balkhi (p. 38).
64. Others were allowed in the Garden.
65. Cf., however, San. 38b, Pesiq. Rabbi Kahana, BR 18:6, and Fathers of Rabbi Nathan ch. 1, which maintain that he was expelled the day he was created.
66. See Tosefta Sota 4:18, Sanhed. 9b, and Fathers of Rabbi Nathan, ch. 1.

beauty." (Ezek. 28:16–17) Of his punishment [it says:] "And I will cast you as profane out of the Mountain of God; and I will destroy you, O covering cherub from the midst of the stones of fire . . . I will cast you to the ground, I will lay you before kings," (ibid.) and also: "I will bring forth a fire from your midst." (Ezek. 28:18) It splits these verses into two, the reason for which I shall abstain from explaining here. The first half of the verses mentions the sin and the second mentions the punishment. From here we learn that a person repents to his Master Who accepts his repentance for God says to the king of Tyre: "Do you not seal the plan?" (Ezek. 28:12) It alludes by this to man which was the completion of the act of Genesis. It calls him "full of wisdom" (ibid.) and were he not forgiven his wisdom would not be worth anything for it says: "Behold they have rejected the word of the Lord and what wisdom is in them?" (Jer. 8:9) It calls Him "perfect in beauty" and were his repentance not accepted neither their grace or nicety would be worth anything for they have no good fortune except with obedience to God as it says: "Pleasantness is false and grace is deceitful; it is a God-fearing woman that is praisewor-thy." (Prov. 31:30) Were one to think "Do you not seal the plan" is not the question "are you such and such" but an assertion,[67] we shall find for them in this section something that is an inquiry: "You are wiser than Daniel?" (Ezek. 28:3) and it is impossible that this should be an assertion that he is wiser than Daniel. Similarly: "With wisdom you have made . . . and silver in your stores?" where it is impossible that [any] collecting of gold or silver is [with] wisdom for it says: "Do not toil in seeking to become rich; abstain from this thought of yours." (Prov. 23:4) This is like one were to say: Have you done or made this by means of your intelligence in a denigrating manner? Our entire nation has had an experience similar to that of man's story. This is that God Exalted brings us into His Garden which is to single us out and commands us to obey Him at the necessary times, but when we do not do so because of enticers and sends us away from the Holiness and deprives us of the esteem. This is what we say in an allegory within an allegory in the Book of Canticles: "I went down into the garden of walnuts to see the fruits of the valley and to see whether the vine flourished and the pomegranates budded. <But when>[68] I did not know, I made myself like the chariots of a noble people." (6:11–12) The meaning of this verse is that this speaker says: "I descended to the garden

---

67. Apparently because there is no particle of inquiry.
68. The Gaon adds these Arabic words into the flow of the Hebrew text.

to observe it and to examine its grapes, pomegranates, and walnuts. But when I did not know this, I made myself this sin a chariot for a noble people after I was the rider." Similarly the nation says in the explanation of the allegory of the text: "Behold we have been given this Book to observe it and investigate what is in it that we should perform in the designated times, but when we do not know and recognize it we make ourselves, by choosing evil, a chariot for the nations," as it says: "In that I have mounted man on our head." (Ps. 66:12) Now why does it say at first "garden of walnuts" and inserts "grapes, pomegranates," and the rest of the profundities in these verses? I shall explain this in [my] interpretation of the Book of Canticles with God's help. The sanctuary <for us> was like the garden for Adam as it makes a comparison with {a garden}: "And He will make its wilderness like Eden and its desert like a garden." (Is. 61:3) It says that flowing water shall issue from it as it did in the Garden: "And a fount from the house of God shall come out," (Joel 4:18) and that He shall form many rivers [as it says]: "For their God the Exalted is for us in a place of rivers of wide banks," (Is. 33:21) and about the abode: "They have forsaken Me the fountain of moving waters," (Jer. 2:13) and the Torah and the ark were like a Healing Tree as it says: "It is a Tree of Healing[69] for those that cling on to it." (Prov. 3:18)[70] The precepts are in place of the Healing Tree and so all that He warned us against are "God's orders not to be performed" (e.g., Lev. 4:2). False prophets were like a snake similar to his statement "You shall not die," they would say to us: "They say still to them that despite me, the Lord has said you shall have peace and they said to everyone that walks after the imagination of his own heart. No evil shall come upon you," (Jer. 23:17) and the repugnant ones will be pleasant for us like { the snake} was as it says: "I have also seen in the Prophets of Jerusalem a horrible thing; they commit adultery and walk in lies, they also strengthen the hands of evildoers." (Jer. 23:14) Our king and leaders were on the level of Eve which believed in falsity, was incited, and incited man so they denied the truth and believed in falsity and incited us as you know of Ahab that received the false words of Zedikiah the son of Kenaanah and abandoned the true words of Micaiah the son of Yamla and also gave permission to smite and assail him as it says: "And Zedekiah the son of Kenaanah made him horns of iron," (I Kings 22:11) <<and "And Zedekiah the son of Kenaanah came near and

---

69. Ad loc. the Gaon has "of life," but see above com. to verse 22.
70. See *Beliefs* intro.:4 (p. 14) for an explanation of this homily.

smote Micaiah upon the cheek and said: 'Which way went the spirit of the Lord from me to speak to you?'" (II Chron. 18:23)>> It also says: "The Prophets prophesized falsity and the priests bear rule by their means." (Jer. 5:31) Now just as it is said to the incited: What is this you have done, so it is said to our people: "And you have not hearkened to my voice, what is this you have done," (Judg. 2:2) and just as He said firmly to the inciter: For you have done this, [so] He said to the kings: "And the Prophet forbore and said: I know that God has determined to destroy you because you have done this and have not listened to my instruction." (II Chron. 25:16) Just as it mentions man's expulsion with the expression "And He expelled him," so He acted toward anyone who deserved it as it says: "Though Moses and Samuel stood before Me, My mind could not be toward this people. Cast [them] out of my sight and let them go forth," (Jer. 15:1) and "For the doings of their iniquity I shall drive them out of My house." (Hos. 9:15) Since it has ancient wonderful myths and ethics that the later [generations] can learn from the earlier, as well as parables of what happened to an individual and to many as we see from the sin of Adam and Eve, it sets the story at the beginning of the Torah.

Chapter IV

Afterwards it embarks on telling us the history of Noah's offspring until it reaches this statement and introduces into the flow of the text many useful ideas which I shall describe. It says:

1) [[1) And Adam had sexual intercourse with his wife and she became pregnant and gave birth to Cain and said: I have been provided a man from God; 2) then she continued and gave birth to his brother Abel and Abel was a shepherd and Cain was a worker of the ground.]]

I

. . . and it is written of him that he is "the father of tent dwellers and owners of cattle" (Gen. 4:20) in the sense of "father," "first," "founder," "inventor," and "creator," of these occupations. Would it say "acquirers of cattle" it would not be able to say "father" for everyone before him was "a man of cattle" but he was "the head of people of cattle." Rather it mentions "tent dweller" first and attributes [this] construct to him and attaches "cattle" to him. In the Scripture we only know of people described as "dwellers in tents" as scholars and teachers as it says of Jacob: "And Jacob was a simple man dwelling in tents," (Gen. 25:27) and regarding Moses it says: "And Moses would take the tent and pitched it." (Ex. 33:7) The first thing that seekers of knowledge need [to learn] is distinguishing every-

173

thing according to its nature and setting everything according to its level. This is the essence and mainstay of logic. As for Jubal it mentions of him: "Anyone who grasped a violin." (ibid.) This is the art of music which I have rendered as: "composition of melodies." This being that the chords of music are built according to the four natures. Being that what has reached me of the art of music is meager and my knowledge of it is minimal, I shall set forth only its fundaments which are the upper chords that ascend to the highs move similar to the nature of fire, I mean black bile because of its similarity they are parallel to the melodies that ascend to some extent until they remain constant in width like the movement of air and are similar to [the movement of] blood. The chords that descend and do not cease going down to the point that they immerse in the ground move according to the nature of phlegm and bear its features for the way of water is to go down as long as it does not come across a hindrance. Every voice that goes down a corridor when it reaches a particular level it stays and is detained there, it moves according to [the characteristics of] black bile for so is the nature of dust to sink and subside. I shall not count what is produced from the composition of these four kinds.[1] The Scripture presents Tuval-Cain as "the master of anyone to craft copper and iron" (v. 22). This means [that] he sharpens and forges vessels of copper and this is what I have mentioned previously [i.e.] that all important trades fall under this one for it is impossible to make a sheet, hammer, or pincers until one knows what they are for in the forging of vessels. It is also impossible to prepare saws, perforators, or axes until one knows the quality of carpentry and all occupations for which utensils are made, copper and steel even for trade since they too are [used] in scales and weights and the like as it says: "Just as iron can crush everything." (Dan. 2:40) These five trades are described at the beginning of the Torah for there was no trade other than them.

Afterwards it tells us that there are auditory precepts that God commanded after {the man} left the Garden when it says:

3) And when it was after the day, Cain collected of the fruits of the Earth as an offering to God; 4) and Abel also brought of the first born of his cattle and its fats and God accepted Abel and his offspring 5) and Cain and his offering He did not accept and Cain was very angered and his

---

1. See Farmer, "Saadiah Gaon on the Influence of Music," and Simon, "Four Approaches to the Book of Psalms," p.

face fell <from embarrassment>[2] 6) and God said to him: Do not be angry and your face should not fall 7) for is it not that if you do good you will be accepted and if you do not do good, to <your> door your iniquity shall lurk and to you is his obedience and you have dominion over him.

I

The first thing that we should explain here is: What caused the [need to wait the amount of] time of which it says: "And it was at the end of days." We say: If not for the second reason that we shall give, there would be the first and if not for the third then there would be the second and since it is impossible without the third, it embraces the other two. The [first reason is] the time for fruits to sprout as it says: "From the fruit of the ground."[3] The second which is broader than {the first} is until the offspring of animals in the land increase to the extent that the amount they may eat and sacrifice [them] without bringing {the animals} to extinction. As we have explained regarding "And for all the beasts of the steppe all the greens" that God prevented the animals from eating each other's flesh so that no species would go extinct at all for God created only a few individuals but when that time passed God permitted them to eat and sacrifice [them] and the "end of days" comes because of "from the first born of his sheep." The third is [yet] broader than {the other two} [and] is: That is the amount [of time needed] that Cain and Abel will grow up and will reach the height of their maturity and will be fit for bringing sacrifices.[4] The smallest that this amount could be is for thirteen years to pass for the smallest of them. And if He instructed them not to sacrifice within twenty, twenty-five, or thirty years then there would be a greater amount of time. Indeed, I have said "if he commanded them of it" for I do not obligate myself to believe any of the opinions regarding the commandments to the people of the twenty-six generations from Adam to Moses as some people do for they say that all 613 commandments were given to all of them[5] or say that only seven commandments were given to

---

2. As opposed to "because of a loosing spirit." This addition was made by the anonymous translator.

3. Following *BR* 22:7, that he brought it in the Atzereth.

4. See *Niddah* 5:6 and *BR* 63:27.

5. See Zucker, *Translation*, p. 448.

them.[6] Some [even] say over thirty.[7] But I discern three levels in them and say that the commandments that I found were given to them explicitly like the sacrifice, the tithe,[8] Leverite marriage,[9] I would say they had then. Those that I find specified that they did not have them like the Passover, matzah, and the Tabernacle I say they did not have then. Those that I find to be neither like impurity of keri and mixing seeds I say it is possible that they had them and also possible that they did not and I shall not make any decision regarding them. This is the correct opinion! For that reason I said here: if they had the commandment to sacrifice from twenty years or twenty-five or thirty, indecisively. I follow this principle in regards to all the commandments of the early generations. The first thing I found in this [category] is <<the meal offering as told of Cain>> animal sacrifice and the sanctification of the first-born as told about Abel. It is impossible for Cain and Abel to have fulfilled these three commandments out of their own initiative but only by the command of an instructor and law of a legislator, for {306} the intellect does not deem this as instinctive. On the contrary it requires study until acceptance of it manifests. This is because the heretics, may God let us pass their tribulations, claim in connection to these [three] sayings: One who has no need for anything will not command to bring Him fruits, grains, oil, and the like.[10] But we say instead God may He be blessed does not need His creations—they however are not un-needing of Him but depend on His goodness and kindness[11] and therefore He gave them this commandment [i.e.] so that they attain their needs by what He recompenses them as it says: "Honor God from your wealth and from the beginnings of all your produce and your granary will fill with abundance of good." (Prov. 3:9–10) The same applies to the sacrifices that {people} pledge to God [for] God made them the cause for saving man from distress and retribution as it says: "Indeed I have commanded you to sacrifice thanks to God and pay your debts to the All-High for your good in order that if you shall call me on the day of your distress I shall be free because you have honored Me." (Ps. 50:14–15) It also says: "I should enter your house with my burnt offerings

---

6. *San.* 56a.

7. *Hul.* 92a.

8. See Gen. 4:20 and 25:22.

9. See Maimonides, *Guide*, 3:29.

10. This is a question of Hiwya al-Balkhi. Cf. *Beliefs* 3:10 (p. 175).

11. See PC.

and I shall pay my pledges if my lips spoke them and my mouth spoke it if it anguished me." (Ps. 66:14–15)[12] Regarding [the question] of the pain caused the animals by this there are two answers: The first is that slaughtering for them in natural place of death is declared for all animals. Their pain is not greater than that which it is possible that God bring upon people [without sin] and recompenses them good for this as we have explained in the *Book of Proof*.[13] The firstborns precede all other things because of their greatness and extreme importance for us. [Accordingly] He commanded to obey Him with a sincere heart as it says of the firstborn and regarding the first dates to ripen as <that they are beloved> as it says: "Shall I give my first-born [for] my negligence," (Micah 6:7) and also "And there shall be bitterness in him as one who has bitterness for his firstborn," (Zech. 12:10) <as I shall explain>. It says of the first ripe fruits that they are beloved as it says: "Like a fruit that ripened before the summer that were one to see it shall not remain in his hand but he shall quickly swallow it." (Is. 17:7) Because the value of the first of something is great and precious in one's mind and has place in the hearts, God commanded to separate them for Himself so that they should serve Him with the greatest thing that is precious for them.

I translated *wayisha* [in the sense of] "acceptance," for these two letters when they are next to each other may have various meanings in our language: [1] "savior" and "help" as it says: "For He is my savior" (Is. 17:7); [2] "acceptance"—"And God accepted Abel and his offering"; [3] "leaving and abandoning"—"Give over from him that he may survive" (Job 14:6); [4] "directing" and "turning": "Man shall turn to his Creator" (Is. 17:7);[14] [5] "involvement"—"He shall not involve himself in futile matters" (Ex. 5:9);[15] [6] "sending"—"And you brought the stolen and the lame and the sick and you brought an offering shall I accept it from your hands, said God" (Mal. 1:13); [7] and "benevolence"—"And to the niggardly it shall

---

12. See Zucker, *Translation*, p. 126. The Gaon adopts the Mu'tazilite view that the auditory precepts were given only for the sake of reward. See *Beliefs* 3:1 (p. 139): "Reason also deems it proper for a wise man to give employment to an individual who performs a certain function and to pay a wage for it merely to confer a benefit upon him." See Zucker 'Book of attainment of the Precepts,' p. 385.

13. It is not certain which book he refers to. The Gaon adopts the Mu'tazilite doctrine that the animals receive recompense as well.

14. Ad loc. however, he translates: "will lean on."

15. Cf., however, Ibn Ezra ad loc. who cites a different rendition in his name.

not be said benevolent." (Is. 32:5) Now these [meanings] should be chosen according to the context. However *pikud, washu,* and *waqu* (ibid.) are names of places in Babylon like Ketarna, Jedam, and Tura.

II

In this matter three things should be clarified: The first is it possible for us to know for what reason Abel's and not Cain's sacrifice was accepted? We say that the Scripture itself hinted to this already as if it said it explicitly. This is because when it described Abel's sacrifice as the choicest it described Cain's sacrifice as vile and lowly[16] and the Torah is destined to command to bring forth sacrifice and to pledge from the choicest as it says: "And the best of your pledges." (Deut. 12:11) Regarding the Dread Offering it says: "And whatever you contribute to God of all your gifts it shall be the best and choicest of them." (Num. 18:29) It says of charity: "Say that when the weak shall live with him so he shall give the gold of the [mines] also," (Ps. 72:15) which is of the choicest. In the books of the Prophets it says explicitly that one who brings forth of what is not his it is not accepted as it says: "I brought that which is stolen, the lame and the sick you have brought the offering. Shall I desire it from your hand? said God." (Mal. 1:13) Moreover, doing so brings a curse not a blessing as it says: "And cursed is the deceiver that has in his flock a male and vows and sacrifices unto the Lord." (Mal. 1:14) The word *nuchal* in this verse has the sense of cheating theft and swindling as it says: "They are enemies for you because of the assassination (*nichlehem*) they committed in regards to Pe'or." (Deut. 25:18)

The second question is: Even if what caused the acceptance of one of the sacrifices and the rejection of the other is known, what is the reason for the acceptance of one man's prayer and the rejection of the other? For it says: "Abel and his offering" and "and Cain and his offering." I say: This is derived from the intellect and the text supports it. Abel was God-fearing and pure in heart but Cain was the opposite of this. For prayer is accepted from purity [of heart] as it says: "He shall accept all of your offerings and shall command of His sacrifices that He shall burn completely," (Job 11:13)[17] but not from a foul one as it says: "The foul of the heart do put

---

16. See *Responsa* to Hiwya #5 and *BR* 22:3.
17. Cf. *Beliefs* 10:19 (p. 407).

on ire and do not seek help from what has bound that ire upon them?"
(Job 36:13)[18]

The third question is: From where did Abel know that his prayer and
sacrifice were accepted and Cain that his were not? I say: As for the
sacrifice [he knew that it was accepted] when fire poured onto it, burned
{the offering} entirely, and turned it to ash similar to what it says
elsewhere: "He shall receive (*yizkor*) all your offering and shall command
of your sacrifice which should be burnt (*yedashne*)." (Ps. 20:4) The word
yizkor here has the meaning of *azkarathah*[19] which means "fragrance,"[20] and
the word *yedashne* is from *deshen*, (Lev. 6:3) which [means] "ashes."[21] These
two [things][22] are an indication of acceptance. As for the [acceptance of]
prayer, if each one asked that God give him a particular thing, it would be
clear that He fulfilled one and rejected the other. If the requests were
about atonement for impurity and similar things that are not visible to the
senses then this would be required to be revealed to them through the
prophet; either he revealed the two things to Adam,[23] or he showed it to
them in a dream free of natural cause as it says: "In a dream or vision of
the night in the time when slumber falls upon men and they sleep upon
their heads and then He changes men and seals their bond by His
command." (Job 33:15)

III

"And Cain was angered"—inside.

IV

"And his face fell" is in the outer side of his body. This is to his praise, not
to his denigration: For one who does not fulfill what he is obligated,
grievous and is stirred results and comes upon him and he regrets his acts,

---

18. Cf. *Beliefs* 10:7 (p. 376).

19. E.g., Lev. 2:2.

20. I.e., He shall smell them. The Gaon renders this idea anthropomorphi-
cally as "remembering."

21. See com. ad loc.

22. I.e., the offering being fragrant and fully consumed.

23. Who was a prophet.

he is more praiseworthy than one whom reprimanding does not stir nor grieve him. It is probable that "and Cain was angered" [means that] {Cain} wished that he should be ill or grievous rather than his sacrifice be rejected and would it have added ["much"] and said "and Cain was angered much" we would say that he asked to die rather than deserving what becomes him as it says of Jonah: "I have been angered to death." (Jon. 4:9) The word "much" (me'odh) is close perhaps to the word hetev and the meaning of "and his face fell" [is as if] he was embarrassed to lift his face to the sky as Ezra says: "My God I am ashamed and abashed to lift, My God, my face to you." (Ezra 9:6) When Adam or Eve saw him they discerned on his face signs of sorrow[24] as was said to Nehemiah: "Why is your countenance sad and you are not sick, this is nothing else but sorrow of heart."

V

We should explain the purpose of God's reproach of Cain when it says: "Why are you angered and why has your face fallen?" and particularly after we have already said that this scowling and his embarrassment are to his praise. We say that the meaning of this matter is that despite that Cain felt the scowling come upon him because of this inadequacy of [his] meal offering [as not being] from the choicest and despite that this is to his praise it would be better and more appropriate for him to improve it and bring forth its fat and [then he] would not need to be embarrassed. [For that reason] God said to him: "Why are you angry?—would you improve you would then be accepted." The improvement may be attained by means of six things: [1] in the kinds of fruits; [2] the quality of their meat;[25] [3] the containers that carry in them;[26] and [4] the place, [5] the time,[27] and [6] the intention of the one who brings forth. It is possible that for that reason it added a waw in the word halo similar to what God says to Cain that improvement is better than grief, He tells us that abandoning sin is better than a sacrifice. Along these lines Samuel says: "Does God delight in burnt offerings and sacrifices as in obeying the voice

24. Conjecture.
25. *Bik.* 1:3.
26. *Bik.* 3:8.
27. *Bik.* 1:6.

of the Lord, to obey is better than to sacrifice," (I Sam. 15:22) meaning that obedience is better than sacrifice. He says that despite that both of them qualify as service of God the first is preferable, just as [some] sins are more severe than others for it succeeds this with the statement: "For rebellion is as the sin of witchcraft and iniquity and idolatry is more severe," (I Sam. 15:23) [i.e.] for witchcraft and sorcery are just sins of misdemeanor but idol worship is more severe and greater. The word *haftzer* indicates "fortifying" and "perpetuation" and just as a sin can be harsher than another so obedience can be greater than another's. It is possible that these two verses, I mean: "Why are you angry" and "If you do not improve," were revealed to Adam[28] for the sake of Cain and it is possible that they were revealed to Cain himself but Cain himself is still not a prophet[29] for so we find Abimelech and Laban that God spoke things[30] to them but they are not among the prophets for this was only reprimanding and threat.

VI

It said *hatath RoveS* and not *RoveSeth* for this is one of the seven [cases] in the Scripture that are both masculine and feminine: [1] *Hatat Rovetzeth*, [2] *Metharaw wi-thedhotheha* (Ex. 39:9), [3] *nas wenimlatah* (Jer. 48:19), [4] *we-dhalyothaw shileHah* (Ezek. 17:7), [5] *yesodho we-nafela* (Ezek. 13:14), [6] *temes yahaloch* (Ps. 58:9), and [7] *be-lo yomam temale* (Job 15:32)[31] In some cases the first follows the second and in others the second follows the first [each] according to the subject. It is more correct is to adjust the first to the second and to say *awon roveS* or *HeT roveS*[32] for the verse ends in the masculine: "And to him is your obedience and you shall have dominion over him."[33]

---

28. As did the Muslims the Gaon followed by Ibn Ezra (5:29, Linetsky, p. 13, n. 15) for example maintain that Adam was a prophet.

29. In *Lev. R.* 1:13 they are, however, considered prophets.

30. According to the *Chapters of Rabbi Eliezer* 36 and *BR* 31:24, the angel Michael spoke to them.

31. See *Criticisms*, p. 98.

32. Ibn Ezra ad loc. cites this opinion anonymously.

33. Cf. Onqelos.

VII

<<It adds "his brother" to indicate that he pleaded, beseeched, and asked him for compassion but he gave him no heed [to him at all] as it shall say: "We are guilty in respect to our brother for we have seen his soul in distress and his pleading with us." (Gen. 42:21)>>

VIII

The Wise One joined three exalted ideas in Cain's reproach to benefit His worshippers with its knowledge. The first [idea] is in reference to the day that man shall stand for recompense for it says: "At your opening iniquity couches," for in this world there are two openings: one for entering and the other exiting. This is indicated in many places by the word "there" like what He says to Job: "And naked I shall return there," (Job 1:21)[34] Elisha's statement: "So they shall scream there . . . and He shall not answer them," (Job 35:12)[35] Ecclesiastes: "When they are in total fear there," (Ecl. 3:17) as we shall explain in the pericope of behuqqothai (Lev. 26:3). The second is one of choice and dominion which is [expressed in]: "And to you is his obedience," similar to what He says to Eve: "And to your husband is your obedience," (Gen. 3:16) just as man was created with the ability to draw his wife to what he desires so He gave all humans [the ability] to direct their thoughts to the good or to the bad and for that reason it says: "See I have placed in front of you today life and the good, death and the bad." (Deut. 30:15) Were one to think that there are verses that tend to heresy I shall mention this in the pericope of "For I have hardened" and shall speak of these verses to my ability.[36]

The third idea is that of repentance to which it alludes with the statement: "And you shall have dominion over him" [and] "And to you is his obedience," [which] refers to the beginning.[37] "And you shall have dominion over him" refers to correction occurring after the sin which is by means of repentance. It has four parts: renunciation, remorse, admission, and acceptance not to relapse [into] sin. We shall explain this well in

---

34. The Gaon translates it as "grave" (Job ad loc., Goodman, p. 171, n. 58).
35. Cf. *Beliefs* 9:4 (p. 332).
36. See *Beliefs* 4:6 (p. 198).
37. I.e., before the sin.

various places in the Pentateuch and books of the prophets.[38] I shall mention its principles in the pericope succeeding this; and they are: [1] Why was Cain punished after this incident and Abel tortured despite his righteousness and how was he punished for his negligence, [2] what act of repentance did he do, [3] what became of him, [4] what did this obedience benefit him? These five things are embraced in the next pericope for it states:

8) Then Cain conversed with Abel his brother and when he was in the steppe Cain got up to Abel his brother and killed him; 9) God said to him <reproachingly>: Where is Abel your brother? He said: I don't know, am I my brother's guardian? 10) He said: What is this you have done? The voice of your brother's blood is screaming to Me from the ground, 11) and now you are cursed because of the ground/more cursed than the ground which opened its mouth and accepted the blood of your brother in front of you; 12) in that you shall work it, it shall not return what you give it its power, moving and wandering you shall be in it; 13) and Cain said in front of God: My sin is too great to be atoned for, 14) and if you do not expel me today from the face of the earth shall I conceal from in front of you and if I become moving and wandering anyone who finds me will kill me; 15) God said to him: Therefore anyone who kills Cain shall be avenged many times and God made for Cain a sign so that anyone who finds him shall not kill him.

I

I translated "and he spoke" as "conversed" for if this were just speech there would be a need to elucidate [what was said] but this is something that is not found. However, conversation, i.e., dispute,[39] does not need explanation of this kind.[40] Similar to this is the statement: "On this day shall say the officers of Persia and Media," (Est. 1:18) i.e., that the wives of the

---

38. See *Beliefs* 4:5 (p. 220) and *Book of Praises* (p. 255) and *Book of Precepts of Rabbi Hefez ben Yazliah* (p. 35). However, Rabbi Samuel ben Hophni (com. to Deut.) criticizes their view.

39. This is the Rabbinic interpretation. See *BR* 22:7. This word is added as a gloss in the anonymous translation.

40. See Zucker, *Translation*, p. 99 and p. 105, n. 417.

officers will argue with the officers. Similar is also: "And I shall bring you to trial . . . just as I was brought to trial with your fathers." (Ezek. 20:36) Argument is between two [people] as it says by means of parable: "Judge between me and my vineyard." (Is. 5:3) Similar is also: *Asher nishbarti eth libbam* (Ezek. 6:9). [*Nishbarti* means] I have been defeated and triumph obtains between two as it says: "Whose words from me or them shall stand mine or theirs?" (Jer. 44:28)

II

The first information in this section is Cain's killing of Abel for it says: "And he killed him." It does not mention "And it was when they were in the field," for he did so when they were concealed from Adam so that he does not save him <<or when the equipment for work will be given to them so that he kill him with it>> or so that he may bury him in a place about which Adam does not know or so that he can feed him to the animals or birds. It adds: "And he attacked him," [which] implies deliberation as it will [later] say: "And he lies in ambush and attacks him until he kills him." (Deut. 19:11)

III

It has been asked elsewhere how did Cain know how to kill?[41] We say by learning from Adam for the needs of commandments or medicine or accidentally.[42] He also asked: Why did the Wise the Able not prevent Cain from killing Abel and would [thereby] do good for the one by keeping him alive and the other by sparing him of sin. They added [further] that this is the result of the desirable sacrifice being accepted. For because of it there was jealousy that lead to killing him and was not saved.[43] We respond to everything saying that Abel's death as well as that of all those who are wronged and especially of prophets would not be regarded as a great deal, would the Creator have just created this world and would not have the ability to bring the dead to life, then every dead

---

41. Cf. *San.* 37b.
42. See *BR* ch. 22.
43. A question of Hiwya (Davidson, p. 40). See *Tanhuma* to Gen. 19.

person would be [permanently] destroyed, his existence expiring forever. [In this case] every evil person would succeed in his evil act before his death and would be freed from punishment for his act. However, since the Creator required that the world should be created with designation for the recompense of the cheated [person] and the punishment of the evil the two worlds were made like two juxtaposed days, the second completing what the first day lacked. [Thus] one who did a wicked act should not rejoice on the first day for he is destined to be punished for it on the second day according to what he deserves. [Likewise] a cheated person should not be grieved on the first day for he is destined to be recompensed on the morrow according to what he shall merit. The only difference is in order. For this reason the deceiver should not take the head of the deceived because on the second day God is required to recompense them and if they die God shall return them as we shall explain [the matter] of reward and punishment in the world to come as I have explained in the pericope of *behuqqothai* (Lev. 26:3) as well as in the section of "I am that is by myself and there is no God with Me" (Deut. 32:29) and as we have explained this in the *Book of Beliefs*[44] the matters of the day of recompense and the day of resurrection. It has become clear that people only lose hope because of the evil that evil people do to the righteous in this world because of the weakness of their belief in the world to come.

The second information is the reproach and is what God said to him—"Where is Abel your brother?" This statement is from God to awaken [him to] admission as we have mentioned in connection to the seventeen questions that are similar to each other[45] and for that reason I have added "reproachingly" in [the translation of] the verse. Would he have admitted and repented to God, He would have forgiven him but he denied and said: "I don't know." He in addition was determined to deceive the angel that his Master sent to him in order to awaken him to admission and said: "Am I his guardian?" as if to turn [God] onto some beast that ate him or perhaps he drowned or was burned or that something similar to this happened to him. By this he added to his punishment similar to his saying: "I don't know," God says: "I shall judge you for saying I did not sin," (Jer. 2:35) and like. . . . would people immerse in this the matter it would be clear for them but they departed from this to the point that they said would it be possible to ask the animals and the birds and that

44. See treatise 9.
45. See his com. to Job 1:7 where he lists all of them.

they would speak a word they would say so,[46] so it says here: "The voice of the blood of your brother is screaming to me from the ground," according to the allegory practiced in the language—since Abel's murder is an overt wrongdoing it would be expected that his blood should yell, scream, and call for help. Likewise, it says: "If my hand had cried out against me and all the folk of its furious have wept," (Job 31:38) and as it says metaphorically that the sin attests in front of the one who was sinned against as it says: "He presses me as thought he were a witness against me and opposed me for making denial testifying to my face," (Job 17:8) and "Though our iniquities testify against us," (Jer. 14:7) and "And our iniquities have attested to us." (Is. 59:12)

It says "bloods" instead of "blood" as is customary in the language [like] *Elodhim* instead of *Elo'ah*, *adhonenu* instead of *adhon*, *bene* instead of *ben*, [and] *pene* which is singular. So *deme* is singular like *dam*. Some[47] refer this to the destruction of seed that would be able to have come out of him.

It adds "to me" in the statement meaning that this is not concealed from Me for all that is hidden is revealed to Me. As it says: "The people that always anger Me in My presence." (Is. 65:3 and Jer. 6:7)

It adds "from the ground" because of what it says afterwards that there are three types of punishment that will befall him in connection with the ground. For that reason it mentions "from the ground" to associate the punishment with it.

The third notification is the punishments. The first of them is his curse as it says: "Now you are cursed." It means by "now" as long as you are in this state.[48] The beginning of the curse is the fineness of the ground as we have explained in the incident with Adam for God says to him: "The ground is cursed because of you." (Gen. 3:17) Just as the beginning of the blessing [of the ground] is fertility as it says: "And he said to Joseph: God He has blessed His land," (Deut. 33:13) and afterwards a blessing for man is happiness and the curse sorrow. Blessing is honor and the curse is shame; the blessing is life in both worlds and the curse is barrenness as it says: "So His blessers will inherit the land and his cursers will be cut off it." (Ps. 37:22)[49] It is also possible that *min ha-Adamah* [means] "more than

---

46. See his com. to Job 12:7.
47. See Onqelos.
48. Of unrepentance.
49. These lines are rather difficult to render.

the ground." This is because the cursing of the Earth is in one thing and the cursing of man is in many, as we have explained.

IV

That it added "which opened" is not the action of the Earth especially since the absorbency of the blood is not considered a sin for it too absorbs it by nature and it has no choice. Rather the intended act refers to Cain as if it said: "The Earth that you have enriched with the blood of your brother shall be desolate for you," and the true meaning is: "which you have made open its mouth," and from what it says at the close of the verse, "to take the blood of your brother," it appears that he killed [him] with a sword or with blood spilling.[50]

V

"You shall work the ground" is an explanation of "You are cursed of the ground" in that he shall work it and it shall not produce anything. Do you not see that God judged as he judges those who were negligent in watching people that caused the spilling of innocent blood for it says: "He shall not work nor sow," (Deut. 21:4) and were that river deprived [of fruits] by nature and if not the Law having prevented him by warning.[51] Now we shall explain what the crime of the elders of the city close to the corpse is it in its place God willing. Of Cain's punishment is: "mourning and wandering." The meaning of both {these words} is that he will not settle permanently in one place and will not find tranquility. But the specific meaning of na' is that he will move little by little as it says: "The heart of the king and the heart of his people waves like the waving of the trees of the forest because of the wind." (Is. 7:2) And in Daniel's words: "And straightened me on my knees and soles." (Dan. 10:10) The specific meaning of nad is uprootment from place to place as it says: "And I shall not continue to pull out Israel's feet from the grove." (II Kings 21:8) These two things together will cause him fear of frost, hunger, thirst, danger of wild beasts, snakes and the like. This is because when man settles in a

50. See BR 22:5.
51. See Mishnah Sota 9 and Talmud 45b.

particular place he builds buildings, something to protect himself from heat and frost, and fortifies himself by something that will protect him from animals and people of bad conduct, he sows and plants and channels water and makes use of any necessity. But when he transfers from place to place it is not possible to prepare his everyday needs at any place and so his needs are not provided and straits come instead of them. Do you not see how these things came upon our fathers in the desert as it says: "The one who made you travel in the great frightening wilderness." (Deut. 8:15)

The fourth information is repentance about which it says afterwards: "And Cain said: My sin is too great to be atoned for." He refers with these three words to three fundaments of repentance. They are four and <<as we have explained:>> Cain alludes to regret when he says: "great," [i.e.] that his regret is great.

"My sin" alludes that he shall not revert to sin again as if he meant: I shall not commit a sin like it.

"From being atoned" alludes to asking for forgiveness for "carrying" is one of those words indicating forgiveness.[52] As for accepting that he should not repeat the sin there was no need to allude to it for it is possible to kill a man only once.

It dilates "For You have expelled me today" in order to arouse pity. This is a manner of [asking] favor and compassion in front of his Master so indeed I have sinned and even though You have declared to kill me for a sinner shall not live in front of You know that I shall not flee from in front of You and even if my limbs were dispersed in the dust for you do not destroy righteous or wicked people rather you disperse parts [of] their [bodies] in dust and afterwards return them [to existence] and no matter how it would be put together or dispersed I cannot depart from Your presence therefore pity me and return to me.

Indeed we find among various [people] that asked for pity from their Master each one's [plea of] desirability is different than the others. One said: "And You forbid, to do like this thing to finish off the righteous with the wicked," (Gen. 18:25) and another: "As the Egyptian shall hear this that you have brought up the nation from among them with your power," (Num. 14:13) another: "And Moses said to God the Egyptians shall hear that you have taken this nation from in front of them with your might," (Deut. 14:13) and yet another: "And what shall you do to your great,"

---

52. Cf. *San.* 101b and *BR* 22:4.

(Josh. 7:9) yet another: "Behold we are here before you in our trespass for we cannot stand before You because of this," (Ezra 9:15) another: "saying what is the use in killing me and me going down to destruction." (Ps. 30:10)

What is the manner of wisdom in the words of the creatures having effect on the Creator settling His anger lifting his punishment? We say it is not that accidents have effect [on Him] nor can He be convinced into anger nor desirability but what is intended with the fine words of the created is being their complete sincerity. This is because one may say "pity me" and "forgive me" regularly and habitually without sincerity but when he takes upon himself to go in the way of appeasement and prayer he collects his delicate thoughts and the purity of his intention to find expression for them. Therefore, the refined and delicate response results in the calmness of temper because of the purity of intention[53] and anyone who reaches the purity of his intended devises something [in his prayer]: Abraham devise that one should not say that he shall not destroy the righteous with the wicked. Moses devised the idea that the nations should not say that because He is not able to keep what He promised them He made pretenses to destroy them[54] and David opened: "If You destroy me because of my iniquity what is the use in this. Moreover, there will be advantage and wisdom there is no use in this but if you erase my sin it will be useful and wise."[55] Ezra devised the idea: "Behold we are in front of you, do with us as you wish," (Ezra 9:15) as we have explained. Likewise many people of the past have stood before their Master devising words of delight to beseech God with them not because they affect Him but because they effect them and anyone who increases in devising ideas and [ways of] awakening with beseeching is praiseworthy. For this reason Cain devised these words: "O my Master I shall not perish if you destroy me nor shall the grave or the like conceal [me] from You. <<This being so>> retain me and keep me alive." Cain succeeded this with another kind of beseeching and said "I shall be moving and wandering and anyone who finds me will kill me." His intention, as we have mentioned previously,[56] is that one who moves about from place to place and travels fears predatory animals and the other living creatures more than one who

---

53. See *Beliefs* 5:6 (p. 224).
54. Deut. 14:17.
55. Possibly the reference is to Is. 51. See also *Beliefs* 4:5 (p. 192). (Zucker)
56. See com. to verse 8, section V.

remains in one place for one who remains in one place designs something to protect him from the evil of ill will.

The fifth information is the use Cain had from his repentance. This is what God told him: "Therefore anyone who kills Cain," and being that killing of people may be by one of two ways: either people like him kill him or predatory animals that tear him, Cain needed that his Master give him protection from both types, [God] gave him protection from both of them, of the evil of man by warning and intimidation and said that "Anyone who kills Cain shall be avenged many times."

VI

The meaning of *shiv'athayim* is "much"[57] as I am accustomed to render according to the norms of the language. He made as protection from the evil of the predatory animals in the land by creating for [Cain something] that will be a divider between him and them.

VII

It says: "And He made for Cain a sign so that one who finds him does not kill him" refers to the animals that God is able to restrain from acts just as He restrained the lions from Daniel and the snakes from our forefathers.[58] God restrained them from Cain by means of a sign. As for people, over whose actions God has no control however, He prevented them from [killing] Cain by means of warning and punishment. For that reason the statement *shiv'athayim yuqqam* refers specifically to people and "all that finds him" refers to the animals. Regarding these two things I shall speak in the section of "As for your blood from yourselves." (Gen. 9:5)

When we observe Cain's words we find that he only complained about "anyone who finds me" and God responds to him: "anyone who kills Cain" before He says: "anyone who finds me." It is most probable that Cain usurped and asked for protection from the animals that existed then [and] God responded to him about animals that [already] were in existence and from people that were destined to be born that may arise upon him will

---

57. So also renders the anonymous translation.
58. He restrained them with a sign.

kill him. These signs that God made for Cain repentance was the cause of it and therefore he began at the beginning of the section with "therefore."

People have already asked: What was this sign that God made for him? [We respond that: it is possible that]* God placed a sign in his body that was . . . the statement: "if he exits the limits" (Num. 35:26)[59] and if he does not leave the confines he shall not be killed. We have already explained that he sought protection . . . of predatory animals. We shall investigate do we find a sign . . . something in explicit in it. We say that this is like God said in the Laws.

Afterwards it says:

16) and Cain went out from in front of God and settled in the land of wandering east of Eden; 17) then he had sexual relations with his wife and she became pregnant and gave birth for him to Enoch and he built a city and called it in the name of Enoch his son; 18) and to Enoch was born Eirad and Eirad begot Mehuyael and Mehuyael begot Methuselah and Methuselah begot Lemech; 19) and he married two wives; one was 'Adha and the other Tzillah; 20) and 'Adha gave birth to Yavel which is first to dwell in tents and owner of cattle; 21) and the name of his brother was Yuval who was the master of anyone who grasped the *tunbur*[60] and lyre; 22) and Tzillah also bore Tuval-Cain who was the master of anyone to craft copper and iron and he had a sister whose name was Naamah 23) and Lemech said to his wives: Lo 'Adha and Tzillah hear my voice, wives of Lemech and hearken unto my words. Behold if I killed a man by my splitting or a child by my wounding and if Cain be avenged many times, Lemech how much more so?

I

Each one of these verses contains various types of benefits and teachings that we are in need of. The first, "And Cain went out from in front of God," teaches that they had a place where the light of the abode appears and there God communicates with a prophet or [with someone] needed to receive reproach or arousal to repentance. Anyone who enters this

---

59. Possibly God confined him to a certain area.
60. An instrument resembling the mandolin.

place it is said [of him that]: "He came in front of God"[61] and vice versa one who leaves there it is said of him: and he leaves from in front of God,[62] as is said of the Mishkan and it is necessary that this sign of assurance that God gave Cain with the statement "Anyone who kills Cain many times shall be avenged" had spread to the people who were born afterwards so that they recognize him and restrain from killing him for it would be insufficient that it be spread by Cain alone for he is the litigant.

II

The land of Nod (wandering) was in the east of the Garden. It is most probable that the place of speech was close to the Garden and when he went out of it he settled in the closest place [to it].

III

It is possible that because the wife of the first to get married, I mean Cain, was his sister and it says [then]: "And Cain had sexual relations with his wife," which is his sister,[63] [that] from here the metaphor that a man calls his wife a "sister" is obtained and this was permitted not only to Abraham,[64] Isaac,[65] and the like that were in danger but also in times that were not of danger. We find in the Chronicles that it says "his sister" instead of "his wife," i.e., the statement: "And Machir took a woman le-Hafim and le-Shafim and the name of his sister is Ma'achah and name of the second (*sheni*) is Tzelaphahadh and Tzelaphahadh had daughters," (I Chron. 7:14) "and his head sister bore Ishhod, Eliezer, and Mahalah." (I Chron. 7:18) This section is of the most cryptic and difficult in the Chronicles but if we assume that it contains five of the forms of metaphor of our language it will become clarified and uncovered. The first is the statement: "And Machir took a wife" is instead of "And Machir took wives" like it says: "For a woman was destroyed from Benjamin," (Jud. 21:16)

---

61. E.g., Ex. 34:34.
62. In his com. to Lev. 17:13 the Gaon gives the other meaning of being in front of God.
63. See also Ibn Ezra 5:29 (Linetsky, p. 115).
64. See Gen. 12:13.
65. Gen. 26:7.

which means "women." The second is le-Hafim and le-Shafim mean mi-Hafim and mi-Shafim as we said previously that the *lamed* comes instead of a *mem*[66] as it says: *ha-ba'im le-Milhamah* (Num. 31:21) and *la-bama asher be-Give'on* (II Chron. 1:13). The third is that "the name of his sister" means "the name of his wife" or a name that they invented having the sense of a female relative. The fourth is that "the name of the second (*sheni*)" is like *sheniyyah*[67] similar to what it says: *le-Hatzer ha-Penimi* (Ez. 40:27) instead of *ha-Penimith*. The fifth is that name Tzelaphahadh exists among woman just as men {3} just as we find among men a woman named Aviha. When these five [ideas] meet the explanation yielded is that Machir married two women from Hafim and Shafim [respectively] the children of Benjamin the name of one being Ma'acha and the other Zelaphahadh which had borne for him daughters and his head wife bore Ishhod, Eliezer and Mahalah.[68] In the Chronicles there are many dubious and cryptic words similar to these [but] there is no place to bring more than we have.

IV

Afterwards it begins to mention the names common to people and places, and brought the name Enoch which may be one of six kinds, names of a man, Enoch the son of Cain,[69] Enoch the son of Jered,[70] the son of Median,[71] and the son of Reuben.[72] The fifth is a name of a city,[73] and the sixth is a verb: "Educate (*hanoch*) the child according to the ability of his age." (Prov. 22:6) Afterwards it mentions the people of the city that was built in the land and as I shall explain in the incident of the Tower the purpose in collecting many people in one city or village. I say if Cain was the one who built the city why did he name it after Enoch his son and not after his own name. We respond: Because Cain was moving and wandering and did not settle in any city and since it was unworthy to call it by his own name he transferred to his son's name.

---

66. See IPC.
67. And that Tzelaphahadh is a female.
68. Ibn Janah (*Riqmah* p. 55) adopted this interpretation.
69. Gen. 4:17.
70. Gen. 5:8.
71. Gen. 25:6.
72. Gen. 46:9.
73. Gen. 4:16.

V

What purpose is there in {the Scripture} recording Cain's lineage for seven
generations: him, Enoch, Eirad, Mehuyael, Methuselah, Lemech, and his
children, I mean: Yavel, Yuval, and Tuval? We find four reasons for this.
The first and most important is [that it waits] until it reaches the
formation of the primal professions as we have already explained in the
first part of the section. The second is [that] it lets us know that Cain's
offspring feared that they will grasp their grandfather's sin until the
seventh generation as we have heard Lemech say. The third is [that it
waits] until it reaches the first to marry two women for it says: "And
Lemech took for himself two wives," as we have previously explained in
the interpretation of the pericope of "Let us make man" (Gen. 1:26) that
the intellect opposes [the marriage of] one woman to two men but does
not oppose [that of] two women to one man. The fourth is until it tells us
the amount of the definition of fruitfulness and multiplication as it was at
early times. It determined that it is two sons or a son and a daughter and
if a man or woman had this many they fulfilled the commandment of
fruitfulness and multiplication.[74] For 'Adha had two sons, Yavel and Yuval,
and Tzillah a daughter and a son: Tuval and Naamah. For this reason it
expands and says: "And Tuval-Cain's sister was Naamah" as we have in the
Law: "two males or a male and female." (Yeb. 6:6) However, this statement
[only applies] to that time because of the lengthiness of life but now
either a male or a female [suffices][75] and if [one of them] dies it is upon
him that he be replaced.[76] If they were born to him while he was a heretic
and repented he is not obligated to replace [them], and how much more
so if they were born when he was a believer and converted.

VI

That it adds "he too" in the statement regarding Tzillah withstands two
meanings: Either that she gave birth after being barren and awaiting
[birth] or to equate two males and a male and a female in fulfilling the
laws of propagation.

---

74. See Rabbi Mubashshir Gaon (*Criticisms*, p. 28).
75. See *Yeb.* 64b. See, however, *Criticisms*, p. 81.
76. Following Rabbi Johanan in *Jeb.* 62a.

VII

The use in stating "and Lemech said to his wives . . . for many times" is one of two estimable ones: Either that what he said is that he felt pain for his sin that was brought about by him, or relinquishing sin that came before him, in both [cases] there is fear of God and the state of . . . from the votary[77] . . . according to the first interpretation . . . affirmatively that he killed a man in truth and this awaits a punishment.[78]

VIII

It adds the statement "and a child by wounding" to add to his punishment for were one to think that the man that Lemech killed deserves death because it is possible that an adult sin but he killed a child which cannot sin. "For many times" fits this idea that one would say: Were Cain avenged for it despite that he killed his brother, Lemech who killed a man and a child certainly will be avenged.

Were we to follow the text according to our second thinking the statement, "For I have killed a man" would be a negation with the omission of the letter *he* as you would say: "Do you think that I bid you to give me some thing," (Job 6:22) and "Is there remaining of the house of Saul." (II Sam 9:1) So here it is a negation with the *he* implied and "For I have killed" means that he killed neither a man nor a child whose value in body and soul and in [the most probable possibility]* . . . his statement: "For may times Cain shall be avenged" is according to this idea . . . if Cain was the one who killed his brother, his Master trusted him that he will not kill [him] again and certainly Lemech who killed neither a man nor a child, one who kills him shall be avenged.

The fifth is that [of] both [those who received what they deserved for]* obedience and [those] awaiting punishment. Moses says: "Admit your sins when their punishment comes upon you." (Num. 32:23) Of who is undeserving of punishment it says: "Then you will raise your face from your faults, and though you were straight you shall not fear." (Job 11:15) It also includes all [of these ideas] when it says: "The precaution of the

---

77. The reference may be to God.
78. See the *Exiled Book*, p. 174 and Zucker, *Translation*, pp. 8 and 17.

iniquitous shall fall upon him and the desire of good God shall give him."
(Prov. 10:24)[79] . . . after it in . . . <the idea is in a manner of
completeness> . . . The statement [refers]* to warning, for the words
said of one who is singled out are more refined than those said of the
masses and not . . . to the statement of his wife as it says: "She is your
friend and the wife of your treaty." (Mal. 2:14) . . . this statement is to
his wife for the words . . . the masses and does not single out the man
from his wife . . . the reason for beginning with "Hear my voice" is in
order to quiet them down for him for his words before he finishes
like . . . will happen to them [they will not give heed]* . . . Now the
repetition of their names is to get their attention so that the beginning of
his words does not escape him.

IX

The addition of "the wives of Lemech" after mentioning Tzillah and 'Adha
and likewise "hearken unto my words" after it says "Hear my voice" is to
soften them and to get their attention. It tells us by this that one should
call the one spoken to in order that the words do not surprise him
[because] he is unprepared for them and their beginning escape him.
Together with this he should quiet him down so that he may exhaust and
hear {the matter} to its end. Also, he should speak softly to him so that the
words enter his heart and leave an impression on him as I shall explain, for
example in [the pericope of]: "Hearken O Heavens," and "Lend an ear and
hear my voice the House of Jacob and all the families of the house of
Israel," (Jer. 2:4) and the like.

X

I have translated shiv'athayim as "much" and shiv'im we-shiv'ah as "even more"
according to the practice of the Hebrews which apprehend multitude by
the numbers 10, 100, and 1000 for they are solid. The number 7 because
the Torah gave it the status of the algebraic numbers for it is proscribed

---

79. Cf. com. ad loc.: "He describes the wicked by the product of their acts
since they commit evil their heart is occupied with worry.

on the <<Sabbath,>> Passover, mourning, drinking feast[80] and confine-
ment each to be seven days for that reason they would say: "Coated many
times," (Ps. 12:7) "And the light of the Sun shall be much stronger than
the light of the seven days," (Is. 30:26) "For many times Cain shall be
avenged," "For the righteous even were he to fall many times he will get
up," (Prov. 24:17) "Am I not better for you than many sons," (I Sam. 1:8)
"And they shall be if many women remain," (Amos 6:9) "Were a man to
beget many and live many years," (Ecl. 6:3) "More than striking the fool
many times," (Prov. 17:10) "Many vines shall be worth much money," (Is.
7:23) and "For existence of a day in your courtyard is better than many
others." (Ps. 84:11) It does not mean in all [these cases] a true 7, 10, 100,
or 1000 no more no less but rather multitude or many. Now because they
assign juridical value to these numbers, the numbers approaching them
from before and after were also singled out. It says: "From many sorrows
will he save you and in the worst of them no evil shall come." (Job 5:19)
They also said: "give a portion to seven and also to eight": (Ecl. 11:2)
despite that there is reference to . . . they went as far as attributing
importance to seven multiplied by ten as it tells: "Many kings having their
thumbs and great toes cut off." (Judg. 1:7) Likewise they singled out
numbers preceding and following their multipliers as it says: "Many are
the queens and concubines." (Cant. 6:8) This is the true [meaning] of
shiva'athayim and *shiv'im we-shiv'ah*.

It then says:

25) and Adam had sexual relations again [with Eve his wife and she
became pregnant] and she bore a son and named him Seth. He said
because God has replaced for me another son instead of Abel whom
Cain killed; 26) and to Seth too there was born a son and he named him
Enosh then calling with the name of God began.

I

The most probable reason for the statement "And Adam had sexual
relations again" is that "again" refers to the giving birth for it is possible
that he copulated with her many times but she did not give birth until this
time.

---

80. Gen. 50:6 and Gen. 29:27 and *Jer. Keth.* 1:7.

II

The most probable [reason] for giving him the name by stating: "Because God has replaced for me another child" is that Cain's killing of Abel was around 130 years [before] and he gave his name according to the nearest event.

III

Az huHal liqro beshem hashem ("then calling with the name of God began") withstands just four interpretations. The first and closest to the text is that at the time of Enosh people began to append the Creator's name to theirs. An example of this is in the naming of Mehuyael, Methuselah for Seth and Enosh are similar Enoch and Eirad. Whereas Cain who preceded them by a generation and after Enoch was born the men Mehuyael, Mehalel were born. [This] spread to Yemuel, Yehabel, Ami-Shaddaim Suri-Shaddai, Shvai, Amazya, and the like.

The second is that they began to pray in the name of God in congregating <and made for themselves places for bowing down and assembling> as it says: "To call all of them in the name of the Lord." (Zeph. 3:9). The third is that they began calling in the name of God to another, like forms, likeness, and idols as it says: "And they said this is your master." (Ex. 32:4) The fourth is that they began to profane calling in God's name and were denouncing prayer.[81] *Huhal* according to this fourth interpretation is derived from the word *hol* which means "denouncement" as it says: "And I am profaned among them." (Ezek. 22:26) Some of the Ancients prefer this latter over the ones that have preceded. The strength of the tradition is well surely without a doubt.[82]

---

81. So Onqelos.
82. See *BR* 22:26.

Chapter V

1) This is the book <of the elucidation> of the offspring of Adam as he was in the day that God created him in His form—a ruler He made him; 2) and He created them male and female and He blessed them and named them "Man" in the day of their creation. 3) So when Adam lived 130 years he begot a son as his likeness in his form and named him Seth 4) and his lifespan after this was eight hundred years in which he begot sons and daughters; 5) his entire lifespan was 930 and then he died . . .[1] 28) and when Lemech lived 180 years he begot a son; 29) and he named him Noah, saying this one shall ease us of our work and of the toil of our hands in the land that God cursed. . . . . . .

I

It is necessary in all these verses that ten matters be explained—seven of them fundamental and the other three supplements and additions. The first of the seven is: What is the use in repeating "that God created him in His form—a ruler He made him;" 2) and He created them male and female," for it has already elucidated all this in what precedes. We say that it tells [us] that the seven characteristic attributes that came about with

---

1. The intermediate verses containing lineage have been omitted because of the uniformity of their structure.

the marriage of Adam and Eve continue onto all their offspring and for that reason it repeats {the attributes} of the offspring. But why does it not reiterate them in connection to Cain and Abel? Because their offspring was abrogated. As for Abel, he was killed and Cain, because of the flood, none of his offspring survived.[2] [Only] Seth's offspring remained. One of the seven repeated things is that God formed him and he is attributed to Him [for] despite that He only created {Cain} with the intermediacy of Adam and Eve, the intermediacy does not exclude him from being created by {God}. The manner in which it attributes Seth to his Master is like it attributes Adam.

The second is that Seth too is made in the estimable and ruling form though his form does not resemble Adam's in all its features but [only] the impression and the composition is the same. It therefore says of both men: "In His form a ruler He made him."[3] The same applies to the rest of the people.

The third is that it requires that all males and females get married like Adam and Eve, a man having no wife and a woman having no husband.[4] The fourth is that every man should have precedence as the ruler <<in the affairs of>> his wife like Adam and Eve.

The fifth is that he should have dominion over the rest of the wealth, im-movables and movables, that she has just as he had before Eve came but she should be a partner with him and it says: "And they shall rule" by his command or under his dominion.

The sixth is that it requires all the offspring to publicize their marriage just as Adam and Eve's marriage was announced, praised, and blessed by God's statement: "And He blessed them."

The seventh is that every man and his wife should be equal in their righteousness one to the other after getting married according to the religious law as it says: "And He named them Adam on the day of their creation."

The second of the seven is: What is the manner of wisdom in the lengthiness of the life of these first ten generations? We say what we have said already [i.e.] in order to increase their offspring for only two people

---

2. This answer is already given in *Chapters of Rabbi Eliezer* (Ch. 22). So also Ibn Ezra ad loc.

3. Apparently the Gaon speaks only of the idea because these actual words are not said of Seth.

4. I.e., people should not engage in intercourse without marriage.

were created and were their life spans shorter they would compensate equally but God extended their existence so that each one would see his sons and grandsons in his lifetime.[5]

The third is: Why did it not detail all or part of the events during this period from Seth to Noah? We say in order to make it easy for us and so that our reading of the Torah not be difficult for that reason he included these generations with their events.

The fourth is: Why did it expand the words of its statement and add "after he begot" and "and he begot sons and daughters"? We say: Because this is the manner of wisdom if the general is duplicated, the details are expanded on.

The fifth is: That it tells us that it is possible that when we say something we may speak of it as far as one hundred years in time and then return to the event that is fifty years before. The reason for this is to exhaust the events of man as it did with "This is the book," it reached until eight hundred years until it exhausted the events [occurring to] man. It then returned to what precedes it 1935 years until it finished for us the events of Seth. It then returned to what precedes this 1957 years and begins with the events of Keinan. It then reaches until 815 years until it completes for us the events of Enosh, and then reached what preceded it by 745 years and begins with the events of Mehalel. The same applies to the rest of these generations, it goes through the events of each one for a long period of time by which it elucidates and completes the events of the people. It then returns to the time before them [measuring in] the amount that calculations requires when it finishes it begins another event. The same applies to the generations after Noah and in the many events after them [of which] I shall not expand in discussion.

The sixth is: Since we have become accustomed to it being possible that the iniquitous may cheat the righteous and [the] Master does not save him from his hand even when he kills him as occurred with Abel for it is in the benevolence of his Master to give him recompense, it tells us that it is possible that his Master give the righteous a short life despite that He gives someone else a longer life. This is what happened to Enoch for it explains of him that he was righteous as it says: "And Enoch was obedient to God." Now if "with God," "before God," or "after God" is attached to "walking" it signifies obedience and righteousness as it says: "With God Noah walked," (Gen. 6:9) and Jacob says: "The God with which my

5. Cf., however, BR ch. 26.

fathers Abraham, Isaac walked." (Gen. 48:15) Likewise, God says of the
righteous priest: "In peace and justice He walked with me," (Mal. 2:6) "But
in the path of God your Master you shall go," (Deut. 13:5) "For they went
in the obedience of God," (Num. 32:12) and "For they did not go in [the
path of] My obedience," (Num. 32:11) and the like. Enoch lived only 365
years and despite that his kin lived eight hundred and nine hundred, in the
world to come his life will be lengthy according to his righteousness.

. . . <it is possible . . . to this matter that God knew that it is better
for him to die for it was[6] . . . or that should chose to stay away from his
righteousness[7] . . . that is should be similar to tragedies . . . despite
that he shall repent as we have explained in the Book of Beliefs[8] what the
matter of Enoch was. Some say that he did not die for they did not attain
my interpretation of the verse among those that said that Enoch died like
our statement and like the words of the Targum[9]>

---

6. Possibly we may complete this sentence as follows: "for he was grieved to
see the wickedness of the people of his generation" and therefore God took him
out of this world. (Zucker)

7. Following Rabbi Aybu in BR 25:1.

8. Apparently the reference is to 4:4. (Zucker)

9. See Zucker, Translation, pp. 92 and 115.

Chapter VI

[[1) And when man began to multiply on the face of the Earth and daughters were born to them, 2) the noble sons saw the daughters of the masses that they are nice and took for themselves wives of all that they chose; 3) and God said: My essence shall not be sheathed in the people forever for they are of flesh and their [allotted] time shall be 120 years; 4) and the heavenly ones were in the land at that time and after this too the noble sons would have sexual relations with the daughters of the masses <prohibitively> and they would be for them, they are the mighty ones who had a name from antiquity; 5) and when God saw that man's evil had increased in the land and all the inclinations of the thoughts of their hearts are absolute evil all the time, 6) God resented that He made man and God threatened them by that He made them and brought sorrow to their hearts; 7) in that God said: I shall erase the people that I have created on the face of the Earth from man to animal to crawler and the birds of the heavens for I have threatened them by that I created them; 8) and Noah found favor with God; 9) this is <the elucidation of> the offspring of Noah; and Noah was righteous and veritable in his generations in [the path of] God <'s obedience> Noah walked 10) and Noah begot three sons, Sem, Ham, and Japheth; 11) and the Earth corrupted in front of God and the Earth filled with despoliation; 12) and when God saw it that it was corrupted in that all flesh had corrupted its way on it, 13) He said to Noah: The deadline of all flesh has approached before Me for the Earth has filled with despoliation from before them and I shall destroy them on accord of it; 14) make for yourself a box of

Box-tree[1] and make it levels and coat it from inside and outside with cement; 15) and this is the measurement that you should make it: three hundred cubits its length, fifteen its width, and thirty its depth; 16) and make for it an illumination and to a cubit you shall finish it from above and make for it a door at its side lowers, firsts, seconds, and thirds you shall make it; 17) behold I bring a flood of water on the Earth to destroy anything of flesh that has a living spirit.]]

I

. . . "Their souls wish filth I too shall choose their tyranny." (Is. 66:5)

The statement "And God said . . . shall not contain" was conveyed to them by means of a prophet for they were in need to know a deadline so that they fear and repent but if they do not repent the threat is fulfilled upon them.

II

I rendered *lo yidon* as "shall not be sheathed" for the sheath of the sword is called *naddan* as it says: "And God said to the angel and He returned the sword to its sheath." (II Chron. 21:27) An example of this is what Daniel says: "And when my spirit became troubled I, Daniel, in my body," (Dan. 7:15) which means that his spirit was destroyed in his body, which is like a sheath. When these letters combine into *din* or *dun* may have [one of] six meanings: [1] "to turn away the feeble from the law" (Is.10:2)—judgement; [2] *Midyan* (Josh. 15:61)—a city; [3] "those that dwell in *middin*" (Judg. 5:10)—caravan; [4] "it shall not be sheathed"; [5] *yadhon* (Neh. 3:7)—the name of a man; and [6] "and the entire nation was *nadhon*" (II Sam. 19:10)—[in] light dispute.

III

I have rendered *beshaggam* as "for" as in a general sense[2] for the essence of the word is *gam* and when a *shin* is added it becomes *shaggam* as you say:

---

1. See Low, *Die Flora der Juden* I, p. 319.
2. As opposed to breaking the word up into components.

"That this too is a thought of wind," (Ecl. 1:17) and a *beth* attaches to {these two components} and it becomes *beshaggam*. This is parallel to its saying: *kevar—shekkevar* (as in "beshekkevar" (ibid 2:16). The meaning of this is that their spirit shall not function in the world but will give them life in the other whether for punishment or reward according to what we have previously explained [to the effect] that man shall not desist.[3]

IV

It does not mean by "And his days shall be 120 years" that God shall make peoples' life[span] 120 years neither from that time, for Sem and Arpachshad and their children lived more, nor from Moses' time, for Jehoyada' the priest lived longer as it says: "And Jehoyada' aged and was satiated in years and died at 130 years when he died." (II Chron. 22:16) Rather God meant that He gave these people an extension of 120 years and this is said with "And it was when man began" before "And Noah was six hundred years old"—this statement was in the year before. "And it was when man began" was more than this.

V

It mentions "And Noah was six hundred years" first in order to arrange the offspring one after the other. Similar to what we have laid down there are many [cases of] dates in disorder in the Scripture which are mentioned first. You already know that [in] the beginning of the Book of Deuteronomy [it says]: "And he spoke at the first of the second month," (Deut. 1:1) while in the middle [it says]: "in the first month," (Deut. 9:1) and many similar cases. Isaiah says to Ahaz: "And in sixty-five years Efrayim shall rise from its people." (Is. 7:8) This was after twenty-two years and this statement indicates that the beginning of the date was from forty-three years before this time. Likewise God says to Daniel: "And they are seventy weeks have already been declared upon your nation," (Dan. 9:24) which is 590 years that begin with the first destruction and end with the second. The beginning of the dating is fifty-three [years] before He

---

3. As opposed to the view of the Rabbis. See *San.* 10:3, *Tos.* 13, *Bab.* 108a.

said [this] to Daniel. Similar to these embellishments there are many in the Scripture.

VI

I rendered *Nefilim* as "heavenly ones" for this is a noun from the name . . . and the word *nafal* has [one of] thirteen meanings: [1] "falling onto the ground" as it says: "And the horns of the alter had been slashed off and they fell to the ground" (Am. 3:14); [2] "dropping in level" as it says: "Babel has fallen as it has fallen" (Is. 21:9); [3] "making someone take oath" [as it says]: "And the fallers that fell upon him" (Jer. 39:9); [4] "waging war" [as] in regards to Joshua [as it says]: "And they fell upon them" (Josh. 11:7); [5] "shame" and "embarrassment" [as it says]: "And Cain was very angered and his face fell" (Gen. 4:5); [6] "dejection" [as it says]: "They were much cast down in their eyes" (Neh. 6:16); [7] "amputation of a limb" [as it says]: "And her hip fell" (Num. 5:27); [8] "cowardice and weakness of heart" [as its says]: "Let not man's heart fall upon him" (Dan. 9:24); [9] "canceling determination" [as it says]: "And make them fall in their determination" (Ps. 5:11); [10] "resting" and "staying" [as it says]: "In the presence of all his brothers he dwelled " (Gen. 25:18); [11] "attainment of fortification and strength of body" [as it says]: "My portion has fallen" and the like; [12] miscarriage in a woman: "A miscarriage (*nefel*) is better than it" (Ecl. 6:3); and [13] . . . <<[when it says]: "the *nefilim*.">>

VII

"And after this too" refers to after He allotted them 120 years—they continued in their iniquity and persisted in their sins, the most well known and worst [of which] is: "That noble sons would have sexual relations with the daughters of the masses." Were one to think that "They are the giants" refers to the noble sons and that this supports that they were angels, the matter is not as he thought. Rather it says "The heavenly ones were in the land in those days" because of the lengthiness of their life[span] for it is known that the persistence of any body is according to the amount of its strength. Being that they had ten times ours [lifespan] it must be then that the strength of their bodies was approximately ten times ours. For that reason it says: "They are the mighty ones who had a name from antiquity." All that was said in the last three verses shows in truth that the noble sons were humans and none other than this for wisdom requires that people of similar sin be similar in their denigration, threat, warning, and punishment and we see that the Scripture mentions only man in connection with the four of them without attaching anything else to them. Therefore, we know that the noble sons and the "daughters of man" are all human for of the denigration it says: "And when God saw that man's evil had increased" and not "And the evil of the noble sons." Of threat it says: "And God resented that He made man on the Earth" and does not say: "And the noble sons in the Heavens." Of punishment it says: "And He destroyed the people" (Gen. 7:23) and nothing else judged to destruction added to it.

VIII

"The evil of man" applies to everything there being three particulars. [1] idol worship as it says: "Jerabo'am did not return from his evil path," (I Sam. 24:7) [2] illicit sexual relations [as its says]: "How shall I commit this atrocity?" (Gen. 39:9), [3] in spilling blood [as it says]: "If I do this thing to my master to the Lord's anointed to send upon him my hand." (I Sam. 24:7) The worst of all of them is their lack in the belief in matters of the Godhead and worship [as] it says: "And the inclination of the thoughts of his heart is evil all the time." (Gen. 6:5) What shows that "all the inclinations of the thoughts" refers specifically to belief, Godhead, and worship is David's statement: "And now Solomon my son know the God of your father and serve Him," (I Chron. 28:9) and also "Observe this forever for the inclination of the thoughts of the heart of your people." (I Chron. 29:18)

IX

The expression "only evil" [means] absolute evil, likewise "only good" [means] absolute good and likewise "only truth" is absolute truth and whatever else is along these lines.

X

I rendered "And he repented in his heart" (*wayyinahem*) as "threatened" for this word may have [one] of six meanings: [1] "regret" according to the known meaning "And the people had regret toward Benjamin" (Judg. 21:15); [2] "threatening"—"Behold Esau your brother threatens you to kill you" (Gen. 27:42); [3] "consolation"—"And Isaac was consoled after the death of his mother" (Gen. 24:67); [4] "forgiveness"—"and He forgave them with the abundance of His esteem" (Ps. 106:45); [5] "heating up"—"Those that are heated up by sheep" (Is. 57:5); and [6] "looking"— "And I looked (*nihamti*) at the evil" (Jer. 18:10). This is of the language of the people of the Land of Israel: *ana Hamay* [which is] instead of *ana Haza* and the *nun* is an augmentation among the meticulous Hebrews as they take words from the language of the *Targum* connecting it in *mul mahaze el mahze* (I Kings 7:5). According to this rendition, "And he was saddened in his heart" modifies "man" for it uses the singular through out [the verse].

XI

It adds "That He made man" (v. 6) and also "That I have created him" (v. 7) according to what we have posited [i.e.] that it is in that He made him from nothing and He is able to destroy them, for destroying them is no more difficult for the intellect [to apprehend] than creating them but easier! Do you not see how to bring a proof similar to this in the incident regarding Babylon for it says: "The Lord of Hosts has sworn by Himself: Surely I will fill you with men as with caterpillars . . . He has made the Earth by His power . . . when He utters His voice there is a multitude of water in the heavens . . . every man is brutish by his knowledge." (Jer. 51:14–17) It is also possible that *wayyinahem* should mean "regret" according to its popular meaning and that "And He was saddened" refers to God's act without infringing on His abilities, according to this path that I shall describe. Do we not say that God fears evil for His votaries as it says: "If not for me fearing the anger of the enemy," (Deut. 32:27) since anger does not apply to Him rather He warns them of it. We say further that He desires something for His creation as it says: "Shall they desire that this heart remain for them," (Deut. 5:26) for desire does not apply to this rather the desire is theirs. [It] also [says] that He is glad with the acts of the righteous despite that happiness does not form in Him as it says: "God shall be gladdened by His acts." (Ps. 104:31) The true meaning of the statement is that He will gladden them by their acts.[4] Accordingly, it would be correct that we say of "And He saddened" that sorrow and worry do not befall Him but those that have denied, sinned, and have replaced Him. Likewise "And God threatened" necessarily [means that] He placed in them regret. They would be complete were they not in the world, would God not have created them. The is the meaning of the completion of [the verse]: "That God made man in the land." Do you not see that when a sickness befalls upon a person he seeks death instead of it, for example: "Who await death but it is not and dig up burial grounds for it," (Job 3:21) and "And said to the mountains 'cover us.'" (Hos. 10:8) Moreover, he wishes that he were never created as it says: "As though I had not been or as if borne from the womb to the grave," (Job 10:19) and the like.

XII

Regarding the statement "And I said: I shall destroy man that I created," people have asked: If man sinned, what sin did the animals and the birds commit? and add to this preceding the question: what sin did the babies commit? Some conjectured that the Creator blessed be He did not create babies . . . the flood this is a claim of a wonder which can not be sustained without proof. This would mean that . . . they all copulate with their wives for many years but they did not become pregnant for it is a wonder that is greater than many others and their claim can only be sustained with a thorough proof. Furthermore, it is not impossible to claim that the animals were not created because of what is recorded. Rather we say, and on God we rely, we already know that according to the intellect it is possible that the Wise One should bring ills upon a person or people and [that] this should be the reason that they prey for delight and fortune. If we see that our Master brings ills upon someone who did not sin we know without a doubt or distrust that God will recompense him with good in the world to come and this a consolation that results of the Creator's will. Now whoever He wants, He gives recompense and if He wishes He does not. Rather we see that one of the reasons for this recompense is that if they deserve destruction for [their] sins, He adds the

---

4. Ad loc. "God shall gladden His votaries with His acts." The causative sense. See Zucker, *Translation*, p. 263.

children to them and He destroys them and recompenses them accordingly. Sometimes the plants are added to them despite that they have no recompense, rather this is so this strikes the heart of one who hears of their events and that He destroyed their land, its people, animals, and plants they will be frightened and will correct themselves to obedience. He judged these with truth and recompense and those with truth and ethical lesson for the sake of those that heard [this] as it says here: "From man to beast to crawler." It says elsewhere: "Therefore thus says the Lord God: Behold My anger and My fury shall be poured out at this place upon man, upon beast, upon the trees of the field, and the fruit of the ground," (Jer. 7:20) and "They tell of Him who are it companions as do their cattle and their rising plants," (Job 36:33) for it had previously mentioned the sword when it says: "And he commanded a *mafgi'a* upon him," (Ezek. 5:17) which is a kind of killer as it says: *"pegha' bo* and he struck him and he died." (II Sam. 1:15) It then adds his friends as it says: "his friends," and the friend of swords are hunger, wild animals, and pestilence. The statement "as do their cattle and rising plants" refers to their animals and of their plants it says: "And the rising plants."

XIII

"And Noah found favor," favor according to what he deserved not more than that similar to what it says: "Favor and esteem God will give us and will not hold back His goodness from those that go in purity," (Ps. 94:12) and "Good intellect gives favor." (Prov. 13:15) The true meaning of "favor" is the complete supply of needs as it says: "God said to Moses: This thing that you said do it to for you have found favor with Me and have elevated your name. (Ex. 33:17)[5]

---

5. The fragment (Or 5563) which begins with section VIII (according to Zucker. See "Genesis" p. 100, n. 81) has the following scribal note at its end: [This] has been completed with the aid of the Creator. Its completion was on the third of the fifteenth month, Marhesewah, the first year, 1098 according to the secular calendar. Wrote Isaiah the son of Rabbi Nissim the Rabbi in blessed memory is his soul. Let the Merciful merit him to lear the entire Torah as well as his offspring and theirs until the end of the generations. Amen, Eternity, Selah.

Chapter VII

1) [[And God said to him: Enter the ark, you and all that belongs to you for I have seen you as righteous in front of Me in this generation; 2) from among all the clean animals you shall take seven of each male and female and of the animals that are not clean a male and female pair you shall take; 3)and also from the bird of the sky seven of each male and female to sustain their offspring on the entire face of the Earth; 4) for lo after the seven days I rain on the earth forty days and forty nights and shall destroy all the people[1] that I have made on the face of the Earth. 5) And Noah did everything God commanded him; 6) and Noah was six hundred years old when the waters of the flood were on the ground; 7)and Noah entered ark and his sons and his wife and his son's wives with him before the waters of the flood; 8) of pure animals and of those that are not pure and of the birds and of the rest of what walks on the ground, 9) pair by pair they entered to Noah to the box male and female as God commanded him of it; 10) and after it was after seven days the waters of the flood were on the ground; 11) in the six hundreth year of Noah's life in the second month in its seventeenth day on that day the springs of the great depths broke open; 12) and the rain stayed on the earth forty days and forty nights; 13) in that day itself Noah, Sem, Ham, Japheth, his sons, and the three wives of his sons with them to the box; 14) they and all the animals according to their kinds and all the animals

---

1. See the Gaon's com. to Gen. 9, part 2 section IV.

according to their kinds and the rest of what walks on the earth according to its kinds and all the birds according to its kinds any bird that has wings; 15) and they entered to Noah to the box pair by pair by pair of all the flesh that has living spirit in it; 16) and all that entered male and female of all humans entered as God commanded him and God sheltered him; 17) and when the flood had persisted forty days on the earth the waters increased and carried the box and it was raised off the earth; 18) and when the water increased and became extremely great on the earth the box went on the face of the water; 19) and when the water became very, very great on the earth all the lofty mountains under the heavens were covered; 20) fifteen cubits from above the water rose and the mountains were covered; 21) and all flesh that walks on the earth from the bird to the animal to the beast to the rest of what walks on the earth and all people died; 22) all the has a living soul in its nose of all that in draught died; 23) and the water destroyed all the people that are on the face of the earth from man to animals to crawlers to bird of the heavens and were destroyed from the earth and only Noah and who was with him in the box remained; 24) and when the waters became great on the earth 150 days.]]

I

. . . From the first raising but rather after the third ascends above it that what is added is a perpendicular angle when it becomes []. It requires that he make the door at the beginning of its side not for all the animals to enter it without . . . it is close to the ground.

II

The statement "lowers, seconds, thirds you shall make" does not necessitate that there were only three levels. This is because were we to imagine in our minds that the there were just three levels . . . then it would have levels of ten Hebrew cubits in height which are fifteen arm [lengths] of an average person, what need do the small animals have for it and this would only be a waste rather there were as many levels as needed. However, it mentions two and three and restrains as is its practice to count for it says: "So two or three cities wandered unto one city." (Am. 4:8) Likewise it says: "And picking grapes shall remain in it like the pulling off of olives that there remain two or three berries." (Is. 17:6) So here, "lowers, seconds, and thirds" is the beginning of a count and includes what is additional to this according the needed amount.[2]

III

"Behold I bring the flood of water" is deposition of the punishment for He says: "My essence shall not be sheathed" without explaining how this is. He also says: "Behold I destroy them" without explaining here how He shall execute their destruction that it shall be by means of water. It is possible that we say that the manner of wisdom in choosing water for their punishment is that this is the first general punishment that the Torah records and God made it from the first element closest to the Earth which is water. Afterwards it tells of the punishment of the people[3] of the Tower which He made with stirring winds as it says: "And God dispersed them from there," (Gen. 11:8) [which] we find refers to this like it says: "With wind He dispersed them[4] in front of the enemy," (Jer. 18:17) which is the element above the water. Then it records the punishment of the people of Sodom and executed it by means of the element that is above the wind which is fire as it says: "And God rained on Sodom and Gamorrah with sulfur and fire." (Gen. 19:24)

IV

When it says "And I shall establish My treaty," it obligates one to sustain the treaty of his Master [as well] for God fulfils His treaty [only] for one keeps his as it says: "And you just as you have invested God your Master to be a Godhead . . . so God has invested in you to be a chosen people." (Deut. 26:17–18) The true meaning of the words is that God had commanded him and all his people to sustain their righteousness so that He upkeep His treaty with them.

---

2. However, the Rabbis maintained that there were actually three levels. See *San.* 108b, *BR* 31 for example.

3. I.e., dispersion by means of wind. So also in the *Book of Jubilees* 10:26. The Rabbis, however, maintain that the Tower was burned (*San.* 1090b) or destroyed by water (*BR* ch. 38).

4. Ad loc. "I shall disperse them "

V

There are those that say that it places the men next to each other when it says "you and your sons with you" and places the women next to each other when it says "and your wife and the wives of your sons," that it prohibited them copulation so long as they were in the box and this is a probable opinion. What proves this is that it reverses this conjunction when they leave [the box] when it joins the husband to his wife when it says "You and your wife and your sons and the wives of your sons."

VI

When it says "two from each" it does not mean just two individuals for it shall command after this to take seven of all pure and two of all impure and there is no contradiction, rather the meaning of "two" is "pairs" [it] not being specified how many pairs there are until the explanation comes afterwards.

VII

It says in the first verse "You shall bring to the box" and in the second "shall come to you." {The Scripture} indicates to us by means of this that He did not trouble Noah to climb mountains and go down springs to gather every animal from them for this is not within his reach and also his knowledge does not encompass all their genera and kinds.[5]

VIII

. . . In the *Book of Distinction* and in the *Responsa* to Anan I have already answered in length to those that cite proof from the section of "And the box rested," that if the moon is not visible we count the month as thirty days. I should mention here too some of their words and some responses to them. As for their opinion that the holidays are determined according to sight, we have already mentioned some of this previously and we shall

---

5. Cf., Leviticus Rabbi 27:7 and *Chapters of Rabbi Eliezer*, ch. 23.

mention yet another part in connection to the pericope of "this month" (Ex. 12:2). In order to cite a proof for this that if the moon was not visible we count thirty days [they said]: Being that Noah did not see the moon during the five months [of the Flood] he made each one of them thirty days [long]. This was the number reached to 150 days for the rain began to fall on the seventeenth of the second month and the box rested on the seventeenth of the fourth month, we have five months that are 150 days at the end of which the waters reduced. For we do not find another reason that box rested other than the reduction of water. There can be only 150 days in five months according to the opinion of sanctifying the month according to sight. When I investigated their words I found that they are invalid from every aspect. We should present here the ten essential claims against them. The first is that they have no proof that the sky was cloudy all the five months and their proof is definitive only in regards to one month within the forty days. This is the first response. The second is that they have no proof that the calculation is Noah's and it is possible that it is that of God who said to Moses: "On such a day it was so and on such a day it was so." Even if we were to extend the cloudiness to all time nothing is concealed from God, neither the moon nor anything else. The third is that they determined that on the 150th day the box rested but they have no proof that [the forty] mentioned before are included in the 150 and what shall they do? The fourth is that they claimed that the box rested only because the water settled but it is possible that it rested on something as we have explained. The fifth is that they said that you will not find five months of 150 days unless it is by the method of observation but we have found them according to the method of calculation for this could be a leap year and [both are] complete.[6] Were we to start with the seventeenth of Marheshwan and seventeen days pass of it and of Kislew thirty and Tebeth twenty-nine and from the second Adar seventeen this would be exactly 150 days. The sixth is that the Scripture records the history of the life of Noah and it is known that the years of people's lives are all solar like that of any growth like trees and the like. The seventh is that it is possible that all these dates were solar before the holidays were commanded to Israel. The eighth is that it is possible that "And Noah's box rested on the seventh month" is from the time of his entrance into the box as we find that it sets a specific date for something specific as it says: "And Hannaniah the prophet died on that year on the fourth

---

6. See *Arachin* 9b.

month." (Jer. 28:17) This is from the time of Jeremiah's prophecy for were it the seventh month [i.e.] the month of Tishri, the other year would have already entered. The ninth is that it is not usual that there be five consecutive months of thirty for if the moon would be seen after this it would be required to make the month or two months twenty-eight days. Were one to claim that the course of the moon follows the calculation of Noah so there is no contradiction, his manner is of one who claims a wonder that can only be established with an overt passage, but this is an improbable opinion.

Chapter VIII

[[1) God remembered Noah and all the beasts and animals that were with him in the box and God brought by a wind on the earth with which He settled the water; 2) and the springs of water and chimneys of the heavens were plugged and the rain was suppressed from the heavens; 3) and the water retreated from the earth continually and the water recede after 150 days; 4) and the box stationed on the seventh month on its seventeenth day on the mountains of Qurda; 5) and the water continually receded until the tenth month and on its first the tops of the mountains became visible; 6) and when it was after forty days Noah opened the window of the box that he made; 7) and he freed the raven and he stood entering and leaving until the water dried off the earth; 8) then he freed the pigeon from with him to see had the water lightened from the face of the earth; 9) but the pigeon did not find a resting place for its feet and returned to the box for the water was on all the earth and he stretched out his hand and took it and brought it to him to the box; 10) and he waited also seven more days and freed it from the box again; 11) and it came to him another time and behold an olive leaf is cut in its mouth and Noah knew that the water had lightened off the earth; 12) and he also waited another seven days then freed and it did not continue to return to him anymore; 13) and when it was on the 601st year on the first day of the first month the water dried of the earth and Noah removed the cover of the box and saw and behold the face of the earth had dried; 14) and on the second month on its seventeenth the earth dried;]]

It then says:[1]

15) And God said to Noah saying: 16) Go out from the box, you and your wife, your sons and the wives of your sons together with all the animals that are with you; 17) from all flesh and birds and the rest of the animals as well as the rest of the insects that swarm on the Earth to procreate on the Earth and they shall be fruitful and multiply on it; 18) and Noah went out and his sons and his wife and his sons' wives with him; 19) and all the animals and the insects and the birds and anything that walks on the Earth according to their kind left the box.

I

The first thing we should ask is what is the manner of wisdom in God delaying Noah 57 days after the settling of the water? We say to prepare the Earth to receive rain and seeds and for that reason it said: "Go out from the box." Another manner is to prepare the habitats and dwelling places of all the animals for that reason it succeeds it with the statement: "Any animal that is with you of all flesh."

II

It means by "According to their kind they left the box" that just as they entered so they left, He required that every animal enter its habitat as He will show it its sustenance.

It then says:

20) and Noah built an altar for God and took a clean animal and clean bird and brought upon it his ascending offering; 21) and God accepted his offering; and God said through His prophet:[2] I shall not revert to curse the Earth because of man for his heart thinks evil from the

---

1. The commentary to verses 1–14 is lacking.

2. However, see III in the commentary below where he has a different rendition of the word.

youngest and I shall not revert to destroy all living as I have; 22) never shall the length of the life of the Earth, sowing, harvest, cold, heat, summer, winter, and day and night shall cease.

I

As for the description "And Noah built" . . . around the two sacrifices is something that is always known . . . as we have explained.

II

The word "And He smelled" . . . has an argument from the intellect . . . an accident in all manners whichever one . . . the Scripture mentions it from observation . . . The fifth it means by that statement . . . the knowledge that we may know by means of it that he already knew likewise . . . for that reason he made this phenomenon for us . . . in any proof. From the linguistic point of view I rendered "And he smelled" as "received" similar to what it says: "And he broke the withs as a thread of tow is broken when it smells fire." (Judg. 16:9) It also says: "Still at the odor of water will it branch and spread out its roots," (Job 14:9) and "And they smelled the fear of God." (Is. 11:4)[3] All these cases mean "acceptance" or "inclination."

III

I rendered "And God said to His heart" as "of Himself" for "heart" in the language refers to the self and essence of a thing as it says: "The inundation collected in the heart of the sea," (Ex. 15:8) "And the mountain was ablaze with fire until the center of the heavens." (Deut. 4:11) It also says: "He still lives in the midst of these," (II Sam. 18:14) and "And to the essence of their detestable things and their abominations their heart goes," (Ezek. 11:21) and the like.

---

3. Ad loc. "fear of God was just for them."

IV

The approximate meaning of the statement "of Himself" is that no one asked Him for this but that He initiated this by Himself, approximately. But why did Noah not ask of this for it is the manner of those who bring offerings to ask their needs. We say that Noah only brought a thanks offering to God for giving peace to him and everyone that is with him. Being that it was thanks for the past he did not mix into it anything that shall be in the future. It is possible that we say . . . Noah for he saw . . . in it . . . it was decided . . . that he ask he did not ask of others . . . in him like the Flood . . . He had accepted his sacrifice . . . considering accepting . . . and whatever is part of it . . . we say is it possible that we know the reason for the people of this period . . . we say in connection to this eight things: . . . that in this . . . created in the duration of time . . . deliberation . . . of wonders he obligated the matter and the which is the obligation of correction. The second is to teach him that he should put the rest of the people in this order from . . . they persisted. The third is that those that preceded then were . . . it is possible for them to deal with all the animals and give them sustenance something that the others would not be able. The fourth is that they were long lived so that is possible that they [will toil]* and plant what will provide . . . the plants and animals as we have explained. The fifth is that because of their financial situation, the Earth could be abandoned for twelve months after which it would be implanted and would produce. Nothing could damage this thing nor could anyone maintain it in such a way. The sixth is because their temperament then gave them strength [to tolerate] if cold or heat is to be held back from them and nothing would damage them. This is because the temperament of the animals is [such] that if it needs cold it obtains it in the winter that comes upon it, it then balances the heat that comes upon it in the summer and requires that the heat that comes upon it in the summer . . . will balance the cold . . . this statement of [something] distant . . . since the seeds and some . . . their manner is to exist . . . and the air upon it . . . after this it does not . . . permit that they exist . . . and whereas it hears this . . . this . . . and since we have already explained . . . it is . . . the declaration . . . but causing . . . I mean by this the rest . . . the wonder . . . .

Chapter IX

[[1) And God blessed Noah and his sons and said to them: Be fruitful and multiply and populate the earth; 2) and your fright and terror shall be upon all the beasts of the earth and all the birds of the heavens and all that walks on the ground and all the fish of the sea in your hands are submitted; 3) any pure living crawler shall be for you as food like the green herbage I have given you everything; 4) as for meat do not eat it with its blood for it is its soul; 5) as for your blood from yourselves I shall demand <by warning>[1] from all the beasts I shall demand it <by prevention> and from the hand of man <meaning > a man who kills his brother I shall demand him by his soul; 6) if there will be one who spills the blood of man by means of a man <like him> his blood shall be spilled for in a noble ruling form He made him; 7) and you be fruitful and multiply and swarm on the earth and multiply on it.]]

I

. . . . any ill person.

_____

1. This addition is found in Kafih's edition (p. 21) but not in Derenbourgh's.

II

"As for meat" is the prohibition that any meat of animals that is alive be eaten for it says: "For it is its soul." It prohibits eating any blood for it says "its blood." It is [also] possible that it prohibits them [to eat] blood vessels, the fat <and the membranes> covering it as it prohibits Israel when it says: "Any fat and any blood you shall not eat," (Lev. 3:17) at the start.

III

It collects three ideas in the statement "as for your blood." The destruction of the animals by means of animals. This being either when a person kills himself or when a predatory animal kills him. It prohibits man from killing himself by the warning: "As for your blood from yourselves I shall demand," without explaining by what [means] this will be [executed] but if we turn to the transmitted and written we find the warning prohibiting this <<for he is denigrated and punished>>. This is because if a person chooses to kill himself because he seeks by this to free himself of <sorrows that will come upon him>, if his Master tells him that suicide leads to retribution like the . . . he will consider and not commit suicide.[2] Were one to say: Do we not see that Samuel committed suicide and afterwards is called "God's chosen" (II Sam. 21:6) and the entire nation counts him among the eight princes?[3] We say that Saul did not succeed in killing himself for when he leaned on his sword he lost his strength and this killing was not completed until he encountered that Amolekite who killed him. Were one to think that the Amolekite lied, were we to search what is written we would find that it says: "And Saul took the sword and fell on it," (I Sam. 31:4) and the Amolekite said: "As I happened by chance upon him, the mountain of Gilbo'a and Saul is leaning on his spear and the chariots and the horsemen caught up to him . . . and he said to me again: 'Stand now upon me and kill me.'" (II Sam. 1:6–9) The statements "He leaned on his bow" and "and he fell on it" (I Sam. 31:4) are in accordance each other.[4] In the end the Amolekite is the killer. It is also possible to say regarding the incident with Samuel that when he asked the

2. Following Rabbi Eliezer in *Bab. Qama* 91b. See *Beliefs* 10:11 (p. 387).
3. *Suk.* 52b.
4. Rabbi Mubashshir (*Criticisms*, pp. 99–100), however, argued against this kind of reasoning.

Amolekite to kill him, he waited to save himself from great sorrow than this, just as Hannaniah, Mishael, and Azarya gained being burnt for themselves to be saved from something greater than that.[5]

IV

God prohibited animals to kill man by means of [placing] the fear of him upon them [and] even [on] the predators unless this is at time of sin, [when then] God compels and gives them rule over him as it says: "And I shall set loose unto you the animals of the steppe." (Lev. 26:22)[6] The prohibition to kill another like him is by threat as it says: "From the hand of a man," and "If there will be one who spills the blood of a man." Were one to know the hater of his friend who wanted to satisfy him[self] by killing him knowing that he killed but he sees that if he kills he will have more satisfaction by [killing] someone else than him he should abstain and not kill him.[7] This is the first of the different interpretations of "by man." This is because "by man" has five possible meanings. The first is that the killer shall be killed for the sake of the people so that they do not destroy each other. This is with wisdom similar to one who chooses to amputate his infected finger so that his entire body not be lost. Likewise it is with wisdom that killers be killed to protect by them the rest of humans.

The second is that the interpretation of "by man" is among people promptly, i.e., in this world before the one to come.

The third is that the interpretation of "by man" means by barrages as it will say: "And I shall make for you judges and authorities." (Deut. 16:18)

The fourth is that the meaning of "by man" is by testimony as it will say: "According to two witnesses." (Deut. 17:6)[8]

The fifth is that "by man" is in the open in front of people so that he not be killed in concealment as it says: "This is so you gather all the men and women . . . so that they hear . . . and fear God," (Deut. 31:12) as it commands of baring the skin of the wicked.[9, 10]

---

5. See Dan. 3:19.

6. See *Sab.* 151b and *San.* 38b.

7. This line is difficult.

8. See *Beliefs* 3:9 (p. 168).

9. Apparently the reference is to giving "lashes," which is done in the open. See Deut. 25:2. (Zucker)

V

Now it has been asked regarding the last commandment, "And you be fruitful and multiply," for did it not already say: "And God blessed Noah and his sons and said to them: Be fruitful and multiply," (Gen. 9:1) why does it repeat this here? We say that the first is a declaration [given] to them and a power that God added to them. The second is that were God to command them to use this power to complete the offspring just as He commanded of seeking sustenance by means of a cause that He made for it, for He established a cause for everything.

VI

In the statement "shall swarm on the earth," God commands them to spread out on the face of the Earth so that they do not all gather in one place for there are some negative respects [to this] which I shall explain in the incident of the Tower, God willing.

8) **Then God said to Noah and to his sons saying: 9) And I establish My treaty with you and with your offspring after you, 10) and with every living soul that is with you and with every beast of the steppe that is with you, anyone who left the box, of all the beasts of the Earth; 11) and I shall establish My treaty with you from the water of the flood and there will never be a flood; 12) and God said: This is an indication of the treaty that I make between Me and you and all the living souls that are with you for every generation forever and the bow shall stand so in the clouds, I shall show it in remembrance to the treaty that is between God and all living souls of all the flesh that is on the earth; 13) and the statement of this was to Noah that this is an indication of the treaty that I have established between Me and all the flesh that is on the Earth.**

I

This section is divided into two parts. The first is giving man assurance against the recurrence of a flood. This constitutes four verses: "And God

---

10. Zucker (*Genesis*, p. 346) has the following rearrangement in his translation: "in concealment . . . 'so that the entire nation listen' (Deut. 17:3) and as it commanded to publicize the smiting of the wicked. . . ."

said," "And behold I establish," "And every living soul," "And I shall establish." The second is giving an indication of the establishment of this preceding assurances which is the statement: "This is the indication of the treaty," to the end of the other five verses. The sixth verse, "And God said to Noah this is the indication of the treaty," was needed for it states in the verse: "And God said to Noah this is the indication of the treaty" to whom did he say . . . this is a statement according to His wisdom . . . similar to: "Do I conceal from Abraham what I do?" (Gen. 18:7) . . . He benefited us by this in that it is not strange for God to inform man what He does. This is like it reiterates "the rural area of Yair" (Deut. 3:15) that it was given to Yair the son of Menasse. His giving them assurance against the Flood did them good so that they [be able to] spread out on the Earth and populate it . . . and building and the like. If not for this they would abstain from populating. We may also say in regards to this that it is possible that one of the reasons for building the Tower was fear of the Flood and He gave them assurance so that they have no excuse for this. It is also possible to say that would it not be for Him giving assurance against the Flood the other generations would only fear punishment of it by means of water but when He made this treaty with them they began to fear that He may punish them in various forms of retribution to no number but they asked for forgiveness and savior from one of them. Do you not see that God presented punishments to men and it is not possible that He present and tell him of two of them . . . the third is similar to what He says . . . destruction and hunger: and shall not be . . . the third. Likewise in the incident with Amos three elements: ground, fire, and wind were mentioned to him. The punishment that is by means of the ground He presented to him . . . <and when he asked for pity> He gave him it as it says: "So the Lord God showed me and behold He forms grasshoppers . . . and it came to pass that when they had made an end of eating the grass of the land then I said, O Lord God forgive." (Am. 7:1–2) He presented fire to him as it says: "Thus has the Lord shown me and behold, the Lord God called to contend by fire." (Am. 7:4) <And from Him too he asked savior and it was given him . . . > <<He also showed him wind as it says:>> "two years before the quake." (Am. 1:1) We know that wind exists between two layers of the Earth and when the two layers touch each other the wind between them leaves and the Earth quakes. This quaking that the Creator made is a harsh act upon the Earth in the likeness of [a wall of] lead until the two layers touch and the wind begins to move. The Earth quakes as it says: "Thus he showed me and behold the Lord stood upon a wall made by a plumbine . . . and the

Lord said to me: Amos, what do you see? Then said the Lord: I shall set a plumbine in the midst of my people Israel." (Am. 7:7–8) For no other kind of punishment exists for there is a lengthy explanation in its place.

II

We say now being that is known among the meteorologists and experimenters that the colors that appear in clouds as a rod, a stick, a bow, or Sea Monster and the like are mists that ascend from the Earth to the upper . . . this does not let them disengage rapidly distancing it from the place of . . . which are places that are close to earth whose path of disengagement . . . which is opposite the Earth because of the heat of the Sun and this . . . the dryness which is sustained by this . . . fire will disengage slower . . . transmission . . . redness . . .

. . . presented from the time of Noah to the end of the existence of the Earth and [then] how did the rainbow be an indication of the assurance against the Flood? We say first that this is only that it exists and persists for because He was able to remove it by making the cloud permanent and lifting [it] when he rebels but he did not do this and therefore its existence for them is an indication <<together with this it is possible that he conceals and intensifies it and creates for it a shape for . . . that reason I rendered "given in the cloud" as "which have made in the clouds">>.

III

From the beginning of the sequel of the Flood, which is "the deadline of all the flesh," (Gen. 6:13) until now, which is its end, it records for us all this so that we deliberate it and that we know that our status regarding the pleasures we deserve, the danger, threats, and receiving punishment and the promise He gave us, is like that of the people of the Flood for just as He endowed them with multiplicity of population as He succeeds with the statement: "When man began to multiply," (Gen. 6:1) then by the statement: "When man began to increase on the face of the Earth," so He says of us: "Judah and Israel are many like the sand that is at the sea, eating, drinking, and rejoicing." (I Kings 4:20) Just as it says of the people of the Flood: "For the inclinations of the thoughts of the heart of man," so it says of Israel: "For I know its inclinations." (Deut. 31:21) . . .

drowning as it says: "Thus said the Lord waters ascend from the north," (Jer. 47:2) and just as He took the confined out of the box and spread them out in the land as it says: "You shall say to the captives go out, to that which is in the darkness reveal yourself," (Is. 49:9) and just as He gave them assurance from the Flood so He gave them assurance against enslavement and sorrow as it says: "And this for me is like the epoch of Noah . . . so I have sworn that I shall not be angry at you and shall not rebuke you." (Is. 54:9) It also says in another place that just as He decreed a flood once and then stopped it so He declared the enslavement once and afterwards stopped it and established a king for His nation. This is the statement: "Just as God prepared the world for a flood for a time so he prepared His kingdom for the world." (Ps. 29:10) The meaning of "shall sit" is "shall judge them" as it says: "You have placed Your chair of Just Judge." (Ps. 9:5)

IV

What is related to the pericope of the Flood . . . is what we find that one of our people thought that the waters of the Flood had not flooded the land of Israel. We say that the one who believed this thought that the statement "You are the land that is not cleaned nor rained upon in the day of indignation" (Ex. 22:24) refers to the time of the Flood[11] . . . We should explain his error in this matter. We say that if there did not remain at that time any populated land that was not flooded by water, then there is no reason to flood the mountains that are unpopulated for the goal was to destroy the animals as it says: "I rain on the land and destroy all the animal life,"[12] (Gen. 7:4) and these places, I mean those that fall into the first and seventh climate, have neither animals nor plants—in the south because of drought and in the north because of frost—for the destruction of the animals there is natural so there was no need to set forth something to destroy with. This is a veritable explanation, for Israel is between these two places and there is no doubt that it was flooded by water. The second

---

11. See *Zeb.* 113a.

12. Derenbourgh's edition referred to ad loc. has specifically "people," but this rendition does not fit the context here. This would appear to a discrepancy between the aforementioned edition and the missing translation accompanying the commentary.

possibility is that he thought that Ezekiel's statement "the uncleansed land" (22:24) is [positive]*. We should explain that it is not only just denigrating but utter indignation and denigration. The meaning is that He said to them: Your land had not been purified nor rained on . . . with anger until God purifies him . . . and to the masses for those who prophesy falsely, the priests, the officers, and the masses are all iniquitous. Of the false prophets [it says]: "There is a conspiracy among her prophets inside it like a roaring lion." (Ezek. 22:25) Of the priests [it says]: "Its priests profaned my teaching." (Ezek. 22:26) It repeats of the false prophets: "And her prophets have daubed them with untempered mortar." (Ezek. 22:28) Of the masses it says: "The masses used oppression and exercised robbery." (Ezek. 22:29) Now "on a day of anger" (Ezek. 22:24) refers to Nebuchadenezzer's army and those accompanying them which He compared to inundating water as we have explained! Even in the Book of Ezekiel itself it compares him to rain for it says: "And there shall be an overflowing shower in my anger." (Ezek. 13:13–14) The land of Israel does not need to be elevated by water . . . for it suffices by truth not by falsity.

It says then:

18) And the sons of Noah that exited the box Sem, Ham, and Japheth dwelled and Ham was[13] the father of Canaan; 19) these three that are Noah's sons from them man was dispersed upon the entire earth. 20) Behold, Noah[14] began <doing some working of> the ground and planted a vineyard; 21) then he drank of the wine and got drunk and uncovered himself in his tent; 22) and Ham the father of Canaan saw his father's nudity and told his brother coming out; 23) and Sem and Japheth took a garment placing it on their shoulders and walked turned away and covered their father and their faces were turned away and the nudity of their father they did not see; 24) and when Noah came out of his drunkenness and knew what his little son had done, 25) he said: Cursed is Canaan<'s father> an enslaved slave he shall be to his brothers; 26) then he said: Blessed is God the God of Sem; 26) Canaan shall be a servant to him; 27) God shall do good to Japheth and he shall occupy Sem's tent and the father of Canaan shall be a servant to him. . . .

---

13. Derenbourgh has "termed" inserted here. See below in the Gaon's com.

14. The Gaon omits "a man of," found in the original.

I

The word *baya* may mean either existence, formation, persistence, or staying.[15] "Existence" as it says: "that there be light." (Gen. 1:2) "Formation" [as] it says: "She became as widow." (Lam. 1:2) "Persistence" as it says: "she shall not continue to bereave." (Ex. 23:26?) "Staying" as it says: "All the time that they stayed at Carmel." (I Sam. 25:7) Now I connected {this case of *baya*} with what belongs to it and [accordingly] the statement means: "After people had stayed in the land Noah began and planted."

II

I render *baHuS* as "outside" for it would not be correct for me to render it as "in the market place"[16] because of the proximity of the incident to the time of their departure as it says: "And Noah began," whereas markets had not yet been organized.

III

I rendered "cursed is Canaan" as "cursed is Canaan's father" for Ham was cursed by his surname for the one who first raised him is known as we see our fathers are termed after their children in their childhood Abu Ishaq and Abu-l-hasan. This becomes their permanent name and so was the practice {of the Ancients}. For that reason it introduces the story saying "And Ham was Canaan's father" for only he of all his brothers is [known] so, for he was cursed by his surname because he was known by it.

IV

I rendered "servant of servants" as "enslaved servant"[17] for I am not able to say "servant of servants." I made it an exaggeration of servitude as it says "for all generations" (Is. 51:8) and "for all eternity" (Is. 34:10) and the like.

---

15. In the sense of "dwelling."
16. Derenbourgh, however, has this rendition.
17. Following Onqelos.

V

I rendered *evedb lamo* as "to him" and not as "to them" for the language permits adding a *mem* for eloquence . . . of the [*beth*]* . . . I found making eloquent with a *mem* in a similar context for it says: *yashar yaHazu penemo* (Ps. 11:7) [which] means *panaw* and we also say: *yaspiq 'alemu'* (Job 27:23) which is instead of *yaspiq 'alaw kappaw*. It is possible to say of . . . his wife and that they both entered . . . or at the time of his intercourse . . . [He made an indication]* . . . servitude: "And if the tooth of his servant," (Ex. 21:26) as we shall explain in its place.

VI

People have asked two questions about this story. The first is what is the sin Ham committed? This is because some think that he cut something off his father's limb while others conjecture something else.[18] Were it to be said to them that his sin was looking at him they will not believe and argue by the word "did." We will demonstrate to them that a bad word said of a person the language calls "doing" as Solomon says to Shim'I the son of Gera: "You know all the wickedness that your heart is privy to that you did you did to David my father," (I Kings 2:44) which is that he cursed him as it says: "which cursed me with a grievous curse." (I Kings 2:8) We add to this that the act that the Scripture denigrates Ham for is itself not doing the act for which Sem and Japheth were praised. For that reason it says before this: *wayithgal*, which is uncovering, and denigrating Ham for not concealing but revealed this too in his words and praised Sem and Japheth for covering [him] up as it says: "And they covered the nudity of their father."

VII

<<We say now>> what is the reason for repeating "And their faces were turned away" when it already says "And they walked turned facing away." It is possible the first "facing away" is upon their entrance and the second is during their departure . . . for that reason it [denigrates him]* or he

---

18. See *San.* 70a.

awoke . . . and Noah knew by this when it says: "And Noah knew" . . .
The second question . . . that Canaan himself and why does he not
curse by his name but by surname for this is most common practice in the
language of Israel to conceal the absolute "father," "brother," and "son" as
for "father" it says: "And Keluv the brother of Shuhe begot Mehir the
father of Ishtan and Ishtan begot Beth Raphe" (I Chron. 4:11–12) means
"and the father of Ishtan." "Brother" as it says: "And Elhanan the son of
Jaare-oregim, a Bethlehemite, slew Goliath the Gittite," (II Sam. 21:19)
but [the reference] is [to] the brother of Goliath as it says in the
Chronicles: "And Elhanan the son of Jair slew Lahmi the brother of
Goliath." (I Sam. 20:5) As for "son" is like Jeremaiah's statement: "In front
of the eyes of Hanamel my uncle," (Jer. 35:12) [which] means "the son of
my uncle." So here in the three statements "And he said cursed is Canaan,"
"And Canaan was," and "and Canaan was" the meaning is "the father of
Canaan" as we have explained.

VIII

In his statement "Blessed is the Lord God of Sem" he alludes that
prophecy and heavenly abode are among the children of Sem and his
domain. For that reason we find all the prophets to be of his seed.
Likewise, all the places where the abode rests is in his domain,[19] for the
word *Eoldhim* when it is used regarding something specific, not general,
has these two meanings: as He says to the prophets: "the Lord your God,"
(e.g., Jer. 42:2) and of Jerusalem: "the God of Jerusalem," (II Chron. 32:19)
"the God of Zion," (Ps. 146:10) as for . . . in that Noah brought upon
them servitude because he slighted him . . . to his father and the servant
to his master . . . the first after . . . but for one who accustomed
himself to be a slave it is not a punishment. Similar to this we have
explained in the questions . . . those that are not of their seed and shall
punish them with servitude. This is because he shall enslave and destroy
them . . . of property and they will be strangers between servitude as it
says: "When they shall be for him as servants and shall know my worship
and the worship of the kingdoms of the lands." (II Chron. 12:8) . . . He
gave us [this] to contemplate the greatness of parents and disrespecting.

---

19. Following *BR* 36 and *Mekhilta 'bo'* ch. 1. See also *Beliefs* 3:5 (p. 154).

Chapter X

It then says:[1]

I

. . . The meaning is that during these three years were not born . . . no sons and daughter in their likeness. The Tradition has regarding the city Cuthi Rabba . . . which is called Ur Kasdim (the Furnace of the Chaldeans) in the name of the furnace that Abram was thrown into and the All-Able and Exalted intervened and saved him.[2] What supports their statement is that furnaces and flames are called by this name like the statement: "Said God that prepared for him a furnace in Zion and an oven in Jerusalem to burn with," (Is. 31:9) "Nor a flame to sit against it," (Is. 47:14) "And he said: For I have become warm and felt the fire," (Is. 44:17) and "Were you to be stricken of fire." (Is. 50:11) What further supports their statement is that we find many cities and places named after the event that happened in them as it says: "And He called the name of that place, 'of trial and argument' for that Israel disputed with God and tested Him," (Ex. 17:7) "And he named that place the graves of desire," (Num. 11:34) and "And he called that place 'blazing' for God's fire was ablaze in

1. *Persuhe* ad loc.
2. *Baba Bathra* 91a and BR 44.

it." (Num. 11:3) Cases similar to this abound but I shall not expand on this [topic].

II

It first states "the name of Abram's wife" because it shall tell her history. The same applies to Milkah for it explicates who begot her. So also "And Sarai was barren," since the sign that God made for healing her will follow—"and she became pregnant and gave birth."

III

The statement "And Terah took Abram his son" is without mention of its cause and it shall mention the cause . . . in what follows this . . . from this . . . the attainment we see him ask and say were Terah and the rest of the people of his house[hold] . . . and went out of Iraq meaning the Israel by themselves without God's command until they reached Haran, how can He tell Abraham in Haran that they should go out to Israel for they had already gone out to Israel on their own accord.[3] Now we say that they saw God's statement to Abram, "from your land and your birth place," and thought that this was said to him in Haran and forgot that Haran is not "his land" nor "birth place" nor the "house of his father" and he errs in all this. We say that what was stated first is "And God said to Abram go for yourself from your land." This was in Cuthie Rabba and for that reason he and Terah his father and all that were with him went out but it mentioned the act before the cause. We say that this is like the Torah exhausts the life each one of these nine generations[4] before it begins the detailing of the life of his children for it completed the life of Sem before it mentions Shelah and went into the time one hundred fifty years. It then returns and mentions the birth of Shelah. It completes the life of Arpachshad before it mentions the birth of Eber and goes 428 until it reaches thirty years in Isaac's life. Similar to this it does with the rest of the generations. So it does in the matter of Terah wishing to complete his life before telling us anything about Abraham's event, being that Terah's

---

3. See Zucker, *Translation*, p. 35.
4. From Noah to Abraham.

death was not in its place he needed to tell us the story of this travels and was brief in mentioning the exit and did not mention the cause until it said: "And they came to Haran and Terah died in Haran." It reaches sixty years in turn after Abram's exit from Haran. And when it told the story of Terah in its entirety it returned to tell us the cause of his and Abraham's exit and said that the reason for this was: "And God said to Abraham go for yourself," and for that reason . . . to what I have rendered this statement is the most correct the connecting what preceded in Haran and the essence.

Chapter XI

[[1) And all <the people of> the land were <people of> one language and one speech; 2) and when they traveled from the east they found a valley in the land of Shinur and stayed there; 3) and one of them said to the other: Let us go and make bricks and cook <them>, and the bricks were for them like stone and the cement was for them like mortar; 4) and they said: Let us go and build us a city and a tower whose head shall come near the heavens and we shall make ourselves a name so that we do not be dispersed upon the ground; 5) and God brought down[1] <an instruction of intimidation> to see the city and the tower that the [2]people built. 6) Behold they are a single kinship and all of them have a single language and this <what> they began to build and now all that they have distressed to make shall not escape them; 7) Let us go and I shall bring down[3] <an instruction of intimidation> and I will disperse their language by it until one cannot hear the language of his friend; 8) and God dispersed them from there on the face of the earth and they ceased to build the city . . . . . . 31) and Terah took Abram his son and Lot the son of Haran the son of his son and Sarai Abram's wife and they went out with them from the Furnace of the Chaldeans to go to the land of Canaan and they came to Haran and they stayed there. . . .]]

---

1. The Gaon renders "and he went down" in the causative sense.

2. Kafih (*Perushe*) inserts here "began." I.e., "which they began to build"—apparently because it was not completed.

3. See note 1. See *Responsa to Hiwya* #21.

Chapter XII

1) Since God said to Abram: Go from your land and your birth place and from the house of your father to the land that I will show you 2) and I will make you into a great nation and I will bless you and I will make your name great and you will be a blessing; 3)and I will bless those who bless you and I will curse those that revile you and all the peoples of the earth will be blessed by means of you.

I

The first thing I did was to connect the cause to the action when I translated the passage as "Since God said to Abram: Go for yourself."[1] There it announced the departure in the name of Terah since he was the father. For this reason it associated those accompanying them with Terah and Abram and said "When they departed" and not "when he departed."

II

Now I say: What is the manner of wisdom in moving Abram from land to land and putting them[2] through the weariness of travel? I say this is for

---

1. The Gaon maintains that this verse is connected to the previous chapter.
2. Abraham and those accompanying him.

two reasons. The first is so that the people[3] benefit as it says regarding
Samuel (I Sam. 7:17): "And he would go from year to year and would go
around Beth El, the Gilgal and Mispe and would judge Israel." The second
is in order to test him and to add to his reward as it says regarding the
people of Israel: "Which the Lord made you go in the desert these forty
years in order to weary you and to test you," (Deut. 8:12) and further it
says: "In order to weary you and test you to make it good for you in the
end." (Deut. 8:17) And further to show signs and wonders for they were
in various troubles and God freed them[4] from them as He did for Israel in
Marah and Rephidhim and the wilderness of Sin, in the land of Edhom
and in the other remaining forty-two places where they dwelled which I
shall elucidate. Likewise when kings would rise up against them they
would not be able to do anything to them despite that they lived among
them as it says: "And they went from band to band from kingdom to other
peoples, but despite this I le did not let anyone wrong them," (Ps. 105:13)
and in the other version it says: "He did not let a person." (I Chron. 17:20)
By means of conjecture "person" refers to the Pharaoh since this word is
specifically used for tyrants as it says: "And a person arose to pursue you,"
(Ps. 124:2) and similarly: "When a person arises upon you," (I Sam. 22:29)
whereas "man" is a reference to Abimelech for this word refers to
righteous people in the majority as David says to Solomon: "And you shall
be strong and shall become a man and you shall watch the watch of the
Lord your God." (I Kings 2:2) We find that God said to Abimelech: "I
know that with the purity of your heart you did this." (Gen. 20:61) And
further to provide them with hapiness, the opposite of what alienship
causes, for it uses up money, or much of it, and also leads to the
bereavement of a father[5] and separates or destroys kin. Therefore God
promised Abram things that were opposed to these conditions. As for the
first thing He said: "And I shall make you into a great nation" . . . And
this is the specification of five[6] general ways.[7] As for the two specific ways
for Abram our father the first, which is the sixth,[8] shall be clear to anyone

---

3. In those lands.
4. See note 2.
5. This statement is difficult to make out.
6. Missing from here is an entire section that apparently spoke of the original
question of the wisdom involved in Abraham's travels.
7. The Gaon apparently refers to the general promises God made regarding
Abraham's descendents, not those specific to him.
8. Of the promises as a whole.

who has left his land and much of his belongings and took little and left
ascetically. For this he shall have great recompense and if Ruth who left
her land unhappily as it says regarding her: "And you shall leave your
father and mother and the land of your birth . . . God shall recompense
your actions," (Ruth 2:3) how much more so someone who leaves happily?
The seventh is in order to add esteem to the land of Israel when we see
people flocking to it from east and west. Abram from the east and Moses
and Israel from the west.

III

We say: What is the import of specifying "from your land, from your birth
place, and from the house of your father?" We answer: This is in order to
endear the land to him and this is the opposite of what humans do for
when a person asks something of his friend he reduces the thing and
makes it light in his eyes. However, the Creator may He be blessed and
exalted when He demands something from the righteous He augments it
in their eyes and makes it difficult for them in order that if they accept His
words nothwithstanding what is beloved to them, their reward as well as
their estimation in our eyes[9] will be increased because of it. This is the
reason for saying: "Take now your son your only one," (Gen. 22:2) as we
shall explain. This accords the fact that he did not incorporate [which]
land it was [into the text][10] and did not tell him which one it was but said
to him just "to the land I will show you." The manner of wisdom in this
is that if God would have specified to him which one it is, one would say
that Abram only obeyed God and went to the land because he asked
about it and God told him of its goodness and fineness and if not for this
he would not have obeyed God. Similar to this is the fact that God did
not immediately reveal to him the place of the binding but said: "On one
of the mountains that I shall tell you." This too we say regarding the fact
that He did not specify Jonah's second prophecy and said: "And call upon
it the call that I speak to you" (Jon. 3:2) and also regarding the fact that

---

9. See next note.

10. Apparently the Gaon means that not only did He not tell Abraham which
land it was, He did not even reveal it to the reader during the unfolding of the
story. This is in order to underscore Abraham's obedience of God and to increase
his estimation in the reader's eyes.

God did not reveal to Ezekiel what he shall prophesy about for He said: "Get up and go to the valley and there I shall speak to you." (Ezek. 3:22)

IV

Since we have said regarding the three parts of the first verse what we thought correct, we say regarding the promises: What is the manner of wisdom in that which He said to Abram: "And I shall make you into a great nation?" And would one ask and say: If God would not have promised him anything he would not have left his land? And would also say: Was not Sarai more obedient than him for she left without any promise? Or would say further that Terah was more obedient than any of them for he went out with Abram just to accompany him as we have explained. We say God only made him all the promises in advance in order that the first troubles occur to him and he tolerates them and [as a result] God will increase his reward for we see that in opposition to the promise of "And I will make you into a great nation" . . . Abram did not begat as it says: "And Sarai was barren" (Gen. 11:30) . . . and in opposition to His statement "And I will bless you," there was a hunger in the land and in opposition to "I will make your name great," Pharaoh says to him "Why did you say 'She is my sister?'" (Gen. 12:19)[11] and other similar events that occured to him . . . but he was expelled—"And Pharaoh assigned upon him men." (Gen. 12:20) Similarly these things happened to him despite the promises and when he tolerated them the promises were realized for him and his children manifold. According to this idea his obedience was greater than that of all of those that accompanied him for they were not promised anything that then changed on them.

V

What the statement "And I will make you into a great nation" indicates is multiplicity of kinships and their number[12] as it says: "And they were

---

11. The assumption is if Pharaoh would have considered him to be a man of stature he would not have to worry about his wife being taken.

12. The kinships were numerous and each kinship had many members.

there an awesome and great nation." (Deut. 26:5) The second meaning is that his children will be answered when they call to God as it says: "For which awesome and great nation has a god near it like the Lord our God whenever we call him." (Deut. 4:17)[13] The third is that God will give them the Torah and its precepts as it says: "Which nation has upright orders and laws like the entire Torah?" (Deut. 4:8)[14]

VI

"And I shall bless you"—these are all the blessing in the priestly blessings . . . and this shall be . . . "In every place that I shall mention My Name." (Ex. 20:21) . . . and in the statement "And I shall increase your name" includes . . . matter of kingship and in . . . included . . . some of . . . God . . . the first thing he shall say.

[[4) and Abram went as God commanded him and Lot went with him and Abram was seventy-five years old when he left Haran; 5) and Abram took Sarai and Lot his relative and all their belongings that they acquired and all the souls that they attained in Haran and went out to go to the land of Canaan and came to it; 6) and Abram passed in the land to the place of Nablus and to the field of Mamre and the Canaanite was then residing in the Land; 7) then God revealed Himself and said: To your offspring I shall give this land; and he built there an altar for God that revealed Himself there; 8) then he moved from there to the mountain in the east of Beth El and pitched there his tent; Beth El in the west and the 'Ay in the east and built there an altar for God called in His name; 9) then Abram continued to travel to the Qiblah; 10) then there was a famine in the land and Abram went down to Egypt to dwell there for the famine had become strong in the land; 11) and when he came near enterting Egypt he said to Sarai his wife: I know that you are a woman of good appearance; 12) I fear that if the Egyptians see you and I would say 'This is his wife,' they will kill me and leave you; 13) say of me that you are my sister so that it be good for me because of you in that

---

13. In this case as in the next "great" is taken in stature, not in number as in the previous case.

14. Making him into a great nation is marked by the receipt of the Torah. This interpretation orginates from *Tanhuma*.

my soul shall be kept alive because of your sin; 14) and when Abram
came into Egypt, the Egyptians saw that the woman was very attractive;
15) and Pharaoh's officers saw her and praised her to him and the woman
was taken to Pharaoh's palace; 16) and it was good to Abram because of
her and he had much sheep, cattle, asses, servants, maid-servants,
she-asses, and camels; 17) and God threatened Pharaoh and his
household with great calamity because of Sarai Abram's wife; 18) and
Pharaoh called Abram and said: What is this you have done to me? And
have not told me that she is your wife; 19) and why have you said to me:
'She is my sister,' so that I take her to be a wife for me and now here is
your wife take her and go! 20) And Pharaoh placed men over him and
accompanied him and his wife and all that is his.]]

I

Were one to say: How did God punish Pharaoh if he did not sin? The
answer to this is that "And God struck Pharaoh" is not in action but by
warning.[15]

---

15. Accordingly the Gaon translates "and God threatened."

Chapter XIII

[[1) and Abram went up from Egypt, he and his wife and all that is his and Lot with him to Qiblah; 2) and Abram was extremely great with property, silver, and gold; 3) and he came in his travel from Qiblah to Beth El to the place where his tent was at first between Beth El and the 'Ay; 4) to the place of the altar that he made there at first and there Abram called in the name of God; 5) and Lot, who went with Abram, also had sheep, cattle, and tents; 6) and the land could not withstand both of them residing in it for their property was much and it was not able [to sustain] both of them 7) and there was a dispute between the shepherds of the cattle of Abram and the shepherds of the cattle of Lot and the Cananite and the Perizite were then residing in the land; 8) so Abram said to Lot: There shall not be dispute between me and you and between my shepherds and your shepherds for we are people of relation; 9) is not all the land in front of you separate from me if to the left then I shall go to the right and if to the right I shall go to the left; 10) and Lot raised his eyes and saw the entire meadow of the Jordan that it is all watered before God destroyed Sodom and Gammorah like the garden of God like the land of Egypt until you reach Zaghr; 11) and Lot chose for himself all the plain of the Jordan and travled to the east and separated everything from his brother; 12) Abram resided in the land of Canaan and Lot resided in the cities of the meadow tented until Sodom; 13) and the people of Sodom were extremely evil and iniquitous to God. 14) Then God said to Abram after Lot had departed him: Raise your eyes and see from the place which you are there north and south, east and west; 15) for all the land that you see to you and to your offspring I have given it for eternity; 16) and I shall make your offspring like the dust of the earth so that if a man be able to count the dust, your offspring too he will be able to count; 17) get up and walk in the land its length and its width and I shall give it to you. 18) and Abram pitched tents and came and stayed in the meadow of Mamre which is in Hebron and he built there an altar to God.]]

Chapter XIV

[[1) Then it was in the days of Amraphel the king of Shinur and Aryoch the king of Elasar, Kedarlaomer the king of Arbistan, and Tidh'al the king of nations; 2) and they waged war with Bela' the king of Sodom, Resha' the king of Gammorah, Shinab the king of Admah, Shemeber the king of Sevuyim, and the king Bela' which is Zaghr; 3) and all these gathered in the meadow of Sadin which is the salt sea; 4) twelve years they obeyed Kadarlaomer and on the thirteenth they rebelled against him; 5) and on the fourteenth year Kadarlaomer and the kings that were with him came forth and killed the giants that are in Ashtaroth Qarnayim and the heads of the villages which are the "threatening ones" that are in Shawe Qiryathayim; 6) and the Hurites that are in the mountain of Shar'ah; 7) then they returned and came to the Spring of Judgement which is Raqim and killed everyone who was in the field of the Amalekite as well as the Amorites that resided in the the gathering of date palms; 8) the king of Sodom, the king of Gamorrah, the king of Admah, and the king of Bela' which is Zaghr and waged war in the field of the Amalekite; 9) with Kedarlaomer the king of Arbistan, Tidh'al the king of the nations, Amraphel the king of Shinur, and Aryoch the king of Elasar, the four kings with the five; 10) and the field of Sadin in which there are wells that bring forth asphalt and the king of Sodom and Gammorah fled and fell there and the rest fled to the mountain; 11) and they took all the possesions of Sodom and Gammorah and all their food and went; 12) and they took Lot the the son of Abram's brother and his possessions

and went and he resides in Sodom. 13) Then the refugee went and told
Abram the Hebrew that resided in the meadow of Mamre the Amorite
the brother of Eshkol and the brother of 'Aner which are of Abram's
pact; 14) and when he heard that his relative had been captured he
hurried his followers born in his house 318 and pursued <them> until
Banias;[1] 15) and the night divided upon them, him and his servants, and
he pursued them until Hobah which is to the left of Damascus; 16) and
he returned all the possesions and Lot his relative and his property he
returned <to them> and the women and the rest of the people; 17) then
the king of Sodom went out to greet him after he returned from war of
Kedarlaomer and the kings that are with him to 'Emeq Shawe which is
the place of the king's recreation; 18) and Malkizedek the king of
Jerusalem brought out food and drink[2] for him and he is the priest for
the All High [and] All Able; 19) and he blessed him and said Abram shall
be blessed by the All High [and] All Able that is the Ruler of the
Heavens and the Earth; 20) and blessed is is the All High [and] All Able
who has supplied your enemies to your hand and he gave him a tithe of
everything; 21) and the king of Sodom said to Abram: Give me the souls
and the possessions take for yourself. 22) Abram said to him I raise my
hands in oath to God the All High [and] All Able the Ruler of the
Heavens and the Earth; 23) from string to shoelace if I take from all your
property and you shall not say I have made Abram not needy; 24) except
for what the lads and part of the of the people that went with have eaten
'Aner and Eshkol and Mamre they shall take their part.]]

I have interpreted "And thirteen years they rebelled and on the
fourteenth year Kadarlaomer came" as on the thirteenth and fourteenth
year, for I have made each one a year so that there is not thirteen and
fourteen years, all together twenty-seven, excluding the first twelve.[3]

---

1. A river in Syria (according to Kafih).
2. Not specifically bread and wine as in the original text.
3. See Criticisms, p. 100 against this view.

Chapter XV

[[1) After these things were God's words to Abram in a vision saying: Do not fear Abram I am your shield, your reward is great. 2) Abram said: O God my Master what shall You give me when I am going barren and the conductor of my house is Eliezer of Damascus? 3) And he said: Since You have not provided me with offspring behold the son that is in my house shall inherit me. 4) And behold God's words were saying to him: This one shall not inherit you but one that shall come out of your loins he shall inherit you. 5) Then He took him outside and said to him direct your eyes to the Heavens and contemplate the number of stars, are you able to count them? Then He said to him: So shall be your offspring; 6) And Abram believed in God and merit was written for him; 7) and said to him: I am God that took you out of the Furnace of the Chaldeans so that I may give you this land for you to take possession of it. 8) He said: O God the Master by what shall I know that I shall take possession of it? 9) He said to him: Bring forth before Me a three-fold calf, a three-fold goat, a three-fold ram, a three-fold turtle-dove, and a three-fold young pigeon. 10) And he brought forth in front of Him all this and split them in their middle, then he placed every part across the other and the bird did not split it; 11) then he placed the bird on the corpses and moved them and Abram moved them and they moved. 12) And when it was during the setting of the sun a sleep fell on Abram and behold a great fog of darkness fell upon him; 13) and He said to Abram: Be sure to know that your offspring shall be a stranger in a land not theirs and they shall enslave and torment them four hundred years; 14) and also the nation that shall enslave them I shall judge them and after this they shall go out with much possessions; 15) and you shall come to your fathers in peace and shall be buried in good old age; 16) and the fourth generation shall return here for the sin of the Amorite had not been completed until now; 17) and when the sun set and there was great darkness behold in the likeness of an oven smoke and flames of fire passed in between those slabs; 18) on this day God made a treaty with Abram saying: To your offspring I shall give this land from the river of Egypt until the large river the Euphrates river; 19) the Keynites, the Kenizites, and the Kadmonites; 20) the Hittites, the Perizites, and the giants; 21) the Amorites, the Canaanites, the Girgishites, and the Yebusites.]]

I

. . . "The slabs"—when the four kindoms shall cease the resurrection of the dead shall take place.[1] They began with the statement: "Until the day shall inflate," (Cant. 2:17 and 4:6)[2] meaning until what is compared to the day of my light shall become visible <<as it says: "Arise, illuminate" (Is. 60:1) and the like. "And shadows shall flee" (ibid.) means that the shade of their kingdom and their state shall be removed>> as it says: "And they shall depart from them." (Num. 14:19) They compared the savior to the deer and the ram because of how swiftly they move.[3] It is possible that a pigeon is a comparison to Edom and Ismael together in the sense that they rule part of the world just as the pigeon appears in Israel only sometimes as it says: "And the voice of the pigeon is heard in our land," (Cant. 2:12) "It is like a pigeon whose wings were coverd with silver and its claws with the yellowness of gold," (Ps. 68:14) and "And like the pigeon to its chimneys." (Is. 60:8) It arranges the five kingdoms by including Israel.

II

"And when it was during the setting of the sun and a *tardema*"—a sleep and *eima* is great darkness. This is the prophetic vision that is called *mar'eh* and

---

1. Apparently the Gaon sees these verses as alluding to the resurrection of the dead.

2. The Gaon gives this verse in Arabic translation.

3. Cf., com. to Gen. 1:24.

also *tardema* and is what is said of Abram here. This *mar'eh* is a term for prophecy. It is the state in which the prophet is found as in a confined circle so that he is unaware of the state of other people just as people do not sense his prophecy.

III

The meaning of *hashecha* is darkness of clouds and fogs surround it similar to what it says: "He made the darkness a cover for Him," (Ps. 18:12) <and: "Darkness, cloud, and fog." (Deut. 4:11)

IV

It adds *eyma* <in order to distinguish between the darkness> and the natural fogs.

V

It adds "great" in the sense of "a large cloud and ignited fire." (Ezek. 1:4)

VI

It specifies "had fallen upon him" means its vicinity and around none of it can be seen like Daniel says: "And I Daniel alone have seen" (Dan. 10:7).

VII

The meaning of "Be sure know" is that he should be certain to know and to inform his children of the length of the end of Egypt. The manner of wisdom in [giving] this information is so they do not negate the enslavement when it comes upon them but will hope for savior that they were promised and will not give up. . . . There are none among the children of Jacob who lived more than Levi. Remove this 117 years until it reaches eighty. According to the Scripture it is impossible that they should stay in Egypt for five hundred years for were we to add the years

Kehath, Amram, and Moses with the majority it will come to just 350 years. Were we to imagine in our minds how much each one of them lived with his father and put the years of one into the other we would have the date of 210. The four hundred years are not all torment nor servitude either. For it includes three things. All of them were five hundred years as it says: "Your offspring shall be a stranger in a land not theirs." This is like were one to say I stayed in Baghdad, Kawfa, and Basra twenty years. It is possible that he was twelve in one place, seven in another, and one in another so "For a stranger your offspring shall be" is five hundred years and "And they shall serve them" is 210 and "And they shall inflict them" is eighty years. This measurement applies solely to his offspring for it says "Your offspring shall be." For that reason it should be counted from the birth of Isaac. The 530 years includes Abraham's journey which is the thirty that we have mentioned in the section of "And Terah took Abram his son," (Gen. 11:31) for it does not say there "Abram's offspring" but "And the residence of the people of Israel" (Ex. 12:40) and Israel is Jacob. Were one to say "the sons of such" this applies to his sons and his family like: "And these are the sons of the city." (Ezek. 2:1) This refers to the entire family and Abraham is included among the sons of Israel. Now "that dwelled in Egypt" (Ex. 12:40) refers to the region of Egypt[4] until the river Euphrates since we find it belonging to Egypt as it says: "The king of Egypt did not continue to leave his land for the king of Babylonia took from the river of Egypt until the Euphrates everything that belonged to the king of Egypt." (II Kings 24:7) This is the interpretation of "the end of Egypt." The statement "and the nation too" refers to the plagues. "And afterwards they went out with great inheritance" refers to silver and gold vessels and garments as we shall explain.[5]

VIII

"And you shall go to your fathers in peace" means in peace from servitude—none of this shall come upon you. The statement to Yoshiahu, "And you shall be gathered to your grave in peace," (II Kings 22:20) in peace from the Temple not being destroyed in his days.[6] His statement to

---

4. Ad loc. the Gaon adds "regions."
5. See *Seder Olam Rabba* ch. 3, *Mek.* ch. 14 and *BR* ch. 43.
6. So *Moed. Qat.* 28b.

Zedekiah, "In peace you shall die," (Jer. 34:5) which is peace from the sword as Jeremiah says: "You shall not die from the sword." (Jer. 34:4). Some say that this means that is protection from the enemy for Nebuchadenezzer died in the life of Zedekiah,[7] but the first [interpretation] is more correct.

IX

The statement "in good old age" contains two ideas. The first is because Terah repented and the other is because Ismael did so [too].[8] Likewise the statement of David, "And he died in good age," (I Chron. 29:21) is that God forgave [him] for the sin that he is known for.[9] Likewise in the statement regarding Gideon, "And he died in good age," (Judg. 8:32) is that Israel did not sin in his lifetime so that one does not think that [the entire event of] "And Gideon made an *ephod* thereof and put it in his city in Ophrah and all Israel went thither a whoring after it" (Judg. 8:27) is during his lifetime. We should explain that making the *ephod* for the priests was during his lifetime but the people after he died made it into an object of worship as it says: "And it was when Gideon died and Israel returned," (Judg. 8:33) and of him it says: "abhoring after it." This is similar to that Moses made the copper snake and after his death the people made it into an idol.[10]

X

<<"The fourth generation shall return here" refers to the fourth generation from the descent to Egypt for Kehat, Amram, and Moses are three and the children of Israel entered the land.>>

XI

"And when the sun set and there was great darkness behold in the likeness of an oven smoke and when the sun set and there was great darkness." It

---

7. See ibid.
8. Following *BR* ch. 38.
9. See *Sab.* 30a.
10. See II Kings 18:4.

adds "smoke." which is a sphere around the fire. It compares it to an oven in order to liken it to what it is familiar to us as it says: "And its smoke ascended like the smoke of a furnace." (Ex. 19:18)

XII

"To your offspring I have given this land" is giving by decree and it is the land of the ten nations as they are counted.[11] Although ten are decreed for us only seven have come to us in the past. The Kenite, Kenizite, and Kadmonite were not obtained but they will be at the time of the Savior as it says: "And if God were to broaden your border." (Deut. 19:8) Some say that for that reason Isaac says "these (ha-el) lands" (Gen. 26:4) and not ha-ele for only three of them remained.[12] Likewise, it says "to these (ha-el) men" (Gen. 19:8) for the third departed from them. The same applies to "all these (ha-el) abominations" (Lev. 18:27) to exclude the eight secondary ones that were transmitted about it.[13] Likewise, "Three other cities shall be added to these three." (Deut. 19:9) This at the time of the Savior when "And if he shall expand" (ibid.) will be fulfilled.

---

11. Gen. 15:19–21.
12. *BR* 63:3.
13. See *Jeb.* 21a. See also the Gaon's com. to *BO* 3:35 for a similar passage.

Chapter XVI

[[1) And Sarai Abram's wife did not bear for him and she had an Egyptian maidservant, her name was Hagar; 2) and she said to Abram: Behold God had held me back from giving birth, come upon my maidservant perhaps my house shall be built from her; and Abram listened to Sarai's words; 3) and Sarai Abram's wife took Hagar her maidservant after twenty years after Abram's stay in the land of Canaan and gave her to Abram her husband so that she be for him a wife; 4) and he came upon Hagar and she became pregnant and when she saw that her pregnancy was intense her mistress was belittled by her; 5) and Sarai said to Abram: My anger is upon you, I have given you my maidservant into your lap and when I saw that she had become pregnant I had become belittled by her, God shall judge between me and you; 6) Abram said to Sarai: Behold your maidservant is in your hands, do with her what you find proper and Sarai tormented her until she fled from in front of her; 7) and an angel of God found her on a spring of water in the desert at the 'Ayn on the way to Hajir Hijaz;[1] 8) He said: Hagar maidservant of Sarai where do you come from and where are you going? She said: From in front of Sarai my mistress I flee; 9) and the angel of God said to her: return to your mistress and serve under her; 10) then the angel of God said to her: I shall surely multiply your offspring until it cannot be counted because of its multitude; 11) then he said to her: Behold you

---

1. A western territory in which Mecca is situated. (Derenbourg, Tafsir, ad loc.).

252

are pregnant, you shall give birth to a son and shall name him "Ishmael"
for God heard your feebleness, 12) and he will be a barbarous of
people, his hand in everything and the hand of everything in him and in
the presence of all his brothers he will dwell; 13) and she called the
name of God that appeared there: You are the All Able and Seeing for
she said: I have seen here Your pity after I had seen <the feebleness>;
14) Therefore she named the Well "the Well of the Living and Seeing."
Behold she is between Raqim[2] and Beredh; 15) then Hagar bore for
Abram a son and Abram named his son that Hagar bore "Ishmael"; 16)
and Abram was eighty-six years old when Hagar bore Ishmael for
Abram.]]

I

"Come upon my maidservant" this refers to a case when the husband
desires something that belongs to his wife that he can only take it with her
permission. Likewise he may only take her maidservant with her consent.[3]

II

"Perhaps my house shall be built from her" teaches us that one who has no
children his house is destroyed.[4]

III

The date "at the end of ten years" serves to require compliance in this,
which is anyone who stays with his wife for ten years and she does not
give birth nor miscarries, he is obligated to marry someone else in
addition to her if it is within his ability to sustain two wives and if not he
shall free the first and marry the other.[5]

---

2. A territory in the Negev. (according to Kafih, in *Perushe*).
3. *BR* 45:1.
4. *BR* 45:1.
5. Ibid.

IV

The date of "after twenty years after Abram's stay in the land of Canaan" is to tell us that the years during which they travelled are not included in the whole for it is possible that accidents along the way delay him. According to this we have by Tradition that when sickness, imprisonment, travel, and other delays come about they are not counted into the amount of ten years for people ever[6] . . . recompense it is upon you to pay good with good according to your ability and if not at least by gratitude.

V

"And Sarai said to Abram my anger is upon you" implies an argument between them because of Hagar which the Scripture eliminates without mention of it. This is because you do not see in the text anything other than "I have given you my maidservant in your lap"—none of this implying an argument existing between Abram and Sarai. "My anger" indicates an argument about which the Scripture is brief. We think it to be as if she said: "It should be that I should take her lightly" . . . but he says this is not permissible and during this she said: "The Lord shall judge between you me and you." She did not want the Lord to judge him but that the Lord should clarify who is correct. God Exalted and Glorified clarified that the truth is with Sarai and that Hagar should remain a servant until she returns to obedience to her to Sarai for when she tormented her when it says "And Sarai tormented her," the angel says to her: "Return to your mistress and be tormented under her." From here we know that Sarai did not sin in forcing upon Hagar what she does not deserve for would it be so the angel would not have agreed to this. . . .

VI

. . . The reason for dividing the speech of the angel is that he commanded her of serving her mistress and that she should submit to her and will not need to correct her. In the second she announced to her that she shall have much offspring and that He made this recompense for her

---

6. *Jeb.* 61a.

for serving Sarai. If one who acts of obligation has recompense then one who serves superogatorilly he should certainly hope to come close to his Master. The third is that he lets her know that the pregnancy will be complete and that he will be male and that she must name him Ismael and that the reason for naming [him so] is "because He heard your feebleness." He [also] let her know that he will dwell in the desert. This is by his statement: "He will be the barbarous of man" as if to say that he shall be the first to dwell in the desert and shall choose it . . . He also says to her that despite this his hand shall be in everything and the hand of everything shall be in him, meaning that he shall mingle with people despite that he is in the desert; he shall mingle with them in marriage, commerce, controversy, and whatever else his matters include in time the like . . . in this matter there is a ramification in the Book of Daniel? . . . which shall mentioned in its place . . . this indicates that he shall not penetrate into the desert . . . but he shall be near the inhabited part of Israel.

VII

<"After I had seen feebleness" she sees torment and [then] God's pity in what happened to her after this. She adds "of the Living and Seeing" to tell [us] that He is so all the time, for all people he is the Seeing and pitiful and not just for her.

VIII

"And she called the name of the son that she bore" lets us know that he believed her and accepted her words because she said that the angel told her that she will give birth and she did indeed. Perhaps he had a sign from the incident that happened that he must believe her.

IX

It specifies "and Abram was eighty-six years old" to tell us of his condition at that time for after this section comes the commandment of circumcision. These verses and their interpretations have many purposes. . . .>

Chapter XVII

[[1) And when Abram became ninety-nine years old God revealed Himself to him and said to him: I am the All Able the Sufficient, go in [the path of] My obedience and be righteous, 2) and I shall make My treaty between Me and between you and I shall multiply you very, very much; 3) and Abram fell on his face and God spoke to him saying: 4) Behold I make a treaty with you and you shall be the father of masses of nations; 5) and your name shall no longer be called Abram but your name shall be Abraham for I have made you the father of masses of nations; 6) and I shall make you flourish very, very much and I will make from you nations, and kingdoms shall come out of you; 7) and I will establish My treaty between Me and between you and your offspring after you for their generations a treaty of eternity so that I shall be for you a God and for your offspring after you; 8) and I will give you and your offspring after you the land of your dwelling the entire land of Canaan as an eternal possession and I will be for you a God.]]

I

< . . . just as Abraham was circumcised after he passed one hundred. This argument is possible but the argument that God wanted it to be so is more preferable.[1]

---

1. Apparently the Gaon refers here to the words of the Rabbis to the effect

256

II

Since God says to him: "I am the All Able the Sufficient," we may say that God devised this name for himself for various reasons. [1] As if He said to him: "I am sufficient for you," for the word *shad-dai* (that is sufficient) is derived from "And what they brought was sufficient (*dayyam*) for the entire job." (Ex. 36:7) God was required to tell him this because of the commandment of circumcision in order that he should not feel that his body will become weak when something is amputated from it or that his enemies will rise upon him during his sickness or that the nations will . . . when he will be . . . for that reason God said to him: "I stand for you against all these things . . . and He is mentioned with the name Shad-dai, "Sufficient" . . . and it says: "Wherefore do they not descry their fate from the All Sufficing?" (Job 24:1) for His knowledge is without a cause. It also says: "That he may trifle with the All Sufficing," (Job 27:10) meaning: "My retribution will not cease." And also: "Like spoils from with the Sufficing will come," (Is. 13:6) for its punishment will not . . . >. So that Abraham knows that this is for estimation.

III

"Walk in front of Me" means obedience similar to what we have mentioned in the incident of "And Noah walked." It adds . . . the commandment shall complete your obedience for it is the greatest[2] . . . people were a male to cut something off his body . . . is the act? That will not add or remove and as long as the foreskin was not removed from his body he shall not be complete[3] and for that reason God commanded him to cut off this addition from him and [then] he shall be complete. The third is that one should not think that Abraham's name was changed for the purpose of magic omens[4] for that reason it says before: "And be righteous," for one who uses magic and omens shall not be righteous as it says: "There shall not be found among you one that burns his son or daughter and who uses magic." (Deut. 18:10)

---

that Abraham was not circumcised until he passed ninety-nine to show how beloved proselytes are even in their old age. (Zucker). See *Mek. Mishpatim*, ch. 18.

2. See *Ned.* 32a.

3. A response to Hiwya (Davidson, p. 64). See also *Beliefs* 3:10 (p. 177).

4. A response to another of Hiwya's questions.

IV

It says: "I will make My treaty," but did He not do this already when it says: "One that God made a treaty with Abraham saying"? We say that that treaty is that God will give the Special Land to His children as it says: "To your offspring I have given." This treaty [however] is that He will multiply their number as it says: "And I shall multiply you very, very much."

V

We then say: Why does the [commandment of] circumcision have to be connected to the multiplication? So that it not be thought that his body would weaken and his seed reduced because of the circumcision . . . or that this is [an exaltation]* of the Torah when they become fruitful by means of it.

VI

"Behold my treaty is with you" has an elliptic word [and means]: "I make a treaty with you."

VII

"And you shall be a father of many peoples" has four meanings. The first and closest to the test is that it refers to the three nations: Israel, Edom, and Ishmael and Abraham is the father of all of them. [The second] is that prophecy, which is called *hamon* (mass) as it says: "And the voice of his words is like the voice of the mass," (Dan. 10:6) is among his children. [The third] is that prayer to the Creator and response to it, which is called *hamon* as it says: "The mass of your mercy and compassion that will be aroused upon us." (Is. 63:15) [The fourth] is the Torah which will be brought down to his children and of which it says: "I was with him a mass." (Prov. 8:30)

VIII

"No longer shall your name be called Abram and your name shall be Abraham" means that one [name] replaces the other. However, what it says elsewhere: "No longer shall your name be called Jacob but Israel shall be your name" (Gen. 35:10) means that he shall not be called just Jacob but both Jacob and Israel. It is according to the usage of the language that in regards to Abraham the meaning was "one instead of the other" and in regards to Jacob "one together with the other."

IX

It repeats "a father of masses of nations" to give the derivation of "Abraham."

X

"And I shall multiply you very, very much" refers to Keturah and her children.

XI

"And I shall establish my treaty" . . . that "between Me and between you" refers to the circumcision of the men [that] Abraham owned . . . and his possessions. "And between your offspring after you for their generations" refers to the circumcision of the children after eight days.

XII

"To be a God for you" is an introduction to "the God of Abraham" and "and to your offspring after you" is an introduction to "the God of Isaac and the God of Jacob." These names are something . . . estimation.

XIII

"And I shall give you and your offspring after you . . . and I shall be for them a God"—He is called the "God of the Armies" after they enter the land. Now they have become "armies" according to what the Ancients said: "The Holy Blessed He was only called 'Armies' because of the Armies of Israel." (Shav. 35b) This means that you will not find this name until after they enter the land as it says: "And a man would go up every year to bow and sacrifice to the God of the Armies in Shiloh." (I Sam. 1:13)

XIV

Then it says:

[[9) Then God said to Abraham: And you observe My treaty you and your offspring after you for their generations; 10) this is My treaty which you shall observe between Me and between you and your offspring after you: Every man among you shall be circumcised; 11) and if you circumcise the foreskin of your bodies it will be an indication of My treaty between Me and between you; 12) and a son of eight days every male of you shall be circumcised for their generations one who is born in <your> house<s> and one who is bought for money from any foreigner that is not of your offspring; 13) being that one who born in your house and bought by you for money My treaty will be in your bodies an eternal treaty; 14) and if a man did not circumcise the foreskin from his body and this man shall be cut off of his people since he annulled My treaty. 15) Then God said to Abraham: Sarai your wife do not call her Sarai but call her Sarah; 16) and I shall bless her and I shall provide for you from her a son and I will bless her and a nation shall be from her and kings of peoples will come out from her; 17) and Abraham fell on his face and laughed and said to himself: Shall a one-hundred-year-old beget and Sarah is ninety years old; 18) and Abraham said in front of God: Lo Ishmael should live in front of You; 19) God said to him: But Sarah your wife will bear a son and shall name him "Isaac" and I will establish a treaty with him an eternal treaty and to his offspring after him; 20) and of Ishmael I have heard you. Behold I have blessed him so that I may make him fruitful and multiply him very, very much <and> twelve nobles he will beget and I will make of him a great nation; 21) and My treaty I will establish with Isaac that Sarah will bear for you at this time next year; 22) and when He completed His speech God['s light] departed from Abraham; 23) and Abraham took Ishmael his son and all that was born in his house and bought with money any man from the people of Abraham's house and he circumcised the foreskin from their bodies in that actual day as God commanded; 24) and Abraham was ninety-nine years old when he circumcised the foreskin from his body; 25) and Ishmael his son was thirteen years old when he circumcised the foreskin from his body; 26) in that actual day Abraham and

Ishmael his son were circumcised; 27) and every man in his house that was born in it or bought for money, any foreigner were circumcised with him.]]

I

[The meaning of] "This is My treaty which you shall observe" is dependent on the Tradition for it is not clear to the listener what the circumcision is and how it is [to be performed] and there is no way to determine what it is other than by means of the Tradition for one would be confused as to which limb it is.[5] Were one to attempt to cite proof from the word *orlah* (foreskin) he would find it used in reference to three limbs: [1] the foreskin of the heart—[6] "And you shall circumcise the foreskin of your heart," (Deut. 10:17), [2] foreskin of the lip—"and I am uncircumcised of the lips," (Ex. 6:12) and [3] foreskin of the ear—"behold their ear is uncircumcised." (Jer. 34:14) So he would be confused when he would look which one of these three limbs were amputated from him . . . Were one to think to cite proof from "the flesh of your foreskin"[7] . . . you will find it in the Scripture that it is possible that it should refer to meat, body, or mass . . . when it says: "This is the description of the dissolution in which his impurity will be either the genitals produce the dissolution like drool or," (Lev. 15:3) it means . . . we do not know that the reference is to the organs of excrement for it being that . . . and "His flesh drooled" could refer to the mouth.

II

"This shall be an indication of the treaty between Me and you"—we find various interpretations, each one of which is in the sense of giving assurance against retribution. The rainbow, which is the first, is assurance against the flood as we have explained that it is an assurance.[8]

---

5. See *Shab.* 108a regarding proofs of where the circumcision is performed. See also Anan, *Book of Precepts*, p. 79.

6. The following three verses do not follow the Gaon's rendition but are kept literal for the purpose of showing the usage of the word "foreskin."

7. See *Shab.* 108a.

8. The section following is garbled and has therefore been omitted.

III

"Born in your houses" is one born in the Trustworthy[9] of a maidservant that converted. "Bought with money" one was bought when he was an adult and was circumcised on the day {of acquirement} and one who is born in the house <is circumcised after eight days.>[10]

IV

"This man shall be cut off of his people"—this is mentioned before the commandment of the Sabbath so that circumcision can push aside the Sabbath. Likewise, the sacrifice is mentioned [before] the Sabbath to push aside the commandments of the Sabbath and should go ahead and circumcise on the Sabbath.[11]

V

"And when God completed His speech" lets us know that God did not appear to the fathers in beasts, *ophanim*, or cherubs but only in pure light so that you know <that they were pure and holy like cherubs.>

VI

It reiterates "On that actual day Abraham was circumcised," which is on the day that Abraham became exactly ninety-nine as Moses says: "I am 120 years old today." (Deut. 31:2) God says to him : "on that actual day" (Deut. 32:48).

---

9. I.e., a Jew.
10. See *Sab.* 135b.
11. See *Beliefs* 3:9 (p. 169).

Chapter XVIII

[[1) And God revealed Himself to him in the plain of Mamre and he is sitting at the opening of the tent at the heat of the day; 2) and he lifted his eyes and saw and behold three individuals stand in front of him and when he saw them he ran to greet them from the opening of the tent and bowed to the Earth; 3) and he said <excitedly>[1]: God<'s prince>[2] if I have found favor with you do not pass by your servant; 4) a little water shall be brought forth to you and wash your feet and recline under the tree; 5) and I shall bring forth a chunk of bread and you recline, feast your hearts [content], after this you shall go for you have passed by your servant for this. They said: So you shall do as you said; 6) and Abraham rushed to the tent to Sarah and said: Rush three *seahs*[3] of fine flour, kneed it, and make it into cakes; 7) and to the cattle Abraham ran and took a calf tender and good and brought it to the boy and rushed <him> to prepare it; 8) then he took butter and milk and the calf that he prepared and placed in front of them, while he stands in front of them under the tree and they eat; 9) then they said to him: Where is Sarah your wife? He said: Behold in the tent; 10) he said: I shall return to her at the same time next year and behold Sarah your wife will have a son and Sarah heard at the opening of the tent and it is behind him; 11) and

---

1. Not a command.
2. See *Beliefs* 2:6 (p. 108).
3. A cubic measure of varying magnitude.

Abraham and Sarah were old and satisfied in years and Sarah stopped having the manner of women; 12) and Sarah laughed in her soul saying: After I have become old I shall have decoration and my master is old; 13) and God said to Abraham: Why did Sarah laugh saying: Will indeed I give birth for I have grown old; 14) is anything concealed from with God. I shall return to you at this time next year and Sarah will have a son; 15) and Sarah denied inside saying: I did not laugh for she was afraid and he said: No for you laughed; 16) then the people got up from there and looked on in the direction of Sodom and Abraham is with them to accompany them;]]

I

. . . Because they are. Here [it says]: "And God revealed Himself in the plain of Mamre" for it is a command for {Abraham} to remain in this place.

II

We should know that the place named "elone mamre" had just one tree in it for it says: "And recline under the tree." It is possible that the appearance of the light and speech came to be because of the tree because prophecy and communication manifest through the elements which [amount to] four. Accordingly, we find the Wise One speaking at various times from light, wind, plants—which are attached to the Earth—and water [respectively].

As for light, God revealed Himself and spoke at Sinai where He brought down His Torah in fire, as it says: "And God spoke to you from in front of the fire." (Deut. 4:12) It associates [the Torah] with fire for seven reasons. The first is because like fire, it makes light for those who observe it, as it says: "Your words for me are a torch and light on my road." (Ps. 119:105) [The second is] because, like fire, it scorches those that dispute it, as it says: "And I will set my face against them and they will go out from one fire and another fire will consume them." (Ex. 15:7) [The third is because] like the sphere of fire that ascends above everything, its votaries are exalted, as it says: "Your Master shall make you above all the other nations." (Deut. 26:1) <<[The fourth is because] like [the bottom] half of the sphere of fire that is under everything, it returns those that go down, as it says: "The path of life on top is for the intelligent in order that he depart from the lower fire." (Prov. 15:24)>>⁴ [The fifth is] because "recompense" is associated with it, as it says: "But unto you that fear My name shall the Sun of the righteous arise with healing in his wings." (Mal. 3:20)[5] [The sixth is] because the ten commandments given on this day are compared to it, as it says: "'Are not My words like fire?' God spoke." (Jer. 23:29) [The seventh is] because the light of the [Heavenly] Abode resembles the appearance of fire, as it says: "And the appearance of the light of God is like consuming fire at the top of the mountain." (Ex. 24:17)

As for the wind, God reveals Himself to Job when He challenges him telling of His power [in comparison with] the power of the created beings, as it says: "Then God answered Job from the storm wind." (Job 38:1). We find six reasons for this [association]. The first is because the revolution of the largest sphere occurs by means of the wind as it says: "For I have spread you abroad as the four winds of the Heavens." (Zech. 2:60) [The second is] because the life force of the animals exists by means of the wind as it says: "And that which has a living soul in it." (Gen. 7:13) [The third is] because the divider between the upper and the lower [existences] is the air that mediates [between them] as it says: "And God's wind was hovering on the face of the water." (Gen. 1:1) [The fourth is] because all views and traits of man, [both] positive and negative, are associated with it. Of the positive it says: "And God's wind rested upon him, the wind of wisdom and understanding." (Is. 11:2) Of the negative it says: "A wind of whoredom caused them to err." (Hos. 4:12) Also because prophecy is referred to by it [as it says]: (Num. 11:29) and because when {the wind} storms it destroys much as it says: "And a big and strong wind separates mountains and breaks stones in front of God." (I Kings 19:11)

A tree is the place [of revelation] in three instances: with Abraham, Moses, and David. It is probable that the light for Abraham appeared between two trees for five reasons. The first is <<because this occurred right after the circumcision one should not think that cutting something off a man>> bears no good. <<It therefore drew a comparison with a tree because cutting some branches off a tree improves it until *its fruits ripen* and despite that Abraham resembles>> . . . for him in the people . . . <<in the tree. Moreover,>> a person cannot have life without something

---

4. Perhaps the Gaon has in mind the rotation of the sphere of fire, half of which surrounds the uninhabitable part of the Earth referred to as the bottom.

5. Apparently "Sun" is to be equated with "fire."

being cut off his limbs [i.e., from] the naval. [The third is][6] because he announces to him the birth of Isaac after some days and there is nothing more similar to this idea than a tree . . . it moistens it and its leaves return: "For a tree there is hope. It may be cut down yet return, its sprouts not finished. Though its roots grow old on the earth and its trunk be near dead in the soil, still at the odor of water it will branch and spread out its roots like a sapling." (Job 14:8) [The fourth is] because the righteous are compared to trees that have roots and branches as it says: "The righteous whose roots entwine about a well and reach the inwards of the stone." (Job 18:6–7) [The fourth is] because all righteous people have been compared to a tree all parts of which have a use, the fruit, the branch, and the leaf as it says: "And it shall be like a planted tree." (Ps. 1:3) [The fifth is] because the announcement to Abraham concerning the increase of his offspring is like that of the leaves and fruits of a tree which are innumerable as it says: "And the righteous shall sprout like a leaf." (Prov. 11:28)

As for water, [God revealed Himself] for Ezekiel and Daniel [in it]. Of Ezekiel it says: "God's word was to Ezekiel the son of Buzi in the land of the Chaldeans in the river of Kebar." (Ezek. 1:1) Of Daniel it says: "In the twenty-eighth day of the first month and I was next to the river Hiddeqel." (Dan. 10:4) This means that this was the time when the nation entered into the servitude of the kingdoms which are compared to water as it says: "Were you to pass in the water." (Is. 43:2) As for Daniel, God announces to him that Israel shall be saved from the exile which is compared to water along the lines of what it says: "and shall raise me and draw me out from the sorrow compared to much water." (Ps. 18:17)

III

<<It says then: "He is sitting at the opening of the tent" . . . because it will say after this: "And Sarah listens at the opening of the tent," for were it to be far from the place of meeting Sarah[7] would not hear the conversation.>>

---

6. It is also possible that this is the second.
7. Who was in the tent.

IV

It adds: "At the heat of the day" as a *pretext* to the time of the meal as well for one of the reasons that compelled in hastening Sarah was [preparing] the food for the people. We should mention that "at the heat of the day" according to our Fathers is after four hours for it says: "And it was on the morrow that Saul put the people . . . in the morning watch and slew the Ammonites until the head of the day and it came to pass that they that remained were scattered so that two of them were not left together." (I Sam. 11:11) *Ashmoreth habboker* is a watch and the measurement of a watch is four hours of the night. Likewise, from the morning as it says: "So Gideon and the one hundred men that were with him came to the outside of the camp in the beginning of the middle watch and they blew the trumpet and broke the pitcher that was in their hands." (Judg. 7:19) Also from the first moment of the heat of the day until sunset for [two hours]* is called "twilight" (*sohorayim*) as it says: "The sons of Rimon the Beerothite and Baanah went and came about the heat of the day to the house of Ish-bosheth who lay on a bed at noon." (II Sam. 4:5) Then from sunset until the commencement of the day is called *ben Ha-arbayim* as we shall explain. For that reason these limits have become our designated times for prayer. The prayer of the morning is up to four hours.[8] There are two hours that are not the time of prayer.[9] The major *minhah* is from six to nine hours [into the day] and the minor one is until the night.[10] The prayer of the night is throughout the entire night.[11]

V

It says then: "And he lifted his eyes." The first question that is asked here is: Why does it say: "And God appeared to him," when we do not see that He communicates anything to him? We say that the purpose of "And God revealed himself to him" was to communicate [to him] about the incident of "the scream of Sodom and Ghammorah for it is great." Now it mentions

---

8. *Ber.* 4:1 and *Tal.* 27a.

9. Cf., *Book of Prayers* (p. 31) where the Gaon has, perhaps more specifically, two and a half hours.

10. *Ber* 26b.

11. *Ber.* ch. 4 and *Tal.* 27b.

the appearance of light before the passing of the individuals so that
Abraham be certain that they are God's votaries. Likewise, [the purpose
of] the appearance of light for the prophets is for them be certain that
what they hear is the words of God and of them . . . Abraham says to
them: "God if I have found favor with you," with "prince" implied. This
error, [i.e.] that he thought that they are people, is all through [the story]
because of how minimal the distinction is between prophets and angels
is[12] as Manoah's wife says to him: "The man of God came to me and his
appearance was like that of an angel of God very awesome." (Judg. 13:6)
These . . . prophets but only resemblance . . . the truth. It is inevitable for Abraham and Sarah from . . . the proofs for these individuals . . . when this individual entered into the . . . "And it was when
the flame ascended." (Judg. 13:21)

VI

"Then he knew" . . . I shall explain that *'al* in the language has [one of]
seven meanings. The first is the popular one: "on the top of the mountain"
(Ex. 34:2); [2] "before": "And the people stood before Moses." (Ex. 18:14);
[3] "attachment" [as it says]: "And attach to them forty-two cities." (Num.
35:6) . . . [4] "And he threw upon the people." (Ex. 24:8); [5] "to": "And
he prayed to God." (I Sam. 1:10); [6] "like": "And like the field of the land
it shall be considered." (Lev. 25:31); and [7] "until" [as it says]: *'al
hamarecheth* (Josh. 2:7) instead of *'ad hamaarecheth*.

VII

It states: "And God appeared" twice for various reasons. [1] He saw that
the Abode stayed for them and understood from this that they were
Noble. [2] He saw that he is sitting and they are standing and this not
well-mannered. [3] He saw that they turned to him from the middle of the
road. [4] He saw the time of the meal. [5] He saw which of them is most
estimable so he spoke to him individually and he answered for all of them.

---

12. See the Gaon's intro. to Ps. (p. 28).

VIII

"And he bowed to the ground" is a practice of [giving] honor for we know that bowing is of two kinds: [of] worship, which is for God specifically, and [giving] honor, which is permissible for one human to another.

IX

"And I have now found favor with you" refers to the most estimable of them with "Man of God" implied. For that reason I rendered "prince of God." This is similar to what it says: "I am the Lord your God from the Land of Egypt," (Josh. 12:6) the meaning being: "the one who brought you up from the land of Egypt" and: "A month they shall be in the Lebanon and two in his house," (I Kings 5:28) meaning each in his own house, and: "to the Gazites saying," (Judg. 16:2) means "still saying."

X

<<His request: "Do not pass in front of your servant," is [the request to] attain what he wishes for were he to respond to him saying: "I shall pass," his request: "A little water shall be brought forth," would be rendered needless. It is possible that what occupied him [and thus prevented him] from realizing that they are angels was one of three things or [perhaps] all of them together: [1] the fear of the light of the Abode, [2] the pain caused by the circumcision, and [3] his rejoicing because [of the chance to] give hospitality.>>

XI

I rendered "shall be taken" as "shall be brought" because this word may be used in this sense [of "bringing"] as well as Jacob says: "Bring them to me," (Gen. 48:9) and as it says of the ram of supplementation: "Then you take the second ram." (Ex. 29:19)

XII

"a little" [reflects] the practice of the abstemious righteous people to reduce [things] in their words. Similar to this is: "a little honey-drink and a little honey" (Gen. 43:11) and "You were few and evil." (Gen. 47:9)

XIII

"Wash your feet"—washing is by means of the [servant] boys so it is possible that he meant by instruction or perhaps we say "and wash" means "as you like," and likewise "and recline" [means] "as you wish."

XIV

"Piece of bread" is according to the abstinent manner of reduction [practiced] by the righteous.

XV

"And feast"—according to your abilities.

XVI

We-ahar taavoru is instead of *we-ahar kach* like: *We-ahar telechu* (Josh. 2:16) and *we-ahar hotethi* (Josh. 24:5), in all {cases} "this" is implicit.

XVII

"For you have passed" has four imports. [1] It is possible that he says: "Forgive me for you have surprised me." [2] It is also possible that he said: "this is my obligation to you for I have seen you," [3] or "because you have been turned to me," or [4] "This is your obligation to me for I have run after you."

XVIII

[In] their answer to him: "So you shall do," it is possible that they hint to him saying: "This is your practice to eat and drink." It is also possible that they only refer to taking of water, washing, leaning, and taking bread, which are apart from the meal. If any act had been performed by them, this [then] is something possible and [even] probable.

XIX

What is the manner of wisdom in leaving Abraham to think them to be humans until the end of the sequel? To tell us of how great his hospitality was. This is a general reason. [Also] so that he hears the announcements from rest and appeasement after the food. This is the specific reason.

XX

The reason for [mentioning] "hastening" three [times] in the story: "And Abraham hurried," and "And Sarah hurried," and "And he hurried to make it," is because he thought them to be hungry. Since bread takes longer than meat to prepare he served it first. {Abraham's} instruction to Sarah takes the longest of all [to complete] and it is therefore mentioned first, while butter and milk are common-found and need no preparation. It is [then] unnecessary to mention in the repetition that he brought them bread for this something inevitable. It is possible that it should be . . . the reason He mentioned the things in a reducing manner: "a little and piece of bread" is in order that his honor be great when he brings much of what he mentioned as little, as is known that three *seahs* are forty-five *rotels* for each *seah* is 1400 [*danks*]*. Despite this he brought a calf, butter, and milk—all of them being [just] three people. For that reason the quality of generosity is attributed especially to Abraham as it says: "Then the magnanimous of the nation gathered." (Ps. 47:10) Because of him the entire nation is called "the daughter of the generous." (*Cant.* 7:2)

XXI

The word *wayokhlu* has two [possible] interpretations: [one is] "destruction" [i.e.] "And you shall destroy all the nations," (Deut. 7:17) and also "a land that destroys its inhabitants," (Num. 13:32) and "And a sword shall destroy flesh." (Deut. 32:42) The destruction is with burning as it says in the story about Gideon despite him being a man:[13] "And God's angel sent the edge of the leaning stick that was in his hand and it touched his flesh," and "A fire ascended from the rock and destroyed." (Judg. 6:21) The other is that "And they ate" refers to one who is capable of eating <because Abraham, Ishmael, and the servant boys were present there.> This usage is much found in the Scripture for so it says of 'Akhan: "And they burned them with fire and stoned them." (Josh. 7:25)—everyone deserving it.[14] Likewise it states: "And whose drinking of wine is with the accompaniment of the mandolin, the trumpet, and drum," (Is. 5:12)[15] . . . and whose drink were with the accompaniment of wine" (Is. 5:12)—that which is fit for drinking from among the mentioned things. So also it says: "Those that came from the captivity the children of exile brought burnt offerings to the God of Israel, twelve bullocks for all of Israel, ninety-six rams, seventy-seven lambs, twelve he-goats, all this was a burnt offering to God." (Ezek. 8:35) There were also sin-offerings, rather it means whichever of these is fit for burnt offerings.[16] Also: "Why shall we die in your presence, our land too we have acquired?" (Gen. 47:19)—they mean that which is vulnerable to death for it is the people not the ground that dies.

XXII

The {man's} question "Where is Sarah your wife?" is an opening [of discussion.] The indication by dots on top of it is fine,[17] meaning that they knew her place, and did not ask as an inquiry.

XXIII

{Abraham's} statement "Behold in the Tent" is connected to the beginning of the section for it says: "And he is sitting at the openings of the tent."

---

13. Even though God appeared to him to be a man.
14. See *Sanhed.* 44a.
15. This translation does not seem to agree with the context here.
16. Cf., however, *Tos. Parah* ch. 1, *Horayoth* 6a, *Temurah* 15a.
17. According to the Gaon as in tract. *Sof.* ch. 6, the word *ayeh* has dots.

We should explain what the purpose of this promise is for he says to him: "Behold Sarah your wife has son," after God already told Abraham: "I shall give you of her a child." We say that the statement was on a condition for God says: "And you shall observe My treaty," (Gen. 17:9) and when he was circumcised the condition was fulfilled which was [at the time of] the meal when Sarah will listen as it says: "And Sarah listens."

XXIV

What is the meaning of "And it is behind him?" We answer that it is the tent behind him. Likewise we ask: What is [the meaning of] "And if he was on her couch"? (Lev. 15:23) We respond that this is a pure vessel for it says before this: "And anyone who touches any vessel that shall sit on top of her," (Lev. 15:21) meaning: If this was not a vessel that she sat on but was on the bed, then only [the one who touches it] is impure. We should also ask what does "For from Israel and he" (Hos. 8:6) mean? We respond: This is the king meaning the advice of the Israel and the king was to make an idol. But where did it mention the king?—in what precedes this verse for it says: "These have made my king and not from me." (ibid.) We should ask further: What is the meaning of "What shall I speak and he threatened me but he shall do this"? (Is. 38:15) We respond: This is the cheating mentioned previously as its says: "My Master, my soul has been deceitful." (Is. 38:14) Now that we have spoken of unclear usages of "he," so we should mention some cases of the word "she" that are unclear. We ask: What is the reference to in "She walks among the beasts"? (Ezek. 1:13) We respond: It is the fire as it says: "And a glister to the fire." (Ezek. 23:43) What is the reference to in: "And with the entire land it is mine"? (Jer. 45:4) We respond: It is the sorrow, the destruction and plucking mentioned previously. We ask further: What is the reference to in: "Now they will commit whoredom with her and she"? (Ezek. 23:43) We say: It is the thought spoken of at the beginning of the verse in feminine language: "and I said to the savant ballah in adultries" <and when it describes thought that is impulsive [it does so] in masculine it says "Put [his] mind [bal] to save him"> (Dan. 6:15) and when it describes it in feminine it says ("ballah") like "or" and "orah" and "Lev" and "labba."

XXV

<<[People] were surprised by the statement "And Abraham and Sarah were old" . . . the statement, for 139 years of his life remained as it says

of him: "And he begot sons and daughters." (Gen. 5:4) These people do not know the existence of doubt for the sons of their men . . . that something new came about in the time of Abraham and became . . . and giving birth before one hundred years . . . were Abraham . . . because of the new creation or because of the circumcision like. . . .

XXVI

. . . People have asked of the statement: "Why is this that Sarah laughed," as if he is reproaching her [for this], and say: Did not Abraham already laugh before this and God did not reproach him? As it says: "And Abraham fell on his face and laughed." (Gen. 17:17) We say: His reproach of Sarah was deserved just as Abraham was but the Scripture waited and did not state the reproach of Abraham until the same thing happened to Sarah and God reproached her and equated them in regards to reproach.

XXVII

The angel's announcement of something that Sarah concealed in her heart is the first sign of wonder and when {Sarah} and Abraham spoke between each other and she said: "I did not laugh," and the angel revealed what she said to him and said to her: "No for you have laughed," is the second sign.

XXVIII

His statement "At this time I shall return" requires that he returned to him even though this is not [explicitly] written [in the Scripture].

XXIX

Abraham's accompaniment of [the angels] which is mentioned [according to] one of the laws of hospitality and also in order that he should see the end of the matter in Sodom.

Now it states idea intended when it states: "And God revealed Himself to him," and says:

17) and God said: Shall I conceal from Abraham what I do; 18) from Abraham shall be a large, great nation by which all the nations of the earth shall be blessed; 19) and I know <him> that he will command his children after him to preserve the way of God and shall act with righteousness and lawfulness in order that it be fulfilled for Abraham what he was promised; 20) and He said to him: The evil of Sodom and Gamorrah has increased and their iniquity has become very great; 21) I shall now bring down <a command of intimidation> and they shall see that if like this evil which reaches Me they have <all> done and if not I shall inform them of this; 22) and Abraham continued to stand in front of God; 23) and Abraham went forth and said: Shall You indeed slay the righteous with the evil? 24) Perhaps there shall be found fifty righteous people in the middle of the land; shall you slay them too? And shall you not spare them because of the fifty righteous people that are among them? 25) Forbid You that You do something like this that You kill the righteous with the wicked and the righteous shall be like the wicked forbid You shall the one who judges the entire world not act in justice? 26) and God said: If I will find in Sodom fifty righteous people in the midst of the land I shall spare all the people because of them; 27) and Abraham answered him and said: I have gone too far in speaking in front of my Master and I am dust or ash; 28) perhaps if the fifty righteous people are reduced by five shall You destroy the entire land because of the five? He said: I shall not destroy it if I shall find there forty-five; 29) let it not be burdensome in front of my Master for I shall speak. Perhaps if there shall be found forty? He said: I shall not do this because of the forty; 30) then he said: I have gone too far in speaking in front my Master; perhaps if thirty shall be found there? He said: I shall not destroy them because of the twenty; 31) then he said: Let it not be burdensome that I speak these words, only perhaps if there be found there ten? He said: I shall not do this because of the ten; 32) then God<'s Abode> departed when He finished speaking to Abraham and Abraham returned to his place.

I

<<I shall explain what I have revealed in this section that any yyy when it is with an *aleph* [and] *daleth* the prophet would find in it a Godly statement and were it with a *yodh* [and] he would find in it the Godly name. For that reason you find [the name in] Abraham's speech as well as

in Moses' [speech] of the thorn bush, written with an *aleph daleth* that it refers to specific mastership.

II

"And God said" is not to the prophet but rather refers to wisdom likewise it says: " . . . "[18]() which is with wisdom">>

III

It says in question form: "Do I conceal from Abraham" for seven reasons. We say that the first is because his children will multiply and inherit the meadow and the cities, I mean Sodom and its suburbs . . . I mean his land and God made a condition upon him that they will [both] inherit it . . . and will dwell in it. For that reason it says: "And Abraham shall be a great nation." The second is . . . and its name . . . the destruction that he threatened them with . . . in his prayer and for that reason it said: "And all the nations of the world will be blessed through you." Since he was a prophet and the prophet's merit is great for that reason it says: "For I know him," [which means]: "For the times that I knew him." The fourth is because he fears [God] and the merit of God fearers is great for "God's secret is for His votaries and he shall not tell them of his treaty," (Ps. 25:14) and for that reason it says: "That he shall command." The fifth is because he was honest and the merit of the honest is: "And His secret is with the proper," (Prov. 3:32) and for that reason it says: "And shall preserve the path of God." (Gen. 18:19) The sixth is in order to increase his reward for his effort in saving people and returning them in repentance. <<For that reason it says afterwards. The seventh is to set for the people of Sodom a small extension after>> the big one as it shall say: "I shall descend now," and as I have explained of the people of the Flood and the people of the Tower.

IV

From the statement "that he shall command" (verse 19) we can prove that the transmission of the intellected precepts or the auditory precepts that

---

18. The verse cited is uncertain.

reach the offspring by the Tradition of the fathers without being committed to writing, is unadulterated and God's proofs are sustained by it. As we know that the Torah says: "so that he shall command," this suffices to watch God's path without a Scripture. This removes the stubbornness of the one who says: The Mishnah is not to be accepted because it is not written. We say to him just as there is no difference in the obligation [of fulfilling] the commandments of the ten commandments and the rest of the commandments even though the former were [given] by hearsay and the latter by hearsay and in writing as it says: "And it shall be when you hear," (Deut. 5:20) so there is no difference in the obligation [in the fulfillment] between the Scripture and the Mishnah even though the latter is transmitted while the other is transmitted and written. This is supported in the Tradition. We have already designated for these precepts . . . the auditory precepts and have gathered all of them. . . .

V

It says: "the scream of Sodom"—this is the primary reason for God destroying them for {screaming} alludes to [1] cheating as it says: "Know that at times the oppressed cry out," (Job 35:9) [2] abstinence from charity as it says: "One who plugs his hearing from the cry of the poor, he too shall call and not be answered," (Prov. 21:13) "And the hand of the poor it did not hold." (Ezek. 16:49)

VI

It adds "For the evil is great," referring to haughtiness as it says: "And they were haughty and committed an abomination before Me." (Ezek. 16:50) It also says: "pride fullness of bread." (Ezek. 16:49)[19]

VII

"And their iniquity" refers to prohibited cohabitation which is what it says: "And they committed abominations in front of Me." (Ezek. 16:50)

---

19. See *Sanhed.* 109a.

"For it has become heavy" also refers to a kind of prohibited relations. Likewise, it adds: "to God much" refers also to prohibited cohabitation.

VIII

"And I saw" is a determination of a period: He sent to them His angel [to set] a small extension, perhaps they will return in repentance on that day. This was after the twenty-five years that God extended for them from the time of Abraham arrived in the land.

IX

If it was like its scream "I shall make waste of them"—"I shall finalize the judgement upon them," as it says: "That it was determined of his father," (I Sam. 20:33) but if they do not continue in their sins but will pull away from them I will inform and reveal this to them by pushing the destruction off them.[20] Now Abraham heard these words and the people went away. Before he began to ask for pity for Sodom he prefaced: "And I am ash and dust," in a form of subduing found among people when their enthusiasm <grows> . . . the ash for fire acts on its essence until it weakens . . . also in nature and what is with it . . . fire and dust change to . . . in its inner . . .

It is possible that what he means with this statement is that would the desire of Nimrod been fulfilled to burn him, he would be dust, and if Amraphel would have succeeded in killing him he would have been dust . . .

X

He said "Perhaps there are," he means by this to inform us . . . he did not think of the place. . . . He informed us that there were not any righteous people in Sodom and if there were he would save them.

---

20. See Zucker, *Translation*, p. 263.

XI

Now we say what is the meaning of his statement "lest you" in this section . . . that those who interceded . . . so that he understand . . .

XII

The reason he repeats—forfend [means forfend] that you do like this to Sodom or anyone else. The reason for the *yodh* lacking [in] the three [instances of] *halilah*—two here and the third is: *halilah le-el mi-resha* (Job. 34:10), meaning that there is not even an iota of wickedness in him, even like a *yod* which is the smallest of letters. This explanation is merely conjecture.

XIII

"To do like this thing" means whatever resembles injustice and unfolds from it. It did not say [just] "this thing" for this would include only one idea.[21]

XIV

"To kill the righteous with the wicked" in God's words is Abraham's expounding.

XV

"And the righteous to kill like the wicked," meaning one will make one like the other and will be devoted to worshipping God like those that say: "All is alike to all," (Ecl. 9:2) but they do not know that the prophet named idea this: "Full of evil and madness is in their heart," (Ecl. 9:2) they also say: "Does the one who judges the entire Earth not act with justice," (verse 25) since he is at advantage and they are lacking intelligence in this like

---

21. See *BR* ch. 49.

we have explained seven matters in the section of: "How can one who hates justice prevail in his own affairs." (Job 34:17)

XVI

God says: "If I find in Sodom," he means, if they will be overt, but not the hidden ones. This is similar to what it says: "Run through the streets of the city and see now and search in its streets." (Tal. Jez. 5:1)

XVII

"In the city" is like "in its streets." (ibid.)

XVIII

We say that there are two imports in regards to the descent from fifty to ten. The first is that God Exalted and Lofty is not the one who first mentioned fifty but Abraham did so hoping that there will be fifty. The second is that God left him to reduce [the number] little by little in order to increase his reward for each and every effort and attempt.

XIX

After this we say it is said that the prayer has an effect on our souls and our effort [. . .]

XX

We say further: Why did Abraham reduce [the count] at first by fives and then by tens? We answer this by means of conjecture that [he reduced] twice by five and then twice by ten so that were there to remain enough to reduce by twenty He would do [so] in the order that we have seen. Some say that He broke the tens only once and said forty-five because we find the [numerical] value of Lot to be forty-five.

XXI

For what reason did Abraham stop at ten and did not ask for less than this? For this we find four reasons: The first is so there be a count for a group by which prayers and many other commandments can be fulfilled as it is known that a congregation is ten. The second is since there were five regions as he alluded that there be five in each reagion. The third is that experience had determined for Abraham there were eight righteous men in the generation of the Flood and {the people} shall not be given grace because of them. The fourth is that he thought that in Sodom there were ten righteous men: Lot, his wife, his four sons, and his four sons-in-law.[22] A proof that he had four daughters is that it says: "And he spoke to his son-in-law who married his daughter," (Gen. 19:14) which were married and when they did not come out with him the two angels present said to him: "And your two daughters that are present." (Gen. 19:15) Abraham thought that four of them were already married.

That Ezekiel says: "And these three men were inside of it," (Ezek. 14:14—15) and said: "Shall these deliver the sons and daughters?" (Ezek. 14:16) [is not in contradiction]* to what is in this account for it considers only the males. Now that it specifies here these three righteous people, I mean Noah, Daniel, and Job, it has been said each one of them saw a world and its destruction. What comes to my mind is: Because he counted the destruction hunger, wild animals, and plague, it specified here these three that were saved of the four: Noah from the hunger as we have explained in the pericope of: "From the ground that God cursed," (Gen. 8:29) Job from the plague as it says: "For now had I died I had been at rest," (Job. 3:13) and Daniel from the sword of Nebuchadenezzer as it says: "And he exiled those that remained from the sword of Babylonia," (II Chron. 36:20) and also from the lions in the den as it says: "My Master sent His angel." (Dan. 6:23)

XXII

That Abraham did not pray for just Lot[23] but placed his trust in his Master to kill him if deserves this is a testimony to Abraham's righteousness. This

---

22. See *BR* 49:12.
23. Cf., however, *Chapters of Rabbi Eliezer,* ch. 25.

is one of the qualities of the righteous people as it says of the children of Levi: "And you found one who says of his father and mother as if he had not seen them and does not recognize his brothers and does not know his sons." (Deut. 33:9)

XXIII

The purpose of the Scripture recording this story is [1] so that we know the origin of our progenitors, [2] make effort in honoring guests, [3] that we not be surprised if God tells us of something that will defy nature, [4] that we should command our children and the people [of our household] to do righteousness and correct judgment, [5] we will not have doubts that our Master is righteous and does not wrong, [6] it will not be hard on us when He passes judgment on those who are close to us, and [7] that we should ask pity for all his servants according to our ability.

Chapter XIX

Afterwards it says:

1) Then the two angels came to Sodom at evening time and Lot is sitting at the gate of Sodom and when he saw them he got up opposite them and bowed on his face on the ground, 2) and said:[1] I am at your service my Masters, come to the house of your servant and spend the night and wash your feet, then at nightfall you can set on and go on your way. They said: No, we shall spend the night in the street, 3) until he beseeched them greatly and they came to him and entered his house and he made them a place to convene and unleavened bread and they ate. 4) Before they could lie down the people of the city, the people of Sodom had already surrounded the house from youngster to elderly as well as all the people that were in its vicinity; 5) and they called Lot and said to him: Where are the people that came in to you this night? Bring them out to us so that we may be ignited by them; 6) and Lot went out to them to the door and blocked the hemistich behind him, 7) and said: Lo my brothers do not harm them 8) behold I have two daughters who never knew a man, I shall bring them out to you and do to them what you find fit but to these two men do not do anything for they have entered under the shade of my roof. 9) They said: Come here; then they said: Shall one who has come to live <with us> judge us? Now we shall harm you more than them? and they pressed on Lot very much and

---

1. Derenbourgh's edition has the following addition here: "in excitement."

neared to break the door; 10) and the two angels extended their hands and brought Lot with them into the house and locked; 11) and the people who were at the door of the house they were struck with [dim-sightedness] from small to large and they were incapacitated from finding the door; 12) then the two angels said to Lot as well whoever remains, anyone related to you by marriage, your sons, your daughters, and whatever else you have in the city take them out of it; 13) for we are destroying this place for their iniquity has increased in front of God; He sent us to destroy you; 14) and Lot went out and spoke to all those married to his daughters and said to them: Get up and go out of this place for God destroys it and shall be to them like a mockery; 15) and the more the outbreak would strengthen the two angels would press on Lot saying: Take your wife and your children that are present or that you are not blown up for the sin of the people of the land. He hesitated so the two angels grasped his and his wife's hand and his daughters since God pitied them and the two of them took them out and they left the entrance of the city; 16) and when the two of them took them outside he said to him: Make for safety, do not turn to your back and do not look at anything in the meadow and make way to the mountain so that you are not blown up; 17) and Lot said to the two of them: No my masters, 18) behold your servant has found favor with you and your esteem is great which you have done for me to keep me alive and I may not repair to the mountain so that tragedy does not befall me and I be destroyed; 19) behold this city is close so I shall flee to it and it is small, I shall take cover there [[despite that it is small]] and my soul shall be kept alive; 20) he said to him: Behold I have done good for you in this matter as well not to turn over the city that you ask for; 21) hurry take cover in it for I cannot do anything until you take cover there. For that reason he named the city Zaghr; 22) and when the Sun rose upon the land he went into Zaghr; 23) and God rained on Sodom and Gammorrah sulphur and fire from with Him from the heavens; 24) and overturned that city and the rest of the meadow as well as the people of the city and the plants of the ground; 25) and his wife turned around and saw it and turned into a pillar of salt; 26) and Abraham set out at nightfall to the place where he stood in front of God; 27) and he glanced out at Sodom and the rest of land of the meadow and saw that its smoke has ascended like the smoke of a furnace; 28) and when God destroyed the cities and He remembered Abraham and sent Lot away from the midst of the overthrow after He overturned the cities in which Lot dwelled; 29) and Lot went up from Zaghr and stayed in the mountain and his daughters were with him [for he feared to stay in Zaghr] and he and his daughters stayed in a cave; 30) and the older said to the younger: Our father has grown old and there is no man in the city to come upon us in the manner of men; 31) come up and let us give our father wine to drink and lie with him and we shall remain alive through our father by means of offspring; 32) and they gave their father wine to drink on that night and the older one got up and lay with him and he knew neither of her laying nor of her getting up; 33) and when it was in the morning the older said to the younger I have lain the day before yesterday with my father, let us give him wine to drink tonight also and you go and lay with him and we shall remain alive through him by means of offspring; 34) and they gave their father to drink on that night also and the younger one got up and lay with him; 35) and the two daughters of Lot became pregnant from their father and the older gave birth to a son and named him Moab and he is the father of the Moabites to this day; 36) and the younger one also gave birth to a son and named him Ibn 'Ami and he is the father of 'Amon until this day.

I

Since we have translated the verses of this pericope we should review them in detail. We say: Since the Scripture opened first with a story within a story [and said:] "And Abraham saw three men," and then said here: "And the two angels came," it lets us know of two things by this. The first is that these two individuals are of the same three and [that] the other is the one that was sent to announce [Sarah] which departed after he completed his messengership and two were left; one of which was to save Lot and the other to overturn Sodom[2] as shall be clarified in the middle of this story.

II

Now, calling men angels and angels men is much, not little, found in our language. As it says: "And Haggai the Lord's angel said . . . and behold six men are coming from the path of the upper gate." (Hag. 1:13) Were we to compare what happened with these angels with Lot to what

---

2. See BR ch. 50.

happened to them with Abraham we find seven praises. The first is that to Abraham they came in the day: "in the heat of the day," but to Lot in the evening. This is because of Abraham's great righteousness for it says: "And He shall manifest your righteous like fire," (Ps. 37:6) and because of the meagerness of Lot's [righteousness]* for he is like the [shadow]* of the night. The second is that it says of Abraham: . . . [3] what it says of Abraham: "And he ran," and of Lot: "And he got up" now.[4] . . . for that reason of the people of Gideon they were offered two individuals but they only accepted one as it says: "Behold is my virgin daughter and his concubine," (Judg. 19:24) while aferwards it says: "And the man grabbed his concubine." (Judg. 19:25) For the first was intended but not brought out and the second he brought out to them.

III

"for so you have come" implies that they asked for his protection and entered his house. This statement necessitates that one who asks for sanctuary the one he lives with is obligated to save him in whichever way he can. They have said of one of the students of Rabbi Meir that a man asked sanctuary in his house and Rabbi Meir sat at the opening of his house to protect him. When someone stood against him, he said to the one who demands him: We shall not fulfill our obligation to him [if he will be killed] for he is like one who enters . . . protection of [sanctity]* . . . in the dawn of the night.

The statement *gesh hal'ah* means further yourself from . . . they should bring him in. It is possible that the statement should . . . and not . . . that with a wonderous sign . . . in Abraham's presence.

IV

. . . For it says: "And they surrounded the house from small to big." The one who started the sin is the one with whom the punishment was begun.

---

3. Zucker (pg. 131) has here: "rest" (i.e., the rest of) but upon inspecting Ant. #213 it has become evident that this word is from the page under this. The lacuna was not totally apparent.

4. Zucker (ibid.) has here: ". . . parts of time . . . a sense of estimation" but these words are from the page below as well.

V

With their statement: "Who else for you is in here"—they refer to the relatives that shall return him in repentance, [i.e.] son-in-law, your sons and daughters that are the furthest in the neighborhood.

VI

"Were taken out of the place" means "were taken outside."

VII

"For we destroy" entails three acts: "Turning over" as it says: "And the vessel that he makes was destroyed," (Jer. 18:14) "burning" as it says: "And I prepared for you destroyers," (Jer. 22:7) and "smiting with plague" as it says "and each one had his vessel of smiting in his hand." (Ez. 9:1)

VIII

It says afterwards: "Pass in the city after him and smite." "And Lot went out and spoke to his sons-in-law the takers of his daughters," meaning his married daughters.

IX

"And it shall be to them like a mocker" means that they laughed [and said]: "you can see drums and trumpets in the city and you say it is turned over!" And when the angels saw that Lot's sons-in-law do not believe [them] and do not come out with him they said to him: "Leave these in the fire and take your daughters that are present"—this being the meaning of "the ones to be found"—but when he began to hesitate because of his two daughters that were coming out—which is the meaning of "and he hesitated"—they grasped him and the three women and took them out as it says: "And the men grasped," for there are three women altogether.

X

That it says "And they took him out" is instead of: "And they took them out and they left them," for it includes the three women in the whole.

XI

That it elaborates [and says]: "And they said: Make for safety," after it says in plural: "And it was when they took them out," supports what we have [been] transmitted [viz.] that one angel was sent to rescue Lot and the other to overturn Sodom but that the overturner is unable to do anything until Lot is saved as it says: "For I cannot do anything."

XII

The angel says to him: "Behold I have raised your face," {6} even though we know that neither God nor an angel "raise faces." We respond as it is our manner to, and say that: "He raises the face of the righteous" is with prayer as it says: "And God raised the face of Job." (Job 42:9) . . . and further a second sign the saving of the city that he sought now these two signs become and it is . . .

XIII

. . . Its statement that Zaghr is near . . . is not in the entire region but a small region that was given to the rulership of Sodom.

XIV

It says *hashemesh yatsa* [*shemesh*] modified in masculine for one of two reasons: either that the Sun comes in masculine just as it does in feminine as it says: *Le'ene hashemesh hazzoth* (II Sam. 12:11), or that: "The light of the Sun came out" is meant, this being more probable. Likewise regarding anything that we find to be either masculine or feminine interchange these two explanations are possible.

XV

It says "And He rained" and then repeats "from the lord"—in truth is indeed in place of "from with him" in the language of the Hebrews for they practice that one Reuben says to Simeon: "I wish that you fulfill the needs of Reuben," and he refers to himself or that he says: "I already fulfilled the needs of Simeon," and referring to his listener. Belonging to the first usage are the words of Lemech to his wives: "Lemech's wives," (Gen. 4:23) and Samuel's statement: "and Yiftah and Samuel," (I Sam. 12:11) referring to himself. David's statement: "Take with yourselves the servants of your master," (I Kings 1:13) likewise Ahasaurus's statement to Mordechai and Esther: "And you write of the Jews as fits in your eyes in the name of the king." (Est. 8:8) The second usage is like in the words of Moses to the Pharaoh: "No longer shall Pharaoh continue scoffing," (Ex. 8:25) and Jonathan's words to David: "Nor when the Lord cuts off David's enemies," (I Sam. 20:15) and the like.

XVI

Despite that it says [just] Sodom we should know that Adamah and Seviyim were [destroyed] with it as it says: "Like the turnover of Sodom, Gammorah, Adamah, and Seviyim." (Deut. 29:22) It also mentions them individually: "How shall I place you like Sodom?" (Hos. 11:8) It is possible that it was brief in stating "these cities" because Soar was saved as we have explained.

XVII

"The entire meadow"—this is all the meadows and gardens of which it says: "For it is all drink."

XVIII

The addition of "and all the inhabitants of the city" refers to the people of the land and whoever was a stranger and lived among them as well as those who left the land and traveled to another land, the wind chased them until it caught up to them and destroyed [them] as we shall explain

in the sequel of "amidst the children of Israel" (Deut. 11:6) in connection
with Korah.

XIX

It adds "the plants of the ground" despite that the plants are too lowly to
mention in such an instance, because it meant that the air too was
destroyed. It is tested that were a person in the land of Sodom to take a
little rainwater to water seeds with it, it will dry up before it falls onto the
ground.[5]

XX

"And his wife looked" has two purposes. The first is to tell us the
punishment of one who defies God's command and the second is to make
it a preamble to fit the story of "And the two daughters of Lot became
pregnant," when [their] mother was [no longer] in existence.

XXI

It makes "And he sent Lot" contingent upon "And God remembered
Abraham" for two [possible] reasons: The first is he was not righteous but
was saved because of Abraham, and the second is that he was indeed
righteous and should have been tested and recompensed like the rest of
the tolerant, righteous people but because of Abraham he was absolved of
this.

XXII

"And Lot went up from Soar," for were he not to have remained in Soar
the events of the people could have reached him and it would not come
to the minds of his daughters that the entire world has been destroyed.

---

5. *BR* ch. 51.

XXIII

It specifies "And he dwelled in the cave" because it will mention drink of wine. Were we to hear this we should say from where did he get [it]? It therefore tells us that their dwelling in the cave brought this upon them for it is the practice of mountain dwellers to hide in caves.

XXIV

"And there was no man in the land" requires that they thought that just like the entire inhabitable land was destroyed by water and only Noah and his offspring remained so now the entire inhabitable land was destroyed by fire and only Lot and his offspring remain for the story of the Flood was close, less than four hundred years had passed. Because of this it says: "There is no man in the land."

XXV

As for "to come,"[6] the word has [one of] seven meanings: [1] reaching a place it he was at a distant place as it says: "Each from his own place." (Job 2:11) [2] "Coming" may also mean "entering" and if this is from a place that is close as it says: "And Judah and his brother entered to the house of Joseph." (Gen. 44:14) [3] Copulation: "And there is no one to copulate." [4] Loss: "His pay has passed."[7] (Ex. 22:24) [5] Acceptance: "My prayer shall arrive in front of me?" (Ps. 88:3) and likewise "Is it like the cry that comes to me?" [6] Arriving with promises: "When your word shall come," (Judg. 13:12) "For their day has come when they say: And we shall lie with him," and "Behold I have laid two days before," and the other eight recurring expressions in this sense show that the language calls one who lays and the one is laid with *shochevim* for that reason there is no reason for proving the prohibition[8] . . . in cohabitation and its punishments.

---

6. Translated as "capulate."
7. See *translation*, p. 346.
8. Another meaning should be provided in the lacuna.

XXVI

"He did not know of her lying down or getting up" does not mean that at the time of the act his senses were not aroused for he would not feel or enjoy, rather all this was during the time of the act but he did not know which one he cohabited with for in the morning he did not remember anything of what happened similar to drunks [who] are desensitized but do not remember this. Of this it says: "He did not know." It is possible that because of this knowledge there are dots on top of "When she got up," meaning not that he did not know but that he did not remember.

XXVII

As for the punishment, were Lot's daughters liable? We say that they are not liable of punishment for intentional [acts] for they did not know that another man does [indeed] existed in the world but believed that just as Adam's children were permitted to marry their sisters because of the absence of other women so it is permissible for them to obtain seed from their father because of the absence of another [man]. They are guilty of error, unawareness, and inexactitude for they did not wait until it would be clarified for them . . .

XXVIII

It records this sequel for us as ethical lesson [1] so that we do not do like Sodom; [2] so we do not act irresponsibly with new incidents, apprehending them by means of conjecture and presumptions; [3] so that we be weary of drinking for it often leads to evils in this and the next world; [4] that we do not give up praying, humility, and asking from the One who hears [us] is close and answers.

Chapter XX

1) Then Abraham traveled from the land of the south and stayed between Reqim and Jefar and resided in KhuluS; 2) and Abraham also said of his wife Sarah that "She is my sister," Abimelech the king of KhuluS sent and took her; 3) and God's angels came to Abimelech in the dream of the night and said to him that: You shall die because of the woman that you have taken while she has a husband; 4) and Abimelech had not come near her and said: Master shall you kill a guiltless person? 5) Did he not say to me: "She is my sister" and she too said: "he is my brother?" With the purity of my heart and the cleanliness of my palms I have done this. 6) God's angel said to him in the dream: I too know that with the purity of your heart you have done this and I have spared you from sinning to me <by informing [you]> and for that reason I did not leave you to come near her; 7) and now let the wife of this man alone for he is a prophet and he shall pray for you and you shall live and if you will not return her then you should know that you will die—you and all your possessions; 8) and Abimelech set out in the morning and called his officials and related all these words to them and the people feared greatly; 9) and he called Abraham and said to him: What have you done to us and what sin have we committed to you that you have brought upon me and my kingdom a great sin, acts that have never been done you have done with me; 10) and Abimelech said to Abraham: What have you seen that you have done this thing? 11) And Abraham said: I said perhaps there is no fear of God in this land and they shall kill me

because of my wife; 12) but in truth she is my relative from my father['s]
not my mother['s side] and she became my wife; 13) and when God took
me out from the house of my father I said to her: This is the kindness
you shall do with me, any place we go say of me: He is my brother. 14)
And Abimelech took sheep, cattle, servants, maidservants and gave them
to Abraham and returned Sarah to him; 15) and he said to him: Behold,
my land is in front of you, what finds favor in your eyes stay in it; 16)
and to Sarah he said: Behold I have given your relative one thousand
drachmas that shall be for you in nice clothes for your accompaniment
that is with you and behold all is opposite you; 17) then Abraham
prayed to God and God healed Abimelech and his wife and maidservants and she gave birth; 18) for God threatened to close all wombs of
Abimelech's pact because of Sarah Abraham's wife.

I

Abraham repeats this act, i.e., that he says that Sarah is his sister, but do
we not see what sorrow and rebuke come upon him in Egypt because of
this? We also have seen the heretics rebuke us because of this [even] until
now saying: "Did {Abraham} not trust and rely on his Master? For were
they to be guilty of sin knowingly it would be more appropriate than for
him to lie and bring Sarah to grief and the people of the land would be
free of they would do with her. We say, and on God we rely, a witness can
see what one who was not present cannot. [Now being that] Abraham was
a trustworthy sage that marshals everything in its proper respects and we
see that he feared death, we know that he was certain that they would kill
the men because of their wives. Abraham [therefore] feared that they will
kill him and will take Sarah prohibitively. Also [that they] will put her
through grief and [consequently] themselves too and the entire nation
may be destroyed together with the king if they help him or if they keep
quiet. He saw that if he would say that "She is my sister," with the
omission that we have mentioned, [i.e.] that she is his relative, as the
language permits, he will save himself from death, her from sorrow, and
them from sin.

II

Were they to have sinned by taking her this would necessarily occur in
one of two ways. [Either] they will be just in speaking of her and if he will
not marry her *off to them then* he will have no sin. Or if they do wrong and

do not have pity[1] on her situation, he is still able to divorce her and make her permissible according to the Law and free them from severe sin despite that they deserve it. Moreover, perhaps it was the practice to divorce a wife forcefully by means of the rulership but Abraham had said "She is my sister," not "She is my wife," and he was honest. This was like when one would go out to war during the time of the children of Israel that he would be obligated to divorce his wife on a condition.[2] Just as we obligate in our time one who departs in the sea to divorce one of his wives on a condition and as the high priest on the Day of Atonement divorces one of his wives on a condition.[3] If he did so and if not he may do so whenever he sees the need and can free all of them. Do you not see that the Torah repeats this act of his and exceeds and mentions the same of Isaac without chagrin? Were there something repugnant and repulsive it would not repeat it. Moreover he would not do it to start with. If the matter is so, what is the place of the punishment of Pharaoh and Abimelech? We say that God Exalted and Augmented wished that Sarah not be taken from Abraham were she just his field as it says: "He shall turn them so that the wicked tribe not rest in the portion of the righteous." (Ps. 125:3) Along the lines of: "No one shall *desire your land.*" (Ex. 34:24)

III

Abimelech's statement "She has a husband" may be interpreted in both ways.[4]

IV

It is possible that in "the nation as well as the righteous" that he refers to himself alone. Similar to what it says elsewhere: "To foreign people it shall not be ruled to sell it." (Ex. 21:8) The meaning being "to a foreign man."[5] It is possible that he refers to himself and his people as it says "upon me

---

1. This phrase is not entirely clear.
2. See *Sab.* 51a.
3. See *Yoma* 11a.
4. It is not certain which ways he is referring to.
5. There appears to be a discrepancy between the Gaon's translation of the verse and his rendition of it here.

and my Kingdom" since they let him do so and how much more so if they assisted him. (Ex. 20:9)

V

The import of "Did he not say to me?" is because these relationships are taken from the words of the individuals, it being impossible to clarify [by another means] and particularly [for people moving] from one land to another.

VI

It adds "and she too" meaning that were they to disagree I would have a doubt.

VII

[By] "with the completeness of my heart" he refers to his thoughts and [by] "the cleanliness of my palms" to his acts. For that reason the angel does not repeat "with the cleanliness of your palms" for no act at all had been committed.

VIII

The meaning of "and I have spared you" is by informing, not by force, meaning: "I informed you that she has a husband so you abstained."

IX

It added "For therefore I have not left you," by warning "I saved you: behold you are dead."

X

Correctly and conjecturally that it writes *mehato'* (from sinning) three ways *MHTW, MHT', MHTW'* is in contrast to three kinds of sin: small, medium and large. The small one was like that of Abimelech for it could have been by means of divorce as we have explained. For that reason it says: *MHTW*. The medial is like the case of Samuel would he not have prayed for the people. For that reason it says: *MHT'* (I Sam. 12:26). The bigger is disobeying God's ruling and speaking of Him what is impermissible. For that reason it writes: *MHTW'* (Ps. 39:2). According to this it is correct to say in regards to the writing of *SLW*, *SL'* and *SLW'* according to three kinds that the level of every man is higher than the other conjecturally.[6]

XI

"For he is a prophet" is not the reason for the return of the woman[7] but an argument for what it says: "And he prayed for her," meaning that because he is a prophet his prayer is accepted as it says: "And if they are prophets, And if God's words is with them." (Jer. 27:18)

XII

He says to him: "You should know that you shall die by the cessation of the womb," as it shall explain afterwards: "for God has stopped" by threat not in act. It is probable that the cause of their fear—the statement: "And the men feared greatly," because of the incident of Sodom and what occurred there and perhaps if we would have mentioned it afterwards {the smoke} would not have settled. It is possible that for that reason it mentions "Its smoke has ascended" (Gen 19:28) first.

XIII

His statement to Abraham: "What have you done to us, and what sin have we committed?" is an augmentation for he did not know his secret of the divorce.

XIV

Now he adds "And what sin have we committed?"—you would not be permitted to do evil to me because of my sin, but Abraham did not answer

---

6. The listing appears to have been omitted by the copyist.
7. See *Bab. Qam.* 92a.

him on for it contains no question but when he said to him "What have you seen?" he replies to him.

XV

"But in truth" indicates that he was a relative of the mother which was worse [in the eyes of the] people than [if he was] that of the father.[8] This agrees with the senses for the mother is a witness that she was pregnant nine months and gave birth. She screams and the neighbors gather and she nurses and raises him. The father [however] knows [this merely] by faith in the mother. We follow the same idea regarding proselytes to Judaism according to the mother, we distinguish between a believer in sorcery and his wife if she is his sister from his mother not from his father. Likewise, between her and her aunt that is the sister of her mother from the side of the mother not of the father whereas his aunt not from the wife of his father herself is not prohibited to her for fatherhood is not detectable by the senses but [only] by a mother who says that he is his father but the Torah does not believe that mother for she is Gentile.

XVI

"And when God threw me off" has [one of] two meanings: [one is] "taking out" derived from: "and the teeth of lions had fallen out (nitta'u)." (Job 4:10) for "falling out" and "taking out" are similar. The other is "confusion" i.e.: "When God confused me from the house of my father and said to me: 'Go for yourself,'[9] I was commanded of this thing and this was not injustice from God's side but a test with recompense.

XVII

The clothing that Abimelech mentioned to Sarah was not for her but for those that served her as it says: "And everything that is against you." It is possible that the statement was made in a manner of propriety as Abigail said of the present: "And she gave it to the lads," (I Sam. 25:27) and everything that he gave Abraham and Sarah was only for the purpose that

---

8. See *San.* 58b and *BR* ch. 52.
9. Go from place to place.

they free him and Abraham had granted him good for this in what shall be mentioned after this.

XVIII

Wenochachta is derived from *nochah*, which means "opposite" or "against," meaning: "Behold everything is opposite and against you." Take what you wish and say what you wish.

XIX

It is asked in this place: If the plague had not struck Abimelech but God [merely] threatened him of it, why does it say: "And God healed"? We say that this *Refu'ah* does not mean "healing" for healing is from sickness but rather "absolving" which is prevention of sickness as it says: "All the diseases that I have afflicted you with in Egypt I will not afflict you with them." (Ex. 15:26) The word *refu'ah* has seven meanings: . . .

Chapter XXI

1) And God remembered Sarah as He said and God did as He promised her; 2) and she became pregnant and gave birth to a son for Abraham in his old age at the time that God told him; 3) and Abraham named his son that Sarah bore for him "Isaac"; 4) and he circumcised him [at] eight days as God commanded; 5) and Abraham was one hundred years old when Isaac his son was born to him; 6) and Sarah said: God has made laughter for me, anyone who hears it will make mockery of me; 7) then she said: Who said to Abraham that Sarah will nurse a child for she bore a son in his old age; 8) and when the boy grew up and was weaned Abraham made a great gathering in the day of his weaning; 9) then Sarah saw the son of Hagar the Egyptian whom she gave birth to for Abraham laughing; 10) and she said to him: Send away this maidservant and her son and he shall not live with my son Isaac; 11) and this thing was extremely difficult for Abraham because of his son; 12) until God said to him: the matter of the boy shall not be difficult for you and watch your maidservant. Anything that Sarah says listen to her for from Isaac shall your offspring remain; 13) and the son of the maidservant I shall make into a nation for he is your offspring; 14) and Abraham set out in the morning and took food and a vial of water and gave this to Hagar and put it on her shoulder and provided her the boy and sent her and she went and lost her way in the "Well of Seven" in the desert; 15) then the water depleted from the vial and she stashed him under a tree; 16) and she went and sat opposite him from afar like the distance of an arrow

300

shot for she said: I shall not see his death and she stood opposite him and raised her voice and cried; 17) and God heard the voice of the boy and God's angel called to her from the Heavens and said: What is it with you, Hagar do not fear for God has heard the voice of the boy that is there; 18) get up and lift him and fasten your hands on him for I shall make a great nation of him; 19) and God opened up her eyes and she saw a well and went and filled the vial with water and gave the boy to drink; 20) and God was with him until he grew up and he dwelled in the desert and became an archer boy; 21) then he settled in the desert of Paran and his mother took a wife for him from the land of Egypt.

I

The "remembering" mentioned at first, peqidah in Hebrew, means pity from God and sustenance for one to whom God [alludes]*.[1]

II

"As he promised" refers to what He said to Abraham: "but Sarah your wife."

II

It repeats "told" referring to what the angels said: "At the same time next year I will return to you."

IV

Sarah's statement: "has made laughter," is the third reason for naming the child "Isaac." The first is the laughing of the parents as was mentioned previously. The second is God's command: "And you shall name him 'Isaac,'" and the third is Sarah's statement: "will make mockery at me."

---

1. See *Beliefs* 2:12.

V

The addition of "anyone who hears" alludes to her trust in people's love for her and Abraham because of [their] righteousness and kindness and [that] they will join in with them in any situation.

VI

Her statement "Who said?" bears [one of] two meanings. The first is: "Who would tell you this if not for the Creator capable of anything?" The second is an augmentation and elevation of the idea as it says: (Is. 41:4)

VII

<"Great gathering" means a gathering for votaries, sages, and righteous people and the like.> Similarly, in regards to Ahasuerus the *mishteh gadhol* was <<because of>> Esther and for her honor.

VIII

The literal meaning of the *MeSaHeQ* that Ishmael would do is that he would mock Isaac and hint that he will not live as it mentions later: *wayehi kemitzaehk bewiyne hothnaw*, "And he was to them like a mocker" (Gen. 19:14) and also because he was weak. Now some people have accused {Ishmael} with accusations of tyranny to which the idea of "laughing" applies, [i.e.], idol worship, prohibited cohabitation, and murder. However, I do not see this [to be correct] for I find it written: "For God listened to the voice of the boy." The Ancients said: "The Holy One does not judge a person except in his time for it says: that is there"[2]

___

2. See *BR* ch. 53, *Rosh. Ha-Sh.* 16:a and *Tal. Jer.* 1:5.

IX

I rendered "shall not be inherit" as "shall not dwell" similar to: "moreover shall **dwell**[3] in it the genus. . . . (Is. 34:11) This is because it was possible that she should hold him back from dwelling [in the house] but not from inheritance.

X

I rendered "in Isaac" as "from Isaac," I mean his son as God says to Jacob "and you are Israel My servant, Jacob whom I have chosen, the offspring of Abraham My lover." (ibid. 41:8) Now only Ishmael is called "the offspring of Abraham" as it says: "For he is your offspring," not his son. Even though they are named so according to [their] natures, God held this back from aspect of greatness and importance.

XI

"Get up raise the child" means raise him by guidance and direction as it says: "Hurry and go up to my father and say to him, 'So said your son Joseph.'" (Gen. 45:9)

XII

"And God opened her eyes" means that God strengthened her sense [of vision] until she saw the well of water from a distance.

XIII

The word *roveh* in the language of the *Targum* is a lad and her sons never ceased to be archers as it says: "And ten of their archers and heroic men were little." (Is. 21:17).

---

3. We have altered the translation to fit the context for ad loc. the Gaon has the literal rendition, "shall take possession of."

XIV

<<"And his mother took for him a wife"—of her origin and land.>>
Afterwards it says:

22) And when it was at that time Abimelech and Pichol the head of his
army said to Abraham saying: God is with you in all that you do; 23) and
now take oath to me here in God that you shall not betray me, my child,
or my grandchild and like the kindness which I do with you do with me
and with the people of the land in which you have settled; 24) and
Abraham said: I shall take oath for you; 25) then Abraham reproached
Abimelech because of the well of water that his servants plugged up; 26)
and Abimelech said: I do not know who has done this thing and you too
have not told me and I too have heard other than [on] this day; 27) then
Abraham took sheep, cattle gave them to Abimelech and they all took
oath; 28) by means of Abraham setting up seven female sheep by
themselves; 29) and Abimelech said to him: What is the purpose of
these seven female sheep that you have set up by themselves? 30) He
said: If you take them from me they shall remain for me a testimony that
I dug this well; 31) for that reason he named the place the "Well of
Seven" for they all took oath there; 32) and when they made a treaty in
the Well of Seven, Abimelech and Pichol the head of his army got up
and returned to the land of Palestine; 33) then he planted a vineyard in
the Well of Seven and called there in the name of God the Master of
Worlds; 34) and he dwelled in the land of Palestine for many years.

I

"And it was at that time" refers to the time of Isaac's birth since Abraham
was complete in all [levels of] estimation leaving only to be provided a
child. When people saw that he was complete in this too they said to him:
"God is with you." The kings began with this statement because they
feared of his children and their [possible] war. The Torah mentioned the
general with king to teach us that it is befitting for a king to have an
advisor for five reasons even if the king is of sound opinion: [1] so that
they support each other; [2] so their natures balance between pity and
harshness; [3] so that his conduct be balanced between fear and hope; [4]
in a case that one of them falls ill; and [5] he directs his colleagues to their
opinion.

II

The primary explanation of "God is with you" is that God shall aid him in any of his decisions as Nathan says to David: "For God is with you," (I Sam. 5:3) and because of this they said to him: "and now etc." meaning before you decide anything and destroy us with .your decision.

III

"Take oath to me" teaches that an oath [must] be according to the consent and conscience of the one sworn to and according to what the one who takes it expresses.[4]

IV

"You shall lie" means "treachery," for in Aramaic the translation of *im tivgod* (delude me) is *teshaqqer*. Many times the word *begidah* in Hebrew has the meaning of cheating and despoliation as it says: (Is. 33:1) and (Is. 21:2)`

V

His statement "my child and grandchild" extends to four generations as it says elsewhere: *shem usher nin waneched* (the names persistence, children, and grandchildren). (Is. 14:22)

VI

It adds "with the land" to say "Do not cheat this land."

VII

It says <"I shall swear" and not "and Abraham swore" teaches us that> one who is obligated in an oath, <it is upon him as if he had already sworn>.

---

4. See *Shav.* 29a.

For that reason the land of the Palestine was not permitted to Israel and they did not enter into it until the fourth generation of which Abimelech says "My grandchild."

VIII

What it says afterwards: "and Abraham reproached," teaches that all reparation and reconciliation between two [people] in which there is no possibility for reproach is not reparation.[5]

IX

"Which his servants plugged up" teaches that a person is obligated to command his household not to sin.[6]

X

Abimelech's response includes three things: "I do not know" by observation, and "you also" [by] claim, and "I too" [by] report from informants.

XI

Why did Abraham not also gift Abimelech servants and maidservants? We say not because he Abimelech was more generous than he but because he is not permitted to take out a proselyte servant from under his domain to another people. The Torah says of this: "You shall not sell a servant." (Deut. 23:16) Moreover . . . and gave his price to his master. From this comes in the Law: "One who sells his servant to a Gentile we fine him up to ten times his value."[7]

---

5. See *BR* ch. 54.
6. See *Sab.* 54b.
7. See *Git.* 44a.

XII

"And Abraham set"—he agreed that there should be seven other female sheep separated in the vicinity as a sign of the treaty between them, the wells were its cause. Whenever one of them dies Abimelech put up {398} a replacement. This is similar to: "This stone is a witness and this is post is a witness," (Gen. 31:52) and "When they cut the calf in two," (Jer. 34:18) and the like.

We should know that were the reason for calling this place in the name of oath and being derived therefrom as it says elsewhere: "And he named that place." How can it say after this that the name Ber Sheva is derived from seven for it says: "And he called it seven." We say that the name of the place of the treaty was ber sheva because they made an oath and then he named the entire city Ber Sheva because of the seven, for that reason he says here "the place" and there "the city."

XIII

"And they made a treaty" . . . Abimelech and his advisor and returned to their land, settling down for their kingdom was secure.

XIV

"And he planted a tree" in order that people congregate around him as it says: "And Saul dwells in Gibeah under a tree Ramah," (I Sam. 22:6) and further that many animals flock there as it says: "Where the birds chirp." (Ps. 104:17)

XV

"And He called in the name of God"—that he would proselytize the people and bring them into the religion. He therefore adds in the naming: "the Lord eternal God," which the act of an actors and the like.

Chapter XXII

[[1) And when it was after these matters God tried Abraham and said to him: Abraham. He said: Behold I am at Your service. 2) He said: Take your son, your only one whom you love which is Isaac and bring him to the land of Work and bring him up there as a sacrifice on one of the mountains that I shall say to you; 3) and Abraham set out early in the morning and saddled his ass and took his servant boys with him and split firewood for the sacrifice and got up and went to the place that God said to him; 4) and when it was on the third day Abraham lifted his eyes and saw the place from afar; 5) and Abraham said to his servant boys sit here with the ass and I and the servant boy will go there and bow and return to you; 6) and Abraham took the firewood for the sacrifice and mounted it on Isaac his son's shoulder and took in his hand the fire and the knife and they went together; 7) and Isaac said to Abraham his father and said to him: O my father. He said: Here I am my son. He said: Behold is the fire and the firewood and where is the lamb for the sacrifice? 8) Abraham said: God shall show the lamb for the sacrifice my son; and they went together, 9) until they came to the place that God said to him and Abraham built there the altar and arranged the firewood and bound Isaac and placed him on the altar on top of the firewood; 10) and Abraham extended his hand and took the knife to sacrifice his son; 11) and an angel of God called him from the Heavens and said: Abraham, Abraham. He said: Here I am; 12) and He said: Do not extend your hand to the boy and do not do anything with him for I now have made it known to the people that you are faithful to God and did not hold back your only son from Me. 13) Then Abraham lifted his eyes after this and behold there is a sheep whose horns are captured in the leaves of the tree and he went and took it and brought it forth as a sacrifice instead of his son; 14) and Abraham named that place "God reveals Himself" as it is said today of this mountain "God reveals Himself "; 15) then God's angel called to Abraham a second time from the Heavens, 16) and said: In My Name you have taken oath says God, for because you have done this thing and have not held back your only son from Me, 17) I shall surely bless you and multiply your offspring like the stars of the Heavens and like the sand that is at the coast of the sea and your offspring shall inherit its enemies; 18) and all the nations of the earth shall be blessed by means of your offspring in reward for you listening to My voice. 19) Then Abraham returned to his servant boys and they got up and went together to the Well of Seven and stayed there.]]

I

. . . It says: "So God tries the righteous but the sinful and the lover of deceit He despises," (Ps. 11:5) [which means] that God puts the righteous through a trial but the sinful and lovers of misdeed He despises and distances them.

It is upon us to know that this trial through which God said He shall put the righteous is not trial [in its] general [sense], I mean in the category of worship or rebellion, for that [kind of] trial may be applied to any person whereas this trial is another kind higher than this one. When a worshipper obeys his Master's [passing] what the other people are obligated to be tested in, it is proper that God should put him through other kinds [of trials] of obedience and should merit him additional reward.[1] One should not say that the one who tests wrongs the one who is tried or the one whom He absolved from the other [kind of] trial for the tried will be granted additional reward whereas the other he leaves in the [level] that he was. For since he did not fulfil what he was commanded first it does not agree with wisdom to place upon him additional [commands]. Moreover, this is for his good for God may He be blessed knows

---

1. See *Beliefs* 5:3 (p. 214).

that this worshipper will not fulfil the additional command that He places upon him and his iniquity will increase. For that reason it says: "God tries the righteous."[2]

We say: For what reason does it describe the righteous with one word, i.e., "righteous," and the sinner by two characteristics, i.e., "wicked" and "lovers of deceit?" We respond: This person that is put through the additional trial is complete in that he believes in good and its performance while the iniquitous that was not tried with the additional trial, whether he does evil or conceives it, in whichever way it may be, he falls outside of {the trial}. Accordingly, it says "and the wicked," which is the one who does an act, and "lover of deceit" is one who conceives it—neither of these shall be tried. It does not say this of the righteous for "the lover of righteousness" is not tried until he becomes righteous in act. The same applies to the story of Abraham, who deserved to be put through an additional trial [only] when he passed the ten trials that have preceded. For that reason the Scripture states "And it was after these things" before [this additional trial], meaning after all the trials had passed.

II

With "And God tried Abraham" it lets us know that wisdom declared that Abraham be tried with this.

III

Now, four estimable [characteristics] are revealed in the trial. The first is of God may He be blessed and exalted. It lets mankind know that God does not chose a votary vainly but only an obedient one, so that one does not say: Would God have wished to chose me I would be like Abraham for when he would see Abraham's trials he would know that he is not like him and would believe that the one that God had chosen [had been so] justly and deservedly. The second is of Abraham [1] that gave away and took upon himself to destroy a son that was given to him {400} at one hundred years of age, in obedience to his Master, and [2] to increase Abraham's reward. The third is of Sarah, that a son that was given her at

---

2. I.e., not the iniquitous.

the time of old age, she gave him away in obedience to her Master. For everything Abraham did was [always] with her consent for it says: "All that Sarah says to you listen to her voice." This means that she knew that {Abraham} took Isaac out to the mountain to slaughter him but did not prevent him in obedience to her Master despite him being her only and beloved one and that he was given to her after she reached ninety years. The fourth is of Isaac so that one does not think that Ishmael gave over of himself to God more than Isaac because Ishmael was circumcised at thirteen years old when he was cognizant of pain and capable of resisting, while Isaac was circumcised when he was [only] eight days old, incognizant of pain and incapable of resisting. For that reason God tried Isaac with a greater trial than Ishmael: One was tried with pain and the other giving himself over to death.

IV

Were one to ask what sake this trial was for? We say It comes for two reasons: One is to inform the people and the other is to increasing his reward.

V

"And Abraham said to him"—it records a call and a response—something it did not do in the previous vision. We say that commandments and warnings were required for the affirmation of their statement, i.e., that He calls the commanded so that the listener should prepare for what he is commanded. Furthermore, so that he should be commanded in the state of ease and comfort.

VI

"Take"—it counts four things: A son, only one, beloved, and Isaac. The intention in this is to show the lavishness of Abraham's obedience for one who has many children and gives one of them over to his Master, it may be said that he obeys his Master. For that reason it says "your son." How much more so if he was the only one, I mean [for] each one of them, for his mother has no other [either]. For that reason it says "your only one."

How more so when he is most beloved and esteemed. For that reason it says "whom you love." How more so if one of them was announced to be singled out with nobility and prophecy. For that reason it adds "Isaac." All four of these [ideas] meet in Abraham's trial by which he followed in obedience to his Master by it.[3]

VII

Were one to ask: How is it possible that he should announce promises of Isaac as it says: "For by Isaac your offspring shall be called," when He had commanded to sacrifice him for then he indicates that promises may be annulled. We say that God would be able to resurrect him after killing him and recompense him for all the promises.[4]

VIII

The beholders of "the annulment" [of the precepts] have asked here: If it is possible that God should command Abraham to slaughter his son and then warns him against this, it is then possible that He gives the commandments of the Torah and then warns against them. Likewise, if it is possible that He should make promises of Isaac and should annul them by the commandment to slaughter him, it is [then] possible that he should annul many of the promises that he was given. Four responses have already been given . . . of which, the one who said that this 'olah does not mean a "sacrifice" but [only] "ascending." We say: Would it be the manner of one who was commanded to bring up his son to a mountain, fire, and wood and to mount them on his son's shoulder and to hold a knife to slaughter him? They said being that the word 'olah withstands two interpretations in the language, "bringing up" and "sacrifice." Abraham was necessitated to prepare for the worst case relying on it being that if the intention is otherwise God will direct me. Since the intention was specifically "bringing up" it was said to him: "Do not send forward your hand to the child." Against this response it has been claimed: If <you maintain that> it is possible that Abraham should go from with his Master

---

3. See *BR* ch. 55.
4. See *Beliefs* 3:9. p. 169.

without being certain of the meaning of what he was commanded, it is then possible that this should happen to many other prophets and that they should command you things that have not been verified by your Master for they went from in front of Him having doubt regarding His words just as Abraham had doubts and did not know what his Master commanded him. Now this [claim] is not obligatory in regards to them, I mean the prophets, for what prompted God to conceal the true intention from Abraham was the trial for it states at the beginning: "And God tried Abraham," and would God have explained to him that this is merely "bringing up," the trial would be annulled.

The second response is of the one who renders the command as a condition and says that God said to Abraham: take [and] sacrifice your son on the mountain if I command you to do so. He renders 'asher as "if" I shall say to you and command you, similar to: asher nasi yeheta (Lev. 4:22) and (Deut. 11:2) "asher tishmeir." Since the command was originally a condition, Abraham prepared himself for the possibility that he will be commanded, the first [thing], which is to be prepared, is still in force.

The third is that there are those that maintain that at the beginning of the trial there is some ellipsis and said that statement of God Exalted, "And raise him," is not directed at Isaac but at the "ram" and that ["ram"]* is elliptic in it. Now it leaves the statement with an allusion and ellipsis so that Abraham should think that the reference is to Isaac and the trial will be executed. They sought proof for this in that when {Abraham} was held back from harming Isaac it became clear to him that the reference was not to Isaac and began to look what was it that he was commanded and whom the reference was to with the commandment. When he saw the ram he knew that the reference was to it, he rushed, took it and sacrificed it instead of his son as it says: "And he lifted his eyes."

The fourth way is that we say that the annulment of a precept is possible where there was no condition that the command can never not be annulled but where there was a condition <that the command can never be annulled> it can never be annulled. Accordingly, when it was said to Abraham to slaughter Isaac since He did not make a condition on this command that he will not annul it, it would be possible to command him [afterwards] not to slaughter him for this [first] command was good in its time but the Law of the Torah is not of this nature so for God made a condition with them and said: I will never annul them and one who will come to annul them do not listen to him for as long as the Heavens stand above the earth they shall not be annulled and after such a condition there is no annulment. Also the promises [to the future] are not like the Laws and God Who is trustworthy in His promise will not permit them to be annulled nor . . . the knowledge that the Creator did not refer . . .

[It then says:]

[[20) And when it was after these things Abraham was told and it was said to him: Behold Milkah has also born sons to Nahor your brother . . .]]

I

It began with "And when it was after these things," meaning after the "remembrance" and the "binding" the rumor had reached Abraham that Milkah had given birth to sons for [how is it possible that]* he not know [this] being that both of them were in Kuth. It was known that Sarah had not given birth as it says "And Sarah was barren," and that Milkah had given birth, for without this Sarah's condition could not be discerned and how could it not mention her giving birth until now? We say that it is possible that this was concealed from Abraham for the good in order that he and Sarah not be grieved by this. After Sarah gave birth and he went out in peace from the trial God Exalted perchanced this rumor in front of Abraham to add to his happiness and <<rejoicing>>.

II

That it specifies the names of the sons has a few reasons. The first is that we should know that Nahor begot twelve sons corresponding to the twelve tribes that were destined [to be born] to Abraham through Jacob and just as [with] these, eight of them were of free woman and four from the maidservant, so [with] these, eight of them from Milkah the free woman and four from Reumah the concubine. Furthermore in order that there be a firm fundament and introduction to Isaac's marriage to Rebecca. Further, to tell us the lineage of Job [i.e.] where he originated from for it says "in the land of US," and so that we know where his friend who spoke sensibly to him, I mean Elijah the son of Berachel the Buzite, originates from. The statement there "from the family of Ram," means "from the family of Abraham" with the mutation of *Av* as it says "yimini" (Es. 2:5)—which means Benjaminite with the abbreviation of *ben*. Shalman

(Josh. 10:4), which means Shalmaneser with the mutation of *Eser*, and "and Nesarim," (Jer. 4:17) which means Nebuchadenezzer with the mutation of *Nebuchad* and like and the like of abbreviations.

The interpretation [of the pericope] "And revealed Himself" is complete with God's aid. The interpretation of "and Sarah's life was" follows it.

Chapter XXIII

1) And Sarah's life was 127 years. These are the years of her life; 2) and Sarah died in the City of Four which is Hebron in the land of Canaan and Abraham came to mourn for her and to cry for her; 3) then Abraham got up from the presence of this dead and spoke to the sons of Heth and said <to them>: 4) "I am a stranger or guest with you, give me a plot of grave with you so that I may bury my dead from in front of me." 5) And the sons of Heth answered him and said to him: 6) Hearken unto us O our master, you are the Noble of God among us, in the best of our graves bury your dead and no man among us shall stint his grave from you so that you may bury your dead. 7) And Abraham got up and bowed <in thanks> to the people of the land and the sons of Heth; 8) He then spoke to them and said to them: If your souls desire to bury my dead from in front of me hearken unto me and plead for me from with Ephron the son of Sohar; 9) that he give me the double cave that he has that is at the edge of his field for full price he shall give it to me among you as a burial ground. 10) And Ephron sat among the sons of Heth [and Ephron the Hittite] and answered him in their presence and the many that enter the gate of his city saying: 11) No my master hearken unto me; the field I have already given to you and the cave that is in it in the presence of my people I have already given it to you, bury your dead in it; 12) and Abraham bowed <in thanks> in front of them; 13) then he spoke in the presence of the people of the land and said to him: But if you <would like to conduct business with me> were you to listen to me

I have already set aside for you the price for the field, take it from me so that I may bury my dead there. 14) And Ephron answered him and said to him: O my master hearken unto me, a land worth five hundred *shekels* of silver between me and you what is it, bury your dead in it. 15) And when Abraham heard this from Ephron he weighed for him the cost according to its worth in the presence of the sons of Heth which is four hundred *shekels* of silver which is approved by merchants; 17) and Ephron's field <known> as "double" in the presence of Mamre the field and the cave that is in it as well as all the trees in the field and all its borders around it 18) became bound to Abraham as an acquirement in the presence of the sons of Heth and the rest of those who enter the gate of the city; 19) and after this Abraham buried Sarah his wife in the cave that is in the field <known as> "double" in the presence of Mamre which is Hebron in the land of Canaan; 20) and the field and the cave that is in it came through for Abraham as a burial ground from the sons of Heth.

I

We return to the explanation we obtained from these verses. The first thing we say is: What is the purpose of dividing these years [into] one hundred, twenty, and seven years as it mentions similar to it regarding Abraham, [i.e.] one hundred years, seventy years and five years and the same of Jacob. We say that from three units, ones, tens, and hundreds, it compares each one to the other approximately. When she was one hundred years old she was like twenty in strength; at twenty she was like seven in righteousness and at seven like twenty in intelligence and understanding and at twenty like one hundred in attainment of good acts.[1] This is in order that we be stirred in every one of these five ideas. We do not find any people in the Scripture whose number of years is mentioned because there was no one whose youthfulness was restored except Sarah.

II

It adds in the verse "the years of the life Sarah," meaning that this is the numbered existence to which years may be applied in this world whereas

1. See *BR* 58:1.

her existence in the other world to which years do not apply has no limit as it says: "Were he to ask for life before you give it to him as well as length of days forever." (Ps. 21:5)

III

It calls Hebron "Kiryath Arba" for [one of] four reason. The first is according to the literal meaning {of the text} is that it is a name of a place or person. The second is that four giants lived in it, Anaq and his three sons as it says: "And Caleb drove thence the three sons of Anaq, Sheshai, Ahiman, and Talman born of Anaq." (Josh. 15:14) The third is that it shall fall in the portion of the four, meaning the tribe of Judah entirely, the Levites in the cities of frontiers,[2] and for the priest in the city of absorption and then its fields for Caleb the son Jephune. The fourth is because the head pairs of righteous people [i.e.] Abraham and Sarah, Isaac and Rebecca, Jacob and Leah according to the written [law] and Adam and Eve before this according to Tradtion.

IV

It says "to mourn for Sarah and to weep for her" is [according] to some of the laws that one is obligated to follow for the dead in various ways. [1] "Eulogy" for one day and crying for three, [2] and seven days for laundering clothes and—hair cutting—thirty days and to come in and make glad the children for a year. [3]

V

I rendered "face" as "presence" because the word may have one of six meanings: [1] "anger" as it says: "I shall make my face fall upon you," (Jer. 3:12) [2] "face" as it says: "The view of the face of the king," (Est. 1:14) [3] "turning" as it says: "And also he turned to island dwellers," (Dan. 11:8) [4] "wish" as it says: "And the light of your face as you liked them," (Ps. 44:4) [5] "against" as it says: "And stopped across from the city." (Gen. 33:18)

---

2. See Lev. 25:34.

VI

That Abraham begins "I am a stranger or guest among you" [he means] that every family has a grave and says that if I am strange I do not have any known family among you and I need a plot of grave. Then he bargained with them after he got up from the presence of his dead according to what comes to us in the law that one who has a dead in front of him neither acquirement nor sale is valid. Likewise, it is not permissible to pray when one's dead is in front of him because he is occupied with it.[3]

VII

By their statement to him, "Hear my master," they mean accept this estimability from us until they always speak to him so. Were he not to have accepted they would not possible for them to do so. Similar to this it says of Yehoash: "And after the death of Yehoiada came the princes of Judah and made obedience to the king," (II Chron. 24:17) in a manner of worship and this does not obligate him a punishment were it not for what he said: "Then the king listened to them." (ibid.)[4]

VIII

Their specification "the Noble of God" for an estimable person is of two kinds an estimable of this world as it says: "And shechem the Son of Hamor the Hiwwite the Esteemed of the land saw her" (Gen. 34:2) and "twelve Nobles will be born" (Gen. 17:20) and estimable in the world to come for that reason they said: "And the Noble of God you are among us." It explains to us that God Mighty and Estimable has elevated you for he . . . out of love you are righteous among us as your acts use up . . . this is the intermediacy that is successful between people.

IX

Their statement "In the choicest of our graves bury your dead."—public burial.

---

3. See *Ber.* 3:1.
4. Following *Seder Olam Rabbah* ch. 18 Yehoash made himself into a deity.

X

They add: "No man among us shall stint his grave," referring to private burial and referring to themselves.

XI

I rendered *lo yichle* as "shall not be niggardly" for this word has [one of] five meanings: [1] "completion": "And Solomon built the house and completed it," (I Kings 6:14) [2] "destruction": "The rod of his wrath perished," (Prov. 22:8) [3] "miserliness": "And to a miser it shall not be said generous," (Is. 32:5) [4] "vacating": "God do not empty me of Your pity," (Ps. 40:12) and [5] "ability": "And she was not able to conceal him." (Ex. 2:3)

XII

The statement "And Abraham stood up and bowed down," alludes to him being elevated in front of them and [that] he wanted to stand up [all the way]. Whereas "and He bowed down" is in a manner of estimation.

XIII

"To the people of the land"—were they not the children of Heth how much more so if they are the children of Heth and are estimable.

XIV

"If you wish" means "If this thing is in your desire," which accords the law that any sale or acquirement and comprise that is by force or accident is invalid for the words *yesh eth nafshechem* is like Yehu's statement: "If you desire and a survivor shall go out of the city to go to tell in Israel." (I Kings 9:15)

XV

Ufag'u li means: "Ask for my good from with Him," for this word means "to ask good." It can also mean: [1] "And do not ask good before," (Jer. 7:16)

[2] "attack": "You turn and attack the priest," (I Sam. 22:18) [3] "reaching" as it says: "And he reached the place," (Gen. 28:11) [4] "perchancing": "And he perchanced at the border." (Job 19:22) The purpose in him asking for good from them is so that they do not oppose him because of the burial and hold him back. It elucidates the name Ephron ben Shahar while being present teaching the necessity in specifying the writing of contracts.

XVI

"And he shall give me." This a manner of giving [meaning] that he will give his agreement to me to sell it and then we will agree on the price.

XVII

It names it "the double cave" to teach that it is a cave inside a cave for the language of *Kifle kiflaim*: "For their *ken* is many times your own." (Job 11:6)

XVIII

It specifies "that is to him" meaning that it impossible that he should sell something which is not his even if he takes upon himself to free the owner.

XIX

It adds "that is at the edge of his field" according to what is known that graveyards at the edges.

XX

I rendered *bekhesef* as "with the price" according to the popular [usage] as it says: "the price of his sale," (Lev. 25:50) and "the price of his acquirement." (Lev. 25:5)

XXI

It specifies "full" supports what is in the Law that the one who acquires land with money so long as he does not pay the choicest of both of the entire price either of them may if the land is indivisible because it is an animal then the sale is invalid.

XXII

He repeats "He shall give it to me" after "And he gave me," for the first is giving and the other is after payment of the price.

XXIII

It adds "among you" for you are the son of his uncle his relative or his neighbors and you shall not demand for me with the Law of pre-emption.

XXIV

We say that since Ephron settles among the sons of Heth what is the use in exchanging words with them instead of with him? We respond firstly as we have said that they do not oppose him. We then say: to let us know that he is a witness for the people, despite that he did not speak, but the speech occurred in his presence and it was said: "attest for him and he is present."

XXV

It adds "among the sons of Heth" for it was necessary to turn our attention to apply the testimony to what they hear.

XXVI

It adds "the Hittite" for at times it is necessary to apply the testimony to his name and the preceding generation. This is when there are two people with the same name.

XXVII

It says "in the presence of the sons of Heth" that the testimony shall be enacted through them hearing. <Likewise any case that he did not pay all

the money for something he already received if it is something that is divisible.>

XXVIII

It adds "and the many that enter the gate of his city" to the sons of Heth for just as they have a specific speaker for their request or the like, so the rest of the people of the city have general speakers for. As for the matter of burial if it is seventy-five cubits away from the city. . . .

XXIX

Ephron demands two things with "No my master." One is not only the cave by itself "I give to you," but both the field and the cave. The second is "Not with the full price I shall give to you but without money and without a price."

XXX

That it specifies the field with giving and the cave with giving separate for every two things of grand has different ideas and the testimony should name both.

XXXI

That it attaches to "which is in it (bo)" shows that "field" in the language is masculine.

XXXII

"And Abraham bowed down in front of the people of the land" includes the sons of Heth and all that come to the gate of his city as well as anyone who has the right to attest to him.

XXXIII

"People of the land" refers to Ephron.

XXXIV

"If you" means one of two things. The first is: "You have done." The second is: "If only you would do," for the word *lo* is divided into two kinds. One is something that the speaker has no part nor utility in like Job says: "Were my agony weighed out," (Job 6:2) and "Were they to become wise they would have intelligence," (Deut. 32:29) as it says what exception this is in two other ways.

XXXV

"I have given the price of the field" means "I have already set it aside." This indicates that the seller should first set aside the money and then testify and he pays. For that reason you find in Jeremiah's sale "weighing money" twice [?] as it says: "And I weighed him the money seven *shekels* of silver and I subscribed in the book and sealed it." (Jer. 32:10) The first weighing is for balancing and the second for measuring for the payment after the contract.

XXXVI

"Take from me" indicates that he did not give over money unless . . . him choosing it.

XXXVII

"A land of four hundred *shekels* of money" has an ellipsis [and it means] "the price of four hundred *shekels* of silver."

XXXVIII

This statement is of good words . . . It says: "And Abraham heard Ephron . . . to the time of weighing. By means of conjecture . . . Abraham said to Ephron in the contract . . . also another one of it.

XXXIX

It says "passing through," the merchant requires that people not buy nor sell unless it is with . . . visible . . . This statement permits whenever people who agreed to bargain in the visible even though it is . . . not pure gold . . . the grandchildren to bargain with.

XL

"And Ephron's field . . . became bound" is connected with what [it says] afterwards: "To Abraham for acquirement," meaning "became bound to Abraham as an acquirement," as it says elsewhere: "The house that was in the city was sustained . . . for the one who acquires it." (Lev. 25:30)

XLI

The meaning of "<known as> 'double' in the presence of Mamre" refers to the definition of the place of the sale by what it may be identified and what structures it has.

XLII

It adds "and every tree that is in the field" teaches us that the trees are not included in the process of the sale of the land unless he explicates this meaning two . . . this land each one of which were explicated . . . explanation of four complete limits and if he specified three [then] he had three . . . it is like whose sides are equal and kept quite—detracting from it.

XLIII

"In the presence of the Sons of Heth." This is a manner of payment. The completion of the story is in the repetition: "and Ephron's field came through," for the first "bound" is necessary and the second possible.

XLIV

"And after the" means "And when Abraham buried Sarah his wife the place became a grave plot for the future." We should know that the entire land of Israel is for us declared justly and that some or many of us seized it by warfare and in it are three places we acquired for a price which is the best of what is in it. The first is Hebron the place of the burial of the fathers according to what [is recorded in] this story and to this the [fore]fathers would go up for the holidays before the Temple was built and one who wished to worship in this . . . in it as Absalom says to David: "I shall go and pay my oath to God in Hebron." (II Sam. 15:7) The second is the place of Mt. Gerizim and Abal on which we were given the blessings and the curses and there we made a treaty. It says of it: "And He accepted the portion of the field where he pitched his tent." (Gen. 33:19) The third is the Temple that David bought from Armon as it says: "And David brought the grain, the cattle with the price of 150 *shekels*." (II Sam. 24:24) It says in the second version: "with six hundred *shekels*." The difference between the two versions is fifty *shekels* from the tribe of Judah and it says six hundred *shekels* from all the tribes. Like God Exalted and Estimable: "which God the Lord your God from all your tribes" . . . twenty Abraham's wife . . .

Chapter XXIV

I

[[1) and <when> Abraham became old and advanced in years and God blessed him in everything; 2) Abraham said to his servant the elder of his house having control over everything that is his:[1] "allude now with your hand to my treaty";[2] 3) and I shall make you take oath by God the Master of the Heavens and the Earth that you will not take a wife for my son from the daughters of Canaan among which I dwell; 4) rather to my land and my birth place you shall go and take a wife for my son Isaac; 5) and the servant said to him: perhaps the woman will not wish to follow me to this land shall I return your son to the land from which you have come out?; 6) Abraham said to him: be careful lest you return my son there!; 7) God the Master of the Heavens who took me out of the house of my father and from the land of my birth who said to me and swore to me saying: to your offspring I shall give this land He shall send His angel in front of you and you shall take a wife for my son from there; 8) and if the woman will not agree to go after you then you shall be cleared of this oath but you shall not return my son there!; 9) and the servant alluded with his hand to the treaty of Abraham his master and

---

1. Or perhaps 'all his possessions' as in the parallel in the v. 36 of the preserved section.
2. Instead of literally: place now your hand under my thigh.

took oath to him on this matter; 10) then the servant took ten camels of the camels of his master and went and all the goodness of his master was with him and he got up and went to Aram Naharayim to the city of Nahor; 11) and he left the camels to kneel at the entrance of the city at the well of water at the time of the evening the time of the coming out of the <women> which water; 12) and He said: O God, the God of my master Abraham make perchance today <my need> and do good by means of this to my master Abraham; 13) Behold I stand at the spring of water and the daughters of the people of the city go out to draw water; 14) and whichever girl I shall say to her lean your vial so that I may drink and she says: drink! And your camels too I shall give to drink, You have found her fit for Your servant Isaac and by means of her I will know that You have done good for my master; 15) and before he finished his words behold Rebecca who was born to Bethuel the son of Milkah the wife of Nahor the brother of Abraham had come out and her vial was on her shoulder; 16) and the girl was very nice in appearance a virgin and a man did no know her and she went down to the spring and filled her vial and went up; 17) and the servant went to greet her and said: let me try a little water from your vial; 18) she said: drink my master! And she rushed and lowered her vial onto her hand and gave him to drink; 19) and when she finished giving him to drink she said: your camels I shall also give to drink until their drink finishes; 20) and she hurried and emptied her vial in the aqueduct and went further to the well to give water until she gave all his camels water; 21) and the man observed[3] and kept quiet to see if God made his way successful or not; 22) and <when> the camels finished their drinking the man took gold rings whose weight was half a shekel <and gave them to her and put> two bracelets on her hand whose weight was ten shekels of gold; 23) <after> he said to her: tell me whose daughter are you and will I find place in the house of your father for us to stay the night in; 24) and she said to him: I am the daughter of Bethuel the son of Milkah which was born to Nahor; 25) then she said straw and hay are plenty with us as well as a place for staying the night; 26) then the servant kneeled and bowed to God; 27) and he said: Blessed is God the God of my master Abraham who did not stint His esteem and goodness from my master. I am on <the correct> path [in which] God lead me to the house of my master's brother!; 28) then the

---

3. Derenbourgh's edition has: "asked for water" but we have altered this reading according to the Gaon's comment ad loc.

girl went and told these matter to the house of her mother; 29) and
Rebecca had a brother whose name was Laban and he went to the man
outside the spring; 30) and when he saw the ring and the bracelets on
the hands of his sister and heard her words saying: so said the man to
me, he came to him and behold he is standing over the camels at the
spring; 31) and he said come Blessed of God why should you stand
outside when I have made space in the house <and have prepared> a
place for the camels; 32) and the man entered the house and freed the
camels and threw them straw and hay and <he gave him> water to wash
his feet and the feet of the men which were with him; 33) then he
brought in front of him to eat but he said: I will not eat until I shall say
my words. He said: speak!;]

I

[4]"And God blessed him with everything." We say: after it says: "And
Abraham was extremely great with property, silver and gold" (Gen. 13:2),
what remains [to be blessed with]? However, "with everything" means
"with land", for after he returned he gained some land for himself.

II

<Now Isaac had never been in the city of Nahor but {the Scripture} refers
to this [act] as returning in respect to [his] father as it says: "Shall I return
your son to the land from which you have come out?"</>

III

. . . as it says: "And also upon the servants and maidservants in those
days I will pour out My wind" (Joel 3:2) < . . . > and this is the general
reason [including] all servants. The second particular one is the reason . . . for this [particular] servant[5] is the statement: "elder of the

---

4. This section is rendered according to Zucker's translation because in the
Arabic section the text is lacking and garbled.

5. Of Abraham.

house" meaning that he was knowledgeable in people's conduct, ordinances, marital [practices] and conventions similar to what it says elsewhere: "And he took ten men of the elders of the city and said: sit here and they sat" (Ruth. 4:2) for he was to mention marriage at the end of the section.

IV

Some people say in regard to: "Put now your hand under my thigh" that there was such a practice, e.g. "seven female sheep" (Gen. 21:28), "and until this mound" (ibid. 31:52), "and this pillar is a witness" (ibid.), "and the calf which they split into two" (Jer. 34:18), "and this stone shall be for us a witness for it has heard" (Josh. 24:27) and the like.[6] Others say that "under my thigh" refers to the place of bowing, bending, and [thus] prayer just as people take oath by Jerusalem and the synagogue and the like. What appears correct to me is that he wanted to make him swear by his circumcision because of two [of its] characteristics. The first of these is that we find oaths to be [executed] by one of six things: [1] God, [2] His Torah, [3] His precepts, [4] His holiness, [5] the life of a prophet, and [6] the life of the one who takes oath. [1] By God as it says: "And God's oath shall decide between them" (Ex. 22:10). [2-3] By the Torah and the Precepts as it says: "By[7] the teaching or the testimony, even though they did not make this statement" (Is. 8:20). [4] By His holiness as it says: "God the Lord takes oath by His holiness" (Am. 4:2). By some votary as it says: "And it became like My trodden or the substance of mortar" (Is. 21:10). [5] By the life of the prophet as they say: "Living is God and Living is your soul" (I Sam. 20:3). [6] By the life of the one who takes oath himself[8]—if not God shall act with him and do with him [such and such] as it says: "So God shall do with me and so He shall add, if I will taste bread or anything else until the Sun sets" (e.g. II Sam. 3:35). Now the circumcision is a

---

6. To use an object to swear by.

7. As did Ibn Janah after him (Riqmah p. 68) the Gaon understands the lamedhs prefixed to 'teaching' and 'testimony' to allude to oath. However, his translation ad loc. has no indication of this which would imply a change of mind. Our addition of 'by' is therefore conjectural.

8. Arabic text has here: "which is the fifth [thing]" but this number does not seem to be correct.

commandment![9] The second characteristic is that we know that they would take oath with any recent original or novel thing of theirs and [the commandment of] circumcision was [indeed] recent! We find Saul taking oath "for living is God which saves Israel" (I Sam. 14:38) referring to the incident of Michmash.[10] David took oath: "who redeemed my soul from all sorrow" (II Sam. 4:9). Solomon takes oath: "Who prepared me and sat me on the throne of David my father" (I Kings 2:24). Of the time of the Redemption it says that the nation will no longer take oath by the Redemption from Egypt because it is distant but rather by the redemption from slavery which is recent as it says: "Therefore behold the days come says the Lord that it shall no more be said, the Lord lives, that brought up the children of Israel out of the land of Egypt, but the Lord lives that brought up the Children of Israel from the land of the North" (Jer. 16:14).[11] It also says: "And one who takes oath by the world, by the True God shall swear, he shall say: and the one who made me forget my first sorrows and concealed them from my eye" (Is. 65:16)—each one will swear: "one who has made me forget my sorrows and worries." If this is so why did Zedekiah swear to Jeremiah: "Living is God which has made us this soul I will not put you to death" (Jer. 38:16) and did not take oath by some thing recent? We explain that this was close to what they were occupied with for were one to ask for protection: "he shall have his life for a prey and shall live" (ibid. 2) while were Zedekiah to ask for protection: "And your soul shall live" (ibid. 17) and that he will not kill Jeremiah.

Now there is [also a case of] an oath by the heavens taken by God and His angels. [By God] as it says: "And I shall swear by the Heavens" (Deut 32:40). By the angels it says: "And I heard the angel suspended above the waters of the Tigris and he lifted his right and his left and swore by the Vitality of World" (Dan. 12:7). The allusion with all this is to the appearance of heavenly signs. Similarly an oath by <<the right [hand] and powerful arm—however by God—is also found as it says:>> "God has taken oath by His strength (lit. his right) and the strength of his might (lit. His powerful arm)" (Is. 62:8). The reference is to appearance of earthly signs. Now "God takes oath by His soul" (Jer. 51:4 and Am. 6:8)

---

9. And therefore can be used to take oath with. Accordingly, the Gaon takes "under my thigh" to be a euphemism. See BR ch. 59.

10. (v. 31) Where Israel defeats the Philistines.

11. See Ber. 12b.

of the first thing he negates but the rest is true. However, if he says: he is a person, an animal, a bird a tree, silver, gold and water—he tells the truth of the first thing he affirms and the rest but the false.

VI

"The daughters of the Canaanite" refers to all the seven nations for the appellation Canaanite applies to them as [being] the name of the father, as it says: "and behold God brought you into the land of the Canaanites" (Ex. 13:5). Similarly, the name Amorite applies to them for they are the first to be conquered, as it says: "and I walked you forty years in the wilderness to inherit the land of the Amorite" (Am. 2:9).

VII

"In whose midst I live" means being that I am in their neighborhood I know their acts. Similar to this it says: "like the acts of the people of Egypt among whom you have dwelled you shall not do" (Lev. 18:3).

VIII

"But to my land"—to the East, "to my birth place"—[to] such specific river.

IX

Now it is brief here [and omits] what it will [say in the] repetition "to the house of my father" (v. 38) [which] means 'my grandfather' but "and to my family" refers to the family itself.

X

Some ask here: Were not the people of {Abraham's} house also idol worshippers?[22] As it says, "Terah the father of Abraham and the father of

---

22. Like the Canaanites.

Nahor and they worshipped other gods" (Josh. 24:2) whereas Abraham was the exception to them from the statement: "the choicest of your fathers gave no heed to them" (Deut 32:18). We give two responses to this. The first is that he knew that the people of his house were more obedient to him to convert to the religion than the others. The second is that the people of his house were more inclined to let him deal with them and to convert them than any others.

XI

We then ask: We see that were {Abraham} not to have made him take oath and gone and brought him a girl who is not from his family would Abraham not realize this from here language and words and question. Rather Abraham was wont to reduce [both] his and her toil and his servant as well!

XII

"And you shall take a wife for Isaac" lets us know that marriage can be arranged by a messenger being that {'taking'} is one of the sixteen known expressions for marriage that people have: [1] 'behold you are my woman' as it says: "and this should be called a 'woman'" (Gen. 2:23); [2] 'mine', [3] 'my helper', [4] 'my opposite' as it says: "I shall make him a helper opposite him" (ibid. 19); [5] 'my rib'; [6] 'my confined'; [7] 'in my place' as it says: "and He took one of his ribs and filled in its place with flesh" (ibid. 21); [8] 'my sole one' as it says: "and they shall be like a single body" (ibid.); [9] 'my designated one' as it says: "which he designated for him" (Ex. 21:8)[23]; [10] 'my engaged one' as it says: "and she is an engaged maid-servant" (Lev. 19:20); [11] 'my possessed one'[24]; [12] 'my acquired one'; [13] 'my bought one' as is known; [14] 'which is mine'; [15] 'in my domain' and [16] 'contingent to me' according to the words of the Mishnah.[25]

---

23. The Gaon renders this phrase in its general sense as: "which shall marry her."

24. translated according to the Gaon's rendition of the word in Deut. 20:7.

25. See Kid. 6a.

XIII

Regarding his statement "perhaps," we say that every 'perhaps' is doubt if something will or will not happen. Were one to ask us about the statement "perhaps there is hope" (Lam. 3:29) [and] "perhaps you will be concealed in the day of God's anger" (Zeph. 2:3). We respond to him that it is also a doubt but this is not something his Master promised him but is their own acts—it is possible that will do it or not.

XIV

"To go after me to this land"—the condition refers to before the marriage, i.e. that {she and Isaac} should remain in her land, for after the marriage plainly she does not have this [option] for the law requires every woman to go out to the land of her husband if his land has four things: [1] an assemblage for the Believers[26], [2] a judge[27], [3]a bath house . . .

XV

"Shall return your son to" . . . .
. . . .

XVI

. . . Levels [1] one who is answered before he [even] prays, as it says: "and it will be before they call I will answer them" (Is. 65:24) [2] one who is answered towards the end [of his prayer], as it says here: "And before he finished his words behold Rebecca" [3] one who is answered after he finishes [his prayer], as it says: "And it was when he finished speaking these word the earth split" (Num. 16:31) [4] one who is answered after finishing in some time or times as it says, "And it was at the end of ten days and God's word was to Jeremiah" (Jer. 42:7), "at that time I Daniel

---

26. I.e. a synagogue. See San. 17a.
27. Zucker has 'Physician' in his translation.

was mourning three weeks of days" (Dan. 10:2)[28] and then "and on the twenty fourth of the first month" (ibid. 4).[29] The most relevant question is: how is it that the answer of Abraham's servant came more hurriedly and faster than that of Moses our teacher? There are two answers to this. The first is that Abraham's servant asked for virtue while Moses asked for revenge. One of our Master's attributes is expediting [the payment of] goodness and delaying [the payment of] revenge . . . The second, and the best, is that Abraham's servant's plea was for himself and the faster He would provide his answer the more certain he would be of himself for he would know that what he asked for <has been fulfilled>[30] whereas Moses' request was to reveal power and signs to Israel[31] and were the signs created before he finished speaking the listeners would not attribute them to him but to trickery [i.e.] since he saw that something was created he came forward with words with which he acclaims them for himself.

XVII

What it says of Rebecca: "and her pitcher is on her shoulder" is not a denigration of her but emphasizes the extent of the certainty and freedom of her people. We find that it gives more descriptions of Rebecca than that of Avisagh for it says of the latter: "and the girl is extremely (adh me'odh) pretty" (I Kings 1:4) while of the former it says: "and the girl is of extremely good appearance" adh comes to reduce.[32]

XVIII

That it says, "no man had known her" after it already says: "virgin" it lets us know by this that if a man had intercourse with a woman despite that

---

28. Ad loc. the Gaon explains that Daniel's mourning is connected with the time period given to him after his prayer in ch. 9.

29. The following section speaks of Daniel's prophecy.

30. The fact that the sign he prayed for came to be immediately gave the servant confidence that God was with him and that Rebecca was the girl to be chosen to be Isaac's wife.

31. Ex. Ch. 4.

32. See San. 39b.

she is still a virgin the Law of copulation befalls her whether it is permissible or prohibited [copulation].[33] <<He too is befallen by it.>>

XIX

His statement to her—*baghmi'ini*—the true meaning of the word is "let me try a little water" if you refer to the intensive act you say: "give me to drink".[34]

XX

[As for] her statement: "for your camels too I shall draw water"—it appears that it was their custom that they would give water to the guest and his animals.

XXI

I rendered as . . . two letters[35] when they are connected have one of seven meanings: [1] the name of a man, as it says: "Er the first born of Judah" (Gen. 38:7); [2] the name of a place as it says "the city of ('ir) date palms" (Deut. 34:3); [3] awakening, as it says: "men cannot awaken" (Job 14:12); [4] 'excite,' as it says: "and God excited against Jehoram the spirit of the Philistines" (II Chron. 21:17); [5] 'revealing,' as it says: "now will He manifest this upon you" (Job 8:6); [6] accompanying something and emptying it, as it says: "and emptied the chest and took it and carried it and returned it to its place" (II Chron. 24:11); and [7] 'stripping naked,' as it says: "strip and then strip it naked" (Ps. 137:7).

XXII

That "she drew water for all his camels" is not a denigration for four [kinds] of service are not denigrating but are honorable and noble. The

---

33. See Kid. 9b.
34. Following BR 50:6. I.e. much water.
35. 'Ain and Resh.

first is: service of God Exalted and Augmented as Moses says to Korah: "Is it too little for you that the God of Israel separated you from their congregation and brought you close to Him to do the service of his Mishkan" (Num. 17:9). [The second is:] service of parents as you know of Jacob's and Esau's attempt to serve Isaac.[36] [The third is:] a student's service of his master <<as it says of>> Elisha' ben Shafat: "which poured water on the hands of Elijah" (II Kings 3:11). [And the fourth is:] a man serving his guests, as it says, "while he stood in front of then under the tree and they ate" (Gen. 18:8).

XXIII

The most compelling interpretation of Mishta'eh is 'deliberating'[37] However, some people maintain that it means 'drinking',[38] but this is incorrect <<for he had already finished>>.

XXIV

As for "kept quiet to see" we have already explained its meaning [i.e.] that not everyone who prays is answered.[39]

XXV

"And the man took a gold ring" has three elements of in—literalness. The first is that it has the ellipsis of two words [and should be understood as]: "and the man took a gold ring and put it on her nose and put the bracelets on her hand." The second is that it mentions what comes after this first as if it says "and the man took the gold nose ring" at the time that "and the daughters of Bethu'el said to him I am the daughter of Bethuel." This is

---

36. See Gen. 27:4.

37. Following BR ch. 60.

38. Ibn Ezra attributes this rendition in various places to Onqelos (see intro. to Pentateuch.) although our texts have shahe not shathe. See Rashi ad. loc. who appears to imply that in his day too this latter reading of Onqelos was existent.

39. See Beliefs 5:6 (pg. 223).

similar to: "until He made it destroyed" (Ex. 14:21) followed by: "and the waters split" (ibid).

XXVI

Now the reason he gave her few ornaments is because they were [just] symbolic in place of a ring [used] in our times, while the presents themselves it shall mention afterwards when it says: "and he took out gold and silver vessel and clothes and gave them gave to Rebecca." It is possible that it reveals a little [of what he gave them] to imply [that he gave them] much and did not detail which vessels there were to relieve us [and tell us] only of what is essential for the laws of the Torah are for the paupers[40] for were they for the rich they would apply [only] to them not the poor.

XXVII

Conjecturally the difference between lalin and lalun is that the former is a single stay while the second is many[41] for he answered him with more than he asked.

XXVIII

"And the man bowed to God" for this is one the ten things that the Believer is to bow down for [1] good news, as it says "And the people believed for they heard that God had remembered the Children of Israel and saw there feebleness and they kneeled and bowed down" (Ex. 4:31); [2] fortune for an individual, as it says: "And then you shall put it in front of the holiness of God your Master and bow down in front of God your Master" (Deut. 26:10); [3] [promise of] fortune heard from God in general, as it says: "And Moses hurried and kneeled to ground and bowed down . . . He said behold I make a treaty against all of your people I shall make wonders the like of which have not been created in the entire world" (Ex. 34:8–10); [4] [during] prophetic inspiration as it says: "And Moses heard this and fell on his face <to seek and hear prophecy from

---

40. See Intro. XVIII.
41. Following *BR* 50:22.

God>"[42] (Num. 16:4); [5] during the appearance of the Light of the Abode, as it says: "like the sight of the bow that is seen in the clouds on a rainy day and I fell on my face" (Ez. 1:28); [6] upon entering the Temple, as it says "So exalt God our Master and bow opposite His Holiness" (Ps. 99:9); [7] [while bringing] a public sacrifice, as it says: "and the entire congregation bows" (II Chron. 29:28); [8] [during] a personal crisis, as it says: "Then Job arose and rent his mantle and shaved some of the hair on his head and fell down prostrate on the earth" (Job 1:20); [9] [during] a public crisis even if it does not effect that individual [who bows], as it says: "And Joshua tore his garments and fell on his face to the ground" (Josh. 7:6) and [10] when one sees wonders as it says: "By the fire coming from before God . . . and they fell on their face" (Lev. 9:24).

Now how long must a worshipper bow for? We say as long as is it takes to pronounce a phrase of more than twenty letters similar to what Israel said at the Mountain of Carmel: "And they fell on their faces and said, the Lord is God the Lord is God" (I Kings. 18:39) which is twenty six letters long or like what they said in connection to the building of the Temple: "And they knelt on their face on the floor and they bowed and gave praise to the Lord for He is good for His kindness is forever" (II Chron. 7:3) which is twenty five letters long, or as it says regarding the Day of Atonement:[43] "they fall on their faces and say, 'Blessed is the name of the esteem of His kingdom forever'" which is twenty four letters long or like we have by tradition that one says during the other fast days: "we have sinned our Rock forgive us our Creator"[44] we have sinned our Rock forgive us our Creator" which is twenty two letters long. If one bows and does not wait [the time needed] to pronounce the smallest of the aforementioned lengths [of letters] it is as if he did not bow down [at all].[45]

XXIX

<<[when] {Abraham's servant} states at the beginning: "Which did not stint His esteem and goodness from my master" he means: for me, who is

---

42. The bracketed part is not found in Derenbourgh's edition but is added in a manuscript used by Kafih ('Perushe' ad. loc.) and similarly "to see vision" in the Polyglot (see Derenbourg's note ad. loc.).

43. Yoma 6:2.

44. The source is uncertain.

45. Cf. Shav. 16b

his follower, too he did [so] similar to: "You shall decide a thing and it shall be established for you upon your way the shall shine light" (Job 22:28) which God promised to the nobles>>⁴⁶

XXX

"And she told the household of her mother" [and] not [of] her father[47] for two reasons. The first is because of the embarrassment of telling this to men and the second is because women are the ones who will notice the rings and bracelets first and will ask about them.

XXXI

"And Laban ran" possibly because of [his] youthfulness, quickness, haughtiness and the like. [Also] "and Laban ran" is belated and belongs after "and it was when he saw the rings and the bracelets on the hand of his sister" according to what we have explained about [verses] which are out of sequence.

XXXII

"And when he heard Rebecca's words" refers to one of two things. Either that he told her of explicitly of marriage with Isaac or that she heard him say: "Blessed is the Lord God of my Master Abraham" in addition to what he himself told them "to marry off the daughter of my brother of my master to his son."

XXXIII

It adds: "the place of the camels" after "I made space in my house" for the accommodations of a person is easier for anyplace will suit them whereas the accommodations of their animals is more difficult.

---

46. This section appears out of place on p. 420 in Zucker's translation.

47. The Arabic section has "brother" but this appears to be a mistake and accordingly Zucker translates "father."

XXXIV

"And he gave straw and hay to the camels" refers to Laban for it attributes: "and water to wash his feet" so the one who did both is the same [person].

XXXV

Now {Abraham's servant} brought with him [other] men to this land for it says: "And the feet of the men which were with him." It is possible that at first they were for his service and later to attest of his credibility and of the marriage if they were in need of it. If among them there was someone who they knew went out with Abraham when he was twenty years old who is now ninety years old this would be even better! Perhaps: "the elderly of his house" was also [mentioned] for this purpose.

XXXVI

"And it was placed in front of him." The meaning is as if Wayiyyasem (and he placed) had been written. Conjecturally this is because of the hesitation and delay that happened to the food whereas Abraham's servant acted only correctly by speaking before eating by making use of them being embarrassed of him.

Then he begins and says:

34) he said: I am the servant of Abraham; 35) and God blessed my master very much and made <him> great[48] and gave him sheep, silver, gold, servants, maidservants, camels and donkeys; 36) and Sarah my master's wife gave birth to a son for him after she had become old and he gave him all his possessions; 37) and my master made me take oath and said: do not take a wife for my son from the daughters of the Canaanites in whose land I dwell; 38) but to the house of my father you shall go and to my kin and shall take a wife for my son; 39) and I said to him: but what if the woman will not follow me? 40) and he said to

---

48. The Gaon apparently understands the original "and he grew" in the causative sense.

me: God in [the path] of whose obedience I have gone shall send His angel in front of you and will make your way successful and you will take a wife for my son from my kin and the house of my father; 41) then you shall be cleared of my oath if you have come to my kin and if they will not give you then you been cleared of my oath; 42) and I came today to the spring and I said: O God the God of my master Abraham would You[49] accomplish my need after which I go! 43) and behold I stand at the spring of water and whichever girl will come out to draw water and I will say to her: give me a little water from you vial; 44) and she will say to me: Drink! And your camels I will also give to drink, then she is the woman which He has found fit for my master's son; 45) I before I finished speaking <these words of mine> to myself behold Rebecca comes out and her vial is on her shoulder and she went down to the spring and drew water and I said to her: let me have water now!; 46) and she rushed and unloaded the vial off herself and said: drink! And your camels I shall also give to drink and I drank and she gave the camels to drink; 47) then I asked her and said: whose daughter are you? She said the daughter of Bethuel the son of Nahor for whom Milkah bore him and I placed the rings on her nose and the bracelets on her hands; 48) and I knelt and bowed in front of God and praised God the God of my master Abraham which led me in the correct path that I marry off the daughter of my master's brother to his son; 49) and now if you would do bounty and goodness with my master tell me and if you do not tell me then I will turn right or left; 50) and Laban the son of Bethuel responded to him and they said: from with God this matter came out how can we speak to you of it either bad or good; 51) behold Rebecca is in front of you. Take her and go she shall be a wife for your master's son as God has decreed; 52) and when Abraham's servant heard their words he bowed to the ground <in thanks> to God; 53) and he took out vessels of silver, vessels of gold and clothes and gave them to Rebecca and sweetmeats he gave to her sister and her mother; [[54) and they ate and drank, he and the people with him and they stayed the night and <when> they got up in the morning he said: let me go to my master; 55) and her sister and mother said: the girl shall stay with us a year or ten months and after this she will go; 56) he said to them: you shall not delay me! And God has made my way successful; 57) they said: we will call the girl and ask her of her opinion; 58) and they called Rebecca and said to her: will you go

---

49. Or perhaps: "I accomplish" but this would not follow the biblical text.

with this man and she said yes[50]; 59) and they sent Rebecca their sister
and her midwife and Abraham's servant and his men; 60) and they
blessed Rebecca and said to her: our sister, there shall be from you
thousands and myriads and your children shall gain possession of the
cities of their despisers; 61) and Rebecca and her servant-girls got up
and mounted the camels and went with the man and the servant took
Rebecca and went; 62) and it was [when] Isaac had come on his way
from the desert which is of the Living [and] Seeing and he was standing
in the land of Qablah; 63) and Isaac went out to pray[51] in the steppe at
the approach of night and he lifted his eyes and saw and behold there are
camels coming; 64) and when Rebecca lifted her eyes and say Isaac she
almost fell off the camel; 65) and she said to the servant: who is this man
walking in the steppe to greet us? The servant said: he is my master and
she took the veil and cover herself with it; 66) then the servant related
to Isaac all the things that he did; 67) and Isaac took her in to Sarah's his
mother's tent and took Rebecca and she became for him a wife and he
loved her and Isaac was consoled after <the death of> his mother.]]

I

Just as all the points of the first part of the story have a significance
[which] we can apply to [matters of] obedience, Law, judgement and
ethical lesson as we have explained, so this second section, in all its points
serves to elevate Abraham's servant and to reveal his wisdom for he gave
encouragement to the people[52] in twelve ways. The first is his statement:
"I am Abraham's servant." [i.e.] Behold you see how [great] my stature and
esteem is and how much more so is his. [The second is that] he
encouraged them in respect to wealth and coming near them as it says:
"and God blessed my master." [The third] is with a wondrous sign, which
is Sarah's giving birth for it says: "And Sarah the wife of my master gave
birth." [The fourth is] by singling out Isaac who was the most estimable
of the children as it says: "And he gave him everything that was his." [The
fifth is] that he gave them preference over all the kings and wealthy
people which are in their land as it says: "And my master made me take

---

50. Instead of "I will go" in the Hebrew.
51. Following the rabbinic interpretation. See Rashi ad. loc.
52. To give their daughter to him.

oath and said, do not take a wife for my son from the daughters of the Canaanites." [The sixth is] by [alluding to them Abraham's] missing people and relatives as it says: "But to the house of my father you shall go." [The seventh is that he said] if you say: "How shall we send our daughters to a distant land" but this is something thing we are finished with, for this shall be executed only by such [a manner] as it says: "And I said to my master: perhaps the women will not wish to follow me." [The eighth is by telling them that] {Abraham} is a man of complete faith and righteousness and there is no need to fear that he will do harm [to her]. Of this it says: "In [the path of] whose obedience I have gone shall send His angel" and he did not . . . you it shall be decisive and doubtless as it says: "Then I shall be cleared of my oath." [The tenth is that he told them] that "I trusted in God" as it says: "And I came today to the 'Ayn" [The eleventh is that he told them] that "He answered my prayer" as it says: "I before I finished speaking." [The twelfth is that he told them that] this is something which I have concluded and ascertained[53] and have thanked my Master [for it] as it says: "And I kneeled and bowed down to God." [The thirteenth is that he told them that] nevertheless this is not the only possibility as it says: "And I shall turn to the right or to the left" as if he hints [to them] that if not he would marry her off to the righteous of the nations and one who tends to trust in him. And when he underlined these thirteen ideas successively, they answered him.

II

It mentions Laban before Bethuel for [various] reasons.[54] The first is because Laban had already had dealings with him for he met him at the spring where whatever happened between them happened. [The second is] because the father is more reserved in these matters than the brother.[55] [The third is that] perhaps Laban was Rebecca's brother from the mother[56] and [for a brother] to take such personal interest is [indeed] common.

---

53. Apparently that this incident is God-sent.

54. In v. 50.

55. Apparently the Gaon wishes to say that the father usually deals with issues of marriage calmly and the brother tends to butt in.

56. Perhaps he means that the Scripture wishes to say that despite that Laban

III

<<When they say: "from God this thing came" they mean what you said: "I before I had finished speaking and behold Rebecca goes out.">>

IV

We say now: How did they believe him in this [account] for it is possible that he exaggerated? This [fact] is indicative of the accident was placed upon them as a result of Abraham's request: "He shall send His angel in front of you and shall make your path successful"[57] [or] it was by means of something that they saw, heard or sensed as we have previously stated.[58]

V

Is it possible that they should not speak evil of him but why should they not speak good of him?. We say that this bad and good is not of Abraham's servant but of themselves—whether the dowry be great or little and the like.

VI

Their statement: "Behold Rebecca is in front of you take and go" is [their] agreement but as for quickness they have still to await.

VII

His bowing down [as it says]: "And when Abraham's servant heard their words" is in thanks a second time.

---

was not actually related to Abraham and Bethuel, he played an active role in the discourse about the marriage.

57. Possibly he means that the fact that they believed him without any evidence was proscribed by God in response to Abraham's prayer.

58. Perhaps he means that they had some evidence of his account.

VIII

The statement: "And the servant took out vessels of silver, vessels of gold, and clothes"—some were for dowry while others for gifts according to what people usually give.

IX

It adds "and sweetmeats" as is customary for people until today to divide fruits and sweets and the like. But that the kin of the woman should give money to the groom, is neither in the Law nor in Tradition and even at the time that the condition of the woman was the worst when most men were killed [in war] as it says: (Is. 3:25) It was in need of "and seven women shall grab hold of one man on that day saying: our bread we shall eat and our dress we shall wear." (Ibid. 4:9) This is what they said. But if they were to say to him: "You shall eat our bread and shall wear our dress" then not. We find giving money to the groom makes the daughters of Israel widows and reduces their offspring and forces both to marry one who is not fit for them and places evil between the man and the [woman]* and forces that she have dominion over him." And if she dies he people hasten to take inheritance in the nations and if he dies most of his legacy goes to waste and his widow remains . . . what it says of giving a Tithe of property[59] and Poseq ma'oth."[60]
[61]

---

59. Keth. 68a.

60. ibid 6:2 and 13:5.

61. There is some discrepancy between the original text of the opening section and Zucker's translation. We have therefore omitted it.

Chapter XXV

[[1) Then Abraham returned and took a wife and her name was Keturah . . . 5) and Abraham gave all that was his to Isaac; 6) and to the children of the midwife that Abraham had, Abraham gave them gifts and sent them to Isaac his son while he was living to the east to the land of the East. 7) These are the days of the years of the Abraham's life that lived 157 years; 8) then Abraham came to an end and died in a good age old satisfied by life and went to his people; 9) and Isaac and Ishmael his sons buried him in the double cave of the field in the field of Ephron the son of Sahar the Hittite which is in the vicinity of Mamre; 10) the field that Abraham bought from the sons of Heth. There Abraham and Sarah his wife were buried; 11) and when it was after the death of Abraham God blessed Isaac his son and Isaac stayed at the well "to the Living of Vision"; 12) this is <the elucidation of> offspring of Ishmael the son Abraham which Hagar the Egyptian Sarah's maidservant bore for Abraham . . . 16) these are the names of the sons of Ishmael according to their outworks and fortresses twenty princes to their nations; 17) and these are the years of the life of Ishmael which lived 173 years and terminated and died and went to his people; 18) and they dwelled from Zawila until Jafar which is in the vicinity of Egypt <until> you come to Mawsal in the vicinity of Egypt he dwelled; 19) This is <the elucidation of> the offspring of Isaac the son of Abraham after Abraham <was

[found to be] the only one to> begat Isaac;[1] 20) and when Isaac was forty years old he took Rebecca the daughter of Bethuel the Aramean from Paddan Aram the sister of Laban the Aramean for him as a wife.]]

I

We would expect that since it opens with "And this is <the elucidation of> the offspring of Isaac" that it would cite for us the names of the children or their history but it opens saying "And Abraham begot," something that does not accord the opening. However, using our mind we find that it wishes [to say] with this statement that these two sons were born to Isaac after Abraham had singled him out and sent the rest of his sons; the first is in general and the second in particular. The actual purpose of this statement is that it had already mentioned prior to this that Abraham gave the rest of his sons presents and while he was still alive he separated them from Isaac but it did not mention in how many years. Since it says here that he begot sons before he sent the rest of the sons and the time of their birth was known as it shall say: "And Isaac was sixty years old when they were born," and fifteen years remained of Abraham's life, we know by means of this calculation that <<the sending of the sons was before the fifteenth years>>. This calculation in essence requires that they were born to him and remained with him some time and then he sent them. All this was before twenty years because he did not marry Keturah until Isaac was married.

II

Now what is the manner of wisdom in their birth being delayed until he singled him out? We say that this is giving esteem to Jacob just as the birth

---

1. However, his statements in the immediate point to the rendition found in Derenbourgh's edition: "After Abraham singled out Isaac from his children." Ruling out the possibility of a scribal error we would have to assume that the Gaon refers with this rather unexpected addition to *Bab. Mez.*, where it is recollected that there were those who accused Abraham of not being Isaac's father but that he was born of Abimelech when Sarah was taken away from Abraham when they descended to Moab.

of Isaac after the circumcision is giving of esteem to him. So the birth of Jacob after being singled out is esteem for him.

III

We say further also: Why did {Abraham} make him special and single him out for we do not find among children anyone who was tested except for him as is explained in the sequel of the "Mountain of Moriah" and there was no one with which a treaty was made except for him as it says afterwards: "And Ismael I have heard you and My treaty I shall establish with Isaac." Nor was there anyone who was placed [in his house] other than him as God says: "Anything that Sarah says to you listen to her voice." Nor anyone who calls himself the offspring of Abraham except for him as it says: "For by Isaac shall be called for you offspring." Now were there not the general law that permits the father to give most of his money to his child, it would be permissible in regards to Isaac the son of Abraham for the reasons that we have mentioned. How much more so if the rule is for the masses as long as he is alive. For that reason it says: "for while he is still alive." It explains to us that the measurement of this was a year prior to his death.

IV

Being that it had already says: "the daughter of Bethuel the Aramean," why does it repeat and says: "from Paddan Aram"? [This is] because there is Aram that is not this one, i.e., Aram the son of Seth as it says: "The sons of Seth were Eilam, Ashur . . . and Aram." (I Chron. 1:17)

[[21) Then Isaac pleaded in front of God for the sake of his wife for she was barren and God endowed him and Rebecca became pregnant and gave birth; 22) then the children hustled in her stomach and she said: Were <I to know that the matter is> so I would not have inquired of it[2] and she went to seek <knowledge> from with God; 23) and God said to her that there are two <fathers> of nations in your stomach and two nations shall split apart from them and one shall be strengthened by the

---

2. See com. which may indicate a different reader.

other and the big shall serve the small; 24) and when the days of her birth were complete, behold there are twins in her stomach; 25) and the first came out all red like a garment of hair and they named him "Esau"; 26) and after this came out his brother and his hand holding fast to Esau's heel and he called him "Jacob" and Isaac was six hundred years old when they were born; 27) then the two children grew up and Esau was a man <knowledgeable> in hunting, a man of the steppe, and Jacob was a simple man[3] dwelling in tents; 28) and Isaac loved Esau because <of his knowledge> of hunting and Rebecca loved Jacob. 29) Then Jacob cooked some food and Esau came in from the steppe and he was hungry; 30) and he said to Jacob: Give me to eat of this extremely red thing for I am hungry. For that reason Esau was named "the red one." 31) Jacob said: Sell me today your primogeniture. 32) Esau said: Behold I am going to die and for what is this primogeniture for me? 33) He said: Swear to me; and he swore to him and sold him his primogeniture; 34) and Jacob gave him bread and food for the lentils and he ate and drank and got up and went. And Esau made light of the primogeniture.]]

I

We should say: What is the manner of wisdom in Rebecca and other righteous woman being barren? We find two answers for this: The first which is the general one is that it is just that the created creature have need for savior from their Creator were these events to come upon them. If they hunger He satiates them, if they become ill He heals them, if they become poor He makes them not needy. This obligates them to persist in worshipping Him. Barrenness is just a sickness. The second answer which is specific to the righteous people has three ideas. The first is trial; if they pass it they are rewarded with good. The second is that they call [God] and pray. One who is singled out in calling receives additional reward. The third is that their children be beloved to them, for making each one beloved contains various kinds of wisdom and guidance. What we say regarding Isaac we say regarding Jacob, Joseph, Samson, Samuel, and of any child whose mother was barren of the votaries despite that the Scripture does not mention it. Even Zion was called so because of

---

3. Or, possibly, "ingenuous."

affection for her people as it says: "Rejoice the congregation which is like a barren woman that has not given birth." (Is. 54:1)

II

The manner of wisdom in the response being endowment for it says: "And He endowed him." . . . for one who prays believes four things:[4] [1] that the Creator exists, for one may ask only of one who exists; [2] that He is capable [to fulfil] what He is asked and he lowers himself in front of God by asking; [3] <<he knows his own strength>> and is obligated to thank Him for the response. For that reason calling to God is beneficial for one who does so and [1] adds to their wisdom as it says: "And they gathered in order to ask for pity from God in regards to this secret." (Dan. 2:18) [2] It adds sustenance as it says: "And when Hezekiah and the princes came and saw the heaps, they blessed the Lord and his people Israel," (II Chron. 31:8) and then: "We have had enough to eat, and have left plenty for the Lord has blessed His people." (II Chron. 31:10) [3] It frees one of troubles as it says: "When this anguished me because of them I would call to God and seek savior from Him." (Ps. 18:7) [4] It forgives sin as it says: "Take with you words and turn to the Lord. Say unto Him: Take away all iniquity." (Hos. 14:3) One heals sicknesses by means of it as it says: "Or he might recompense him, too, for torments upon his bed," (Job 33:19) and it says at the end of the incident: "He has implored God and is accepted by Him. He shall look upon his face with favor, in the midst of the tumult of people, and He will requite that man because of His righteousness," (Job 33:26) means: God's righteousness, kindness, and truth.[5]

III

From the statement "And Rebecca his wife became pregnant and gave birth" we should know why the early people were anxious for children.

---

4. It is uncertain how these items are to be divided into four.

5. Our translation differs with Goodman's, who has "for his righteousness," the reference being to man. This rendition was possible because the Gaon does not disambiguate this clause ad loc.

We say: in order to teach them matters of religion so they be benefited by its reward as it says: "And a father shall tell his sons of Your truth," (Is. 38:19) after the Torah says: "And teach it to your sons," (Deut. 11:19) and after it says of Abraham: "And I know that he will command his sons." (Gen. 18:19) Together with this we know that fathers derive benefit from the righteousness of their children if there is a righteous one among them for four generations for by means of it they spare some investigation that they are obligated as we shall explain in the passage of: "Exacts the iniquity of the fathers with the sons," (Ex. 34:6) which is in [the section of]: "And when God's Abode passed," (ibid.) together with the other kinds of pity for which Moses beseeched for Israel at the time of the spies and said: "O Lord give them time as You have promised, perhaps some of their children be righteous." This is what it says: "And now the greatness of Your strength is evident O Lord as You have said to me," (Num. 14:17–18) [and] "God the All Able the Merciful" and the rest of what is in this section. However, the matter [does not work] in the opposite of this, I mean if one of the four generations is wicked that the father should be held responsible for this at all if he was not deficient in educating and teaching him just as Ezekiah was not held responsible for the sin of Menasseh. There is no merchandise that has [only] gain but no loss that one who is endowed with intellect shall not strive to obtain it!

IV

What is the purpose of "And the sons shoved"? We say: So that she goes and asks about this and she should know who punishes them. Were they not to hustle she would not ask about anything. These two letters in the language have [various] meanings: [1] the meaning of "running" as it says: "Then the girl was present," (Gen. 24:28) and [2] the meaning of "desire" as it says: "My soul desired my chosen," (Is. 42:1) [3] "finish off" as it says: "Then the land shall finish off its abstinence," (Lev. 26:34) [4] "shatter" as it says: "And she shattered his head," (Judg. 9:53) [5] "injustice" as it says: "Who have I done injustice to?" (I Sam. 12:3) [6] "shoving" as it says: "And the sons shoved in her stomach," [7] "glittering" as it says: "Like lightning they sparked." (Nah. 2:5) This [adds up to] seven.

V

The true meaning of "If so why is it I?" is that she means: "If the matter is so why is it that I am pregnant?" and "pregnant" is elliptic. Therefore I

have rendered it as: "Would I have known that the matter is so I would not
have asked for them."

VI

That it calls them "sons" while were [still] embryos alludes to the second
state. It says: "And those that shall become sons shoved," similar to what
it says: "You have stripped the clothing of the naked," (Job 22:6)[6] and the
like.

VII

In the statement "And she went to seek knowledge from with God,"
"seeking knowledge with God" is by four manners: [1] "seeking knowledge
of what is concealed by means of a prophet" as it says: "Is there not here
another prophet of God that we may inquire of him?" (I Kings 22:7) [2]
prayer as it says: "For whenever I have asked God He has answered me,"
(Ps. 34:5) [3] observing the religion as it says: "And they entered the pact
to ask God," (II Chron. 15:12) and [4] repentance as it says: "Seek the
Lord and you shall leave." (Amos 5:6) Similarly, "asking" in regards to God
may be in four ways: [1] seeking knowledge of secrets as it says: "And
David inquired of the Lord" (II Sam. 21:1) because of the hunger, [2]
prayer that is by means of a sacrifice as it says: "They shall go with their
sheep, cattle to seek the Lord," (Hos. 5:6) which can also be without a
sacrifice as it says: "For my heart says of you O my face inquire of Him,"
(Ps. 27:8) [3] observing religion as it says: "Seek the Lord all you meek of
heart," (Zeph. 2:3) and [4] repentance as it says: "And I faced God my
Master seeking prayer and sympathy." (Dan. 9:3)

VIII

"And God said to her" was by means of a prophet as it says: "And God
spoke to Menasseh and to his people but they did not listen." (II Chron.
33:16)

---

6. Ad loc. he translates as follows: "And stripped people of their clothing
leaving them naked."

IX

When it says "There are two nations in your stomach," it implies "two fathers of two nations."[7]

X

The meaning [in that] it reiterates "Two nations from your stomach shall split" is that when the two children will grow up it shall become clear that each one of them differs from his brother in his acts and choices. This is that as long as the children are little they are associated with the stomach, the intestines, and the womb as it is in many places and it was so as it says: "And the children grew up," and then separated.

XI

"And one shall be strengthened by the other" is at their offset as it says of Esau: <<"And he went to another land from in front of his brother," (Gen. 36:6) and did not return.

XII

"And the big shall serve the small" in their last matters as it says: "And Edom shall be destroyed as well as Sei'er and the rest of his enemies." (Num. 24:18)>> Were one who hears this matter to have doubt that the announcement should be for those born in a much later time we say: It has already been said to Abraham of Ismael: "And I shall make him into a great nation," (Gen. 17:5) but he only had a kingdom after two hundred years as we have explained.

XIII

Conjecturally, why does it state "two nations" so that the singular be *goy* which means a river as if it compares the two progenitors to two rivers from which will flow out two nations. We already find fathers compared

---

7. For she did not carry actual nations.

to their children by means of *maqor, ma'yan, nahar,* and *nahal* and the like. Some say that the *waw* written in *goym* indicates that they were back to back and derive the word from *gaw* but this is a claim of a wonder that has no proof by allusion of what is written. In this matter, [however,] it would be more correct to write *shene gowyim* and for that reason {this claim} is invalid!

XIV

The statement about Esau that "He was all like a garment of hair" refers to the majority of his body, not to all of it.

XV

"And his hand holding fast to his heel" is a wondrous sign no doubt and this was the reason for calling him "Jacob." This name is a reference to what it will say: "For he has pursued me twice." (Gen. 27:35) We may say that this wonder that is a child holding fast to his brother's heel, the Scripture makes a parable that Jacob shall have defeat at the end of time for the one who holds fast to his heal is defeat as it says: "And the trap catches his heel, its mask holds him fast." (Job 18:9)

XVI

<"Dwelling in tents"—a place of Torah [study] for so it was called before the giving of the Torah as it says: "And Moses would take the tent . . . and any one who would inquire of God would go out to the tent of meeting (presence)." (Ex. 33:7)

XVII

"And Rebecca loved Jacob" [teaches] that Jacob's advantage was told her when she sought out God and not to Isaac.>

XVIII

In the incident of the cooking and primogeniture there are four [pieces of] information. The first is: How does it name Esau "red"? It tells us that it is because of the redness of the lentils, apart from the reason it gives when it describes him as "red." The second is Jacob's acquirement of the primogeniture so that he can say: "I am Esau your firstborn." The third and the fourth is that Jacob aspired to obedience while Esau made light of it as it says: "And he made light of the primogeniture." The Scripture did not intend by this to denigrate Jacob in that he grieved Esau his brother with eating the lentils until he took much of it but intended to denigrate Esau for selling such an exalted level for such a poor amount for it says: "And Esau made light of the primogeniture."

XIX

The reason it adds "today " to "sell" and "take oath" is because at the time that it tells us the events of these people its status was not to be sold or bought. In order that we not be surprised when we hear about this it adds "today." It says: "According to what was permissible among people at that time."

XX

"And Jacob cooked something" [means] that he cooked lentils which is food of mourners and wanted to bring it to his father when Abraham died.[8]

XXI

"Behold I am going to die" [means that] since he knew of his father's death he denied and said: "This master died, how much more so the rest of the people."

---

8. See *Bab. Bath.* 17b and *BR* ad loc.

Chapter XXVI

[[1) Then there was a famine in the land other than the first famine that came upon the people of Abraham, and Isaac went to Abimelech the king of Palestine to Khulus; 2) and God revealed Himself there and said: Do not descend to Egypt. Stay in the land which I shall tell you. 3) <As for now> reside in this land and I will be with you and I will bless you and I will give you and your offspring this land and I will upkeep My oath that I have made with Abraham your father, 4) and I will increase your offspring like the stars of the Heavens and I will give them all of this land and all the nations shall be blessed by means of them 5) as reward for Abraham listening to My words and observing all My ordinances, injunctions, and laws that I have obligated him; 6) and Isaac stayed in Khulus. 7) Then the people of the land asked him about his wife and he said she is my sister for he feared to say: She is my wife, saying: So that the people of the land do not kill me because of her for she was of nice appearance; 8) and when his days of his dwelling there had become long Abimelech the king of Palestine glanced out of his window and saw and behold Isaac is playing with Rebecca his wife; 9) and he called him and said: If she is your wife why did you say: She is my sister? He said: I feared I shall be killed because of her; 10) Abimelech said: What is this you have done to us, if shortly one of our people would have cohabited with your wife, you would have brought misdeed upon us; 11) and he convoked all the people saying: Anyone who harms this man or his wife shall surely be killed. 12) Then Isaac sowed in that land and found in that year one hundred in amount and blessed God; 13) and the man multiplied until he became extremely great; 14) and he obtained much possessions, sheep, cattle, and a large entourage that the Palestinians envied him; 15) and the well that Abraham's servants dug in pact with Abraham his father the Palestinians plugged them up and filled them with dust. 16) Then Abimelech said to Isaac: Go from with us for you have grown too much for us; 17) and Isaac went from there and went down to the spring of KhuluS and resided there. 18) Then he returned and dug the wells of water that were dug in the days of Abraham his father and the Palestinians plugged after his death and he named them as Abraham his father did; 19) and when Isaac's servants dug in the spring they found a well of flowing water; 20) and the shepherds of KhuluS and the shepherds of Isaac fell into dispute saying: The water is ours; and he called the well "dealing" because they were engaged with it; 21) and they built another well and disputed over it and they named it "of resistance"; 22) then he moved from there and dug another well but they did not dispute over it and they called it "of wideness" for now God shall widen for us now and shall make us sprout in the land; 23) then he went up from there to the Well of Seven. 24) And God revealed Himself in that night and said: I am God of Abraham your father, do not fear for I am with you, I will bless you and I will multiply your offspring because of Abraham My servant; 25) and he built there an altar and called in the name of God and pitched there his tent and Isaac's servants dug there a well. 26) And Abimelech came to him from KhuluS and Ahuzath his confidant and Pichol the head of his army; 27) and Isaac said to them: What do you think that you have come to me and you have hated and have sent me away from you? 28) They said: Behold we have seen that God is with you and we have said: There shall be now an oath between us and between you and we shall make a treaty with you; 29) that you not do evil to us as we shall not harm you and as we have done absolute good with you and have freed you in peace and you are now blessed by God; 30) and he made for them a sitting in which they eat and drank; 31) and they got up early in the morning and each man swore to his brother and Isaac sent them away and they went from with him in peace. 32) And when it was in this day Isaac's servants came and told him of the well that they dug and they said: We have found water; 33) and they called it "seven" and for that reason the name of the city is "the well of seven" to this day. 34) And when Esau was forty years old he married a woman named Yehudith the daughter of Be'eri the Hittite and Bosmath the daughter of Alon the Hittite; 35) and they would dispute the views of Isaac and Rebecca.]]

I

"Other than the first famine"—why did it need to [mention] this, we know that these are different hungers? Perhaps it was to tell us that the condition in it was as dire as in the time of Abraham.

II

"As reward for" alludes to fear of God and humbleness.

III

"Abraham listening to My words" refers to the travel of which it was said to him: "Go for yourself from your land."

IV

"And observing all My ordinances what I obligated" refers to the commandment that require [observance]*.

V

"My ordinances"—tithe and the like.

VI

"Laws"—laws of prohibited cohabitation and the laws of circumcision.

VII

"Shortly one of our people would have cohabited with your wife" means "This is what almost happened since you were not killed."

VIII

Those that the Scripture says of them: "continually growing" are <five>:
Isaac, Samuel, Jehoshaphat, David, and Mordechai. Isaac in worship,
Samuel in wisdom,[1] Jehoshaphat in judgement,[2] David in wealth, and
Mordechai in strength.

IX

The purpose of telling us of the plugging and opening of the wells is so
that we know that Isaac did not change their names but followed his
father in this as it says: "And he named them as his father Abraham did."
We have an ethical lesson that one who honors his father by not changing
the names of his wells, the Torah writes good of him, especially someone
who does not change the customs of his father and does not sway after
their tradition. Of Isaac's reward for not changing the names of their
names is that God Exalted did not change his name as he did Abraham's
and Jacob's.

X

"Ahuzath" is a name like Pichol. We say: What is their necessity in saying:
"Let there be an oath between us," did Abraham not make a treaty with
them that he will not do evil to them, their offspring, or their and their
successors as it elucidates? We say that they annulled the treaty with Isaac
and sent him away as it says: "from with us," and their treaty was freed
from them and for that reason they were in need of renewing it.

XI

They repeat "between us and between you," they mean: "We would like
that you give a treaty to me, my son-in-law, and grandson as was between
us and between your father."

---

1. I Sam. 2:26.
2. II Chron. 17:12.

XII

It made sure to mention the wells here because of people's need in them for a land that is barren for a long time and its water is impure. <<And even bad>> as the prophet made a comparison saying: "and now what do you have to do in the way of Egypt to dr'nk the waters of Sihor or what do you have to do in the way of Assyria to drink the waters of the river." (Jer. 2:18) "To drink the waters of Sihor" refers to dug water because it had impure water bitter and salty and it is the place of the Philistines. "To drink the water of river" is bad and stenchy and this is in the path of Jezirah.

Chapter XXVII

[[1) Then when Isaac grew old his eyes weakened from seeing and he called Esau his older son and said to him: O my son. He said: I am here. 2) He said: Behold I have grown old and do not know the day of my death; 3) and now lift up your weapon, your armor, and your bow and go out to the steppe and make a hunt for me; 4) and prepare it for me as kinds of delicacies as I like and bring it to me; I shall eat of it so that my soul may bless you before I die. 5) And Rebecca heard when Isaac spoke this to Esau her son and when Esau came to the steppe to make a hunt she brought him; 6) she said to Jacob her son: I have heard your father speak to Esau your brother saying: 7) Bring me a hunt and fix it for me as delicacies; I shall eat of it so that I shall bless you in front of God; 8) and now O my son hear from me what I shall command you: 9) Go to the cattle and take from it two goats of the good goats and prepare them as delicacies as he likes; 10) and you shall bring them to your father and he shall eat of them so that he may bless you before his death. 11) He said to her: Behold Esau my brother is a man of hair and I am a hairless man; 12) lest my father feel me and I shall be with him as one who mocks him and I shall bring upon myself a curse, not a blessing. 13) His mother said to him: <Warding off> your sin is upon me! 14) And he went and brought it to his mother and his mother fixed it as delicacies as his father likes it; 15) then Rebecca took Esau's her older son's most splendid clothes and dressed Jacob her younger son with them; 16) and the skins of goats she dressed his hand and the smooth parts of his neck;

364

17) and she gave him the delicacies together with the bread that she made; 18) and he went in to his father and said: O my father. He said: Behold. Who are you O my son? 19) Jacob said to his father: I am Esau your firstborn; I have done as you have commanded me. 20) He said: What is this that you have hurried to find? He said: Because God your Master had perchanced in front of me. 21) Isaac said: Come forward so that I may feel you my son, are you my son Esau or not? 22) And Jacob came forward to Isaac and he felt him and said: The voice is the voice of Jacob and the hands are the hands of Esau; 23) and he did not recognize him for his hands were like the hairy hands of Esau and he blessed him; 24) <moreover> he said to him: You are my son Esau. He said: I am he. 25) He said: bring forward to me so that I may eat of your hunt so that my soul may bless you and he brought forward to him and he ate and he brought him wine and he drank; 26) then he said to him: Come forward and kiss me, 27) and he came forward and kissed him and he smelled the odor of his clothes and he blessed him and said: See the smell of my son is like the smell of the field that God has blessed; 28) God shall give you of the dew of the Heavens and the fatness of the Earth and abundance of wheat and prime; 29) and the nations shall serve you and the bands shall submit to you and be a master over your brothers and sons of your mother shall submit to you for the one who curses you is cursed and the one who blesses you is blessed. 30) And when Isaac finished blessing Jacob, it was when he was about to leave, Esau his brother had come from his hunt; 31) and he too made delicacies that he brought to his father and said to him: My father shall get up and shall eat of the catch of his son so that your soul may bless me. 32) He said to him: Who are you? He said: I am Esau your firstborn son. 33) And Isaac trembled very greatly and said: And who is it that made a catch and brought it to me and I eat of it before you came and I blessed him and he shall also be blessed? 34) And when Esau heard the words of his father he cried greatly very bitter and said to his father: Bless me too father. 35) He said: Your brother came in delusion and took your blessing. 36) And he said: It is correct that he was named "Jacob" for he has pursued me already twice. 37) Isaac responded and said: Behold I have made him your master and all your brothers I have made servants for him and the fat and the wheat I have divided for him. Now what shall I do my child? 38) Esau said: Do you have just one blessing my father, bless me too; and he raised his voice and wept. 39) And he answered him and said: Behold of the fat of the sky earth shall be your dwelling and of the dew of the sky from above; 40) by your sword you shall live

and your brother you shall serve and it shall be if you rebel and loosen his yoke from your neck. 41) And Esau harbored anger against Jacob because of the blessing that his father gave him and Esau said in his soul: The days of my father's mourning shall come near and I shall kill Jacob my brother; 42) and Rebecca was told Esau's her older son's words and she sent and called Jacob her younger son and said to him: Behold Esau your brother threatens you to kill you; 43) and now my son hear me and get up and go to Laban my brother to Haran; 44) and stay with him a little days until your brother's wrath settles; 45) until his anger settles and he forgets what you have done to him and I shall send and take you from there so that I do not bereave both of you one day. 46) Then Rebecca said to Isaac: I am disgusted at my life from before of the daughters of Heth and if Jacob is to marry a woman from among them like these or from the daughters of the rest of the people of this land then why do I need life?

I

"I do not know the day of my death"—he thought that his life was as long as his father's and when he lived longer than his father by three years he said: "I do not know the day of my death."

II

"And make a hunt for me"—he was not in need of what Esau is to bring for he had much sheep and cattle but bringing something as a result of his effort and toil is good for soul.

III

"Lift now your vessels" means to defend him were an enemy human or predatory beast to come upon him. <"Your vessels" is armor and the like. *Talyecha* is the sword that one hands on himself.>

IV

Isaac had a doubt as to which one it was and blessed him on the condition that whichever one he is the blessing shall be his no doubt. For were it

Isaac's intention to bless a known individual, the blessing would not befall someone else.

V

Isaac's statement to Esau, "Behold the . . . " God sustained for him and said: "For as inheritance to Esau I have given it."

VII

Rebecca's statement, "And I shall send and I shall take you from there," had already been fulfilled . . . . . . this is that we see Deborah [coming]* with Jacob at the time of his return.

VII

"Why shall I bereave both of you in one day"—this is he kills him like Esau and Jacob and the Judge shall come and kill for his blood.

Index

About the Author

Michael Linetsky was born in the former USSR and came to the United States in December of 1978. He resides in New York and attends Yeshiva University.

Recommended Resources

The Book of Genesis: A Commentary by ShaDaL
(S.D. Luzzatto)
translated by Daniel A. Klein   0-7657-9993-6

Rabbi Abraham Ibn Ezra's Commentary on the Creation
by Michael Linetsky   0-7657-9982-0

Available at your local bookstore
online at *www.aronson.com*
or by calling toll-free 1-800-782-0015